ADVANCED PRAISE

"America's Conscience *breathes new life into activism today. We have choices to make and so do our public servants both those elected and appointed. This book helps us see what we can do now that denial won't work anymore."* ~H. Margret, Artist

"America's Conscience *cries out for the average American to wake up and question authority! You will be inspired to critically evaluate the "common knowledge" as Bernadette Vadurro exposes the truth behind the rhetoric in Washington. Her thoughtful analysis clearly explains the urgent need for our political leadership to reflect the will of the people,* America's Conscience." ~Deborah Ulinski Potter, Scientist

"It's all here in a well written, concise single volume, the manipulation of the American people exposed and the machinations of arrogant public officials revealed. Whatever your political affiliations, be baffled no more. Be informed, be angry and throw the bums out! Take back America." ~Robert Morgan Love, Architect

"Bernadette T. Vadurro's book America's Conscience *presents a very important social gospel. The modern social gospel is a story that brings light and truth to today's world and it reveals how we affect humanity. The author provides a truth and an account so that people can fully understand what is really going on in our nation. We must take responsibility for our lives and our country."* ~Richard Gundrey, Archbishop Catholic Apostolic Church of Antioch-Malabar Rite

"Bernadette Trujillo-Vadurro's America's Conscience *is a sobering overview of the assault the American ethos has endured with the ascension of the neo-conservative philosophy to the highest levels of our government and media. Read this book! You will be moved to preserve the America we all cherish. Read it for yourself, for your children and for your country.* ~Stephen McCabe, Small Business Owner

"If you are a busy patriotic American who feels a need to know what is going on politically in the U.S., the meticulous research in this book will provide you with a concrete foundation. It is our responsibility to search out this information for the sake of our nation, our planet and future generations." ~Ruth Solomon, Bookkeeper

As an engineer who worked in Saudi Arabia and Kuwait for six years and who voted for Ronald Reagan in the 80s, I found America's Conscience *to be concise, informative and easy to read. Since the era of Harry S. Truman our nation has been consumed with fear and terror caused first by Nazism, then the new enemy which was communism, to 9/11 which brought on the newest fear of Islam and terrorism. At what point will Americans ask how these fears are being used to manipulate them and their tax dollars? Let us be cautioned by the words of Dwight D. Eisenhower quoted below.*

~Emilio B. Duran, Professional Engineer

"...we must guard against the acquisition of unwarranted influence, whether sought or unsought, by the military-industrial complex. The potential for the disastrous rise of misplaced power exists and will persist. We must never let the weight of this combination endanger our liberties or democratic processes... Only an alert and knowledgeable citizenry can compel the proper meshing of the huge industrial and military machinery of defense with our peaceful methods and goals, so that security and liberty may prosper together."

~Dwight D. Eisenhower

AMERICA'S CONSCIENCE

AMERICA'S CONSCIENCE

Facing Threats to Democracy,
the Middle Class and Our World

Bernadette T. Vadurro

Speakers LIVE
Books

America's Conscience © 2007 by Bernadette T. Vadurro

Speakers Live Books
41 Vista Calabasas
Santa Fe, NM 87506
(800) 736-8986
www.speakerslive.com
www.AmericasConscience.com

The author may be reached at:
    BernadetteVadurro@speakerslive.com

INTERIOR DESIGN/PRODUCTION: SunFlower Designs, Santa Fe, New Mexico

COVER DESIGN: Frank Wechsler, fw graphic designs, Santa Fe, NM

First Edition 2007. **Printed in USA**

ISBN: 978-0-9793580-0-5 • 0-9793580-0-0

Library of Congress Control Number: 2007900982

This book is dedicated to my father, who said
we must believe in the strength of our convictions.

"Then you will know the truth, and the truth will set you free."

John 8:32

Acknowledgements

Thank you to the love of my life, my husband Rob. Your patience and support has meant the world to me. A huge thank you to my daughters, Christy and Kate — I know it's been hard to sacrifice the presence of your mother for the better part of a year. Thanks to my Mother for your positive affirmations and to Chuck for the constant bantering that drove me only harder to write the best book possible. I am grateful to my four younger siblings, the two whose mindset convinced me of the absolute necessity of this book and to the two who encouraged me to keep writing.

Thank you to Anjali Pai, Roberta Hunt and especially Debby Ulinski-Potter, Ph.D., who scoured the manuscript over and over again for accuracy. A debt of gratitude is owed to friends, colleagues and clients who served as readers and provided critical feedback, Drs. Yolanda Briscoe, Joseph Neidhardt, Carol Brown and Rob Love, Tommy Archuleta, Margaret Henkle, Jeff Potter, Benny Duran, Roxanne Rivera and Betty Brand and to the countless patriotic Americans whose honest opinions and perspectives gave depth to this book.

The generosity of the Center for Public Integrity and the National Priorities Program is deeply appreciated for data, charts and graphs used in this project. My deepest appreciation is extended to Richard Polese of Ocean Tree Books for shepherding me through this project. Finally, thank you to Dottie DeHart and the staff of DeHart Public Relations for your expert guidance in getting this book into the hands of the American Public.

Contents

Introduction

*"I was born an American; I will live an American;
I shall die an American."*

Daniel Webster

T HE WORDS OF JOHN F. KENNEDY were seared into my mind and heart. He told us in 1961 during his inauguration, "Ask not what your country can do for you; ask what you can do for your country." While I was growing up in New Mexico, several important values were instilled in me about our individual responsibility to the world. My four siblings and I were raised to believe we had a duty to make a difference in the world. My father taught us to speak the truth, regardless of the consequences. My mother emphasized the benefit of speaking as diplomatically as possible so people would listen. In our American, middle-class, devotedly Catholic, Hispanic home, we engaged in fiery discussions on politics, religion and social issues around the dinner table. Dad would take the lead and any topic was fair game. We were challenged to become independent thinkers, and when we didn't understand something, we were encouraged to ask questions. Interestingly, the five of us grew up to represent the entire political gamut, from conservative to moderate to liberal.

I deeply appreciate how fortunate we are as Americans to have freedom of speech and a voice in our government. I cherish our way of life and believe that, as Americans, we are incredibly lucky to have the ability to achieve the American Dream — becoming whatever we dream, if only we are willing to work hard to accomplish our goals.

Traveling the country as an extroverted motivational business speaker, I've been able to have conversations with many different people and sometimes it feels like Americans are living in parallel universes because their perspectives on the political issues of our day vary so greatly. But the passion and love for our country is enormous and most evident, regardless of the individual differences.

Using a non-threatening interviewing technique of asking questions and listening, Americans have generously shared their views on political issues and the social concerns that are most relevant to them. I've met and talked with strangers in airports, restaurants, hotel gyms, and store lines. Seminar attendees from all over the country have shared their thoughts and feelings about our current political climate.

My clients represent a wide range of industries from different parts of the country. A number of them have revealed their perceptions concerning the state of our nation. It has been fascinating to listen to the insights of my colleagues, other professional speakers and consultants, who also have access to a wide variety of national and international audiences. And, of course, there have been the many conversations with friends and family. I've kept track of scores of comments, insights, responses, and opinions. I will refer to some of these conversations, using the first names or pseudonyms of the people as they may have requested. Their reflections and concerns provide intriguing commentary throughout this book.

This book is for those who love America and who, despite the unsettling events of late, still believe it is the best country in the world in which to live. It is for those who are passionate about democracy and care about the truth. It is written for those who feel a need to know more about our foreign policies, especially the wars in Iraq and Afghanistan, the oil connection, and how our very political system seemed to change overnight.

It is for those who have little time for independent research yet thirst for the whole story of how we got to this particular point in American politics. It is written for those who want to leave the world, and especially our country, a better place for future generations. It is a gift of love from me to you, with the hope that somehow you, too, will be touched to live your life differently.

Bernadette T. Vadurro

★ 1 ★

The American Apple Turnover

"Whosoever wishes to know about the world
must learn about it in its particular details."

Heraklieto of Ephesos

PRIOR TO THE 9/11 ATTACK ON AMERICA, I had not kept up with global events. When newspapers and magazine articles emphasized world conflict and strife, my eyes glazed over and I simply skipped them. I asked, "What does discord and war half a world away have to do with me?" And according to documented studies I was not alone.[1] As a matter of fact, American's interest in foreign affairs had declined dramatically in the last forty years, with Americans more preoccupied with the state of the economy than with any other issue until after the 9/11 attack. According to the Gallup Poll, the number one issue for Americans from 1972 until the election of 2004 was the economy.[2] Prior to 1972 the top issue was foreign affairs. The U.S. involvement in Vietnam, worry over Soviet Union communist threats and concerns with "Red China" were matters prompting greater and more acute citizen awareness in foreign affairs.

Fewer and fewer Americans travel abroad and the number of students studying foreign languages today is half the number who studied foreign languages in 1965.[3] Less than 8 percent of U.S. college students take a foreign language class in any given year and less than 2 percent study abroad.[4] There has been a consistent drop in foreign news stories in American newspapers since the late 1980s, according to a 2004 Columbia University study.[5] We have a very limited focus on matters beyond our own borders.

Our nation is so large that it is easy for Americans to become isolated in our homes and individual communities. Most Americans are preoccupied with earning a living and tending to family, home and local matters. We tend to take care of our local community while relying on our government to develop honest and ethical foreign policies that will ultimately serve us. As a matter of fact, most Americans will spend more time researching their next cell phone purchase, or deciding which sporting event or movie to watch, than researching and understanding our nation's foreign policies and practices.

I'll bet only a few of us know exactly how our congressional representatives have actually voted on domestic issues that directly impact us. I would venture to bet still further that even fewer of us know how they have voted on foreign matters.[6] The U.S. is the greatest superpower in the world and our foreign policies have a massive impact on the nations of the world. As such powerful global citizens, Americans have an obligation to know and understand how the policies and practices of our nation are affecting the world today.[7] As Americans, many of us are fat, happy and fairly comfortable. My European friend Gerard says he sees Americans "as fiercely patriotic, fairly ignorant and rather naïve about foreign affairs."

Debby, a retired scientist who has traveled around the world, says, "Americans know little about the rest of the world. We live like kings and queens while most of the people on this planet spend their day searching for their next meal." Futurist Andrew Zolli said recently, "Most garbage disposals in America eat better than the majority of the people on this planet."[8]

Opportunities of life, liberty and the pursuit of happiness should be available to every human being around the globe who desires them. We touch others outside our borders through U.S. policies and practices. Ultimately, the voting public is responsible for electing government officials who institute policies and practices that reflect, or should reflect, our values as Americans.

But how many Americans can honestly say that they fully and completely know and understand U.S. foreign policies? How can we really trust what is going on, especially if we are not familiar with or do not understand U.S. policies abroad? By increasing understanding and encouraging participation and involvement we can make a fair assessment. U.S. foreign policies should be transparent, easy to understand, free from greed, economic inequality and human rights violations. Policies ensuring sound environmental protections must be in place to preserve the quality of life for future generations. By becoming involved, we can assure that America is kept safe and secure while still respecting and safeguarding the fundamental ideals of our great nation.

Unfortunately, we have developed a culture that encourages naiveté and ignorance. Because Americans are so consumed with their day-to-day lives, and because we expect our government officials to share our values of honesty, integrity and a strong sense of ethics, we tend to give them a free pass. We do not pay as close attention to governmental matters as we might if we suspected otherwise.

Others think it is all right to be disengaged, ill-informed or naïve about governmental matters and foreign affairs because they believe there are mechanisms in place to protect us from abuse. As Americans, we think that if our elected officials are unscrupulous, our free press will expose the culprits. Further, we think that if our free press fails to identify these culprits, then there is a safety net in the form of a system of checks and balances that will ultimately reveal offenses. My research has uncovered three major reasons why Americans have failed to be as politically engaged as perhaps we should be and why we offer justifications for our disconnected state of being.

JUSTIFICATION FOR AMERICAN DISCONNECTEDNESS

1. The "busyness" factor.
2. Too much, too little or conflicting information.
3. The apathetic attitude.

WE THINK WE HAVE CHECKS AND BALANCES

1. Trust in our public servants to serve with honesty, integrity and a strong sense of ethics.
2. Belief that the media serves as a whistle blower to disclose the truth in a timely manner.
3. Confidence that a check and balance system is in place and that it works.

Justification for American Disconnectedness

1. **The "busyness" factor:** With all the new technologies we possess, one would think that Americans have more time, but in essence we seem

to have less and less time. We work longer hours yet have more family commitments and community obligations than ever before.[9] Americans have a profound need to trust government so that we can place our time and attention on our families and develop our personal and professional lives.[10] We are simply too busy to stop and do the necessary research required to find out what is really going on in the world, and what our government is doing.

2. **Too much, too little or conflicting information factor:** We may be experiencing the too much, too little or conflicting information factor. Karen, a business management consultant, explained to me that she feels "media overload." As Americans, we are confronted with hundreds of choices in television, radio, newspapers, magazines, websites, and books. This variety, combined with the overwhelming negative content and perspective of the reporting, makes her shut down. When the messages get fuzzy or conflicting, it becomes even more challenging to know what the truth really is and who is telling it.

Ron, a landscaper who owns his own business, says that when he gets conflicting information, his tendency is to postpone analyzing it. He says he hopes someone he trusts within his network of friends or family figures it out. He says, "I don't have time to figure out who is telling the truth." He describes feeling anxious and frustrated when 2 plus 2 doesn't add up to 4.

Traveling around the country, I have noticed that newspapers in diverse locations are decidedly different in content and perspective. The quality and quantity of information a U.S. citizen is exposed to vary greatly depending upon where they live. Frequently, in one day I can obtain several local newspapers from many different communities and get a totally different perspective on the same story. For example, right before the war in Iraq was being routinely covered by the press, I picked up a local paper before leaving the West Coast. Highlighted on the front page were reports of numerous anti-war demonstrations, complete with photos from around the U.S. and the world.

Yet on the very same day in Salt Lake City I found their local newspaper had nothing about the impending war in Iraq. The only exception was a short letter to the editor. Whether the newspaper is owned by a corporate conglomerate or whether it is a small independently-owned newspaper makes a difference in what international information is presented, where in the paper it's found, and how that information is covered, or simply omitted. Another factor may be geographic and cultural differences that often determine how the news is reported.

If you have too little information, it becomes difficult to make an accurate assessment. It's like trying to solve a puzzle with only half the pieces. You can attempt to fill in the blanks, but you may never be certain the picture is right. More information on this phenomenon will be addressed in depth in the chapter, "When Watchdogs Become Lap Dogs."

3. **The apathetic attitude:** This attitude is made up of three fundamental causes:

- **Cause one** is disenfranchisement whereby people believe their opinions, ideas and votes don't matter anymore and they feel nothing they say or do will change the outcome.

- **Cause two** is the belief that our political system has become poisoned by giant corporate influences and unethical lobbyists. People feel powerless, and without leadership they engage in ostrich behavior, meaning they think if they stick their "head in the sand," the problem will go away by itself.

- **Cause three** is fear. This is a state in which people not only don't know what is going on, but they are also terrified of what they might discover if they were to begin seeking the truth.

We Think We Have Checks and Balances

1. **We trust our public servants to serve with honesty, integrity and a strong sense of ethics:** Like the idea of innocent until proven guilty, most Americans hold high standards of ethics, honesty, integrity, and behavior. We hope our elected government officials adhere to the same standards by which we live our lives. U.S. citizens are outraged, and then deeply disappointed, when they discover that politicians have willingly engaged in unethical and devious behavior. So many government officials of late have broken this sacred trust. Today, many Americans are totally disgusted as they learn of one political scandal after another, asking, "Where does it end?" or "Does it ever end?" Unethical behaviors designed to defraud and cheat the American public can be better controlled when a fully educated electorate demands complete accountability and is willing to closely monitor all its branches of government.

2. **We believe the media serves as a whistle-blower to disclose the truth in a timely manner:** Because of the purported freedom of the press,

most Americans believe that we have a vigorous and unintimidated media that strives to keep citizens informed in a timely manner.

With television, print media and the Internet all protected by our guaranteed freedom of speech, we think the media will tell us if politicians or their policies have violated the sacred public trust. According to recent studies, 59 percent of Americans trust the media "to operate in the best interests of society."[11] Fox News and CNN, according to a June 2006 Harris Poll, remain the two top news television sources for a majority of Americans.

3. **Confidence that a check and balance system is in place and that it works:** This confidence is rooted in the deep-seated belief that the three branches of government—executive, judicial and legislative—operate with integrity and in the best interest of its citizens. We think that because of checks and balances we are protected from one branch monopolizing the others.[12] Through this system, Americans hope to be sheltered from blatant abuses of public trust. But what happens if all of these entities become corrupt, infected or disproportionately influential?

If Americans have access to complete, accurate and reliable information, I believe they will unite to insist upon accountability and justice, regardless of their political affiliation. We need courage to seek out the facts in order to draw our own conclusions. Knowledge provides a feeling of empowerment to participate in the process. These three need to work in concert: *honest public servants, an informed and unbiased press, and a viable working system of checks and balances.*

Is Our Country Headed in the Wrong Direction?

There is a growing level of anxiety among people in our nation, a feeling that things aren't right and a sense that we have gotten off track. Seventy percent of respondents in a May 2006 poll said the country was heading in the wrong direction.[13] People are frustrated as they attempt to identify the problems. I've found the politics of our nation have become increasingly polarized for many. Here are two examples:

> **Tom** *says he's frustrated with his 40-year-old twin sister Leslie, who accused him of being "brainwashed and ill-informed" because he supported President Bush's decision to go to war in Iraq. Tom says every time he calls Leslie, she brings up the fact there were never any weapons of mass destruction, and he hates feeling he might have been manipulated. On the other hand, he tries to explain*

to her that he believes "we are engaging the enemy in the Middle East" and that this keeps our nation safer. Tom says Leslie doesn't believe this and he ends up feeling irritated and defensive. Tom reports that he and Leslie used to talk at least once a week, but now they rarely speak.

Melissa says she feels very uncomfortable when her congressional representatives bring up the issue of gay marriage. Melissa's husband Peter supports the President and other politicians' stand on the gay issue. Melissa says she believes the gay issue has nothing to do with national priorities. As a life-long Republican, Melissa says, "it's an attack on traditional Republican values, values that used to advocate protection against governmental intrusion, especially into the private lives of people." Melissa thinks it's a trick to distract Americans from more pressing issues. She feels annoyed with Peter, who after many conversations now refuses to discuss it with her.

These are just two instances of the divergence in political ideology. Americans appear to be committed to a strong stance on particular topics and are not receptive to information that may alter or negate that position. Each person accuses the other of not listening when one or the other brings up differing views. We will further examine how dangerous divisionary tactics have fractured us as a nation in the chapter, "Push, Push Back: Distraction, Division and Polarization."

Conservatives charge the media with a liberal bent and Liberals charge the opposite. While working out in a hotel gym prior to the 2004 elections, I witnessed a verbal scuffle between two people. A young man walked into the hotel gym and asked if he could turn off the television and turn on the radio instead. The television was on a Fox News station. A middle-aged man responded by saying no, he did not want to hear the radio, but would prefer changing the channel to CNN News. At this point, another man bellowed out that CNN was a communist station. The first man barked back that Fox News was the bullhorn for Bush and Company. I was amazed at the level of intensity and hostility exchanged by two people over which news station to watch.

According to a 2006 Harris Poll, over 60 percent of U.S. adults surveyed say there is a media bias. However, there is a disagreement about whether the bias is liberal or conservative.[14] What is going on in our world and who can we trust to present the truth? With all the strife in the world, especially in the Middle East, we can no longer ignore the questions of media bias and the inaccessibility of information. More on this topic is addressed in the chapter, "When Watchdogs Become Lap Dogs."

Personal Stories of the Affected

There may be a few Americans who do not care about what is going on in our nation and beyond our borders, but I believe most Americans simply have not been paying close attention. They are devoted and patriotic Americans who intuitively know things aren't right in our nation, but they can't seem to put their finger on it. They tend to blame the media, one political party, the decline in social morals, the U.S. educational system, Hollywood, and the list goes on. Still others have much greater problems with the state of our nation because it has impacted their lives personally, as in the following situations:

Dale was a participant in one of my programs. He is a dedicated employee who has worked for his company for many years. He is married with children. On September 11, 2006, Dale gave a four-minute presentation. He began his speech by noting the date and talking about how he felt as an American regarding the attacks on 9/11, using words like "angry" and "bewildered." He said that after the attacks he was one of the people who could not wait for us to get to Afghanistan to get "our revenge against those who had attacked us." Dale admitted that he had no idea what or who the Taliban was before the attacks. He said for all he knew the Taliban could have been the name of a mutual fund. Dale said he was disappointed when our troops were unable to apprehend Osama bin Laden.

He then told the group that his son joined the Marines in 2006 and was to be deployed to Iraq. Dale struggled with his conflicting emotions as he now questioned whether this war was worth the life of his son. He described how it felt to be an American invested in America's war in Iraq. With his son's impending active duty service, it was a much heavier investment. I watched Dale with heartfelt sadness as he spoke of this struggle.

Jimmy and Laura, once passive Americans, are now active in the antiwar movement. They track every American casualty and reach out to the families who have lost loved ones. They do not see an end to the death, turmoil and increased conflict in Iraq. Jimmy and Laura vacillate between states of sorrow and bitterness, to resentment over the daily deaths of young Americans and Iraqis who are dying for a war launched expressly in a search for weapons of mass destruction. Weapons, we later discovered, that had never existed.[15]

Sue, a stay-at-home mom, lost her father in the World Trade Center on September 11, 2001. She screams with outrage when yet another transcript from a news agency appears on her computer screen presenting a message from Osama bin Laden, who remains at large some six years after sanctioning the 9/11 attack on America. Sue wonders why President Bush is so consumed with Iraq and why capturing Osama bin Laden is no longer a priority.[16] Sue feels betrayed.

Dave *and his son* **Kyle** *love to go ice fishing in Montana every winter, but this year they were fiercely disappointed because the lake never froze. Dave is irritated because he says "the government is hiding evidence of global warming to protect oil-polluting industries."*

Tina *and her husband* **James** *were devastated when their tiny house in New Orleans was destroyed in the flood waters of Hurricane Katrina in 2005. James is a retired city worker who is downright furious that "American dollars have been appropriated to rebuild Iraq, while American cities like New Orleans continue to be left susceptible and in a state of disarray and disrepair." They say the reconstruction money that was supposed to be for New Orleans never went to the people and places where it was most needed.*

Sam and Louise *lost their children's college savings in the Enron scandal (the global energy company based in Houston, Texas). They had invested their kids' college funds in Enron accounts. As their children reach high school graduation they feel "ripped off."*

Sarita, *a nurse in Northern California, lost most of her retirement savings because of Enron and she worries about how she will ever be able to retire. With the growing U.S. deficit, she wonders if she will be able to realistically count on social security to augment her retirement plan. Sarita hopes to stay healthy so she can keep working.*

Other General Concerns

Each of these persons describes feelings of helplessness, fear, anger, and anxiety. Many working Americans are feeling confused and frustrated. These are Americans who *must* work for a living, without the luxury of trust funds or other economic safety nets. They must be accountable for their actions or they will be fired from their jobs or lose their businesses. They are saving money for their children to go to college and are concerned about the rising costs and declining quality of education.

They worry about the social security system and wonder if it will be around to care for them when the time comes. Approximately one out of three average Americans was without health care insurance during 2002-03.[17] Those who have health care insurance are grateful to have it, but voice concerns about reduced benefits and coverage. They express frustration over the ever-increasing premiums, co-payments and deductibles that take bigger chunks out of paychecks and business profits. Those who don't have insurance pray they don't get sick. Small businesses that find they are unable to afford health care insurance for their employees are at a competitive disadvantage to recruit and keep the best qualified employees.

Overworked, Distracted or Disengaged Americans

Voter turnout is so low that according to pessimists the biggest winner in every election in America is apathy, and they say this sarcastically. According to the U.S. Census Bureau, voter participation in national elections has been at or below 50 percent for the last three decades.[18] This is a sharp decline from earlier decades. In the 1964 Presidential elections, 69.3 percent of the voting-age population exercised their right to vote as compared to 54 percent in the 2000 Presidential elections.[19] Participation is always higher for Presidential elections than it is for mid-term elections, so that makes mid-term election turnout even more pathetic.

Most Americans would rather spend their leisure time with their loved ones, or in front of a good book or television program. Few would be driven to sit at their computer or go to the library to research our county's foreign policies, energy plans, oil dependency, and security threats. But, if one were to research carefully, they would discover American reliance on fossil fuels, security threats from terrorists, a political environment that chips away at freedoms and democracy, a narrow-minded dogma that encourages division and polarization of its citizens, and global warming to be topics that are all deeply interwoven. The fact is, Americans are facing complex moral, emotional, philosophical, and political issues.

Martin, a contractor and builder, said, "I feel overwhelmed and powerless to make any positive changes," and he said he doesn't have "enough reliable information to discuss the issues." Many intelligent people are starting to say: *It is time for me to wake up out of this comfortable slumber, get informed and get involved.*

Because busy Americans might be limited in their knowledge and understanding of the world at large, we tend to create perceptions of how the world operates beyond our borders. The problem arises because many of our perceptions are inaccurate. What problems should we be focused upon to ensure the health, safety and future prosperity of our great nation? How can we come together as a nation to solve the complex issues facing us in the 21st Century?

Let's take each of these issues and break them into bite-sized components. If we can get a handle of each of these issues, we can better understand, evaluate and determine appropriate action.

Let us start with what we do and do not know. I have developed an easy quiz to determine your knowledge of foreign affairs. I challenge you to take this simple yet interesting assessment. Questions 1, 3, 4 and 7 are similar to questions asked by GFK Roper Public Affairs in the 2006 National Geographic Survey conducted among young American adults. Simply circle the answers you believe to be correct. You will find the answers at the end of the quiz.

"In extraordinary events, ignorance of their causes produces astonishment."

Marcus Tullius Cicero

World Knowledge Assessment

1) Sudan is located in:

  a. Asia

  b. Africa

  c. India

  d. Indonesia

  e. Ethiopia

2) Which countries border Iraq?

  a. Niger, Saudi Arabia, Kuwait, and Lebanon

  b. Libya, Syria, Algeria and Kuwait

  c. Saudi Arabia, Turkey, Iran, Kuwait, Jordan, and Syria

  d. Iran, Kuwait, Saudi Arabia, and Libya

  e. Niger, Turkey, Iran, Kuwait, and Libya

3) What primary language is most often spoken in the world?

  a. Spanish

  b. Russian

  c. English

  d. Mandarin Chinese

  e. Arabic

4) As measured in dollars, which country is the world's largest exporter of goods and services?

  a. USA

  b. China

  c. Japan

  d. England

  e. Russia

5) The seven most populated cities in the world are:

  a. Mumbai, Sao Paulo, Karachi, Seoul, Jakarta, Mexico City, and Beijing

  b. Beijing, Xi'an, Istanbul, Cairo, Tokyo, Tehran, and Bangalore

  c. Calcutta, Tokyo, London, Los Angeles, Singapore, Rome, and Mexico City

  d. New York City, Tehran, Rio de Janeiro, Rome, Ho Chi Minh City, Berlin, and Bogota

  e. Manila, Mumbai, Istanbul, Singapore, Buenos Aires, Madrid, and Budapest

6) Which President made a speech to Congress using ten principles, including a comprehensive energy policy: reduced demand for oil, the development of new, unconventional sources of energy and the establishment of a national petroleum reserve?

  a. George W. Bush in 2001

  b. William Clinton in 1996

  c. Ronald Reagan in 1982

  d. Jimmy Carter in 1977

  e. George H.W. Bush in 1990

7) The major religion in India is:

a. Christianity

b. Hinduism

c. Buddhism

d. Islam

e. Sikhism

8) Which of the following statements is true?

a. While Ronald Reagan was President, the Iran-Contra Affair took place and the U.S. National Security Council sold arms to Iran and gave the proceeds to Nicaraguan rebels to fight against their elected government.

b. President Jimmy Carter was given a Nobel Peace Prize for his efforts to find peaceful solutions to international conflicts.

c. The Gulf War during George H.W. Bush's Presidency was launched to repel Saddam Hussein's invasion of Kuwait, and to provide stability in the Persian Gulf where roughly two-thirds of the world's oil reserves are located.

d. In Darfur, Sudan, literally hundreds of thousands of people have died and 2,000,000 have been displaced as of early 2006.

e. All of the statements are true.

9) The number of Americans who have a passport is:

a. Less than 5%

b. Between 6% and 15%

c. Between 16% and 25%

e. Approximately 30%

d. More than 50%

10) Which of the following statements is false?

a. In 1953, the United States CIA covertly worked to overthrow the government of Iran.

b. In 2005, the UN estimated more than 100,000 Palestinians out of the 125,000 that used to work in Israeli settlements or in joint industries had lost their jobs.

c. In 1947, the United Nations created the nation of Israel; this caused conflict with the Palestinians who were living in these lands.

d. All nineteen of the 9/11 suicide hijack terrorists were practicing Wahhabis.

e. Most terrorists come from the Iraqi Shiite faction.

(Answers on next page)

ANSWERS

1) Sudan is located in:

b. Africa.

2) **Which countries border Iraq?**

c. Iraq is bordered by Saudi Arabia, Turkey, Iran, Kuwait, Jordan, and Syria. This is an important fact for Americans considering that the cost to secure freedom in Iraq has been estimated at $283,182,193,000 as of May 24, 2006, and it grows daily (based upon congressional appropriations).[20]

3) **The primary language most spoken in the world is:**

d. Mandarin is the most widely spoken language because it is spoken in China; the most populous country on the planet. Mandarin beats second-place English by a two to one ratio.

4) **The world's largest exporter of goods and services as measured in dollars is:**

a. USA. According to a recent report conducted by the GFK Roper Public Affairs, the United States is the world's largest exporter of goods and services.

5) **The seven most populated cities in the world are:**

a. Mumbai (formerly known as Bombay), Sao Paulo, Karachi, Seoul, Beijing, Mexico City, and Jakarta.

6) **The President that made a speech to Congress to emphasize the importance of national security using ten principles to include: a comprehensive energy policy, reduced demand for oil and the development of new unconventional sources of energy was:**

d. Jimmy Carter, in 1977, made a plea to the nation and Congress to support his comprehensive energy plan.[21]

7) **India's major religion is:**

b. Hinduism.

8) **Which statements are true?**

f. All of the statements are true.

9) **The number of Americans with a passport is:**

b. Between 6% and 15%.

10) **Which of the following statements is false?**

e. Terrorists come from all over the world.

NOTES, Chapter 1

1 Alkman Granitsas, "American's are Tuning Out," *YaleGlobal*, November 24, 2005.

2 Answers cited on Presidential Elections by Gallup Polls, 1972-2004.

3 Granitsas, "Tuning Out."

4 www.statesman.com/news/content/news/stories/local/07/17foreign.html.

5 Granitsas, "Tuning Out."

6 www.votenote.aol.com; www.govtrack.us/. Both sites provide subscribers with regular notification of how congressional representatives vote.

7 Granitsas, "Tuning Out."

8 Andrew Zoli, Keynote Speaker, Northeast Farm Credit Services Conference, October 4, 2006.

9 International Labor Organization Labor Market 2001-2002 study. Americans work longer hours than Canadians, Germans, Japanese and other workers, and American workers are, per person, more productive than their counterparts in other countries as reported in CNN on August 31, 2001.

10 Dale Allen Pfeiffer and Elizabeth Anne Pfeiffer, "The Power of Delusion," *From the Wilderness*, 2004, www.fromthewilderness.com/free/ww3/112304_ power_ delu sion.shtml.

11 Ibid.

12 According to a ten-country, 10,000-person poll by the London-based research firm GlobeScan, in the U.S., the government ranks ahead of the media on trust at 67 percent to 59 percent.
a. "Americans trust government more than media," *WorldNet Daily*, May 4, 2006, www.worldnetdaily.com/news/printer-friendly.asp?ARTICLE_ID=50034
b. William Leggett, *Democratick Editorials: Essays in Jacksonian Political Economy* (Indianapolis: Liberty Fund, 1984), oll.libertyfund.org/ToC/0012.php.

13 Adam Nagourney and Megan Thee, "Poll Gives Bush His Worst Marks Yet," *The New York Times*, May 10, 2006.

14 "News Reporting is Perceived as Biased, though Less Agreement on Whether it is Liberal or Conservative Bias," *The Harris Poll*, June 30, 2006, www.harrisinter active.com/harris_poll/index.asp?PID=679.

15 Fox News reported in June 2006 that tubes of chemical weapons had been found. According to the de-classified memo from Negroponte, the 550 tubes were pre-1991 chemicals and they had been reported as found once before.

16 National Commission on Terrorist Attacks, *The 9/11 Commission Report: Final Report of the National Commission on Terrorist Attacks Upon the United States* (New York: W. W. Norton, 2004).

17 "Facts on Health Insurance Coverage," *National Coalition on Health Care*, www.nchc.org/facts/coverage.shtml.

18 *United States Census Bureau*, www.census.gov.

19 *Public Broadcasting Service Online*, www.pbs.org.

20 "The Cost of War." *National Priorities Project*, May 24, 2006, www.national priorities.org/index.php?option=com_wrapper&Itemid=182.

21 For the complete text see www.pbs.org/wgbh/amex/carter/filmmore/ps_ energy.html. Speech delivered April 18, 1977.

★ 2 ★

We're Addicted

"The entire world is waiting for a substitute for gasoline...
and long before that time the price of gasoline will have risen
to a point where it will be too expensive to burn as motor fuel."
Henry Ford, 1925

H E LAY ON PERSPIRATION-DRENCHED SHEETS, withered and gaunt. His grimy hair was plastered against flaccid skin that hung from an emaciated and worn face. The crazed, blood-shot eyes darted around the room. He twisted and wrenched his body, which was filled with excruciating pain that throbbed through every cell of his being. If there were a sound to accompany such pain, it would be the cacophony of horror. His thin, jaundiced hand reached out as he cried, "Oh God, please..."

Such is the plight of an addict in the throes of detoxification and withdrawal; the pain may be deferred but it is unavoidable if one wishes to recover. Every day we are told in papers, magazines and news programs that America is addicted to oil. America has not yet reached the point described so dramatically above. We are, however, at the itchy desirous state, just about to go over the edge. How and when will America recover?

The Deal: Petroleum for Protection

Concern for oil has been present since the early 1920s. Towards the end of World War II it was discovered that U.S. petroleum reserves were quickly being depleted. If the rate of production continued at its current pace, our nation would be out of petroleum within decades. President

Franklin Delano Roosevelt (FDR) was anxious for the U.S. to have an enduring and dependable source of oil.[1] According to U.S. petroleum geologists, the Middle East had tremendous untapped reserves. America would be called on to provide much of the oil needed to win World War II and to help rebuild a war-torn Europe. Having an abundant energy source would secure our nation's continued preeminence in the world, and FDR showed strong interest in forging a relationship with Saudi Arabia to meet U.S. energy demands.

The British were pumping significant amounts of cash into Saudi Arabia to help increase its stability and were exerting increased pressure on the Saudis to make a deal directly with them. However, since the Saudis had previously experienced unpleasant British domination, they preferred an alliance with their new friends, the Americans. The timing for a mutually agreeable pact was ripe. On February 1945, a meeting in the Suez Canal aboard the *U.S.S. Quincy* took place between FDR and Ibn Sa'ud, the Ruling Monarch of Saudi Arabia. Ibn Sa'ud had fought tooth and nail to establish Saudi Arabia as a nation in 1932. He desperately needed reliable protection from various warring Islamic tribal factions and the aggressions of other Middle Eastern nations. Saudi Arabia also had an urgent need for new cash reserves. At the time, the agreement between the U.S. and the Saudis seemed like a marriage made in heaven.

King Ibn Saud with President Franklin D. Roosevelt on board U.S.S. Quincy *in 1945.*

The U.S. won concessions from Saudi Arabia, guaranteeing long-term, cheap and fairly reliable energy resources. The concessions were made in exchange for a U.S. commitment to be Saudi Arabia's top customer and the protector of the royal family. The U.S. would protect the Saudi kingdom against threats from enemies both internally and from outside the country. The pact would wed our governments, our economies and our security for years to come. Powerful government and corporate influences substantially impacted the public and private lives of citizens from both nations as a result of this union. This merger has been marked by greed, possessiveness, religious fanaticism, covert plundering, and terrorism, all of which will be explored in depth in later chapters.

THIRTY-THREE YEARS
OF PRESIDENTIAL LIP SERVICE

1974: "Let this be our national goal: At the end of this decade, in the year 1980, the United States will not be dependent on any other country for the energy we need to provide our jobs, to heat our homes, and to keep our transportation moving."

Richard Nixon[2]

1975: "These proposals and actions, cumulatively, can reduce our dependence on foreign energy supplies from three to five million barrels per day by 1985."

Gerald Ford[3]

1979: "Beginning this moment, this nation will never use more foreign oil than we did in 1977—never."

Jimmy Carter[4]

1991: "When our administration developed our national energy strategy, three principles guided our policy: reducing our dependence on foreign oil, protecting our environment and promoting economic growth."

George H.W. Bush[5]

2006: "Breakthroughs on this and other new technologies will help us reach another great goal: to replace more than 75 percent of our oil imports from the Middle East by 2025."

George W. Bush[6]

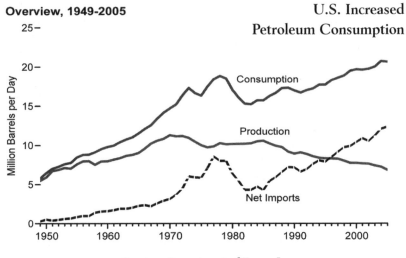

Courtesy Department of Energy[7]

Conserve Less Consume More

Despite the rhetoric and the promises of our elected politicians to achieve energy independence, the U.S. continues to move completely in the opposite direction by increasing foreign oil dependence.[8] The U.S. has an insatiable appetite to gobble up *vast quantities* of oil. In the last twenty-two years, America has more than doubled consumption from 8.8 million barrels per day in 1977 to more than 21 million in 2006.

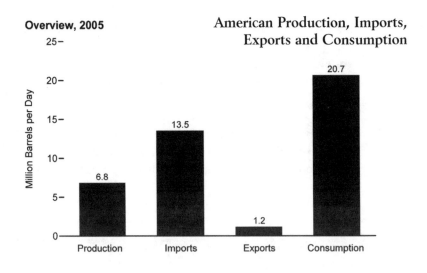

Hidden Costs of America's Foreign Oil Dependency

Reports show that U.S. petroleum production peaked in the 1970s at 9.64 million barrels. As of 2004 the nation was only able to produce 5.43 million barrels of oil. Canada is the biggest exporter of oil to America.[9] The *largest declines* in oil production continue to be in the U.S.[10] American automobiles use *more than half* of the oil upon which we are dependent. As more fuel-efficient cars have been slow to appear on the market, our government continues to subsidize inefficient, gas-guzzling SUVs through tax incentives.

In the summer of 2006, Americans paid an average $3.00 per gallon for gasoline. According to a study commissioned by the U.S. Department of Energy (DOE), the true cost of a gallon of gasoline is much higher. We have failed to calculate all the hidden costs paid through American tax dollars. Consider the tax breaks and subsidies given to the gas and oil industry. The cost for the U.S. to secure oil in the Middle East is esti-mated at $50 billion per year. Then there is the cost of two wars. The Gulf War cost $80 billion, and the 2003 Iraq war, which was originally estimated to cost $200 billion, is projected to be double that by 2007.[11]

Additionally, a DOE-commissioned study indicates that Americans have transferred an estimated $1.16 trillion to oil-producing nations over thirty years, thus drastically increasing the U.S. trade deficit. This study also shows that America loses 27,000 jobs for every $1 billion of the U.S. trade deficit. Oil imports account for almost one-third of the total U.S. deficit.[12] Finally, we must take into account the damage that the burn-ing of fossil fuels does to our environment, our air quality and our health. If renewable energy sources such as solar power were given the same sub-sidies as the oil industry, America would be further along toward energy independence.

In Europe, many countries impose a hugely significant gasoline tax that comprises up to 75 percent of the total cost per gallon. In March 2005, gasoline cost $6.48 per gallon in Amsterdam, $5.79 in London, $5.57 in Frankfurt, and $4.24 in Tokyo. Foreign gasoline taxes include an "environmental impact tax," which goes toward funding clean, alternative energy research.[13]

Gasoline Consumption

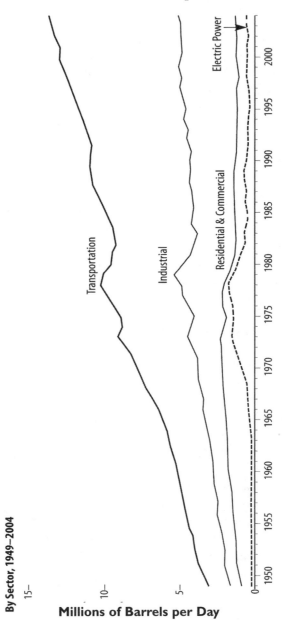

Courtesy Department of Energy[14]

The Pressure to Produce More Oil

Americans are not the only people who have needs for greater amounts of oil—the whole world is getting oil-addicted. As the need for oil increases, so does the pressure to produce more fossil fuels. Chinese oil consumption has risen by nearly 900,000 barrels per day. By 2004, global oil production exceeded 80 million barrels per day for the first time. The Organization of Petroleum Exporting Countries (OPEC) gained market share as output rose by 2.2 million barrels per day to 32.9 million barrels per day.[15] Iraq and Venezuela remained below previous peaks, but Saudi Arabian output reached a record 10.6 million barrels per day.[16]

Oil production outside OPEC increased by 965,000 barrels per day in 2004; this increase was 200,000 barrels per day above the previous ten-year average. Russia was another leading contributor, with output rising by nearly 750,000 barrels per day. Angola, Chad, Ecuador, Equatorial Guinea, and Kazakhstan all recorded growth of more than 100,000 barrels per day.

According to the *British Petroleum Statistical Review of World Energy*, in 2004 the U.S. had about 31 billion barrels of proven reserves, or 2.7 percent of the world's oil supply. If we relied only on domestic reserves, at the current rate of consumption we'd have enough oil to last four and a half years, assuming no more is found. It is important to note that this total includes sectors of the Gulf of Mexico and the Arctic National Wildlife Refuge that are currently off-limits for drilling. This is a huge problem for the U.S., whose economy is heavily reliant on cheap foreign oil.

Worldwide Proven Oil Reserves (billion barrels)[17]

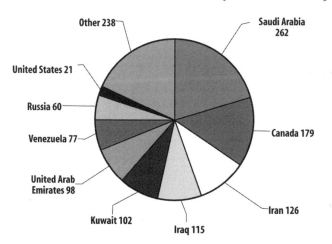

Other 238
Saudi Arabia 262
United States 21
Russia 60
Venezuela 77
Canada 179
United Arab Emirates 98
Kuwait 102
Iraq 115
Iran 126

Floundering Government Initiatives

Richard Nixon, who was hailed as the modern day "environmental President," initiated Project Independence in 1973. The initiative committed $10 billion in federal funds to spur energy independence and development during a five-year period. He predicted private enterprise would invest as much as $200 billion in five years and $500 billion in ten years.[18]

The Watergate scandal that led to Richard Nixon's resignation slowed efforts. However, these endeavors were revitalized in 1977 when President Carter tried to convince the American people and Congress that the country's increased dependence on foreign oil exports was not only bad for our economic future, but that it also threatened the security of our nation. Carter delivered a prophetic speech nearly thirty years ago, warning America about the very scary possibilities we might face if we did not make major adjustments to move away from our reliance upon foreign oil. We did not heed his warning and we failed to make those adjustments. Now we face dire consequences.[19]

Because of the oil embargo in the mid-70s, American politicians were more in favor of conservation and energy-conscious programs. Carter instituted several important initiatives during his presidency. These would start the U.S. on the path of conservation and foreign oil independence. His most notable initiatives affect us still:

- The institution of President Gerald Ford's fuel-efficiency standards for automobiles insisted that U.S. automakers build more fuel-efficient cars with the goal of achieving an average of 27.5 miles per gallon.[20]

- The establishment of the National Strategic Petroleum Reserve assured that the U.S. had at least a six-month supply of crude oil in reserve.

- Carter motivated utility companies to cut their use of oil by switching to electricity and increasing use of natural gas and coal. At the time, this step alone resulted in a decline in oil usage from 20 percent to only 3 percent of electricity generation.[21]

- Carter offered tax deductions for solar water heaters installed in homes and commercial buildings.

- Carter had solar collectors installed on the White House. He turned down the thermostat and role-modeled energy conservation behavior as he mandated federal government agencies to do likewise.

- Carter created the U.S. Department of Energy to manage America's energy resources and prepare for the future.[22]

The Carter Doctrine
and U.S. Foreign Oil Entitlement

Referring primarily to the Soviet invasion of Afghanistan, Carter said in his State of the Union Speech in 1980: *"An attempt by an outside force to gain control of the Persian Gulf region will be regarded as an assault on the vital interests of the United States of America, and such an assault will be repelled by any means necessary, including military force."*[23] This would become known as the Carter Doctrine.

Presidents Reagan, George H.W. Bush and George W. Bush would later expand Carter's statement; it would be used as the basis to assert overt military power in order to control entities that threatened America's oil interest in the Middle East.

The Reagan Doctrine, which featured an enormous military investment in the "Star Wars" program, advocated "peace through power." The George W. Bush Doctrine would push even further, asserting the right to preemptive strikes against "perceived threats," whether real or imagined. A document that explains the new George W. Bush Doctrine, created by the American Enterprise Institute in 2003 and entitled *The Underpinnings of the Bush Doctrine*, declared "it takes little imagination to dream up other scenarios that might call for preemptive military action."[24] This doctrine — and how it became American policy — will be explored in greater detail in the chapter entitled "Neo Caustic."

The Vanishing of the U.S. Energy Crisis

Once Ronald Reagan assumed the Presidency, America's energy crisis simply disappeared; or at least that's what we were led to believe. Because of conservation and decreased regulations, world oil supplies increased and the forces of supply and demand pushed oil prices down. The middle class bought more cars, and those cars got bigger. The upper-middle class continued to move from the city to the suburbs, and commute times increased. Holiday lights were put up, and homes were warmed or cooled to comfort year-round. We created more products using petroleum-based substances, and we ignored all the warnings given to us by President Carter.

Through the years, an occasional, dim recollection of President Carter in his sweater speaking his message about conservation and alternative energy development would flash through my mind. I would be reminded of the image, especially during the holidays, when neighborhoods lit up in celebration. I trusted that somehow our government and the private sector had fixed this problem, but I never bothered to find out how, or if in fact the problem had really been fixed.

Ronald Reagan and Bill Clinton were the Presidential exceptions when it came to providing lip service on the problems related to our nation's foreign oil dependency. Instead of talking about the problem, they took two different approaches. After Reagan arrived in the White House in 1980, the solar panels came down and the solar research program was gutted. This move resulted in the firing of half the staff and all of the contractors, including two people who went on to win Nobel Prizes in other fields.

President Reagan and Congress stopped aggressively pushing new auto-efficiency standards, complying with the American auto industry desire to leave the standards at the Carter-era levels. The solar water-heating industry instantly went from a massive, billion-dollar industry to one that in 2006 installed only about 6,000 solar hot water heaters a year in the U.S. This was according to Noah Kaye, a spokesman for the Solar Energy Industries Association.[25] The solar tax benefit expired, and with it went the life of the embryonic solar industry.

Reagan removed all the oil price controls, resulting in a surplus of petroleum on the market and lower gas prices. His removal of price controls was, in part, an incentive for the oil and gas industries to increase production. Additionally, the industry was supposed to use the tax relief to seek alternatives to fossil fuels. According to Lou Cannon, President Reagan could have helped the U.S. diminish dependence on foreign oil if he had engaged in any one of three simple strategies:[26]

1) He could have filled the national strategic reserves with less expensive oil.
2) He could have imposed an oil import fee and used the funds for alternative energy development.
3) He could have encouraged conservation through increased gasoline taxes.

Because of the many initiatives that Carter had previously set up, and the relaxation of the tax burden under Reagan, dependence on foreign oil basically remained steady throughout the Reagan years, leaving George H.W. Bush with the same problem.[27] In the 1970s, the U.S. attempted to get serious about energy conservation. Under Reagan, motivated by government tax incentives, we switched lanes. Americans began a buying frenzy of oversized SUVs. Many of these purchases were heavily subsidized through huge government tax deductions.[28]

Clinton Attempts Are Overridden

In 1993, Bill Clinton attempted to get a wide-ranging energy bill passed through Congress. The plan would have created a tax increase at the gas pump, costing a typical family approximately $120 more each year and another $200 in indirect costs, for a total of $320 a year, according to the Department of Energy.[29] The bill was geared toward reducing the nation's dependence on foreign oil by reducing gasoline consumption. Ever fearful of impacting the economy, Congress rejected President Clinton's Energy Plan.[30]

Every President from Carter through Clinton who has attempted to move America away from foreign oil dependence has been obstructed by Congress, which is heavily influenced and lobbied by automakers and the oil industry. In 1993, Clinton initiated a $1 billion program called the Partnership for a New Generation of Vehicles (PNGV). PNGV was a collaboration between seven federal agencies, national laboratories and the U.S. Council for Automotive Research, along with DaimlerChrysler, Ford and General Motors. It aimed to produce a prototype car that could achieve approximately 80 miles per gallon by 2004.[31]

While the auto manufacturers have received these funds, they do not have to market vehicles to the public. According to Anna Aurilio of the U.S. Public Interest Research Group, auto manufacturers should not need subsidies to produce "super-efficient cars." She further states, "This program is corporate welfare" that benefits the major U.S. auto and diesel engine manufacturers.

Clinton was able to make a few environmentally responsible changes through administrative orders, but these orders hardly dented the problem of dependence on foreign oil.

The Hypocrisy of Tax Deductions and Credits

Here are two very typical examples of our government's hypocrisy regarding its stated desire to eliminate foreign oil dependence. They are illustrated in the **SUV Tax Deduction Loophole** and the **Hybrid Tax Credit.**

This chart illustrates the cost of six gas guzzling, fuel inefficient vehicles and the average overall miles per gallon that these cars are able to get. Despite their horrific inefficiency, the owners of these vehicles qualify for enormous tax breaks with few strings attached:

SAMPLE OF GAS GUZZLERS QUALIFYING FOR TAX BREAKS

BRAND	STICKER PRICE	OVERALL MPG
Chevrolet Suburban or Tahoe	$41,000	13
Dodge Durango	$39,820	12
Cadillac Escalade	$53,850	13/18
Hummer H3 SUV	$36,915	14
Ford Expedition	$45,180	14/17
Nissan Pathfinder Armada	$41,500	12

In 1997, a provision in the U.S. tax code provided small businesses with a tax writeoff of up to $25,000 for vehicles weighing more than 6,000 pounds. Currently, thirty-eight different passenger SUVs, including the notorious Hummer H2 (estimated 11 mpg), all weigh more than 6,000 pounds.[32] This loophole allowed the least fuel-efficient vehicles to qualify for a significant tax break.[33]

GEORGE W. BUSH PUSHES FOR BIGGER SUV TAX INCENTIVES

In 2003, the Bush Administration requested an increase of the SUV tax deduction to $75,000 for business owners. The Lawmakers reacted by expanding the deduction, not to $75,000, but to a massive $100,000. At the very same time, Congress was ever so stingy with tax credits on fuel-efficient vehicles for Americans.[34]

The House Ways and Means Committee approved a three-year extension of the gas-guzzling $100,000 loophole. This tax deduction created a huge benefit for buyers of the largest and least efficient vehicles. The result of this ridiculous tax benefit is that many of the wealthiest families in our nation qualified for a brand new SUV, tax-free, in addition to writing off the cost as a business expense.[35]

In response to public outrage, Congress introduced a couple of proposals aimed at nixing the gas guzzling SUV tax deductions. These proposals quickly failed. A compromise between the House and Senate, which rolled back the deduction to its original amount of $25,000 plus a 30 percent bonus write-off, was the best that could be done in October 2004. In 2005, the Bush Administration asked for weaker standards for gas-guzzlers and, according to Deron Lovaas, the Director of the National Resource Defense Council, "The Bush Administration's new standards... provide a loophole for the biggest gas-guzzlers like the GM Hummer. Even worse, this plan gives automakers an incentive to boost the size of their vehicles to avoid higher fuel economy standards."[36]

Congress Encourages Foreign Oil Dependence

The Bush Administration and the Republican-controlled Congress sabotaged all real efforts to minimize foreign oil dependence over the ten-year period from 1996 to 2006. To move ahead with more energy efficient and environmentally friendly automobiles simply was not a priority for this administration or Congress. In May 2002, the IRS declared gasoline-electric hybrids eligible for tax credits as "clean fuel" vehicles under the Energy Policy Act of 1992 (PL 103-486). However, the maximum deduction was $2,000 with a $500 reduction in the possible deduction every year until it was intended to be completely phased out in 2006.

On March 3, 2003, Senator Orrin Hatch (R-UT) and Representative Dave Camp (R-MI); along with Senate co-sponsors John Rockefeller (D-WV), James Jeffords (I-VT), Lincoln Chafee (R-RI), Hillary Clinton (D-NY), John Kerry (D-MA), Joseph Lieberman (D-CT), Olympia Snowe (R-ME), Gordon Smith (R-OR), Zell Miller (D-GA), Mark Dayton (D-MN), and others, reintroduced the CLEAR Act (S. 505). The bill was designed to provide tax incentives for clean, advanced vehicles. The CLEAR Act passed the Senate Finance Committee with strong environmental performance criteria intact on April 3, 2003.

However, after the CLEAR Act got to the House of Representatives, the bill was altered and dramatically weakened by the House Ways and Means Committee. The hybrid tax credit was removed and replaced with a credit for diesel vehicles. Diesel vehicles are three to ten times dirtier than hybrids. Other modifications to weaken the bill were made. The weakened version then passed the full House on April 11, 2003.

After much political backlash from U.S. consumers, scientists and environmentalists, the following tax credits were approved on January 1, 2006, with an effective start date of June 5, 2006. The IRS ruled on exact credit amounts for all hybrids, and it posted a summary of the hybrid tax credit.[37] Unfortunately, there were several strings attached to the tax credit and a *very* short time frame within which to take advantage of it. Here is a summary:

- The new tax credit set a limit of 60,000 hybrids per carmaker. Toyota hit the 60,000 mark in June 2006, shortly after the bill took effect. Honda and Ford still had hybrids available as of July 2006.

- Buyers had until September 30, 2006 to purchase one of the five gasoline-electric hybrid models sold by Toyota and Lexus in order to qualify for 100 percent of the credit. On October 1, 2006 the listed credit amount was reduced by half.

- The credit for Toyota hybrids will stay at 50 percent for two quarters, fall to 25 percent in the subsequent two quarters, and then expire on October 1, 2007.

- The credit amount is based on the date of actual possession of the vehicle — not on its order date.

- The new law for the hybrid tax credit might require taxpayers to forfeit their hybrid tax credit if they re-sell their hybrid car or truck.

HYBRID VEHICLE CREDITS

CURRENT MODELS:

MAKE	MODEL	TAX CREDIT
Ford	Escape Hybrid (2wd)	$2,600
Ford	Escape Hybrid (4wd)	$1,950
Honda	2006 Accord Hybrid*	$1,300
Honda	2006 Civic Hybrid (auto)	$2,100
Honda	Insight (auto)	$1,450
Lexus	GS 450h	$1,550
Lexus	RX 400h	$2,200
Mercury	Mariner Hybrid	$1,950
Toyota	Camry Hybrid	$2,600
Toyota	Highlander Hybrid	$2,600
Toyota	Prius	$3,150

*2006 Honda Accord Hybrid AT without updated control calibration qualifies for a credit amount of $650.

UPCOMING MODELS (based on manufacturer's specs):

Chevrolet/GMC	**Silverado/Sierra**	**$250**
Chevrolet/GMC	**Silverado/Sierra**	**$250**
Nissan	**Altima**	**$1,300**
Saturn	**VUE Greenline**	**No info available**
Toyota	**Camry**	**$1,300**

This tax provision is extremely limiting in the time constraints for purchasing an automobile, and in the amount of the tax credit allowed. Also, the types of fuel-efficient automobiles available for purchase are limited. Hardworking Americans might be wondering why the government would give such generous tax incentives for gas-guzzlers. They might also ask why the government isn't providing more generous tax incentives for Americans to purchase environmentally friendly and gas-economical vehicles. Below are examples of the cost of fuel-efficient vehicles and their overall mileage. Not all of these qualify for the tax credit.

SAMPLE OF HIGH-MILEAGE VEHICLES

BRAND	STICKER PRICE	OVERALL MPG	QUALIFIES FOR TAX CREDIT
Honda Insight	$21,045	51	Yes
Toyota Prius	$23,780	44	Yes
Honda Civic Hybrid	$22,700	37	Yes
Volkswagen Jetta	$24,580	34	No
Scion XB	$15,220	30	No
Ford Escape Hybrid 4D	$25,600	30	Yes

How About Renewable Energy?

Despite all the talk, and billions of dollars the U.S. government has spent over the last thirty-five years to develop clean, renewable energy sources, the results are negligible. According to a Department of Energy (DOE) report of May 2006, alternative renewable energy accounted for 6.1 percent of total U.S. energy consumption.[38] The footnote at the bottom of the report discloses, "A small amount of alcohol fuel (ethanol blended into motor gasoline) was included in this percentage...." Our level of utilization of renewable energy sources remains dismal at best.

In June 2002, George W. Bush appointed W. Henson Moore to head the Renewable Energy Exports Advisory Committee. Mr. Moore is a board member of USEC, a leading supplier of enriched uranium fuel for commercial nuclear power plants. USEC, the global energy company, reported revenues in 2005 of $1.56 billion. One might think that an expert in the field of clean renewable energy alternatives would be brought in for this job. There are many safe, reusable, environmentally friendly substances and processes to be considered in lieu of fossil fuel consumption:

1) **Alternative Fuels:** biodiesel, biomass, ethanol, hydrogen, and methanol.[39]

2) **Power Generation:** cogeneration, combined heat and power, distributed power, fuel cells, geothermal, green power, hydropower, micro-turbine, solar photovoltaic, ocean energy, and wind power.[40]

3) **Increased Energy Efficiency:** advanced materials, high-efficiency appliances, high-performance buildings, energy management, intelligent highways, ground source heat and lighting, mass transportation, recycling, smart growth, and solar thermal heat.[41]

The Bush Administration, while granting huge subsidies to the oil, gas, coal, and nuclear industries, has relaxed the environmental safeguards that apply to energy development on public lands.[42] In return, our government asks nothing from those who would benefit from these generous tax breaks. Big oil and gas companies continue to enjoy the tax breaks, but they are not required to provide any tangible guarantees toward ensuring an America free of fossil fuels.[43]

In 2006, George W. Bush had more oil experts working with and around him in appointed positions than any other President since his father, George H.W. Bush. In his February 2006 State of the Union speech, Bush told the nation, "America is addicted to oil." Further into the speech, the President indicated that Americans would find relief from foreign oil dependencies sometime around the year 2025. Rather than a lack of available alternatives, this timeline appears to reflect the lack of political will from our President and Congress. According to many leading scientists, there are a number of alternatives, which range from the electric car produced by GM in the 1990s to the substitution of sugarcane ethanol for use in fueling vehicles. Brazil is now using sugar cane ethanol for 90 percent of its oil needs. We might completely eliminate foreign oil dependence by tapping the huge supplies of available geothermal energy that lie beneath the earth's surface.

Presidential speeches make for good sound bites, but Americans become more skeptical as we are increasingly aware of the realties associated with dependence on foreign oil. The nation is held hostage at the gas pumps, digging deeper into our pockets while dollars are sucked into oil corporations, which show obscene profits, and the rest of those dollars are going to oil exporting nations, many of whom hate America. Regions of oil producing Middle Eastern nations are churning out people who despise us. More is needed than Presidential sound bites and empty promises. To continually postpone our foreign oil dependence at this time is not merely a political ploy; deferring this problem to our children is an immoral act.

Two fact-filled books, *American Dynasty* and *American Theocracy*, by Kevin Phillips, provide much enlightenment. The *Wall Street Journal* described Kevin Phillips as "the leading conservative electoral analyst, the man who invented the Sun Belt, named the New Right, and prophesied 'The Emerging Republican Majority' in 1969."[44]

American Dynasty unveils a disturbing and alarming account of how four generations of the Bush family have systematically used their financial and social influence to gain national power, and build a personal empire. Phillips painstakingly details the Bush family's exclusive contacts within the CIA, the energy industry, military arms manufacturers, Enron, Halliburton, Wall Street, and the Saudi government. In a scathing and precise report, Phillips charges George W. Bush with compromising the economic and national security of our nation by running up the national deficit to the tune of trillions of dollars, and even sacrificing the lives of Americans for the war in Iraq with the express purpose of securing and controlling the vast oil reserves of the Middle East. Phillips claims the Bush Administration has manipulated national security, deceived the American public and thwarted democracy.[45]

In *American Theocracy*, Phillips illustrates how failed British, Dutch and Spanish empires of the past attribute their economic downfall to energy dependence. He offers a chronological, in-depth study of various oil and fuel dependencies. In the late 1800s, England stood on top of the world, boosted by coal power during the Industrial Revolution. A century later, an oil-driven America is the leading world power. American's obsession with fossil fuels and its failure to make other energy source choices threaten our very security, warns Phillips. Additionally, he cautions against further stalling in moving towards alternative energy sources, predicting the U.S. will suffer disastrous economic consequences if drastic changes do not occur quickly.

Phillips says America has become blinded and crippled as a nation due to the influence of high government officials. The two Bush Administrations have been particularly damaging by finding it in their interest to take our nation to war, rather than to promulgate decisions in the best interest of the American public. Three important factors put America at huge risk, according to Phillips:

1) The U.S. has adopted an imperialistic policy driven by hunger for cheap oil supplies in the highly volatile and unstable Middle East.

2) Ultra-conservative "Christians," who are possessed with an apocalyptic allegiance involving Biblical prophecies, hijacked the Republican Party.

3) An attitude of doom and denial, combined with government leaders who are insufficiently invested in the future of our environment and controlling the national debt, has crippled our country.[46]

I spoke with several U.S. troops who served in Iraq. The majority of those with whom I spoke believe that the reasons for our going to war were to fight terrorism, to help with the rebuilding and to protect the "assets" (oil fields) for the people of Iraq.

Vernon, a U.S. Army Reservist who was deployed in Iraq for thirteen months, startled me with his bluntness when he said, "American soldiers are dying daily. We are held hostage in the Middle East so we can protect the oil interests in Iraq for Exxon/Mobile and the profiteers of Halliburton." He then added, "I bet you a thousand dollars we'd never be there if Iraq didn't have any oil."

QUICK OIL AND GAS FACTS[47]

- The U.S. consumes 25 percent of world's oil while representing only 5 percent of the world's population.

- 88 percent of U.S. residents drive to work.[48]

- U.S. vehicle fuel economy averages reached their highest point in 1988, but as gas prices leveled off Americans purchased more SUVs in the 1990s, which sent fuel efficiency backwards.[49]

- Of the ten largest corporations in the world, five are either oil and gas companies, or automakers: Exxon/Mobil, Chevron Corp., Conoco/Phillips, Ford, and GM.

- The Model-T, produced decades ago, got better gas mileage than the average Ford vehicle on the road today.[50]

- Winter temperatures in the Arctic have warmed by 4°F in recent years. Global warming is causing glaciers and sea ice to melt. Ecological changes in the Arctic environment will have a devastating impact on the entire world.[51]

- In the last ten years, the oil and gas industry has received $26.2 billion in federal subsidies.[52]

- Today, the U.S. imports 55 percent of its oil.[53]

- Only 4 percent of the world's proven oil reserves are in the U.S.[54]

- If carrots were the number one export from the Persian Gulf, do you think we would have invaded Iraq?

Oil is a Quickly-Depleting Resource

There is some disagreement as to how long it will take before world production peaks. Optimists, who tend to be economists, say we have thirty years, and pessimists, who tend to be geologists, say that we have only five to ten years.[55] According to the experts, oil will still be available after world production peaks, but retrieving it and getting it to the consumer will be increasingly expensive. In the meantime, if we do not eliminate our dependence on fossil fuel, we will then continue to be dependent upon the Middle East. According to a 2004 poll conducted by the Washington-based Arab American Institute (AAI), 96 percent of Saudis, 86 percent of United Arab Emirate and 85 percent of Jordanian citizens have an unfavorable view of America.[56] I do not believe our nation has done anything to improve our image in the Muslim world since that poll was taken, so I can only imagine that the view of America has deteriorated even further in recent years.

"Across the nation, gas prices went to record highs today....
Will it get to the point that only the privileged can afford gas?"

John Blackstone, CBS *Evening News*, August 11, 2005

NOTES, Chapter 2

[1] Kevin Phillips, *American Dynasty: Aristocracy, Fortune, and the Politics of Deceit in the House of Bush* (New York: Penguin Group, 2004).

[2] President Richard M. Nixon, "State of the Union Address," January 1974. The full text of this State of the Union Address—and others cited below—may be found at www.usa-presidents.info/union/.

[3] President Gerald Ford, "State of the Union Address," January 1975.

[4] Ronald Bailey, "Energy Independence: The Ever-Receding Mirage," *Reason*, July 21, 2004, www.reason.com/rb/rb072104.shtml.

[5] Ibid.

[6] President George W. Bush, "State of the Union Address," January 2006.

[7] Ibid.

[8] "Annual Energy Review: Petroleum Overview," *Energy Information Administration*, 2005, www.eia.doe.gov/emeu/aer/pdf/pages/sec5_4.pdf.

[9] "Canada," *Energy Information Administration*, www.eia.doe.gov/emeu/cabs/ Canada/Background.html.

[10] *Energy Information Administration*, www.eia.doe.gov.

[11] "How much are we paying for a gallon of gas?," *Institute for the Analysis of Global Security*, iags.org/costofoil.html.

[12] Ibid.

[13] "Gas prices around the world," *CNN Money*, money.cnn.com/ph/features/lists /global_gasprices/.

[14] "Annual Energy Review."

[15] OPEC, an international organization whose principal aim is to safeguard the interests and stability of prices in international oil markets, is made up of 11 countries: Algeria, Indonesia, Iran, Iraq, Kuwait, Libya, Nigeria, Qatar, Saudi Arabia, UAE, Venezuela.

[16] "BP Statistical Review of World Energy,"

[17] "World Oil Reserves," *Wikipedia*, upload.wikimedia.org/wikipedia/en/d/d1/ World_Oil_Reserves_2005.png.

[18] Richard M. Nixon, "State of the Union Address."

[19] The entire text of this speech may be found at www.pbs.org/wgbh/amex/carter/ filmmore/ps_energy.html.

[20] Ibid.

[21] Stephen Koff, "Was Jimmy Carter Right?," *Cleveland Plain Dealer*, October 1, 2005, www.energybulletin.net/9657.html.

[22] Ronald Bailey, "Energy Independence: The Ever-Receding Mirage," *Reason Online*, July 21, 2004, www.reason.com/rb/rb072104.shtml.

[23] "Our Broader Strategy," 27 March 1980, Department of State, Current Policy No. 153, as reprinted in *Case Study: National Security Policy under Carter* (Air War College, AL: Department of National Security Affairs, 1980-81), 98.

[24] Thomas Donnelly, "The Underpinnings of the Bush Doctrine," AEI Online, January 31, 2003, www.aei.org/publications/pubID.15845/pub_detail.asp.

[25] Koff, "Jimmy Carter."

[26] Mr. Cannon is a journalist who has covered Ronald Reagan for over twenty-five years. Lou Cannon, *President Reagan: The Role of a Lifetime* (New York: Touchstone/Simon & Shuster, 1991), 823.

[27] Ibid.

[28] T. Klare, *Blood and Oil: The Dangers and Consequences of America's Growing Dependence on Imported Petroleum* (New York: Metropolitan Books, 2004), 104-5.

[29] Robert D. Hershey, Jr., "Clinton's Economic Plan; Indirect Effects of the Energy Tax," *The New York Times*, February 20, 1993.

[30] The bill was rejected by a Republican-dominated Congress.

[31] "Dump Diesel: Partnership for a New Generation of Vehicles," *Green Scissors*, www.greenscissors.org/energy/pngv.htm.

[32] "A Hummer of a Tax Break," *Taxpayers for Common Sense*, December 12, 2003, www.taxpayer.net/TCS/whitepapers/SUVtaxbreak.htm.

[33] "Tax Incentives: SUV Loophole Widens, Clean Vehicle Credits Face Uncertain Future," *Union of Concerned Scientists*, www.ucsusa.org/clean_vehicles/cars_pickups_suvs/tax-incentives-suv-loophole-vs-clean-vehicle-credits.html.

[34] Ibid.

[35] Taxes are reduced by deducting the full cost of the SUV as a business expense.

[36] National Resources Defense Council, "White House proposes weak fuel economy standards for gas guzzlers," The Bush Record, August 23, 2005, www.nrdc.org/bushrecord/2005_08.asp.

[37] "Summary of the Credit for Qualified Hybrid Vehicles," *Internal Revenue Service*, May 2006, www.irs.gov/newsroom/article/0,,id=157557,00.html.

[38] *Monthly Energy Review:* May 2006, Energy Information Administration.

[39] *Green Energy News*, www.nrglink.com.

[40] Ibid.

[41] Ibid.

[42] National Resources Defense Council, "Rewriting the Rules (2005 Special Edition): The Bush Administration's First Term Environmental Record," *U.S. Law and Policy*, www.nrdc.org/legislation/rollbacks/execsum.asp.

[43] National Energy Policy Development Group, *National Energy Policy*, May 2001, www.whitehouse.gov/energy/National-Energy-Policy.pdf.

[44] "American Dynasty: Fmr. Top Republican Stategist Discusses the Bush Family's Rise to Power Since WWI," *Democracy Now!*, January 12, 2004, www.democracynow.org/article.pl?sid=04/01/12/1448237.

[45] Kevin Phillips, *American Dynasty: Aristocracy, Fortune, and the Politics of Deceit in the House of Bush* (New York: Penguin Group, 2004).

[46] Kevin Phillips, *American Theocracy: The Peril and Politics of Radical Religion, Oil, and Borrowed Money in the 21st Century* (New York: Penguin Group, 2006).

[47] Inspired by the *Test Yourself: The Oil and Auto Quiz*, which may be found at www.globalexchange.org/war_peace_democracy/oil/oilquiz.html.

[48] *Mother Jones*, March/April 2005.

[49] *The United States Environmental Protection Agency*, www.epa.gov.

[50] a. *Environmental Protection Agency*.
    b. *New Encyclopedia of Motor Cars*.

[51] *Arctic Climate Impact Assessment*.

[52] National Resource Defense Council, *Green Scissors*.

[53] Energy Information Agency, U.S. Dept. of Energy.

[54] Ibid.

[55] a. Jamais Cascio, "Peak Oil and the Curse of Cassandra," *World Changing*, July 31, 2005, www.worldchanging.com/archives/003224.html.
    b. James Boxell, "Top oil groups fail to recoup exploration costs," Energy Bulletin, October 9, 2004, www.energybulletin.net/2470.html.

[56] *Al-Ahram Weekly*, July 29, 2004.

★ 3 ★

The Premeditated Sin

"A sin takes on a new and real terror when there seems a chance that it is going to be found out."

Mark Twain

SADDAM HUSSEIN, the former dictator of Iraq, had not always been an enemy of the United States. In 1963, when Saddam was in his early twenties, he was allegedly recruited by the Central Intelligence Agency to assassinate the Iraqi prime minister Abdul-Karim Qassem.[1] The United States had grown worried because Abdul-Karim Qassem had backed Iraq out of a pact with the United States and had begun favoring trade with the Soviet Union.[2] Qassem had also legalized the Iraqi Communist Party. More importantly, Iran was an ally of the United States (at that time) that bordered the Soviet Union. The U.S. needed more friendly countries in the Middle East. In order to stop the communist influence in Iraq, the U.S. actively supported the 1963 coup against Abdul-Karim Qassem that placed Saddam's Ba'ath Party into power. This U.S. action provided a counter to the communist threat and gave our nation better control over Iraq and its oil resources.

In the 1980s, Iran was in the midst of an Islamic revolution and pro-American governments in the region, such as Kuwait, Saudi Arabia and Jordan, were showing signs of collapse.[3] U.S. officials began to see secular Baghdad as a buffer against militant Shiite extremism. By supporting Saddam's regime, American policymakers believed they could exert a "reverse domino theory" in the Middle East comparable to what had happened in Southeast Asia.[4] The hope was that if Iraq could be turned into a democratic country, democracy would spread through the region. This theory made Iraq America's strategic partner in the Middle East. In fact, U.S. diplomats in Baghdad routinely referred to Iraqi forces as "the good guys" and the Iranians as "the bad guys." For almost a decade, the U.S. supported Saddam's efforts against Iran in a war that would kill one million Iranians and Iraqis.

While the Iran-Iraq war raged through the 1980s, the Ronald Reagan and George H.W. Bush Administrations provided Saddam with intelligence information, economic assistance, military arms, and biological weapons.[5] The U.S. government sold Iraq poisonous chemicals and deadly biological viruses, including anthrax and bubonic plague.[6] The chemicals were intended for use in the war with Iran. U.S. arms dealers, never missing an opportunity to turn a profit, sold weapons to Iran and the notorious Iran Contra Affair took place during this period. More on the Iran Contra Affair is discussed in the chapter "Neo Caustic."

Saddam Hussein later used chemical weapons on the Kurds in Northern Iraq when they staged a revolt against the government.[7] At this time, the U.S. did not know he would use this weapon of mass destruction on his own people. However, we did find out about this crime long before Saddam was considered a part of George W. Bush's "axis of evil."[8] For most Americans it may be difficult to comprehend the level of brutality that exists within many Middle Eastern dictatorships. But to give you an idea, there is the account of the president of Syria, Hafez al-Assad, who destroyed the entire city of Hama in 1982. Hama was Syria's fourth largest city. An estimated twenty thousand innocent people were killed in order to root out the Muslim Brotherhood who was threatening his rule.[9]

The Reagan and Bush Administrations ignored complaints from international human rights groups who begged the U.S. to rein in the Iraqi government and Saddam Hussein. Senator Claiborne Pell, (D-RI), introduced the "Prevention of Genocide Act of 1988." The bill called for imposing harsh sanctions against Iraq, freezing all exports to that country and eliminating any imported goods. The bill quickly passed in the Senate.[10] President Reagan insisted that Saddam would respond better to a carrot than to a stick, and went on record saying he would veto the bill if necessary.[11] The bill was defeated in the House of Representatives. The U.S. government protected Saddam, but more importantly, it protected its economic interests. U.S. farmers were providing substantial agricultural products to Iraq and the U.S. relied on Iraqi oil imports.[12] It was argued that sanctions would negatively affect the U.S. farm trade and oil sanctions could negatively impact the economy.

One year after the bill was defeated and two years after Saddam gassed the Kurds, the Bush Administration gave Saddam his carrot by doubling the tax credits to Iraq. Details of the United State's involvement in the Hussein government can be found in a chronological listing at the National Security Archives website.[13] The website includes photos of former Secretary of Defense Donald Rumsfeld shaking hands with Saddam Hussein. Americans tend to forget the strong military and strategic alliance the U.S. held with Saddam Hussein in the years prior to his 1990 invasion of Kuwait.

Iraq is made up of several religious and ethnic groups, including Sunnis, Shiites, Turks, and Kurds. These groups have different religious beliefs, cultures and practices. Both Sunnis and Shiites are Muslims, but have a long history of feuding.[14] Saddam Hussein was Sunni, a minority in Iraq. The Kurds in the northern part of the country have a substantial Christian base and have long wished to become separate from Iraq. Because of past injustices spanning generations, each group harbors deep resentments against the others and all of them have shown a determination to rectify past wrongs through hostile skirmishes and warfare.[15]

While Saddam Hussein was notorious for his human rights offenses against the Kurds and Shiites, his government invested heavily in programs that benefited the Iraqi public. Prior to the first Gulf War, Iraqis enjoyed free public school education for both males and females from kindergarten through 12th grade, as well as free college and graduate school entrance. Iraq had a robust economy, adequate electricity, modernized agriculture, and a rapidly growing middle class. According to the World Health Organization, 93 percent of the population had access to free health care and other social programs for over twenty years.[16]

Iraq is twice the size of Idaho and borders several nations, including Kuwait to its southwest. Kuwait lies between Iraq, Saudi Arabia and the Persian Gulf. It is 17,820 square kilometers, slightly smaller in size than the state of New Jersey.[17] At the turn of the 20th century, Kuwait was an autonomous region claimed by the Turkish Ottoman Empire. Kuwait had agreements with the British for naval protection. Because of this protection, Kuwait was able in 1920 to successfully fight off the Saudis, who claimed sovereignty over Kuwait and were seeking to consolidate their territory. In 1930, Kuwait discovered it was practically floating on oil after British and American oil concerns drilled wells. When Kuwait declared itself to be an independent state in 1961, Iraq claimed that Kuwait was Iraq's 13th province. Notwithstanding such claims by Iraq, the Kuwaiti Royal Family, represented by Al-Sabah, has maintained absolute control over the state since 1756.[18] Kuwait is now flirting with democracy. Despite claims of liberalization, all decisions made by voters can be overturned by the royal family. Kuwaiti women were granted the right to vote only in 2002.

Saddam Hussein complained for years about the border between Iraq and Kuwait, arguing that Kuwait was originally a part of Iraq. In the late 1980s, Saddam vehemently accused the Kuwaitis of stealing Iraqi oil through a technique known as slant drilling. According to Saddam Hussein, the Kuwaitis were driving down the price per barrel of oil, and he threatened on numerous occasions to take back Kuwait. For years the CIA thought he was merely bluffing.[19] But if Saddam Hussein were able to successfully take over Kuwait, he would control close to a quarter of the world's oil supply and could possibly pose a threat to Saudi Arabia, according to President George H.W. Bush in 1990.[20]

The United States Approves the Invasion of Kuwait

A little known and even lesser publicized meeting took place on July 25, 1990 between Saddam Hussein and then United States Ambassador to Iraq, April Glaspie. At this meeting Hussein's venture into Kuwait was tacitly approved by the Ambassador!

Saddam Hussein met with Ambassador Glaspie to determine how the United States would react if Iraq *annexed* Kuwait. During this meeting, Ms. Glaspie assured Saddam Hussein that President George H.W. Bush "wanted better and deeper relations" between the U.S. and Iraq. She further stated that the U.S. had "no opinion on the Arab-Arab conflict like your border disagreement with Kuwait."[21] Saddam Hussein, feeling confident and unaware of any potential retaliation from the U.S., marched 100,000 Iraqi troops and 700 tanks to the south of Iraq. Eight days later, on August 2, 1990, his troops crossed the Iraq-Kuwait border.[22]

Transcripts of Ambassador Glaspie's and Saddam Hussein's conversation were made public one month after their July meeting. Two British journalists later confronted Ms. Glaspie about her role in the conflict. The record of that confrontation included the following exchange:

BRITISH JOURNALISTS CONFRONT THE AMERICAN AMBASSADOR

Journalist 1: "Are the transcripts correct, Madam Ambassador?" *(Ambassador Glaspie does not respond)*

Journalist 2: "You knew Saddam was going to invade but you didn't warn him not to. You didn't tell him America would defend Kuwait. You told him the opposite — that America was not associated with Kuwait."

Journalist 1: "You encouraged this aggression, his invasion. What were you thinking?"

U.S. Ambassador Glaspie: "Obviously, I didn't think, and nobody else did, that the Iraqis were going to take all of Kuwait."

Journalist 1: "You thought he was just going to take some of it? But, how could you? ... [T]he Iraqis have always viewed [Kuwait] as an historic part of their country! America green-lighted the invasion. At a minimum, you admit signaling Saddam that some aggression was okay — that the U.S. would not oppose a grab of the al-Rumeilah oil field, the disputed border strip and the Gulf Islands, the territories claimed by Iraq?"

(Ambassador Glaspie says nothing as a limousine door closed behind her and the car drives off.)[23]

George H.W. Bush's Initial Reaction

President George H.W. Bush revealed his concerns regarding Iraq on August 8, 1990. In a nationally televised address, Bush made the following statement: "The stakes are high. Iraq is already a rich and powerful country that possesses the world's second largest reserves of oil and over a million men under arms. It's the fourth largest military in the world. Our country now imports nearly half the oil it consumes and could face a major threat to its economic independence."[24] Four weeks later, on September 11, 1990 in a speech to Congress on the federal deficit and "the crisis" in the Persian Gulf, George H.W. Bush would use the word "oil" fourteen times and the word "energy" seven times in discussing the concerns in the Persian Gulf. He used the word "terror" only once.

Saddam the Baby Murderer

"And after all, what is a lie? 'Tis, but the truth in masquerade."

Lord Byron

In the months leading up to the first Gulf War, an intense and carefully orchestrated media campaign was generated by the United States to personalize the war against a "demonic" Saddam Hussein. Through the power and influence of the media, Americans would come to regard Saddam Hussein as the evil enemy. Conservative editorial opinion writers such as Charles Krauthammer and Morton B. Zuckerman began stirring the cauldron of fear using language and imagery, comparing Saddam Hussein with Adolf Hitler. Highly inflammatory and extremely opinionated stories were fueled by pundits, Neoconservatives and oil interest groups.[25] Drawing a chilling correlation to Nazi Germany, Krauthammer, *et al.* were able to successfully instill substantial levels of alarm and anxiety into the American public when they theorized how Saddam might acquire the ability to obtain nuclear weapons. They went so far as to say that he might be able to do this within four years and could use them against the United States and Israel. It wasn't too difficult to seed fearful images in the minds of Americans especially when imparting that Saddam had gassed over 5,000 Iraqi Kurds, his own citizens.

Six full months prior to the start of the Gulf War, the Saudi government gave American troops permission to set up bases in Saudi Arabia, allowing the U.S. the means and place to prepare to retake Kuwait. Mission Desert Shield, the precursor to Desert Storm, had begun.[26]

LOGICAL FALLACIES DEFINED

Logical: Based on facts, rational thought and sensible reasoning.

Fallacy: A mistaken belief or idea believed to be true; an erroneous or invalid argument or reasoning in which the conclusion does not follow from the premises; deceptiveness, misleading or deceptive.

On October 10, 1990, a 15-year-old girl identified only as Nayirah testified before the Congressional Human Rights Caucus Committee. She told the committee of a horrible summer vacation she had recently spent in Kuwait, a vacation she hoped no other child would ever have to endure.

Nayirah testified that she and her mother had traveled to Kuwait to visit her older sister who had just given birth to a premature baby boy. Nayriah said that she and several women volunteered to help at the Kuwait hospital. Nayirah detailed a grueling account of atrocities she said she witnessed in Kuwait. She told the committee that invading Iraqi soldiers had stormed the Kuwait hospital and, at gunpoint, had taken premature babies out of their incubators, dumped them on the cold hard floor to die and then removed the incubators from the hospital. A tearful Nayirah told the committee that had she not been at the hospital on that day to defend him, her premature nephew, too, would have died.[27]

On October 15, not even a week after Nayirah's testimony, President George H.W. Bush repeated the story, saying that the Emir of Kuwait had informed him of the murders by Iraqi soldiers of babies at the Kuwait hospital. The President repeated this story in subsequent days during his numerous television interviews.[28] After hearing it from President George H.W. Bush, the *London Daily Telegraph* was the first newspaper to print the story. *Reuters* picked it up, followed by the *Los Angeles Times* and *CNN*, and soon thereafter all the other major newspapers and cable news networks were reporting on the mass murder of the Kuwaiti babies. More legitimacy for the story followed when it was reported by the New York Human Rights Middle East Watch Group and the London-based Amnesty International.

Six weeks later, on November 27th, Nayirah's story was further corroborated by Dr. Issah Ibrahim, who gave testimony to the United Nations Security Council, saying that the hardest thing he ever had to supervise was "burying the babies," how he himself had buried forty of the 120 premature babies left to die.[29] After such passionate testimony, the United Nations Security Council passed a resolution paving the way for military force to drive Iraqi troops from Kuwait. The story appeared so believable that on January 12, 1991, the Senate voted to support the Bush resolution to battle against Iraq. The resolution passed by a thin margin of only six votes.[30] On February 15, 1991 Vice President Dan Quayle told Congress, "There are pictures Saddam doesn't want us to see, pictures of premature babies in Kuwait that were tossed out of the incubators and left to die."[31] Most of the world believed this to be the truth, except the Iraqis, the Kuwaitis, and those who cooked up the tale.

The story of the Kuwaiti hospital invasion by Iraqi soldiers was an outright lie. The tale of premature babies being thrown out and left to die on the cold hospital floor was a complete deception. The saga of a young protective girl witnessing atrocities was pure propaganda.[32] It was created by the Citizens for a Free Kuwait, an organization with close ties to the

Bush White House that was seeking U.S. Military intervention against Saddam Hussein. The organization hired the American public relations firm of Hill & Knowlton to mastermind the story and make it credible. Hill & Knowlton consultants coached and prepared Nayirah, Dr. Issah Ibrahim and others for testimonies that were then sold to the public and government officials as "truth." It was later discovered that Nayirah was the daughter of Kuwait's Ambassador to America, Saud Nasir al-Sabah. Dr. Issah Ibrahim was an alias for a dentist named Dr. Issah Behbehani. Neither Nayirah nor Dr. Behbehani had recently been to Kuwait. Their stories were totally fraudulently fabricated. Since the Congressional Human Rights Caucus Committee was not bound by laws covering false testimony and none of the witnesses were under oath, they lied with legal immunity.[33]

The story was created to increase public support for the upcoming Gulf War. The lies were used to heighten fear and hatred against Saddam Hussein, sway public opinion and garner the congressional support required for a military invasion of Iraq. The government, media, and the American public were deceived and manipulated. Based upon this manipulation, the U.S. acted hastily to condemn and convict without taking the necessary time to discover the truth.

For some, the truth has never been uncovered. In 2003, a plumbing wholesaler named Ben told me that one of the main reasons he supported both wars in Iraq was that "we had to get rid of that baby-killing madman, Saddam Hussein." After the first Gulf War, in January 1992, John R. MacArthur wrote an editorial in *The New York Times* describing how several senators had cited the atrocities of murdered babies as being the influential factor in their decision to vote for the Iraqi war resolution.[34]

Another important claim used by George H.W. Bush for launching the first war against Iraq was that Saddam Hussein had 265,000 Iraqi troops and 150 tanks sitting on the Kuwaiti border preparing to invade Saudi Arabia. The President alleged that he had satellite photos of Saddam's troops that he had obtained from a commercial satellite company. Five-time Pulitzer Prize nominee and investigative reporter Jean Heller from the *St. Petersburg Times* was able to obtain the same satellite photos and found absolutely no evidence to support these accusations. The Bush Administration classified the photos so they have never been available for public scrutiny.[35]

Through deceptive tactics such as those cited, the George H.W. Bush Administration, with the help of Neoconservatives and influential oil-interested parties, was able to generate enough support to persuade Congress to agree to launch a war against Saddam Hussein and the Iraqis.

THE ART OF SELLING A WAR

- Hill & Knowlton, the world's largest public relations firm, was hired in 1990 for the Kuwaiti Government to mastermind the PR campaign leading up to the Gulf War. At the time, it was the largest foreign-funded campaign ever aimed towards manipulating American public opinion.[36]

- The Emir of Kuwait channeled $11.9 million to fund "Citizens for a Free Kuwait."[37]

- Almost the entire budget of Citizens to Free Kuwait, $10.8 million, went to pay Hill & Knowlton for the hoax on America concerning the "Kuwaiti Hospital Babies."[38]

- Former U.S. Ambassador to Bahrain, Sam Zakhem, funneled $7.7 million from oil-rich Bahrain for advertising and lobbying by front organizations, The Coalition for Americans at Risk and The Freedom Task Force.[39]

- The Coalition for Americans at Risk prepared and placed TV and newspaper ads and kept fifty professional speakers available for pro-war rallies and publicity events. These advertisements were designed to increase American fear of Saddam Hussein and position the U.S. as having no other option but to go to war against Iraq.[40]

- Craig Fuller managed the Washington offices of Hill & Knowlton during the media campaign.[41] The same Craig Fuller served as George H.W. Bush's Chief of Staff when Bush was the Vice President. Mr. Fuller is one of Bush's closest friends.

- The Wirthlin Group, which conducted polling for the Reagan Administration, is a research component of Hill & Knowlton. They reportedly received $1.1 million in fees for research assignments for the Kuwaiti Government.[42]

- The PR front groups were designed to mask the collusion between the Kuwaiti government and the Bush Administration. By law, the Foreign Agents Registration Act was required to expose this propaganda campaign to the American people, but the Justice Department chose not to enforce it.

Many think it is far more likely that Saddam Hussein went ahead with the invasion of Kuwait because he assumed the U.S. would not respond with more than a verbal condemnation. That was the inference he drew from his meeting with U.S. Ambassador April Glaspie on July 25, 1990, and from statements by State Department officials in Washington at the same time. The State Department made a public statement disavowing any U.S. security commitments to Kuwait.[43] Given the fact that the U.S. government had provided mixed messages to Saddam Hussein throughout the years, he most likely believed that the 1990 Bush White House reaction to the Iraqi invasion of Kuwait was nothing more than political posturing. After all, Saddam Hussein had been publicly condemned before by U.S. government officials only to soon after be rewarded with bigger "carrots."

> *"Obviously, I didn't think — and nobody else did — that the Iraqis were going to take all of Kuwait. Every Kuwaiti and Saudi, every analyst in the Western world, was wrong too. That does not excuse me. But people who now claim that all was clear were not heard from at the time."*

U.S. Ambassador April Glaspie

Before I began my research for this book, I was totally unaware of these details related to the first Gulf War. When made aware of the facts, I lay in bed, restless and unable to sleep, stunned and disturbed. I asked myself, *How is it that this information about the first Gulf War was so far removed from the conscious awareness of most Americans? What else is going on under the radar screen?*

Apparently, President George H.W. Bush, the former head of the CIA and Vice President under Reagan, knew how to win the confidence of the American people and Congress. It appears that using questionable methods that some would describe as ethically wrong and dishonest, the U.S. went to war against Saddam Hussein and Iraq.

NOTES, Chapter 3

[1] a. Paul Roberts, *End of Oil* (New York: First Mariner Books, 2005).

b. Kevin Phillips, *American Theocracy: The Peril and Politics of Radical Religion, Oil and Borrowed Money in the 21st Century* (New York: Viking Penguin, 2006).

c. "Saddam Hussein: America's man in Iraq," Unknown News, www.unknown news.net/saddam.html.

[2] "America's man."

[3] Michael Dobbs, "U.S. Had Key Role in Iraq Buildup, Trade in Chemical Arms Allowed Despite Their Use on Iranians, Kurds," *The Washington Post*, December 30, 2002.

[4] Ibid.

[5] a. Joyce Battle, ed., "Shaking Hands with Saddam Hussein," *The National Security Archive*, February 25, 2003, www.gwu.edu/~nsarchiv/NSAEBB/NSAEBB82/.

b. Kevin Phillips, *American Theocracy*.

[6] Michael Dobbs, "Key Role."

[7] a. "Nerve Gas used in Northern Iraq on Kurds," *Physicians for Human Rights*, April 29, 2993, www.phrusa.org/research/chemical_weapons/chemiraqgas2.html.

b. Norm Dixon, "The Ties that Blind: How Reagan Armed Saddam with Chemical Weapons," *Counterpunch*, June 17, 2004, www.counterpunch.org/dixon 06172004.html.

[8] Dixon, "Ties that Blind."

[9] Robert Baer, *Sleeping With the Devil: How Washington Sold Our Soul for Saudi Crude* (New York: Crown Publishers, 2003).

[10] a. Nathaniel Hurd, "U.S. Diplomatic and Commercial Relationship with Iraq, 1980 – 2 August 1990," *Campaign Against Sanctions on Iraq*, July 15, 2000, www.casi.org.uk/info/usdocs/usiraq80s90s.html.

b. Alan Maass, "The crimes of a U.S. Ally," *Socialist Worker*, January 2, 2004, p.5, www.socialistworker.org/2004-1/480/480_05_SaddamHussein.shtml.

[11] Maass, "Crimes."

[12] a. Ibid.

b. CBC Online, "The Forgotten People: One Man's Battle to Stop Iraq," *CBC News*, March 26, 2003, www.cbc.ca/fifth/kurds/battle.html.

[13] *The National Security Archive at George Washington University*, www.gwu.edu/~nsarchiv/.

[14] HNN Staff, "What Is the Difference Between Sunni and Shiite Muslims—and Why Does It Matter?," *History News Network*, September 9, 2002, hnn.us/articles/934.html.

[15] Christopher Allbritton, "Curious Numbers in Ninevah," *Back to Iraq*, October 17, 2005, www.back-to-iraq.com/archives/kurds/.

[16] Joy Gordon, "Cool War: Economic Sanctions as a Weapon of Mass Destruction," *Harper's Magazine*, November 2002.

[17] "Kuwait," *Countries of the World*, www.theodora.com/wfb/kuwait_geography.html.

[18] "History," *Kuwait Info*, www.kuwait-info.com/sidepages/nat_history.asp.

[19] Melissa Boyle Mahle, *Denial and Deception: An Insider's View of the CIA from Iran-Contra to 9/11* (New York: Avalon, 2004).

[20] Clyde Prestowitz, *Rogue Nation: American Unilateralism and the Failure of Good Intentions* (New York: Basic Books, 2003).

[21] a. Prestowitz, *Rogue Nation*.

b. "Exerpts from Iraqi Document on Meeting with U.S. Envoy," *The New York Times* International, September 23, 1990, www.chss.montclair.edu/english/furr/glaspie.html.

c. "April Glaspie Transcript," *What Really Happened*, www.whatreallyhappened.com/ARTICLE5/april.html.

[22] "1990: Iraq invades Kuwait," BBC News, August 2, 1990, news.bbc.co.uk/onthisday/hi/dates/stories/august/2/newsid_2526000/2526937.stm.

[23] "April Glaspie Transcript."

[24] George H.W. Bush, "Address to the Nation Announcing the Deployment of United States Armed Forces to Saudi Arabia," August 8, 1990.

[25] Sara Dougherty, "The Munich Analogy and the Persian Gulf War," *Empire, Resistance, and the War in Iraq: A Conference for Historians and Activists*, University of Texas at Austin, February 18, 2006.

[26] www.dcs.ftmeade.army.mil/PublicNet/Downloads/HistoryFull.pdf.

[27] Kathy Kelly, "What about the incubators?," *Emperor's Clothes*, April 14, 2000, emperors-clothes.com/articles/kelly/what2.htm.

[28] John Stauber and Sheldon Rampton, *Toxic Sludge is Good for You: Lies, Damn Lies, and the Public Relations Industry* (Monroe, ME: Common Courage, 1995).

[29] David Dadge, *Casualty of War: The Bush Administration's Assault on a Free Press* (Amherst, NY: Prometheus Books, 2004).

[30] Ibid.

[31] Ibid.

[32] "No casus belli? Invent one!," *The Guardian Unlimited*, February 5, 2003, www.walden3.org/No_casus_belli_Invent_one!.htm

[33] David Dadge, *Casualty of War*.

[34] John R. MacArthur, *Second Front: Censorship and Propaganda in the Gulf War* (Berkeley: University of California Press, 1992).

[35] "Casus belli."

[36] MacArthur, *Second Front*.

[37] a. "Citizens for Free Kuwait Files with FARA after a Nine-month Lag," *O'Dwyers FARA Report* 1, no. 9 (Oct. 1991): 2.

b. Arthur E. Rowse, "Flacking for the Emir," *The Progressive*, May 1991, 22.

[38] "Citizens for Free Kuwait."

[39] Ibid.

[40] Ibid.

[41] *O'Dwyer's FARA Report* 5, no. 1 (Jan. 1991): 8, 10.

[42] Ibid.

[43] a. "April Glaspie," Wikipedia, en.wikipedia.org/wiki/April_Glaspie.

b. R.W. Tucker and D.C. Henderson, *The Imperial Temptation: The New World Order and America's Purpose*, New York: Council on Foreign Relations, 1992.

★ 4 ★

The Sixth Commandment

The sixth (Protestant and Jewish) or fifth
(Catholic and Luthan) commandment is
"Thou shall not kill."

THUS, ON JANUARY 17, 1991, the U.S. began bombing Iraq in retaliation for Hussein's invasion of Kuwait in what would be known as the Gulf War. Saddam Hussein and the Iraqi troops were quickly defeated and pushed back into Iraq. Though a relatively brief war, it caused a great deal of destruction and damage to the people and nation of Iraq. George H.W. Bush thought better than to get bogged down with ground troops in Iraq. After Saddam Hussein's retreat back into Iraq, most of the American troops came home but some remained in Saudi Arabia and Qatar.

The Bush Administration believed by pursuing a plan of containment they would be able to eventually eliminate Saddam Hussein. The hope from the administration was that the Iraqis would overthrow the dictator. This, however, did not happen. Shortly after the departure of the U.S. in 1991, a few disastrous and futile attempts by Iraqis were made to fight for independence and freedom. Many may recall watching the Northern Kurds slaughtered after the U.S. encouraged them to stand up to fight against Saddam Hussein. Also, some might remember the Shiites of Basra rising against Saddam's regime in the wake of the American "100 hours to free Kuwait." These battles proved to be nothing more than useless efforts resulting in catastrophe for the challengers. Mass graves allegedly due to these uprisings were later discovered.[1] Widespread fear paralyzed most Iraqis thereafter.

After the Gulf War, Iraq was subjected to some of the harshest sanctions ever imposed upon a nation. The UN deployed inspectors to conduct a search for weapons of mass destruction. This search lasted more than six years. The UN was also to provide stability to Iraq, but because of the lack of funding, resources and ever-political posturing by Saddam Hussein, this became a daunting task.

Containment consisted of a "No-Fly Zone." This allowed the Allies to fly warplanes over northern and southern Iraq to prevent Saddam Hussein from using his military. Eventually, the No-Fly Zones became a means for the Allies to force Iraq to comply with UN demands.[2] Comprehensive economic sanctions would devastate an already fragile war-torn country. Iraq was plunged into dire poverty as a result.

Economic Sanctions against Iraq

"I swore never to be silent whenever and wherever human beings endure suffering and humiliation."

Elie Wiesel

The UN reported that a battered and beaten Iraq was facing a crisis. UNICEF witnessed 200 children dying a day.[3] Lack of food, water, sanitation, and health care threatened the country. Medical conditions broke down due to the shortage of clean water, waste disposal facilities, preventive medicine, and health-care services. The lack of electricity and poor transportation only exacerbated the situation. According to United Nations reports, Iraq was in a state of "imminent catastrophe" and the UN predicted epidemics and famine if massive life-support needs were not swiftly met.[4]

From 1991 through 2002, an estimated 500,000 Iraqi children under the age of five died as a result of the first Gulf War and the impact of the sanctions. This number is close to three times as many deaths as those caused by the U.S. atomic bombs dropped on Japan.[5] By 1999, 13 percent of all Iraqi children were dying before their fifth birthday as an indirect result of contaminated water.[6]

The United States anticipated the collapse of the Iraqi water system early on. The Pentagon's Defense Intelligence Agency projected in January of 1991 that under the embargo, Iraq's ability to provide clean drinking water would fail within six months.[7] Chemicals for water treatment, the agency noted, were "depleted or nearing depletion." Chlorine supplies were "critically low," and the main chlorine-production plants had been shut down. Industries such as pharmaceuticals and food processing were nearly incapacitated.[8]

The sanctions affected virtually every aspect of the country's imports and exports. So, for example, while Iraq was allowed to purchase a sewage-treatment plant, it was blocked from buying the generator needed to run it. The consequence of not having the needed technology to run the sewage plant resulted in Iraqis dumping 300,000 tons of raw sewage into their rivers daily.

The U.S. finally agreed with the UN evaluation in 1996 that Iraq was facing a humanitarian disaster. A "Food for Oil" program was established, thereby allowing Iraq a chance to resolve this crisis in exchange for a limited amount of oil. Iraq's entire infrastructure, including its food, medicine, water treatment, electricity, telephones, roads, equipment, and supplies were subjected to UN Security Council monitoring and review.

On March 18, 1997, Iraq granted Russia the status of most favored nation to receive Iraqi oil exports in exchange for humanitarian goods. Of the first 37 contracts approved by the United Nations in the Food for Oil sale, seven went to Russian companies, representing almost 20 percent of the volume of oil in the sale. On March 22, 1997, Iraqi Oil Minister Amer Rashid announced the establishment of a new Iraq/Russian oil company that would work independently of Iraq's national oil company. Iraq signed other agreements with France and China as well.[9]

Three of the UN Security Council's permanent members, France, Russia and China, as well as other members of the UN, continually requested that the sanctions be lifted from Iraq, but the UN held that the sanctions could not be lifted until the United States and Britain agreed. Both nations would continue to hold firmly to the imposition of sanctions upon Iraq until after the 2003 invasion of Iraq. Mr. Denis Halliday, the UN Humanitarian Coordinator for Iraq, resigned in October of 1998 in order to freely criticize the sanctions on Iraq, stating, "I don't want to administer a program that satisfies the definition of genocide."[10] His resignation came after a thirty-four year career with the United Nations.

*"The great error of nearly all studies of war ... has been
to consider war as an episode in foreign policies,
when it is an act of interior politics ..."*

Simone Weil

The biggest criticism of the Food for Oil program was that Saddam Hussein allegedly used the funds from the program to build palaces and mosques. He was said to have punished segments of Iraqi citizens by denying them food.[11] We now know that while ordinary Iraqi citizens suffered and died, Saddam Hussein continued to enjoy his rich lifestyle inside his many palaces with his well-stocked liquor cabinets, Cuban cigars, parties, and tailored Armani suits. Hussein's dictatorial lifestyle was hardly affected during the years of sanctions but the Iraqis suffered brutally.

Foundation of The Project for a New American Century

It was 1992 and Neoconservative Paul Wolfowitz, who served in the Department of Defense under Dick Cheney in the George H.W. Bush Administration, created the first draft of the "New Defense Planning Guidelines." The defense document prepared by Wolfowitz called for preemptive strikes against Iraq and North Korea.[12] The New Defense Planning Guidelines created a hailstorm of criticism, so much so that George H.W. Bush, embarrassed by the media exposure, ordered Dick Cheney to rewrite them.

These guidelines were later resurrected to become the fundamental doctrine of the Project for a New American Century. In a document entitled "Rebuilding America's Defenses," Wolfowitz campaigns for a future of rapidly increased defense spending and the overthrow of Saddam Hussein. Ominously, he writes, *"The process of transformation, even if it brings revolutionary change, is likely to be a long one, absent some catastrophic and catalyzing event — like a new Pearl Harbor."*[13]

In the darkness of the 9/11 attacks on our nation, Wolfowitz got his "Pearl Harbor." Few U.S. citizens realized that the Project for a New American Century's "Rebuilding America's Defenses" became the United States' new foreign policy. This policy not only included the doctrine of preemptive strikes against other nations, but it also enthusiastically promoted the ideals of American hegemony.

"Imperialism is an institution under which one nation asserts the right to seize the land or at last to control the government or resources of another people."

John T. Flynn

NOTES, Chapter 4

[1] John Sweeny, "Saddam's Mass Graves," *BBC News*, September 23, 2003, news.bbc.co.uk/1/hi/programmes/correspondent/2785095.stm.

[2] "No-Fly Zones," *Global Policy Forum*, www.globalpolicy.org/security/issues/iraq/flyindex.htm

[3] Matt Welch, "The Politics of Dead Children," *Reason Online*, March 2002, www.reason.com/0203/fe.mw.the.shtml.

[4] Joy Gordon, "Cool War: Economic sanctions as a weapon of mass destruction," *Harper's Magazine*, November 2002.

[5] Ibid.

[6] Ibid.

[7] The Research Unit for Political Economy, "Behind the War on Iraq," *Monthly Review* 55, no. 1 (May 2003), www.monthlyreview.org/0503rupe.htm.

[8] Ibid.

[9] "Iraq Energy Chronology: 1980-November 2005," *Energy Information Administration*, December 2005, www.eia.doe.gov/cabs/iraqchron.html.

[10] "Denis Halliday," *Wikipedia*, en.wikipedia.org/wiki/Denis_Halliday.

[11] www.thetruthaboutiraq.org/myths_04.htm. Defunct, December 14, 2006.

[12] a. Patrick E. Tyler, "U.S. Strategy Plan Calls for Insuring No Rivals Develop, A One-Superpower World, Pentagon's Document Outlines Ways to Thwart Challenges to Primacy of America," *The New York Times*, March 8, 1992. b. PBS Online, *Frontline: War in Iraq*, www.pbs.org/wgbh/pages/frontline/saddam/.

[13] The Project for the New American Century, *Rebuilding America's Defenses: Strategy, Forces and Resources for a New Century*, September 2000: 63, www.newamericancentury.org/RebuildingAmericasDefenses.pdf.

★ 5 ★

Neo Caustic

"Any intelligent fool can make things bigger, more complex, and more violent. It takes a touch of genius — and a lot of courage — to move in the opposite direction."

E. F. Schumacher

AMERICANS SHOULD FIRST EVALUATE their own concepts and ideas about how they believe the U.S. government should engage and interact with other nations. By taking a simple ten-question multiple-choice assessment, you will be able to determine your own predominant style and approach to foreign affairs. This understanding can help drive U.S. foreign policy and protocols and be used to direct our government leaders to engage in actions reflective of the values of the American public. Finally, you can determine if your approach corresponds to the approach used by the Bush Administration in foreign affairs:

Foreign Affairs Assessment — What's Your Style?

For each topic, there are four choices. Circle the one that best reflects how you feel about the matter:

On Democracy

1. I believe other nations should figure out their own system of government and that America should mind its own business.
2. I believe the best way to convert other nations to democracy is to live our values of democracy so that other nations may desire what we have.

3. I believe America should help other nations achieve democracy only if they request such assistance.

4. I believe America should invade and occupy other nations with our military so we can teach them about democracy.

On Starting Wars

1. America should avoid all wars. Human life is too precious and war begets more war.

2. To keep America safe, we should invest in educating a large group of American negotiators to speak many different foreign languages, understand different cultures and be able to negotiate in the best interests of our nation.

3. America should wage war as a last resort, and only on those countries or groups who strike at us first, acting in self-defense.

4. To keep America safe we need to practice preemptive strike authority, which means we should start wars and eliminate any government or group which might threaten our security.

On Capitalism Abroad

1. I believe people and the environment come first and corporate profits come second.

2. I believe fair business practices should include in their cost of doing business the protection of human rights and the environment. Corporate profits should only be earned in an ethical manner.

3. I believe it is important to balance corporate profits with human and environmental concerns.

4. I believe corporate profits are more important than people or the environment. The true nature of capitalism is to make a profit at any human or environmental cost.

On Military Superiority

1. I believe we already spend too much money on the military; we need to cut back.

2. I believe the best way to ensure America's military superiority globally is to lead by example, going back to treaties of non-proliferation and making sure other nations comply as well.

3. I believe the best way to ensure our military superiority globally is to fully fund America's anti-terrorism programs, work with allies, and reinstitute the treaties to ban weapons of mass destruction.
4. I believe the best way to ensure America's military superiority globally is to continually invest and upgrade Star Wars and nuclear arms programs.

On Global Cooperation

1. The U.S. should never go to war.
2. The U.S. should go to war only after all other options have been exhausted, and if absolutely necessary. UN approval is required prior to launching a war.
3. The U.S. should only go to war with UN approval and with allies at our side.
4. The U.S. doesn't need permission to launch a war. We have everything we need to win, and our allies are either with us or against us.

On Weapons of Mass Destruction

1. The U.S. should destroy all of its weapons of mass destruction, apologize to the world and ask them to destroy their weapons as well.
2. The U.S. needs to reestablish the treaties and bans, and work with the UN and our allies to lead by example in getting rid of weapons of mass destruction.
3. The treaties voided by the Bush Administration were antiquated instruments that, in the shadows of the 9/11 attack on America, needed to be eliminated in order to develop more aggressive policies.
4. It's good that George W. Bush took the U.S. out of all nuclear proliferation treaties and bans against weapons of mass destruction. We needed to start manufacturing updated nuclear weapons to keep us safe. We should strike other nations we see as a threat before they develop weapons of mass destruction.

On Jobs Abroad

1. Congress should pass laws that make it illegal for American corporations to send jobs overseas.
2. Americans need to understand that we live in a global market and use our creativity and innovation to find niches in the market and develop these for profit.
3. America needs to invest in education to keep our citizens technically and scientifically competitive and institute a variety of corporate tax incentives or penalties to keep jobs in America.
4. The most important element is for corporations to make profits and keep prices low for Americans. It is each person's responsibility to maintain his or her employment competitiveness. It is not the responsibility of the government.

On Oil Imports

1. America should not be subsidizing terrorist nations with our dollars; we must immediately stop using oil and find alternatives.
2. The oil industry should be highly taxed and penalized for not coming up with clean alternatives for automotives.
3. The government should reinstate tax incentives to eliminate oil dependency by providing a 100 percent tax credit for the purchase of hybrid vehicles and adding a large tax to gas-guzzling vehicles.
4. Subsidizing and protecting America's oil interest in the Middle East is best for our economy and our nation.

On Imperialism

1. The U.S. government should take care of its citizens and our nation. We have no business in other parts of the world. If U.S. corporations choose to move outside our boundaries, they do so at their own risk.
2. The U.S. government should assist other nations through the UN with those initiatives deemed essential or important to the financial or security goals of the U.S.
3. The U.S. government has a responsibility as a global leader to invest in other nations and help corporations within reasonable limits.

4. The U.S. government must defend American corporate interests globally, spreading democracy, freedom and free trade through the use of military force and any other resources needed to do so.

On World Policing

1. The U.S. is not the world cop and should stop acting like one.

2. America should act with humility and restraint, taking care of "world crises" as a mediator only.

3. America's interests are best served when we work through the UN to resolve conflicts and issues.

4. It is America's duty and obligation to police other nations, overturn governments, and launch wars (preemptive strikes) if we suspect our interests abroad might be threatened.

SCORING

For each answer you circled multiply by the following:

# of 1s Circled _____ x 0_____

# of 2s Circled _____ x 3_____

# of 3s Circled _____ x 7_____

# of 4s Circled _____ x10_____

Total Number _____   _____

Find your total on the chart on the next page and see which category correspondences to your score.

SCORING TEMPLATE: FOREIGN AFFAIRS PHILOSOPHY

75-100

NEOCON: Your views are consistent with those in the Neoconservative movement. As a Neoconservative, you are primarily concerned with the profits of private corporations. You believe America is kept safe by maintaining highly expensive and dangerous nuclear arms. You agree with the preemptive strike philosophy to eliminate any suspected or threatening nations. You have a strong imperialistic bent for the U.S. and believe in a "go it alone" attitude. Your attitudes are consistent with the George W. Bush White House.

41-74

TRADITIONALIST: Your views are consistent with many Democrats and Republicans. As a traditionalist, you are primarily concerned with balancing home needs with global needs. You believe America is kept safe by participating in UN programs, global collaborations and anti-terrorism programs. You believe in strong investments in education, science and technology to maintain a global competitive advantage. You are not hesitant to use force when necessary but do not look to start wars.

21-40

COLLABORATOR: Your views are consistent with a collaborator. As a collaborator, you value working cooperatively with others in a win-win fashion. You put faith in the negotiation process. While you value balance in profit-making and taking care of people, you also believe in strong incentives or penalties as interventions when necessary to take care of citizens and the environment. You believe the U.S. should fight in wars only after they are proven absolutely essential.

0-20

PACIFIST: Your views are consistent with a pacifist. You prefer that the U.S. government concern itself with matters within its boundaries. You believe that by being a good role model and neighbor, America is kept safe. You believe the priority of the U.S. government should be investing in its people as opposed to providing tax breaks or security for corporations who choose to do business abroad. Taking care of the environment and other priorities within the U.S. are important to you. You rarely, if ever, believe there is a necessity for being involved in a war.

Neocons: A Brief History and Overview

The term "Neoconservatism" has been used to describe two very different groups. I do not consider those affiliated with the religious right or religious conservatives to be Neocons. Neoconservatives, or "Neocons," originated from an exclusive group of white, affluent, well-educated, and well-connected males in the late 1960s and early 1970s. These men had become disenchanted with so-called liberal politics after the 1960s.[1] Much of their early philosophy was derived from a political philosopher, Leo Strauss, who became an American citizen at the age of 50 and was a professor at the University of Chicago.[2]

Albert Wohlstetter was another important founder of the Neoconservative Movement. He was the world's leading nuclear and national security strategist and had previously served as a senior staff member at the RAND Corporation. RAND was founded in 1946 by the United States Armed Forces under a contract with Douglas Aircraft. Later, RAND became an independent "think tank." Like Strauss, Wohlstetter taught at the University of Chicago.[3]

In the 1970s, the U.S. and many Middle Eastern nations were engaged in a tug-of-war over the control of oil in the Middle East. The American military presence in the Persian Gulf was minimal and the prospect of seizing control of Arab oil fields by force was simply unrealistic at the time.[4] A few of the original Neoconservatives were "hawkish Democrats." The term "hawkish" indicates a political stance of military aggressiveness against others to improve the standing of one's own government, country or organization.[5] Some of these Democrats were angry with the Vietnam anti-war protestors and the social programs created by the Johnson Administration. These people moved to the furthest right of the Republican Party to join the Neocons.

George W. Bush Appoints
Iran-Contra Scandal Figures

Under President Ronald Reagan in the 1980s, the Neoconservatives were referred to as Neo-Reaganite Hawks. They included Dick Cheney and Paul Wolfowitz, both of whom served in the Reagan Department of Defense. Several Neocons convicted and involved in the Iran-Contra scandal have been appointed to high-ranking positions within the George W. Bush Administration.

The Iran-Contra scandal involved a group of CIA operatives and Reagan government officials who were caught in defiance of the U.S. Congress and in violation of multiple laws. They helped to overthrow the democratically elected government of Nicaragua in Central America by selling arms illegally to Iran without congressional approval. They then gave the money raised to violent militias. Neo-Reaganites, such as Elliott Abrams and John Poindexter, were convicted of conspiracy, lying to Congress, defrauding the government, and destroying evidence in the Iran-Contra scandal.[6] They were later pardoned by George H.W. Bush.[7]

Both Abrams and Poindexter became part of the George W. Bush Administration, as did several other Neocons involved (but never convicted) in the Iran-Contra scandal. Elliot Abrams was appointed as Special Assistant to George W. Bush and as a Senior Director on the National Security Council in 2002. John Poindexter was appointed to head the Defense Advanced Research Projects Agency, Information Awareness Office (IAO) in 2002. The controversial office was later de-funded by Congress out of fear that a mass surveillance program developed by that office could potentially violate the constitutional rights of Americans.[8]

John Bolton was appointed to the Office of the Under Secretary and International Security from 2001 through 2005 by George W. Bush. The President appointed Bolton as U.S. Ambassador to the UN in 2005. Because of many controversies, including Mr. Bolton's role in the Iran-Contra scandal, his nomination was subjected to a prolonged filibuster in the Senate. It was led by Democrats and Republican Senator George Voinovich. Bush, unable to obtain Bolton's confirmation by the Senate, simply bypassed Congress and made a "recess appointment" of Mr. Bolton, installing him as the interim U.S. Ambassador until 2007.

In 2001, despite substantial opposition from Senate Democrats, John Negroponte was appointed as the U.S. Ambassador to the UN.[9] This nomination was ratified by the Senate four days after the 9/11 attacks on September 15, 2001. In 2004, John Negroponte was appointed as the U.S. Ambassador to Iraq, and in 2005 he was appointed as National Intelligence Director by George W. Bush. Negroponte became top deputy to Secretary of State Condoleezza Rice in early 2007.

I wonder how many American business owners or high-level supervisors and managers would hire a team of ex-convicts and affiliated conspirators to run their businesses? How many average Americans would entrust a group of individuals who were known to have lied to Congress with important life and death issues to oversee their business concerns? I challenge you to think about this.

"In looking for people to hire, you look for three qualities:
integrity, intelligence, and energy. And if they don't
have the first, the other two will kill you."

Warren Buffet, CEO, Berkshire Hathaway

Neoconservatives Hijack America's Foreign Policies

The Neocons had become strong in money, power and influence by 2000. What few people realize is that in the shadow of the 9/11 attacks on America, the Neocons radically changed America's foreign policies. It was reported that within days of the 9/11 attack, nuclear arms and Star Wars programs were pulled from the shelves, dusted off and key elements were reinstated in the new U.S. foreign policy. Terms such as "preemptive strike" became the new dogma.

Neoconservatives promote a philosophy of preemptive strike. They believe the U.S. has the right to start wars with other nations and to overthrow the government of these countries.[10] Neocons insist the U.S. has this right regardless of whether the other nation actually poses a threat to the U.S. In accordance with the Neoconservative doctrine, the U.S. would triumph in the future through imperialistic military strength and power.[11] Their plans for the U.S. include actively working to overthrow the governments of Iraq, Iran, Syria, and North Korea. These plans have been in existence since 1992 and were updated in 2000 in a report entitled *Rebuilding America's Defenses: Strategy, Forces, and Resources for a New Century*.[12] This was one of the most important documents created by the Project for a New American Century (PNAC).

Neoconservatives within the George W. Bush Administration pressured Congress to give the U.S. Military astronomical amounts of money to update and reinstitute formerly prohibited nuclear weaponry. United in their mission to reestablish the nuclear Star Wars program and to increase American dominance in the Middle East using the U.S. Military and American tax dollars, the Neocons' influence had grown to terrifying proportions.[13] They insisted the U.S. Military needed to increase its own cache of weapons of mass destruction, while demanding that other nations disarm. The cost of the wars in the Middle East has long evaporated any U.S. budget surplus left from the Clinton Administration. They have incurred a huge National Debt. This debt will be handed down to future generations. (The impact of the current state of our national budget is examined more thoroughly in the chapter, "Meanwhile, Back at the Ranch.")

Neocons show intense contempt for international organizations and they have worked to undermine the credibility of the UN.[14] They deny the need for multilateralism, and they do not advocate working cooperatively with other nations to achieve global goals. Neocons show impatience with traditional balance of power, and they avoid using diplomatic methods to resolve differences. They subscribe to a unilateral ideology, preferring to "go it alone" if America's allies disagree with their actions.[15]

Outspoken in their belief in Western culture and political superiority, Neocons believe that the U.S. has a responsibility to bring democracy and freedom to the world; this means to them subjugating other nations to American corporate power.[16] This dogma has proven ineffectual, as they have failed to promote either peace or democracy.

Neocons use religious jargon to sway the "religious right." In return, the "religious right" receives little more than lip service. During elections, Neocons support causes motivating the "religious right," only to forget these causes soon after they have achieved their political goals. (More on this topic is discussed in the chapter "Push, Push Back: Distraction, Division, and Polarization.") Neocons are highly aligned with Israel, and have demonstrated eagerness to use American power to protect and further Israeli security interests.[17]

Distract and Attack Tactics

Using distraction to further their aims, Neocons saturate the news media with "moral" issues while surreptitiously moving to further their own economic and political goals. An example is the issue of gay marriage, which has been a subject of intense debate that has no real bearing on actual foreign or domestic policy. While these "wedge issues" distract most Americans, Neocons quickly passed legislation through the Republican-controlled Congress that benefited big corporations and the wealthiest Americans. Protection for American workers has been sacrificed and important domestic programs have been cut.[18] Meanwhile, the workplace is becoming more dangerous for working employees.[19]

This strategy has worked to bring huge tax breaks to those needing them least while driving up the federal deficit. Preemptive attacks are not limited to potential foreign enemies. Neocons take offensive strategies against their American opponents as well.[20] Those who dare to disagree risk having their reputations challenged or in some cases shredded. These challenges are rarely legitimate. By engaging in false accusations, whisper campaigns and innuendo, Neocons have been incredibly successful at tarnishing and destroying the reputations of many good people.[21] More on this topic will be detailed in later chapters.

Neocons profess to be intellectuals, but the radical dogma underlying their ideology from which they write and speak lacks critical thinking and is based upon strong biases and preferences. Neoconservatives operate several "think tanks"—organizations that claim to be impartial research centers used for the purpose of analyzing important public policy issues. These "think tanks" and "research centers" use the tax shelters offered through status as non-profit 501-C organizations.

Most centers are headquartered in Washington, D.C. A few are found in other major cities such as Chicago. In reality, the think tanks and centers are highly sophisticated public relations and lobbying firms whose main function is to sell Congress and the American public on a variety of highly refined Neoconservative initiatives. They write and speak on a wide range of issues, such as the war in Iraq, foreign policy, the environment, global warming, the UN, government regulations, Social Security, public education, health care, and welfare reform. Neocons are brilliant at manipulating their message, using advanced psychological marketing tactics to entice both busy politicians and mainstream Americans. They seldom, if ever, search for common ground among diverse American groups. Their actions are divisive and lead to dissent in America. Several examples are presented later in this chapter.

Advocates of Deregulation

Neocons advocate the elimination of government rules and regulations that they believe will hinder their business interests.[22] Under the Reagan Administration, Neocons supported deregulation of the savings and loan industry. Within a few short years, that deregulation led to the collapse of this industry, costing taxpayers billions of dollars.[23]

Enron provides yet another example of how Neocons have foisted their objectives upon the American public with disastrous results. Wendy Gramm, the spouse of Senator Phil Gramm (R-TX) and the former chairwoman of the Commodity Futures Trading Commission, lifted governmental oversight of energy contracts under which Enron and other companies were traded in the early 1990s.[24]

Shortly after his wife approved the elimination of this oversight, Senator Gramm sponsored legislation entitled "The Commodity Futures Modernization Act" that contained a clause giving Enron the legal exemption it had sought. Enron was then free to hide its illicit deals from the scrutiny of any regulating agency. In turn, Enron would be Senator Gramm's largest political contributor. But even more was to be gained by the Gramm family. A few weeks after the government deregulation, Mrs. Gramm was appointed to Enron's board of directors, where she received three million dollars over an eight-year period to provide oversight as an Enron board member.[25] Normally, when a company collapses, as did Enron, the board of directors is held liable. This did not happen. Enron's tentacles extended to the President but the government's case against the company was limited to Enron employees. Former Senator Gramm and his wife were well-known Bush supporters and no Enron board members were held accountable. Enron had been the biggest financial contributor to George W. Bush's first Presidential campaign.[26]

Well-Funded Corporate Connections

The Neocons, along with their think tanks and research centers, have a long history of heavy funding by corporate sponsors such as Enron and Exxon/Mobil. But more important than direct sponsorship is the direct support of the many Neocon foundations created in the last thirty-six years. These non-profit foundations get direct, tax-free money from the corporations. In return, the Neoconservative think tanks and centers lobby for the corporations' interests. Money for Neoconservative foundations such as the Sarah Scaife Foundation flows from corporations such as Alcoa, Chevron, the Union Trust Company, the Pittsburgh Coal Company, and Mellon Banks.

All of these corporations have done extremely well, some featuring 25 percent stock price increases, while our nation has been at war. Recently, Alcoa announced its highest quarterly income and revenue in the company's history.[27] And in every subsequent quarter, the gas and oil industries surpass the previous quarter with breathtaking earnings. Twelve of the top-funded Neocon foundations are:

1. Carthage Foundation
2. Charles G. Koch
3. Claude R. Lambe Charitable Foundations
4. David H. Koch Charitable Foundations
5. Earhart Foundation
6. Henry Salvatori Foundation
7. JM Foundation
8. John M. Olin Foundation
9. Lynde and Harry Bradley Foundation
10. Phillip M. McKenna Foundation
11. Sarah Scaife Foundation
12. Smith Richardson Foundation

One of the earliest and most influential foundations is the Heritage Foundation. It was established in 1973 by three right-wing Republican billionaires: Joseph Coors, Richard Mellon Scaife, and Edward Noble, along with right-wing activist Paul Weyrich.

Andy, a businessman and warehouse owner in Atlanta, said the Heritage Foundation was one of his favorite organizations for the "philanthropic work it does." Andy says he's a small contributing member of the Heritage Foundation. I quizzed Andy about the foundation and it was clear he did not know anything about Heritage's obsession with Star Wars or nuclear arms.

Rebirth of "Star Wars" and Weapons of Mass Destruction

"War is a racket. It always has been. It is possibly the oldest, easily the most profitable, surely the most vicious."

General Smedley Butler

According to Edward Fuelner, President of the Heritage Foundation, Heritage had authored 22 publications on the need for a Star Wars defense program during the year 2000 alone. In addition, it had published three books on national defense and had set up a website for resources on national security and military strikes. On October 22, 2001, the Heritage Foundation had fifteen "experts" working "full time on issues of national security and foreign policy."[28]

Immediately after the 9/11 attacks, under the direction of Donald Rumsfeld, the Pentagon announced the formation of its Homeland Defense Task Force to develop policies that would help state, local and federal agencies fight terrorism. The task force was conducted in partnership with the Neoconservative think tank Heritage Foundation, and was headed by L. Paul Bremer, who would later become Ambassador to Iraq. The Heritage Foundation was found ready and willing to implement the Neoconservative platform it had worked on for decades. It issued a press release just days after 9/11: *Terrorist Attack on America Confirms the Growing Need for Missile Defense.*[29] The Heritage Foundation people had been itching for a rationale to revive the Star Wars program and, in the emotional heat of the 9/11 attacks, they believed they had been delivered such a rationale.

One short month later, on October 11, 2001, another Heritage Foundation press release stated, "The project will focus on the obstacles that must be overcome quickly to get the various agencies working together, so they can create and implement a master strategy that will protect the American people, economy and infrastructure from attack." What all this meant was that U.S. foreign policy had shifted to the radical right without the benefit of any debate, discussion or oversight. Immediately after the 9/11 attacks, the guidelines upon which the Project for a New American Century was established were implemented as the new U.S. policy under George W. Bush.[30]

> **"Getting Star Wars, a multibillion-dollar strategic missile defense program, had been an ongoing struggle, but it had been the major priority for the Heritage Foundation for years."[31]**
>
> Edward Fuelner, President Heritage Foundation

Donald Rumsfeld, one of the most adamant and well-known Neocons, used his power and influence as the Secretary of the U.S. Department of Defense to accomplish one of his long-awaited dreams. He had long called for the return of America's production of nuclear weapons. Rumsfeld battled throughout the 1990s, arguing for the reinstatement of the production of deadly, devastating and cost-prohibitive nuclear weapons for offensive and defensive purposes, despite repeated professional reports indicating there was no need for the proliferation of these types of weapons.[32] These reports evaluating the need for nuclear defense systems included important input from prominent U.S. Military specialists.

In 1998, against the backdrop of the Clinton impeachment, Rumsfeld demanded yet another commission to determine the need for a nuclear arms defense program. An eight-member commission headed by Rumsfeld, including Neoconservative cohort Paul Wolfowitz, came up with results that supported nuclear expansion. These results were in opposition to findings that had previously been confirmed.[33] Rumsfeld and Wolfowitz used only the slightest evidence to suggest that America needed a vastly expanded nuclear arms defense program.[34]

After the Rumsfeld report was concluded, it was discovered that no one had bothered to ask the professional military what they thought the biggest threat to America was. The Chiefs of Staff of the military would have told the Rumsfeld commission that the biggest threats to America were not from a nuclear attack, but from "unconventional terrorism."[35] The 2001 National Intelligence Estimate concluded, "the U.S. territory is more likely to be attacked by countries or terrorist groups using ships, trucks, airplanes, or other means than by a long-range ballistic missile." The U.S. is more vulnerable to Scud missile attacks, bombs hidden in briefcases or bombs arriving in shipping containers than to a nuclear attack. After implementing the missile defense program insisted upon by the Rumsfeld–Wolfowitz Commission and after spending 65 billion taxpayer dollars, the program was judged to be an absolute failure. Air Force Lieutenant General Ronald Kadish of the U.S. Missile Defense Agency reported on March 18, 2002, "Right now we have zero probability of intercepting a ballistic missile, and some judgment will have to be made as to whether anything greater than zero is useful."[36]

Unfortunately, the Bush Administration, together with former Secretary Rumsfeld and a majority in Congress, believe it is more important to spend obscene amounts of American tax dollars on threats that professionals keep telling us are not the priority. The type of terrorism delivery mechanisms the U.S. faces today makes Star Wars a costly and useless technology because it is either incompatible with, or incapable of, counteracting these threats.[37]

In fact, six months before the 9/11 attacks on America, in February of 2001, when the Senate Armed Services Committee requested $600 million for anti-terrorism activities, Rumsfeld declined the request and went so far as to threaten to recommend a Presidential veto.[38] At the same time, Rumsfeld sought $8.3 billion towards a missile defense program from the U.S. Congress.

Top conservative corporations have given the Heritage Foundation, the American Enterprise Institute and the Cato Institute more than $88 million since 1985.[39] According to Richard W. Behan, writing for the *Baltimore Chronicle and Sentinel,* "These three think tanks have designed almost the entire domestic and foreign policies of the George W. Bush Administration."[40] Jeb Bush served on the board of trustees of the Heritage Foundation.[41] Heritage has pumped out propaganda benefiting corporate sponsors year after year, yet it still manages to enjoy its tax-exempt status. In 2003, Heritage reported assets of $128,750,000.[42]

Another strong advocate of the missile defense industry is the Center for Security Policy (CSP), a corporate-financed advocacy group with at least eight defense executives on its advisory board at any given time. A major chunk of the Center's revenue comes directly from defense corporations.

Using Free Media to Spin and Lobby Congress

The Heritage Foundation uses talk show radio to promote its agenda, and the staff is frequently featured as guests and television pundits on major news and public affairs programs on major networks: ABC, CBS, NBC, CNN, CNBC, C–SPAN, and Fox. Heritage holds lectures, conferences and seminars that are broadcast regularly by C–SPAN, and it provides forums for members of Congress free of charge. Heritage boasted that from 2001 to 2003 it was able to influence American opinion through:

- 2,193 Television appearances
- 3,430 Radio interviews
- 2,225 Printed journalistic documents in major media outlets

Heritage has two broadcast studios in its offices just two blocks from the Capitol in Washington. With state-of-the-art equipment, Heritage produces regular talk shows featuring members of the House and Senate starring as guests in their programming. Each election year, the Heritage Foundation produces a "bible" for its Neoconservative candidates. The foundation offers candidates and lawmakers in Congress an online briefing service to provide instant Neoconservative positions on all issues.[43]

Neocon Talking Points for Politicians

Below are sample statements of how Heritage helps prepare our congressional representatives with specific talking points. These statements come directly from the Heritage Foundation's website and literature:

On Labor

- "Instead of pursuing economically corrosive policies to 'protect' workers, lawmakers should emphasize what is right with the U.S. economy."[44]
- "Congress has not raised the minimum wage since 1996, and it is now undeniable that average wages have risen during that time, proving that a higher minimum wage is unnecessary."[45]

On the Environment

- "... new restrictions on energy use in the name of environmental protection, especially a cap on emissions of carbon dioxide from fossil fuels, are unnecessary and would retard economic growth."[46]
- "Reject calls to crack down on air pollution beyond existing requirements, and avoid any cap on carbon dioxide emissions."[47]

On Health Coverage

- "Today's federal and state tax codes already provide enormous tax breaks for health insurance."[48]
- "Ideally, the federal government and employers should be neutral in treatment of health care."[49]

On Education

- "Dispel the myth that federal education spending leads to improved educational achievement and freeze the growth in education spending."[50]
- "Limit federal education policy to its original intention — assisting disadvantaged children — and pursue reforms that empower parents, not bureaucrats."[51]

On Nuclear Arms

- "Arms control advocates here and abroad want to impose international agreements on the U.S. Military to limit its space operations under the slogan of 'not weaponizing space.' The U.S. should resist these efforts."[52]
- "This includes both the nuclear payloads and the delivery systems and means that the modernization plan should not be curtailed because of demands for a permanent end to nuclear explosive testing and ratification of the Comprehensive Test Ban Treaty (CTBT)."[53]

On Terrorism

- "Avoid linking terrorism to root causes such as human rights or poverty that distract from the core issue of fighting terrorism."[54]
- "Do not press for a precise definition of terrorism, which is very controversial."[55]

The Revolving Door

Another large Neoconservative think tank is the American Enterprise Institute (AEI). It serves as a revolving door for Neocons, placing them into high-ranking U.S. government positions where they make recommended changes in laws and regulations or through executive orders. After serving as government officials, many Neocons go directly to work for the corporations that may have benefited from changes made while they were in office.[56]

While Dick Cheney was the Secretary of Defense, he made huge changes to privatize much of the U.S. Military, steering contracts to the private sector in an unprecedented manner.[57] Halliburton was the recipient of many lucrative contracts during Cheney's term as Defense Secretary.[58] After losing his job in the Reagan Administration, Dick Cheney was housed at the AEI for a short period until his position as Halliburton's new CEO was secured. His salary quickly skyrocketed to over $2 million annually, plus generous stock benefits. It is reported than from 1995 to 2000, Mr. Cheney was paid over $10 million and owned an additional $40 million in Halliburton stock.[59]

Mr. Cheney is reportedly the largest stockholder at Halliburton, which is the parent company of Kellogg, Brown and Root, a company that has received billions of dollars in non-competitive contracts for reconstruction projects in Iraq.[60] The Vice President's financial records reveal he continues to receive between $100,000 and $1 million annually in "deferred compensation" from Halliburton, where he served as CEO for five years.[61] As of 2005, Mr. Cheney reportedly still had multiple millions of dollars in Halliburton stock investments through Vanguard.[62]

Roger, a friend of mine who manages a small hardware store, said it was his understanding that "the Vice President had put all his money into a trust." Apparently, Roger thought that meant Dick Cheney had given it all away. Because most average Americans don't have trust accounts, they don't realize putting money in a trust is like putting all your assets into a transportable suitcase that still belongs to you. Mr. Cheney did not give his money away like Warren Buffet, the billionaire who recently gave most of his money to the charitable Bill and Melinda Gates Foundation. Cheney simply put his assets into a different type of transferable tax mechanism, one that he still owns.

Neocons may serve at the American Enterprise Institute while waiting for the Institute to secure a job for them in private sector corporations, school institutions or media organizations. The AEI provides endowments for schools and these endowments may influence schools to take Neocons as needed. Recently, despite massive objections and protests by students, professors and parents, Georgetown University accepted Douglas Feith, a Neocon and one of the chief architects of the invasion of Iraq. Mr. Feith was also a member of the Project for a New American Century. He was accepted as a visiting professor in the School of Foreign Service.[63]

The AEI board of trustees reads like the "who's who" of big business, with members like Vice Chairman Lee R. Raymond, former CEO of ExxonMobil Corporation, and William S. Stavropoulous, Chairman

Emeritus of the Dow Chemical Company. In 2006, the chairman of AEI was Bruce Kovner, who heads Caxton Associates, the largest single-manager hedge fund firm in the world, with $11.5 billion in capital as of December 31, 2003.[64] Hedge funds use volatile, complicated and risky trading strategies that can greatly affect the market. They have immense influence over financial markets, global economies and corporate decision-making and are not regulated by any governmental oversight despite numerous court challenges.[65]

Vice President Cheney's wife, Lynn Cheney, is a senior staffer at the American Enterprise Institute. At least twenty other AEI staffers have served in the Bush Administration since 2001, though many of these have since left the administration for better corporate opportunities.

ExxonMobil contributed approximately $925,000 to the AEI between 1998 and 2003, and this figure doesn't include other contributions made by individual board members. In return for the sponsored donations, AEI has been an avid opponent of the Kyoto Protocol. Signed by President Clinton, Kyoto was the international agreement designed to minimize greenhouse gases (including carbon dioxide) that are warming the global atmosphere. Power plants powered by fossil fuels are the greatest contributor to global warming.[66] The AEI opposes environmental regulations that might harm its sponsors. AEI climate science skeptics include James K. Glassman, also of ExxonMobil-funded Tech Central Station.[67] These skeptics regularly appear as "environmental experts" on news programs and their direct ties to their sponsors is never mentioned. More will be discussed in the chapter, "The Fifth Commandment."

The AEI frames controversial topics for congressional consideration that helps their corporate sponsors in spite of potential harm to consumers.[68] Take for example the recent congressional battle over "Net Neutrality."[69] Organizations as diverse as the Christian Coalition, Google, MoveOn, and the Gun Owners of America joined forces to fight for Internet freedom. Corporations are desperately trying to control the free flow of information in an attempt to make a profit on the Internet and eliminate dissenting voices.[70] The AEI sponsored a paper that in part recommends congressional intervention and U.S. governmental regulation and pricing of the Internet.[71]

Bona Fide Expert or Fabricated Opinion?

A strategy of the Neocons is to flood the media with highly opinioned position papers created by their "think tanks." Since their papers do not go through rigorous scrutiny or any peer review, they short-circuit the process that ensures information is accurate before publication or dissemination. To the public, it appears that they are presenting a scientific conclusion. Instead, what is presented is biased information or conclusions based upon one-sided, skewed or erroneous information. Using a program of propaganda, distorted pictures and fear, the Neocons have assisted the Bush Administration in successfully changing the hearts and minds of the American people on a number of extremely important issues.

They hide their deceit through carefully crafted words of patriotism. In fact, they have been known to utilize techniques developed by the Nazis to challenge anyone who questions them on issues, especially those pertaining to their "war on terrorism."[72]

> **"The people can always be brought to do the bidding of the leader, that's easy. All you have to do is tell them they are being attacked and denounce the peacemakers for lack of patriotism, exposing the country to danger."**
>
> Herman Goering, 1944, Second in Command of the Nazi Party[73]

Over the last thirty years, Neoconservatives have used multiple platforms to legitimize their propaganda. Of the voluminous amounts of information disseminated by the Neoconservative movement, little is seeded in factual data or valid scientific studies. By using a very thin shred of truth or slight evidence, they create a sense of validity. They create policy papers, columns and press releases and ignite petition drives based on false premises. Neocon think tanks tailor messages, and perpetuate media spin, to create an illusion of authentic news reporting to further their sponsors' positions.

Neocons also attempt to create a sense of legitimacy by conducting polls and surveys. I regularly receive an opinion poll from an organization called the Polling Station, which promises "Results You Will Not See Anywhere Else." Every time I receive survey results from this organization, it is totally different from any other mainstream poll. Upon research, I found the Polling Station, despite its non-partisan claim, to be affiliated with the Neoconservative Project for a New American Century.

Neocons have garnered enormous influence and have shown their effectiveness in using it to instill confusion and sway public opinion. The amount of money available from Neocon supported industries to create confusion and vigorously campaign for their causes is nothing compared to what these companies might lose if the American public demanded some accountability. Take, for example, the oil industry. It is making excessive profits while destroying our environment and threatening U.S. national security with continued foreign oil dependence. Changes in vehicle gasoline standards, alternative fuel sources, large tax credits on hybrid vehicles, and other measures geared towards environmental conservation would immensely affect big oil's bottom line. Demands to bring troops home and account for the billions of lost dollars by KBR of Halliburton would be a huge blow to the war profiteering companies so heavily supported by the Neocons.

Neocons profess to value "freedom," but their values are simply rationales to protect big corporations from having to take responsibility or face accountability. This lack of oversight has resulted in destruction and havoc on the environment and the exploitation of human rights. On their printed literature and websites, Neocons state their philosophy, indicating, "Private owners are the best stewards of the environment."[74] This means private for-profit corporations are free to use and abuse the environment that the entire world depends upon for survival. These Neocon think tanks and "research centers" strategize, support and spin off other Neoconservative organizations as they dispense a flood of disinformation across the nation.

Neocons continually charge the media of having a distinct liberal bias. A *Harris Poll* of heavy viewers found that 69 percent of those who watched *Fox News* felt strongly that there is a liberal media bias.[75] Those who do not watch *Fox News* and instead watch *CNN News* indicate the conservative and liberal biases are about equal.[76] On any given day you will witness disparaging comments about liberals and the purported liberal biases on Fox programs such as *The O'Reilly Factor.*[77] I believe it is these comments and commentators that create the *illusion* of an exaggerated liberal bias in the media.

Clinton and the Neocons

President Bill Clinton was the target of Neoconservative and Republican harassment throughout much of his administration. Led by House Speaker Newt Gingrich, the harassers subjected the Clinton Administration to probe after probe. For example, Republican lawmakers spent over 100 hours reviewing the Clinton Christmas card list to determine if Mr. Clinton had used the list for political purposes. Contrast this level of oversight to the congressional oversight concerning the atrocities committed by American contractors and soldiers at Abu Ghraib. The congressional oversight on Abu Ghraib was limited to less than 12 hours.[78]

Neoconservative Republicans spent over $2.4 million to bankroll the Paula Jones lawsuit against President Clinton.[79] This group included Stephen S. Boynton, a conservative Virginia attorney, David Henderson of the American Spectator Educational Foundation, and Richard Larry, president of the Sarah Scaife Foundation on behalf of conservative billionaire Richard Mellon Scaife. The legal battles consumed considerable attention throughout Clinton's Administration. After a four-year investigation by special prosecutor Ken Starr, and well over $40 million in taxpayer dollars, all that was discovered was an illicit affair, which most Americans would have preferred not to know about.[80] William Jefferson Clinton, in the midst of the impeachment hearings, still held approval ratings well above 73 percent.[81] By comparison, George W. Bush's approval rating, as of June 2006, was only 38 percent. The irony of such investigations was that they were pursued by Gingrich and his Republican Moral Majority. Newt Gingrich, while touting family values, had walked out on two wives and has since confessed to having an affair with an aide all through the Clinton-Lewinsky ordeal.

The impeachment proceedings were a desperate attempt to discredit Clinton, as well as to distract him from his agenda. The Neocons hounded Mr. Clinton on Iraq, baiting him and bombarding him with the same message over and over. They said, "Our work in Iraq is not done." President Clinton ignored most of their bantering during his eight-year term, calling for restraint and humility regarding Iraq. He preferred holding a position of "containment" on Saddam Hussein. However, in 1998, Clinton succumbed to the pressure of the Neocons and bombed Iraq from American warships stationed in the Persian Gulf.[82] A Gulf War veteran from this mission would later describe the act as dishonorable. The veteran said his heart ached when he thought of how the U.S. shot fifty-two Tomahawk missiles from the "safety of our ship into Iraq and [the Iraqis] had no way of attacking back."[83]

In 1998, when Clinton was informed of the opportunity to take out Osama bin Laden, he took it and ordered missile attacks on sites in Afghanistan and Sudan in retaliation for the bombings at the U.S. embassies, and to deter future terrorist attacks.[84] The Republicans retaliated, accusing Clinton of using bin Laden as a distraction from the ongoing probe of the day. Later, these same Republicans would blame Mr. Clinton for not doing enough to get rid of Osama bin Laden. Hillary Clinton frequently referred to the Neocons as a vast right wing conspiracy; much of the public thought she was acting paranoid.

Project for a New American Century

Disenchanted with how the first war on Iraq ended in 1992, a group of Neoconservative warhawks started an organization called a Project for a New American Century (PNAC), a spin-off from AEI and housed in the same building. Officially convened in 1997, PNAC is one of five Neoconservative think tanks that received close to a billion dollars in support from its inception in 1997 to 2003.[85] PNAC provided the U.S. with a grand strategy for a new world order of American hegemony and a blueprint for world domination. Some direct quotes from their doctrine:

- "The United States has for decades sought to play a more permanent role in Gulf regional security. While the unresolved conflict with Iraq provides the immediate justification, the need for a substantial American force presence in the Gulf transcends the issue of the regime of Saddam Hussein."[86]
- "...blueprint for maintaining global U.S. pre-eminence, precluding the rise of a great power rival, and shaping the international security order in line with American principles and interests."[87]
- "American grand strategy" must be advanced "as far into the future as possible."
- The U.S. must "fight and decisively win multiple, simultaneous, major theatre wars" as a "core mission."[88]
- American armed forces abroad should act as "the cavalry on the new American frontier."[89]
- The U.S. must "discourage advanced industrial nations from challenging our leadership or even aspiring to a larger regional or global role."[90]
- Iraq, Iran, Syria, and North Korea could potentially be threatening to the U.S.[91]
- Preventive wars against these nations are recommended.[92]

Neocon Warhawks Beat their Drums

"This is garbage from right-wing think tanks stuffed with chicken-hawks — men who have never seen the horror of war but are in love with the idea of war. Men like Cheney, who were draft-dodgers in the Vietnam War."

Tam Dalyell, The British House of Commons

These men, none of who ever served a day in the U.S. Military, and members of the Project for a New American Century demanded that our Nation go to war against Iraq. Here is a small sampling of their rhetoric as they wrote opinions in newspapers across our nation and letters to Congress. They constantly alleged falsities about Iraq and Saddam Hussein. Many of these same individuals continue their rhetoric, but in 2006 and 2007 they made the accusations against Iran.

ALLEGATIONS OF IRAQ'S WEAPONS OF MASS DESTRUCTION MADE BY PNAC

December 15, 1997

"Three weeks without UN inspections undoubtedly allowed the Iraqis to roll back months if not years of weapons-monitoring work by the UN Special Commission. That was ample time to disperse and conceal facilities for research, production, and storage of mass-terror weapons." [93]

JOHN R. BOLTON, *later appointed U.S. Permanent Representative to the United Nations*

January 19, 1998

"The list of what Hussein has done during Clinton's watch is long... a program to continue developing weapons of mass destruction..." [94]

JOHN R. BOLTON, *U.S. Permanent Representative to the United Nations*

January 30, 1998

"...the Iraqi leader never again uses weapons of mass destruction, the only way to achieve that goal is to remove Mr. Hussein and his regime from power." [95]

WILLIAM KRISTOL & ROBERT KAGAN, *in The New York Times*

February 26, 1998

"The fact that UNSCOM will be allowed to continue its mission in some form, moreover, does not mean the inspectors will be any closer to finding Saddam's biological and chemical weapons than they were before. After all, as administration officials acknowledged just last week, after 6½ years of inspections, the United States still has no idea where the weapons are hidden." [96]

WILLIAM KRISTOL & ROBERT KAGAN, *in The Washington Post*

February 26, 1998

"Saddam has now had four months to conceal his weapons. How many months, or years, will it take the inspectors to get back on the scent?" [97]

WILLIAM KRISTOL & ROBERT KAGAN, in The Washington Post

September 28, 1998

"Saddam will suddenly present the United States and the world with a horrifying fait accompli: He will have his weapons of mass destruction and the missiles to deliver them." [98]

ROBERT KAGAN, THE Weekly Standard

September 28, 1998

"If and when Saddam builds his weapons of mass destruction, the United States will still be able to deter him from aggression against his neighbors." [99]

ROBERT KAGAN, THE Weekly Standard

September 28, 1998

"It has long been clear that the only way to rid the world of Saddam's weapons of mass destruction is to rid Iraq of Saddam. Last week, Paul Wolfowitz, a defense official in the Bush Administration, laid out in testimony before Congress a thoughtful and coherent strategy to accomplish that goal." [100]

ROBERT KAGAN, THE Weekly Standard

November 16, 1998

"The longer the present crisis lasts, the more weeks the United States spends arguing with its allies and with Russia, the closer Saddam comes to his real objective: finally acquiring chemical and biological weapons of mass destruction and the missiles to deliver them." [101]

JOHN BOLTON, THE Weekly Standard

November 16, 1998

"Unless we are prepared to live in a world where aggressive dictators like Saddam Hussein wield weapons of mass destruction — presumably not the legacy for which President Clinton would like to be remembered — then the time has come to take the necessary risks to prevent it." [102]

JOHN BOLTON, THE Weekly Standard

November 16, 1998

"Can the air attacks insure [sic] that he will never be able to use weapons of mass destruction again? The answer, unfortunately, is no." [103]

JOHN BOLTON, THE *Weekly Standard* editorial

November 16, 1998

"After the bombing stops, Mr. Hussein will still be able to manufacture weapons of mass destruction." [104]

JOHN BOLTON, THE *Weekly Standard* editorial

February 26, 1998 and January 7, 1999

"Unless we are willing to live in a world where everyone has to 'do business' with Saddam and his weapons of mass destruction, we need to be willing to use U.S. air power and ground troops to get rid of him." [105]

WILLIAM KRISTOL & ROBERT KAGAN, in *The Washington Post*

PNAC Members Become Influential Public Policy Makers Under Bush

The Neocon hawks, as prolific writers, generated position papers for four solid years, creating a sense of support for a preemptive war strike against Iraq from 1997 until 2001, when George W. Bush moved to the White House.

Money to fund PNAC came primarily from very large conservative foundations, endowed by corporations or corporate executives and founders who support the initiatives of war.[106] The founders of PNAC have become George W. Bush's most intimate circle. At least thirty-two Neocon hawks were appointed to high-ranking positions in the Bush Administration.[107] These appointees were former executives, consultants or significant shareholders in top defense contractors.[108] The Bush Administration gave them free rein to drive U.S. foreign and military policy. Here is the list of the original signatories to PNAC, and the positions they came to hold after George W. Bush was elected President:

Elliott Abrams National Security Council

Dick Cheney Vice President of United States

Eliot A. Cohen Defense Policy Board

Paula Dobriansky Under Secretary of State for Global Affairs

Aaron Friedberg National Security and Policy
Planning Advisor to Vice President

Francis Fukuyama	President's Council on Bioethics
Frank Gaffney	Defense Policy Board
Fred C. Ikle	Defense Policy Board
Zalmay Khalilzad	Ambassador to Iraq
I. Lewis Libby	Chief of Staff to and National Security Advisor to Vice President
Norman Podhoretz	Council on Foreign Relations
Dan Quayle	Defense Policy Board
Peter W. Rodman	Assistant Defense Secretary for International Security Affairs
Henry S. Rowen	Defense Policy Board
Donald Rumsfeld	Secretary of Defense
Paul Wolfowitz	Deputy Secretary of Defense
Gary Bauer	Founder, Campaign for Working Families (pro-life political group)
William J. Bennett	Host, *Morning in America*
Jeb Bush	Governor of Florida
Midge Decter	Board of Trustees, Heritage Foundation
Steve Forbes	Editor-in-Chief, *Forbes* magazine
Donald Kagan	Co-author, *While America Sleeps*
Stephen P. Rosen	Professor of National Security and Military Affairs, Harvard University
Vin Weber	Clark and Weinstock (Neocon think tank)
George Weigel	Ethics and Public Policy Center (Neocon think tank)

Other Neocons affiliated with PNAC who were signatories on documents advocating war include individuals such as **John Bolton,** former UN Ambassador, and the following:

Richard N. Perle	Defense Policy Board
Kenneth Adelman	Defense Policy Board
Devon Gaffney Cross	Defense Policy Board and Donors Forum on International Affairs
R. James Woolsey	Defense Policy

Chris Williams	Defense Policy Board and Deterrence Concepts Advisory Panel
Richard V. Allen	Defense Policy Board and the National Security Advisory
Stephen Cambone	Under Secretary of Defense for Intelligence
Douglas Feith	Department of Defense
John F. Lehman	9/11 Commission to Investigate Attacks on the U.S.
William Schneider, Jr.	Chairman, Defense Science Board
Abram Shulsky	Pentagon's Office of Special Plans Director
Dov S. Zakheim	Dept. of Defense Comptroller
Robert Bruce Zoellick	U.S. Trade Representative
Jeane J. Kirkpatrick	U.S. Representative to UN Human Rights Commission

A letter from PNAC was sent to George W. Bush on September 20, 2001, nine days after the 9/11 attacks. The letter called for the removal of the Taliban and war on al-Qaeda, and stipulated waging a broader and more ambitious "war on terrorism." It advocated cutting off the Palestinian Authority under Yasser Arafat, taking on Hezbollah, threatening Syria and Iran, and most importantly, ousting Saddam Hussein regardless of his relationship to the attacks or al-Qaeda. The letter stated:

> *"It may be that the Iraqi government provided assistance in some form to the recent attack on the United States, . . .* **But even if evidence does not link Iraq directly to the attack, any strategy aiming at the eradication of terrorism and its sponsors must include a determined effort to remove Saddam Hussein from power.** *Failure to undertake such an effort will constitute an early and perhaps decisive surrender in the war on international terrorism."* [109]

> **"Saddam Hussein is a homicidal dictator who is addicted to weapons of mass destruction."**
>
> George W. Bush

Known Oil Reserves in Iraq[110]

> **"By 2010 we will need on the order of an additional fifty million barrels a day. So where is the oil going to come from?...While many regions of the world offer great oil opportunities, the Middle East with two thirds of the world's oil and the lowest cost, is still where the prize ultimately lies."** [111]
>
> Dick Cheney, CEO Oil Services Halliburton, 1999

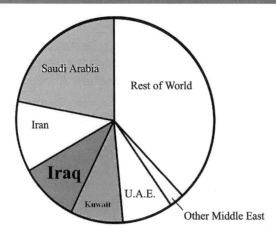

Feeding at the Government Trough

One of the most disturbing qualities of the Neocons is their tendency, as U.S. government officials, to cash in on actions they initiate while supposedly acting as public servants. For instance, it would appear to be unethical to be on a commission investigating the need to reinstate nuclear weapons if you are also a major stockholder, consultant, attorney, or paid lobbyist of a corporation that would directly benefit from such actions. If you were to benefit personally in any manner, it would certainly seem to impede your ability to provide an unbiased and impartial recommendation especially while on a public commission or board or overseeing a government agency.

George W. Bush, his family and many of his appointees appear to have compromised their integrity and public trust. On numerous occasions, Bush appointees have been personally rewarded financially from decisions they have made on behalf of the American public. In 2005, the Senate passed an $8 billion emergency funding bill to deal with the Bush Administration's purported Avian Flu (H5N1) pandemic. Three days after the emergency funding was passed on November 1, 2005, George W. Bush announced at the National Institutes of Health in Bethesda, Maryland that in the U.S. alone, 200,000 to 2 million deaths would occur as a result of the avian flu pandemic.[112]

This claim was used to justify the immediate purchase of millions of doses of Tamiflu, a drug that is allegedly incapable of preventing the Avian Flu. Tamiflu is supposed to decrease the number of sick days, but it has also been reported to possibly cause the mutation of a more lethal version of the virus.[113] The Pentagon was one of the biggest customers for Tamiflu, ordering $58 million worth of the drug in 2004 for U.S. troops around the world. Tamiflu is manufactured and marketed by Swiss pharmaceutical giant Roche, who holds the patent on behalf of Gilead Sciences. They were awarded $2 billion in 2005 by the Bush Administration for the purchase of Tamiflu.[114] Former Secretary of Defense Donald Rumsfeld is the former CEO of Gilead Sciences Inc., and is said to be one of the largest if not the largest stockholder.[115] Incidentally, in 2006 there were a total of 113 deaths due to Avian Flu *worldwide*.[116] Accusations that former Secretary Rumsfeld has benefited financially also point to his stock ownership in other companies receiving no-bid government contracts, such as Bechtel ($11.7 billion) and Gulfstream Aerospace General Dynamics ($30 billion).[117] How did former Secretary Rumsfeld keep a lid on these transactions? It might be helpful to know that he is also a major stockholder in the Tribune Company, one of the top media conglomerates in the nation, boasting 11 leading daily newspapers and 26 television stations.

Former Deputy Secretary Paul Wolfowitz was a consultant for the Northrop Grumman Corporation. The company produces defense electronics, information technology, aircraft, shipbuilding, and space technology. Under Wolfowitz, the Defense Department steered Northrop Grumman $48,074,442 worth of contracts for the preemptive Iraq war that Wolfowitz had planned since 1992.

Richard Perle served as the Chairman of the Department of Defense Planning Board but was forced to step down in March of 2003 after being the target of an investigation into unethical profiting from the war in Iraq. Perle had major holdings in Hollinger International, Trireme Partners L.P., Global Crossings, Morgan Crucible, and the *Jerusalem Post*. When Mr. Perle's questionable business dealings were exposed, he called the investigative journalist Seymour Hersh of *The New Yorker* a "terrorist" on national television. Richard Perle was still able to maintain his position on the board; he was simply removed as the board chairman.[118] Dick Cheney, Donald Rumsfeld, Paul Wolfowitz, and Richard Perle were all members of the Neoconservative think tank, Project for a New American Century, as well as several other Neoconservative research centers and think tanks.

Most contracts given by the Department of Defense have been extended in secrecy, behind closed doors, and have been given without a bidding process, otherwise known as non-competitive bids.[119]

Department of Homeland Security Increase in No-Bid Contracts, 2003 to 2005

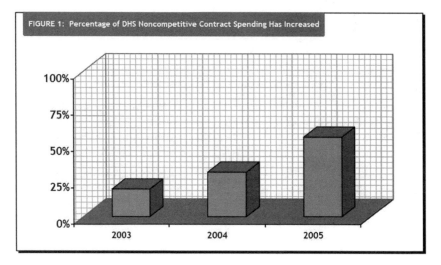

FIGURE 1: Percentage of DHS Noncompetitive Contract Spending Has Increased

Preferential Sole Source Contracts Awarded without Oversight

The number and dollar amount of sole-source contracts awarded by the Department of Homeland Security (DHS) dramatically increased from 2003 to 2005. In 2003, DHS awarded $655 million in contracts without full and open competition. By 2005, this figure had ballooned to $5.5 billion, an increase of 739 percent! In 2005, over 50 percent of the dollar value of all DHS contracts was awarded without full and open competition. Of the $5.5 billion in contracts awarded by DHS without full and open competition in 2005, $2.1 billion was awarded as sole-source contracts without any competition. DHS awarded the remaining $3.4 billion under conditions of limited competition by which only a small number of contractors were allowed to submit proposals.[120]

The Defense Policy Board Members were appointed by Donald Rumsfeld. Members are supposed to provide the Pentagon with independent, informed advice and opinion concerning major matters of defense policy. This board has become a lucrative setup for Neoconservatives and their corporate sponsors under Rumsfeld and board chairs like Richard Perle. Of the thirty Defense Policy Board members appointed by the Bush Administration, at least one-third has ties to companies that won over $76 billion in defense contracts in 2001 and 2002.[121] Four members of the Defense Policy Board are registered lobbyists, and one board member represents two of the three largest defense contractors.[122] Defense Policy Board Member David Jeremiah is a director or advisor to at least five corporations that received more than $10 billion in Pentagon contracts in 2002.[123] Defense Policy Board Member Jack Sheehan has been with Bechtel since 1998. Bechtel has received over $11 billion in contracts.[124] Defense Policy Board Member Ronald Fogleman sits on the board of several companies receiving millions in contracts in 2002.

The direct connections and cozy relationships between Defense Policy Board members and private sector corporations extends to many big names such as Boeing, TRW, Northrop Grumman, Lockheed Martin, Booz Allen Hamilton, Rolls-Royce North America, North American Airlines, AAR Corporation, the Mitre Corp., Symantec Corp., Technology Strategies, and Alliance Corp. These corporations have garnered colossal contracts in recent years.[125]

With that level of corporate influence, it is difficult to believe the Defense Policy Board is providing the Pentagon with impartial and unbiased decisions guaranteed or even intended to make America safer and our citizens more secure. Unfortunately, the evidence points to a Defense Policy Board filled with Neocon warhawks that manufactured a war in Iraq. Americans have put their faith and trust in an administration that has chosen appointees whose primary mission is to sustain wars ("staying the course" in Iraq), to create other wars (in Iran and Syria?) and to ensure hostility and provocation continue in the Middle East (such as between Lebanon and Israel).[126] These actions profit their respective corporations while exacerbating hatred of Americans.

THE CENTER FOR PUBLIC INTEGRITY

www.publicintegrity.org • www.publicintegrity.org/wow

Windfalls of War and Post-War Contracts Over $1 Million in Value Iraq and Afghanistan, 2002 through July 1, 2004

CONTRACTOR	CONTRACT TOTAL
Kellogg, Brown & Root (Halliburton)	$11,431,000,000
Parsons Corp.	$5,286,136,252
Fluor Corp.	$3,754,964,295
Washington Group International	$3,133,078,193
Shaw Group/Shaw E & I	$3,050,749,910
Bechtel Group Inc.	$2,829,833,859
Perini Corporation	$2,525,000,000
Contrack International Inc.	$2,325,000,000
Tetra Tech Inc.	$1,541,947,671
USA Environmental Inc.	$1,541,947,671
CH2M Hill	$1,528,500,000
American International Contractors, Inc.	$1,500,000,000
Odebrect-Austin	$1,500,000,000
Zapata Engineering	$1,478,838,958
Environmental Chemical Corporation	$1,475,000,000
Explosive Ordnance Technologies Inc.	$1,475,000,000
Stanley Baker Hill L.L.C.	$1,200,000,000
International American Products Inc.	$628,421,252
Research Triangle Institute	$466,070,508
Titan Corporation	$402,000,000
Louis Berger Group	$327,671,364
BearingPoint Inc.	$304,262,668
Creative Associates International Inc.	$273,539,368
Readiness Management Support LC (Johnson Controls Inc.)	$214,757,447
Chemonics International Inc.	$167,759,000
Harris Corporation	$165,000,000
Science Applications International Corp.	$159,304,219
DynCorp (Computer Sciences Corp.)	$93,689,421
Raytheon Aerospace LLC	$91,096,464
Lucent Technologies World Services, Inc.	$75,000,000
EOD Technology Inc.	$71,900,000
NANA Pacific	$70,000,000
CACI International Inc.	$66,221,143
Earth Tech, Inc.	$65,449,155
Development Alternatives Inc.	$49,117,857

Vinnell Corporation (Northrop Grumman)	$48,074,442
Abt Associates Inc.	$43,818,278
Parsons Energy and Chemicals Group	$43,361,340
International Resources Group	$39,230,000
Management Systems International	$29,816,328
SkyLink Air and Logistic Support (USA) Inc.	$27,200,000
Ronco Consulting Corporation	$26,131,923
AECOM	$21,610,501
Blackwater Security Consulting L.L.C.	$21,331,693
World Fuel Services Corp.	$19,762,792
Laguna Construction Company, Inc.	$19,536,683
Weston Solutions, Inc.	$16,279,724
Motorola Inc.	$15,591,732
Stevedoring Services of America	$14,318,895
Miscellaneous Foreign Contract	$13,489,810
Raytheon Technical Services	$12,412,573
Kropp Holdings	$11,880,000
Military Professional Resources Inc.	$11,433,491
General Electric Company	$8,525,498
Foster Wheeler Co.	$8,416,985
Inglett and Stubbs LLC	$8,175,245
Stanley Consultants	$7,709,767
Liberty Shipping Group Ltd.	$7,300,000
TECO Ocean Shipping Co.	$7,200,000
University of Nebraska at Omaha	$7,072,468
PAE Government Services Inc.	$7,007,158
Anteon International Corporation	$6,800,000
Michael Baker Jr., Inc.	$5,999,566
Detection Monitoring Technologies	$5,584,482
American President Lines Ltd.	$5,000,000
Ocean Bulkships Inc.	$5,000,000
S&K Technologies Inc.	$4,950,385
Signature Science	$4,704,464
United Defense Industries, L.P.	$4,500,000
Simmonds Precision Products	$4,412,488
AllWorld Language Consultants	$4,051,349
Sealift Inc.	$4,000,000
MZM Inc.	$3,640,896
SETA Corporation	$3,165,765
Chugach McKinley, Inc.	$3,068,407
Diplomat Freight Services Inc.	$2,604,276
Federal Data Corporation	$1,991,770

Stratex Freedom Services	$1,978,175
Social Impact Inc.	$1,875,000
Global Container Lines Ltd.	$1,850,000
Midwest Research Institute	$1,765,000
Camp Dresser & McKee Inc.	$1,700,000
Cellhire USA	$1,465,983
J & B Truck Repair Service	$1,353,477
Artel	$1,254,902
Structural Engineers	$1,113,000
Dataline Inc.	$1,028,851

Reprinted by permission, The Center for Public Integrity[127]

Representative Nancy Pelosi (D-CA) noted, "The American people have spent $20.9 billion to rebuild Iraq with much of the money squandered on no bid contracts for Halliburton and other favored contractors."

Halliburton received a sole-source contract worth $7 billion to implement the restoration of Iraq's oil infrastructure. According to a senior Army Corps of Engineers official, the sole-source contract was "coordinated with the Vice President's office." Iraqi oil production is still below the output level prior to the start of the war according to a news report in November 2006. This means that even under sanctions, Iraqis were producing more oil before the war and the U.S.-led invasion of Iraq than after four years and billions upon billions of dollars spent for the reconstruction.[128]

Sarah, a retired college professor who has closely monitored the rise of the Neoconservative movement, says, "Neocons pretend to be made of high moral fabric, but most of them are nothing more than paid mercenaries compensated to spread the gospel of corporate globalization on behalf of their sponsors."

Noted conservative Clyde Prestowitz, author of *Rogue Nation*, wrote, "The imperial project of the so-called Neoconservatives is not conservatism at all but radicalism, egotism, and adventurism articulated in the stirring rhetoric of traditional patriotism."[129]

"I'm not upset that you lied to me,
I'm upset that from now on I can't believe you."

Friedrich Nietzsche

NOTES, Chapter 5

1   Stefan Halper and Jonathan Clarke, "Origins and Early Development," *America Alone: The Neo-Conservatives and the Global Order* (Cambridge: Cambridge University Press, 2004).

2   Stefan Halper and Jonathan Clarke, *America Alone.* 67-69.

3   Ibid.

4   Neil Mackay, "Bush Planned Iraq 'regime change' before becoming President," *The Sunday Herald*, September 15, 2002.

5   "Hawkish," *Wikipedia*, http://en.wikipedia.org/wiki/Hawkish.

6   Patrick Martin, "Iran-Contra gangsters resurface in Bush Administration," August 1, 2001, www.wsws.org/articles/2001/aug2001/cont-a01.shtml.

7   Ibid.

8   "Information Awareness Office," *Wikipedia*, http://en.wikipedia.org/wiki/Information_Awareness_Office.

9   "Iran-Contra Figure to Lead Democracy Efforts Abroad," News Services, *The Washington Post*, February 3, 2005, www.washingtonpost.com/wp-dyn/articles/A59235-2005Feb2.html.

10 Ibid.

11 The Project for the New American Century, *Rebuilding America's Defenses*, www.newamericancentury.org/RebuildingAmericasDefenses.pdf.

12 Ibid.

13 The Neoconservative Plan for Global Dominance, www.projectcensored.org/publications/2004/1.html.

14 a. Friends of the Earth, "U.S. undermines united nations environment programme," March 31, 2004, www.worldrevolution.org/article/1159.

b. Justice Richard J. Goldstone, "US Withdrawal from ICC Undermines Decades of American Leadership in International Justice," *International Criminal Court Monitor*, June 2002, www.thirdworldtraveler.com/International_War_Crimes/USWithdrawal_ICC_Goldstone.html.

15 "The Project for the New American Century," *Officialssay*, home.earthlink.net/~platter/neo-conservatism/pnac.html.

16 "Twilight of the Neocon I," *Whiskey Bar*, December 23, 2003, www.billmon.org/archives/000924.html.

17 "Twilight of the Neocon II," *Whiskey Bar*, February 29, 2004, www.billmon.org/archives/001131.html.

18 "The Bush Administration's FY 2004 Budget: Missed Opportunities, Misguided Plans and Misplaced Priorities," *AFL-CIO*, www.aflcio.org/issues/bushwatch/2004budget.cfm.

19 Ibid.

20 Joshua Micah Marshall, "Practice to Deceive," *Washington Monthly*, March 4, 2003, www.washingtonmonthly.com/features/2003/0304.marshall.html.

21 "Karl Rove," *RightWeb*, rightweb.irc-online.org/profile/1343.

22 Richard W. Behan, "The Free-Market al-Qaeda," *Baltimore Chronicle & Sentinel*, June 4, 2003, www.baltimorechronicle.com/jun03_behan.shtml.

23 "The S&L Crisis: A Chrono-Bibliography," *FDIC*, December 20, 2002, www.fdic.gov/bank/historical/s&l/.

24 Robert Manor, "Gramms regulated Enron, benefited from ties," *The Chicago Tribune*, January 18, 2002.

25 Jerrold Oppenheim, Esq., "Democratic Public-Private Partnerships," *Democracy and Regulation*, May 22, 2003, www.democracyandregulation.com/attachments/48/DemocraticPublicPrivatePartnerships.doc.

26 a. Aaron Brown, *CNN Newsnight*, January 15, 2002, transcripts.cnn.com/TRANSCRIPTS/0201/15/asb.00.html.
b. Bethany McLean anad Peter Elkind, *The Smartest Guys in the Room: The Amazing Rise and Scandalous Fall of Enron* (New York: Penguin Group, 2003).

27 "Alcoa Announces Highest Quarterly Income and Revenue in Company History," Business Wire, July 10, 2006, www.alcoa.com/global/en/news/news_detail.asp?pageID=20060710005953en&newsYear=2006.

28 Clyde Prestowitz, *Rogue Nation: American Unilateralism and the Failure of Good Intentions* (New York: Basic Books, 2003).

29 Baker Spring, "Talking Points: Terrorist Attack on America Confirms the Growing Need for Missile Defense," *The Heritage Foundation*, September 20, 2001, www.heritage.org/Research/MissileDefense/BG1477.cfm.

30 Clyde Prestowitz, *Rogue Nation*.

31 Bill Berkowitz, "Heritage Foundation hawks," *Working for Change*, October 22, 2001, www.workingforchange.com/printitem.cfm?itemid=12191.

32 PBS Online, *Frontline: Missile Wars*, October 10, 2002 www.pbs.org/wgbh/pages/frontline/shows/missile/.

33 Ibid.

34 Ibid.

35 Ibid.

36 Ron Laurenzo and John M. Donnelly, "Predator Tests Raise Questions," *Defense Week*, March 18, 2002.

37 William Hartung and Michelle Ciarrocca, "The Military-Industrial-Think Tank Complex, Corporate Think Tanks and the Doctrine of Aggressive Militarism, The Business of War," *Multinational Monitor* 24, no. 1 and 2 (Jan/Feb 2003).

38 Ibid.

39 Behan, "al-Qaeda."

40 Ibid.

41 "Heritage 25," *The Heritage Foundation*, www.heritage.org/About/photos.cfm.

42 "The Heritage Foundation," *U.S./Iraq ProCon*, www.usiraqprocon.org/BiosOrg/Heritage.html.

43 "Issues 2006 Candidate's Briefing Book," *The Heritage Foundation*, www.heritage.org/research/features/issues.

44 "Jobs & Labor," *The Heritage Foundation*, www.heritage.org/research/features/issues/issuearea/Jobs.cfm.

45 Ibid.

46 "Energy & Environment," *The Heritage Foundation*, www.heritage.org/research/features/issues/issuearea/Environment.cfm.

47 Ibid.

48 "Reducing the Number of Uninsured," *The Heritage Foundation*, www.heritage.org/research/features/issues/issuearea/Uninsured.cfm.

49 Ibid.

50 "K-12 Education Reform," *The Heritage Foundation*, www.heritage.org/research/features/issues/issuearea/Ed_K12.cfm.

51 Ibid.

52 "Nuclear and Space Forces," *The Heritage Foundation*, www.heritage.org/research/features/issues/issuearea/Nuclear.cfm.

53 Ibid.

54 "Global War on Terrorism," *The Heritage Foundation*, www.heritage.org/research/features/issues/issuearea/Terrorism.cfm.

55 Ibid.

56 a. "Missile Wars."
b. Walter Pincus, "GAO Finds Pentagon Erratic In Wielding Secrecy Stamp," *The Washington Post*, July 14, 2006.
c. Andre Verloy and Daniel Politi, "Policy Board, Have Ties to Defense Contractors," *Center for Public Integrity*, March 28, 2003.

57 a. Scot Lehigh "Revealing the road to 'The Dark Side,'" *Boston Globe*, July 13, 2006, www.boston.com/news/globe/editorial_opinion/oped/articles/2006/07/13/revealing_the_road_to_the_dark_side/.
b. PBS Online, *Frontline: The Dark Side*, June 20, 2006, www.pbs.org/wgbh/pages/frontline/darkside.

58 Ibid.

59 Robert Bryce, "Cheney's Multi-Million Dollar Revolving Door," *Mother Jones*, August 2, 2000, www.motherjones.com/news/feature/2000/08/cheney.html.

60 a. Ibid.
b. Lee Drutman and Charlie Cray, "Halliburton, Dick Cheney, and Wartime Spoils," *Citizen Works*, April 4, 2003, www.citizenworks.org/corp/halliburton.php.

61 a. Frida Berrigan, "Halliburton's Axis of Influence," *In These Times*, March 28, 2003, inthesetimes.com/comments.php?id=138_0_1_0_C.
b. Susan Cornwell, "Democracts Question Cheney's Halliburton Payments," *Environmental Network News*, September 17, 2003, www.truthout.org/docs_03/091803B.shtml.

62 "The Bush Family's War Profiteering," *Democracy Rising*, February 24, 2005, democracyrising.us/content/view/57/164/.

63 "Georgetown Faculty Object to Appointment of Iraq War Architect Douglas Feith as Professor in School of Foreign Service," *Democracy Now!*, May 11, 2006, www.democracynow.org/article.pl?sid=06/05/11/1445248.

64 "*Institutional Investor Magazine's* Alpha Names Caxton Associates the World's Largest Hedge Fund Firm for the Second Year in a Row," *Dailyii*, May 11, 2004, www.dailyii.com/pdf/pressRoom/pressrelease/2004hf100_final.pdf.

65 Rachel Beck, "Dangers lurk in lack of hedge-fund oversight," *Associated Press*, July 1, 2006, www.nctimes.com/articles/2006/07/03/business/news/17_32_447_1_06.txt.

66 "Global Warming/Climate Change," *Washington State Department of Ecology*, www.ecy.wa.gov/programs/air/globalwarming/Global_Warming_site.html.

67 "Exxon Secrets Fact Sheet," www.exxonsecrets.org/html/orgfactsheet.php?id=9.

68 Robert Hahn and Scott Wallsten, "The Economics of Net Neutrality," *AEI-Brookings Joint Center*, April 2006.

69 Elliot D. Cohen, "The Great American Firewall: Why the Net is Poised to Become a Global Weapon of Mass Deception," *BuzzFlash*, www.buzzflash.com/contributors/06/05/con06169.html.

70 "Protect Internet Freedom," *MoveOn.org*, cdn.moveon.org/content/pdfs/MoveOn ChristianCoalition.pdf.

71 Hahn and Wallsten, "Economics."

72 *Independent Intervention*, 2005.

73 *Independent Intervention*, 2004.

[74] "About Us," *The National Center for Public Policy Research*, www.national center.org/NCPPRHist.html.

[75] "News Reporting is Perceived as Biased, though Less Agreement on Whether it is Liberal or Conservative Bias," *Harris Polls*, June 30, 2006, www.harrisinteractive. com/harris_poll/index.asp?PID=679.

[76] Ibid.

[77] *O'Reilly Factor*, August 7,8,9, and 10th, 2006.

[78] Margaret Talev, "109th Congress earns 'Do-Nothing' Label," *The New Mexican*, B-6, October 8, 2006.

[79] Murray Waas, "The men who kept Paula Jones' lawsuit going," *Salon*, April 2, 1998, www.salon.com/news/1998/04/cov_02news.html.

[80] Dan Rather, *CBS Evening News*, August 5, 1998.

[81] "Poll: Clinton's approval rating up in wake of impeachment," *CNN*, December 20, 1998, www.cnn.com/ALLPOLITICS/stories/1998/12/20/impeachment.poll/.

[82] William Kristol and Robert Kagan, "Bombing Iraq Isn't Enough," *New York Times*, January 30, 1998, newamericancentury.org/iraq-013098.htm.

[83] *The Peace Patriots*, DVD, directed by Robbie Leppzer (2005; Wendell, MA: Turning Tide Productions, 2006), www.turningtide.com/peacepatriots.htm.

[84] "Bill Clinton," *Wikipedia*, en.wikipedia.org/wiki/Bill_Clinton.

[85] Rob Kall, "Envisioning a Progessive Counterpart to NeoConservative Think Tanks like Project for a New American Century," *OpEdNews.Com*, April 1, 2003.

[86] PNAC, *Rebuilding*.

[87] Ibid.

[88] Ibid.

[89] Ibid.

[90] Ibid.

[91] Ibid.

[92] Ibid.

[93] John R. Bolton, "The U.N. Rewards Saddam," *The Weekly Standard*, December 15, 1997.

[94] John R. Bolton, "Congress Versus Iraq," *The Weekly Standard*, January 19, 1998

[95] William Kristol and Robert Kagan, "Bombing Iraq Isn't Enough," *New York Times*, January 30, 1998.

[96] William Kristol and Robert Kagan, "A 'Great Victory' for Iraq," *Washington Post*, February 26, 1998

[97] Ibid.

[98] Robert Kagan, "A Way to Oust Saddam", *The Weekly Standard*, September 28, 1998.

[99] Ibid.

[100] Ibid.

[101] *The Weekly Standard* editorial, November 16, 1998.

[102] Ibid.

[103] Ibid.

[104] Ibid.

[105] Kristol and Kagan, "Great Victory."

[106] Hartung and Ciarrocca, "Think Tank."

[107] Ibid.

[108] Ibid.

[109] Jim Lobe, "New American Century Project Ends With A Whimper," *Inter Press Service*, June 13, 2006.

[110] Greg Muttitt, "Crude Designs: The Rip-Off of Iraq's Oil Wealth," *Global Policy Forum*, www.globalpolicy.org/security/oil/2005/crudedesigns.htm#5.

[111] Dick Cheney, speech at the Institute of Petroleum Autumn Lunch, London, November 15, 1999.

[112] "Rumsfeld To Profit From Avian Flu Hoax," *Break for News*, October 20, 2005, breakfornews.com/my/modules.php?op=modload&name=News&file=article&sid =177.

[113] Staff Report, "Tamiflu Gilead Chair Was...Rummy," *FreeMarketNews.Com*, October 21, 2005, www.freemarketnews.com/Feedback.asp?nid=578.

[114] "Donald H. Rumsfeld: Gilead Sciences," *SourceWatch*, www.sourcewatch.org /index.php?title=Donald_H._Rumsfeld#Gilead_Sciences.

[115] Nelson D. Schwartz, "Rumsfeld's growing stake in Tamiflu, Defense Secretary, ex-chairman of flu treatment rights holder, sees portfolio value growing," *CNN Money*, October 31, 2005, money.cnn.com/2005/10/31/news/newsmakers/ fortune_rumsfeld/.

[116] "Bird Flu Death Count Climbs to 113," *FluFactor*, April 22, 2006, flufactor.blogspot.com/2006/04/bird-flu-death-count-climbs-to-113.html.

[117] a. "Bechtel Group, Inc," *Center for Public Integrity*, www.publicintegrity.org/ wow/bio.aspx?act=pro&ddlC=6. From 1990 to fiscal year 2002, the company received more than $11.7 billion in U.S. government contracts—the sixth largest amount received by any of the approximately 70 companies with contracts in Iraq and Afghanistan.
   b. Over 10 years with Lockheed Martin.

[118] "Richard Perle," *RightWeb*, rightweb.irc-online.org/ind/perle/perle_body.html.

[119] Steve Kroft, "All In The Family: Company Official Defends No-Bid Army Contract," CBS News, September 21, 2003, www.cbsnews.com/stories/2003/ 04/25/60minutes/main551091.shtml.

[120] " U.S. House of Representatives Committee on government reform, 2006, www.democrats.reform.house.gov/Documents/20060727092939-29369.pdf.

[121] Drutman and Cray, "Halliburton."

[122] Andre Verloy and Daniel Politi, "Policy Board_Have Ties to Defense Contractors," *Center for Public Integrity*, March 28, 2003.

[123] Ibid.

[124] Ibid.

[125] Jamie McIntyre, "Top Pentagon adviser resigns under fire," *CNN*, March 28, 2003, www.cnn.com/2003/US/03/27/perle.resigns/index.html.

[126] "Iran, Syria, Libya For Regime Change Next; Says Richard Perle," *World Tribune.com*, February 25, 2003, www.hartford-hwp.com/archives/27c/526.html.

[127] "Post-War Contractors Ranked by Total Contract Value in Iraq and Afghanistan." *Center for Public Integrity*, www.public-i.org/wow/resources.aspx?act=total.

[128] Griff Witte, Violence, poor planning plaque reconstruction, *The Washington Post*, November 12, 2006.

[129] Prestowitz, *Rogue Nation*, 277.

★ 6 ★

Suicide Bombers Fly into America

"Bin Laden Planning High-Profile Attacks...
in the United States using high explosives."

June 30, 2001, CIA warning, *9/11 Commission Report*

D O YOU REMEMBER where you were when you first heard that two planes had flown into the World Trade Center, only to discover that a third had flown into the Pentagon and a fourth had crashed in Pennsylvania? What were your initial thoughts and reactions? These horrendous flashes are forever locked in the depths of our minds. Time stands still at the moment of such tragedies and later we can recall the incidents vividly. We remember the confusion, the fear, the anger and the words spoken following the revelation. Similarly, I clearly remember when Mrs. Willard, my third grade teacher, walked into the classroom to announce that President John F. Kennedy had been shot. That memory, like the 9/11 attacks on our nation, will be forever locked in my mind.

On Tuesday, September 11, 2001, I was engaged in a telephone conversation with a friend who had her television on in the background. She informed me that an airplane had crashed into the World Trade Center in New York. My initial thought was that a small aircraft had somehow gotten off course and crashed into the façade of the building. However, when she indicated that yet another plane had flown into the second tower of the Trade Center, we decided to end our conversation. I turned on the television and watched in horror the instant replay of earlier scenes. As the pandemonium unfolded before my eyes, I was shocked and appalled. The news about the atrocious events quickly spread and it was all anyone could talk about. In the immediate days that followed, I, like most Americans, huddled with family, friends and colleagues. We cried, we prayed, we went to church, we donated to the victims' funds, and we hoped for additional survivors to be found.

America pulled together as sympathy and heartfelt grief poured into the U.S. from every corner of the globe. The rest of the world sent their sympathy and stood unified behind America with resolve and determination to help us find out who was behind these heinous crimes. The international community quickly galvanized to assist the United States in finding the culprits. One glaring exception to our unified mourning was the televised image of a few Palestinians cheering and dancing in the streets upon learning of the 9/11 attack on America.

In the weeks that followed, I acted as patriotically as possible. When President Bush asked Americans to get on board and put aside their fears to get back to work, I did exactly as requested. Within two weeks of 9/11, I boarded a plane to Dulles Airport near Washington, D.C. to recommence my work, assuring my clients I felt completely safe in traveling. I went shopping and returned to as normal a life as possible.

Yet in the back of my mind I mulled the question over and over again: Who would do such a thing and why? Two comments have since struck me. The first one came on the day of the attacks when a highly respected architect said while watching the rerun of the collapse of the Twin Towers, "Those son of a b—— *[sic]* did it themselves, buildings just don't fall like that." It was such a gross accusation that I just ignored him.

The second comment that struck me was when I was at a community meeting in the days immediately following the tragedy of 9/11. Beth, a colleague, posed the question, "What would possess someone to do this horrifically destructive act to so many innocent people seemingly without provocation?" And she took it one step further by asking rhetorically, "If this was done by some group against America, does America have a responsibility to look at what we might have done to provoke this?"

Beth, a patriotic wife, mother and member of a 12-Step Program, explained that members of 12-Step Programs are encouraged to engage in regular personal inventories whereby a thorough examination of one's role in any conflict, misunderstanding or dispute is examined. In her rhetoric she touched upon the question that many of us were asking: the *why*.

The Hunt for Osama bin Laden

"The most important thing is for us to find Osama bin Laden. It is our number one priority and we will not rest until we find him."

George W. Bush, September 13, 2001

Within two days of the 9/11 attacks on America, the name of Osama bin Laden was being published as the culprit behind the attacks, and details of previous plots by bin Laden were highlighted in news coverage in subsequent days. Bin Laden had been listed by the FBI as one of the world's most wanted terrorists for the 1993 World Trade Center bombing, the 1996 killing of nineteen U.S. soldiers in Saudi Arabia, the 1998 bombings of two U.S. embassies in Kenya and Tanzania, the October 2000 attack on the *USS Cole* in the Yemeni port of Aden, and now finally the September 11, 2001 attack.

Osama bin Laden was the seventeenth of fifty-seven children, born in 1957 to Mohammed bin Laden, a wealthy Saudi billionaire of Yemeni origins, and a Syrian mother. Bin Laden attended Abdul Aziz University in Saudi Arabia. Though bin Laden studied management and economics, he also showed interest in the study of the Islamic religion and was inspired by the blistering sermons of Abdullah Azzam, who was known to be bin Laden's spiritual mentor.[1] Osama bin Laden aligned himself with the Mujahideen and established an organization called Maktab al-Khidimat.[2] As a wealthy family member with access to Saudi funds, he was to become well known as an organizer and financier who funneled money, arms and Muslim fighters from the Middle East into Afghanistan.

Americans were told it was this man, Osama bin Laden, who had led the 9/11 attacks on America. We were told that U.S. forces would hunt him down and hold him responsible for the pain, anguish, and mass murder of Americans killed on that date. The Bush White House, along with government officials, notified the world through our free press that Osama bin Laden together with his notorious al-Qaeda operatives would be brought to justice for sanctioning the attack on the U.S.

The U.S. government said it knew where bin Laden was hiding and they informed us on how they intended to use military force on terrorists and on nations that harbor them.

NOTES, Chapter 6

[1] Col. Jonathan Fighel, "Sheikh Abdullah Azzam: Bin Laden's Spiritual Mentor," *ICT Terrorism and Counter-Terrorism*, www.ict.org.il/articles/articledet.cfm?articleid=388.

[2] "Osama bin Laden," *Answers.com*, www.answers.com/main/link_to_answers.jsp?topic=Osama%20bin%20Laden&link=/topic/osama-bin-laden.

★ 7 ★

The Seeds of Frankenstein
and their Mutations

"I, the author of unalterable evils, live in daily fear,
lest the monster I had created should
perpetrate some new wickedness."

Mary Shelley's *Frankenstein*

W**HAT KIND OF AN ENVIRONMENT** creates a network of people whose primary purpose is to methodically and demonically mass murder innocent victims? Why would people spend years of their lives dedicated to this destructive purpose and willingly die in the execution of their plans? Who are the Taliban? Are the al-Qaeda and the Muslim Brotherhood the same organization? Why do people say that the U.S. government trained Osama bin Laden?

The Wahhabis: Wahhabis are the fanatical followers of Abdul Wahab (1703–1792). The movement was created to cleanse Saudis from the influence of Sufism. Wahhabism emphasizes the oneness of God and was revived under the al-Saud rule in the 1920s in Saudi Arabia.[1] Wahhabi understanding of Islamic laws and values is based upon the literal interpretation of the *Holy Qu'ran.*

The Wahhabis strictly define appropriate behavior for themselves and others. Public prayer by men is mandated. Prayer is to be practiced punctually at specific times, communally and within prescribed ceremonial services. Consumption of alcohol, tobacco and other drugs or stimulants is forbidden. The Wahhabis advocate modest dress for both men and women.

Women must dress in *hijab* (meaning to hide or conceal) while in public. This normally means wearing a dark, baggy dress and head covering. This dress code as prescribed by the Wahhabis demonstrates good moral Muslim character, geared towards preserving a woman's dignity and self-esteem. This dress code infers that women are not to be identified sexually. Saudi women are forbidden to play sports in school, go shopping or drive a car without a male escort. These women must hide in their own homes when male visitors are received. When dining, men eat together alone, and women and children eat separately. According to one source, Saudi women may not own certain property in their own name and have few personal rights and liberties as defined by most American standards.[2]

According to the Wahhabis, wearing American-style clothes, sporting American hairstyles or listening to music — particularly Western music — is forbidden. Watching television is considered a sin. A *fatwa* (a formal Islamic legal decree) has been issued stating that anyone who owns a satellite dish or system will not go to paradise.[3] The Wahhabis' version of Islam forbids dancing, loud laughter and emotional weeping, especially at funerals.[4]

A Muslim must take an oath of allegiance to his ruler, and this oath is another guarantee of redemption after death, according to Wahhabi tradition. A ruler can expect solid allegiance from his people so long as he leads his society according to the Wahhabi edicts. The purpose of the Muslim population is to become the living personification of God's laws, and it is the responsibility of the ruler to assist people under his domain to know and understand God's laws and to live in compliance.

Wahhabis become hostile against rulers who fail to dole out justice in accordance with the faith. Rulers who appear lenient towards infidels (Americans are commonly referred to as infidels) are subjected to disapproval and condemnation by the Wahhabi clergy. The religious police or *mutawi'oon*, which means "enforcers of obedience," are responsible for maintaining moral order and conduct according to Wahhabi laws.[8] Individuals who appear impure or who practice treachery, or women who commit adultery, are punished.

Failure to strictly obey the guidelines can bring swift and harsh punishments, including flogging, amputation of the hands or stoning to death.[9] A soldier may be told that he is guaranteed immediate access to paradise (heaven) when he successfully carries out the death order, sometimes referred to as *jihad*, especially on infidels.

The influence of Wahhabis is seen throughout the Middle East, Africa and many nations of the former Soviet Union. In Saudi Arabia, the schools, universities and mosques are all under the direct authority of the Wahhabis, and Saudi Arabia has been one of the primary breeding grounds for terrorists. More will be discussed in the chapter, "Why Do They Hate America, Mommy?"

To many Muslims, Islam is touted as an all-inclusive socio-political system.[5] Capitalism is viewed as an enemy promoted by Westerners and infidels. The struggle against communism and capitalism is a typical feature of Islamist writings. The *Qur'an* promotes a type of social justice advocating that the rich are responsible for the care of the poor.

Capitalistic Christianity and Islamic Muslim business models differ. Millions of Muslims believe banking institutions should be avoided. Despite that belief, Islamic banking is widely regarded as the fastest growing sector in the Middle Eastern financial services market. Extending credit or giving a loan is not prohibited. However, Muslims do not believe in charging interest on debts as Americans do. Charging interest is prohibited by Islamic law.[6] There are five basic rules of Islamic financing:

- A lender may not charge any interest or additional cost beyond the original loan.
- The lender must equally share the profits or losses that arise from the loan. Investments that benefit the community are encouraged.
- Money is to be used to make purchases. Making money from money, such as fixed interest payments, is not acceptable.
- Uncertainty, risk or speculation is prohibited. This includes contract options, futures and foreign exchange transactions.
- Investments are only for allowable practices or products. Investments are forbidden for practices involving the trade of alcohol or gambling.[7]

The Muslim Brotherhood: Motivated by his deep hatred of British dominance in Egypt, Hasan al-Banna founded the Muslim Brotherhood at the age of 16 in 1922.[10] The Brotherhood was very similar to the Syrian Young Men's Muslim Association in nature, as both shared a goal of resisting foreign control and dominance in their countries. The primary purpose of the Brotherhood is to stop the proliferation of Western culture, especially in terms of what the Brotherhood regards as the permissive morals of the West.

According to Elaine, the wife of a businessman who lived in Saudi Arabia, Muslims judge our society by the young American girls they see scantily clothed, flaunting their bodies in sexualized commercials. They fear they will be corrupted by what they perceive as an American society lacking morals and obsessed with sexuality. They hear of elderly women forced onto the streets and becoming homeless because they can no longer work and they define it as a lack of respect and compassion for women. They are apprehensive of these attitudes permeating their society and they believe they have a duty to protect their citizens from exposure to "western ways." The Brotherhood also has strong concerns with the Christian missionaries' aspirations to convert Muslims to Christianity.

The Brotherhood has called for a restoration of the Islamic caliphate whereby a representative of God or successor to the prophet is selected as the ruler, as opposed to the leadership being passed down by heredity through a monarchy.[11] Al-Banna contended that Western Europeans had been given the chance to rule over the Muslim world because Muslims had strayed from the true path of Islam. To both the Wahhabis and the Brotherhood, the governance and presence of Westerners (Europeans and Americans) is considered God's wrath on Muslims in the Middle East. Therefore, the struggle against this influence is called the holy war or *jihad*. The *Dictionary of Islam* defines *jihad* as "a religious war with those who are unbelievers in the mission of Muhammad for the purpose of advancing Islam and repelling evils from Muslims."[12] Other meanings of the word *jihad* are "struggle" and "to do one's best to resist temptation and overcome evil."[13]

Al-Banna established three general decrees for the Brotherhood. First, rulers must be responsible to God and the people and the ruler must act as a servant of the people. Second, a Muslim nation must act with purpose and be coordinated and united. Unity is a major Islamic tenet. The third rule is that a Muslim nation is responsible for monitoring the ruler's behavior; providing advice and making sure the ruler respects the will of the people.[14]

The Brotherhood offered many collaborative activities for young Muslim men including religious education, fellowship, physical training, camping trips, and other activities.[15] As they felt little need for any formal government structure, the motto of the Brotherhood was simple: the *Qur'an* was their Constitution. Nothing else was needed. Increasingly, in the latter part of the twentieth century, a number of Islamic extremist movements grew out of the Brotherhood. The world would see more dramatic use of violence in an effort to control the masses and bring Islam to greater fruition in accordance with their defined views.[16]

After the Brotherhood assassinated the Egyptian Prime Minister Nuqrashi in 1948, they were forced underground. The majority of the Brotherhood settled in Saudi Arabia where conditions were ripe to recruit more members and increase influence. Others of their fellowship went to Syria, Sub-Saharan Africa, South Asia, and even West Germany, where Brotherhood cells flourished.[17] A West German cell served as one of the bases for the 9/11 attacks on the U.S. Today, even though it is a highly secretive society, the Brotherhood is considered one of the most influential political and religious forces in the Middle East.[18] It has become an extremely volatile group that vehemently encourages the destruction of what they see as Western imperialism.[19] This includes American citizens and symbols of luxury. The World Trade Center was a symbol of Western business and enterprise.

The Brotherhood has founded hospitals, clinics, pharmacies, and schools. While the Brotherhood preaches social justice and the eradication of poverty, corruption and political freedom, its benefits are promised only amongst Muslims who are committed to their brand of Islam.[20] They are highly conservative on many issues, including women's rights, and have shown hostility towards organizations such as trade unions.[21]

The Mujahideen: The Mujahideen were a loosely assorted group of Wahhabis, Brotherhood Muslims and other young Middle Eastern men who united to fight against the occupation of Afghanistan by the Soviet Union, in 1979. The word *Mujahideen* is another word for "struggler" or a person engaged in *jihad* or holy war. These men fought side by side through the 1980s. The Sheikh Ab-

dullah Azzam was an early supporter of the Mujahideen in the war against the Soviet Union in Afghanistan. Azzam is a Palestinian fanatic with a Ph.D. in the principles of Islamic jurisprudence. Not only did he advocate the religious warfare of *jihad,* but he also promoted the extreme use of violence and force to overcome the enemy.[22] Azzam taught "Allah's rule on earth," which he believed to be the responsibility of each and every Muslim. The *jihad* would be the mechanism to establish Islamic rule over the entire world. This holy war was to be delivered without negotiations, conversations or communications of any sort whatsoever. In other words, Azzam promoted an Islamic "holocaust" against unbelievers. Assam's target for termination was any foreign infiltrator to the Middle Eastern world. Think of medieval Christian crusaders purging the earth of wicked influences, only with modern weapons. Azzam eventually became Osama bin Laden's spiritual mentor. Many people have said that the U.S. government trained Osama bin Laden and I have always wondered if this is true. It appears that bin Laden found his calling when he began working to assist the Mujahideen.

During the Carter and Reagan Administrations, the Saudi government and the United States provided arms, training and huge sums of money towards supporting the Mujahideen in their battle against the Soviet Union.[23] This was before the end of the Cold War, and the United States wanted to stop Communist Russia through any means. President Ronald Reagan honored the Mujahideen as freedom fighters, and in the 1988 film *Rambo III*, featuring Sylvester Stallone, the Mujahideen were portrayed as heroes who assist Rambo in the rescue of his former Vietnam commanding officer held hostage in Afghanistan.[24] Of course, this was a Hollywood version of what was actually going on at the time.

The Soviet occupation lasted until 1989 and was a disaster for Afghanistan. A million Afghans lost their lives and millions more fled the country as refugees. The Mujahideen raced into Kabul as victors upon the exodus of the Soviets. Their victory was soon soured by infighting as the different Mujahideen groups failed to agree on how to appropriate their new power. The Mujahideen turned the fighting against one another and chaos broke out in Afghanistan.[25] Tens of thousands of civilians lost their lives when the Mujahideen took control of Afghanistan, and the country slid into a state of anarchy.

The Mujahideen provided the U.S. with the covert means necessary to fight communism. In return, the U.S. assisted in the creation of the Mujahideen. Unfortunately, the West and its allies totally misjudged the real objectives of these so-called freedom fighters. The future would reveal a dangerous mutation of the Mujahideen that was ever more brutal, treacherous and volatile. Over time, the Mujahideen transformed into a monster whose hostility against America would swell to greater proportions each day. Because support to the Mujahideen was provided covertly through operations in Pakistan, there was little interaction with Americans.[26]

The Taliban was a cohesive group of well-trained young religious militants. They were initially selected by the government of Pakistan to protect trade between Pakistan and the rest of Central Asia. After the Taliban's victory in warding off the Mujahideen and the warlords, they unified in battle and effectively took over the southern Afghani city of Kandahar in 1994.[27] The success of the Taliban lay in its ability to reorganize the Mujahideen factions. Many Mujahideen commanders quickly defected to the Taliban ranks. Soon thereafter, the Taliban was able to take control of 90 percent of Afghanistan.

The Taliban instituted a strict interpretation of Islam. Perhaps most appalling was the treatment of women. According to the Taliban, girls could no longer go to school, nor could they work outside the home. These rules were meant to protect a woman's honor. This caused a disaster in the health care and education systems in Afghanistan. Women were not allowed out of their homes without the accompaniment of a male relative. Women who broke the rules were beaten or sometimes shot.

Under the Taliban, Afghanistan became the training ground for Mujahideen and the Muslim Brotherhood of all nations. Opium poppies were cultivated and used to manufacture heroin products and other illegal drugs, and this activity increased under the watch of the drug lords. "The Pakistan-Afghanistan borderlands became the world's top heroin producer, supplying 60 percent of U.S. demand. In Pakistan, the heroin-addict population went from near zero in 1979 to 1.2 million by 1985. . . ."[28] In 1995, the former CIA director of the Afghan operation, Charles Cogan, disclosed that the CIA had indeed sacrificed the drug war to fight the Cold War.[29]

These transgressions served to ostracize the Taliban from much of the world. Bin Laden returned to Saudi Arabia after the Soviet withdrawal in 1989, and worked in his family's construction business. There, bin Laden and Muhammad Atef created an international terrorist group made up of many of the well-trained and outfitted Mujahideen supporters from Afghanistan. Later, when bin Laden decided to return to Afghanistan, he was not only welcomed, but also enjoyed the status of a privileged guest under the protection of the Taliban.[30]

al-Qaeda ("the Base"): With the assistance and financial support of the Saudi government, bin Laden would spread a much more dangerous philosophy to many in the Brotherhood. This included founding the al-Qaeda, whose mission was to use bloodshed, carnage, force, and violence to oppose all non-Islamic governments, but especially those of the West. Many of the newly recruited al-Qaeda warriors had fought in Bosnia, Chechnya, Somalia and the Philippines. Researchers believe these loosely connected zealots form the core of bin Laden's current network.

Bin Laden denounced the Saudi royal family for the "great deterioration in all walks of life, in religious and worldly matters," and for weakening the economy.[31] Additionally, he accused Arab leaders of lacking accountability, particularly for allowing American soldiers on Saudi soil in 1990 prior to the first Gulf War against Iraq. Osama bin Laden offered the services of himself and the al-Qaeda to defend Kuwait and Saudi Arabia from the invasion, but bin Laden was turned down by the Saudi royal family in favor of the Americans.[32] Feeling spurned by the royal family, bin Laden became infuriated when he discovered that American soldiers would be allowed in the birthplace of Islam. He went public with his condemnation, and plots of revenge against America intensified.

In 1991 bin Laden was expelled from Saudi Arabia, losing his Saudi citizenship and passport, but never losing the cash flow commitment from the Saudi government and his family that would follow him wherever he went.[33] Bin Laden moved his factions to Sudan, where he began purchasing property, setting up operations and working with an exiled group of radical Egyptians.

Darfur, Sudan is currently the site of horrible atrocities that have been going on for more than a decade now. Innocent Sudanese are being murdered by radical Muslims and as of April 2005, it was estimated

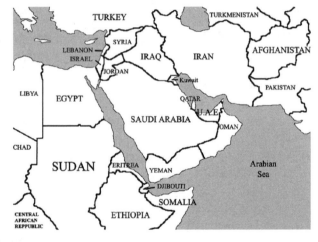

that 380,000 people had died. Civilians continue to die at a rate of 15,000 per month.[34] The CIA revealed that the Sudanese offered bin Laden to the U.S. in 1996, but the U.S. failed to see bin Laden as a significant threat and declined to take him.[35] bin Laden continues to operate as a free man, galvanizing Islamic Muslim rebels in deeds of hatred and destruction. In April 2006, bin Laden made a broadcast calling for al-Qaeda fighters to begin traveling to Darfur to prepare for a "long-term war against the Crusaders...."[36]

In August 1996, while the U.S. Government was turning a blind eye to Osama bin Laden, he issued an order or *fatwa* for Muslims to force American soldiers out of Saudi Arabia. A *fatwa* is an interpretation of

Islamic law by a respected Islamic authority. The document condemned the Saudi monarchy for allowing U.S. soldiers, and especially American women, in a land with sites considered most sacred to Islam. He openly applauded the suicide bombings of American military facilities in the Saudi Kingdom and the 1983 suicide bombing in Beirut that killed 241 U.S. Marines and the 1992 bombing of the USS Cole in Aden. In his message, bin Laden crowed about the United States leaving the 1993 Somalia firefight "carrying disappointment, humiliation, defeat, and your dead with you."[37]

In televised interviews in 1998, bin Laden said, "We are certain that we shall—with the grace of Allah—prevail over the Americans." He warned, "If the present injustice continues . . . it will inevitably move the battle to American soil."[38] Bin Laden made plans to attack the United States with deliberate resolve throughout the 1990s.[39] His al-Qaeda forces had found their purpose in organizing a new kind of war of destruction that would be launched against America to convert the world to Islam.

The 9/11 Hijackers Follow Through on Threats

The 9/11 Commission Report determined that the terrorist attack itself was planned by Sheik Khalid Mohammed, who personally chose the hijackers from the al-Qaeda international terrorist network. But according to the commission report, it was Osama bin Laden who approved the decision to actually carry out the September 11, 2001 terrorist attacks. The attacks on the World Trade Center, the Pentagon and Flight 93 killed over three thousand people and injured many more. There would have been more casualties if the attack on Flight 93 had not been foiled by proactive Americans storming the cockpit.

The 9/11 hijackers were made up of two types of terrorists: those who were considered the brains and could fly the planes, and those considered the brawn who controlled the passengers of each flight. Mohammed Atta is believed to have flown Flight 11 into the north tower of the World Trade Center. Marwan al-Shehhi is believed to have flown Flight 175 into the south tower of the World Trade Center. Hani Hanjour is believed to have flown Flight 77 into the Pentagon, and Ziad Jarrah is thought to have been the pilot of Flight 93 that crashed into the Pennsylvania countryside after a brave assault by passengers on this flight. The perpetrators were well educated. Some were more religious than others. Most of the hijackers were single, but a few were married.

The Mujahideen, the Taliban and al-Qaeda all evolved from early Islamic extremists who have become increasingly prolific and highly endemic across the Middle East. According to the 9/11 Commission Report, as many as 70 percent of al-Qaeda followers were originally recruited from the Mujahideen.

The Middle East proves to be a prolific generator of terrorists for many reasons to be explored in the next chapter. What the perpetrators all had in common was an extraordinarily entrenched hatred towards America, a hatred they were willing to die for.

According to Senator Jon Kyl, an Arizona Republican who chaired the Senate Subcommittee on Terrorism, Technology and Homeland Security, all the perpetrators were practicing *Wahhabis*.[40] The hijackers responsible for the 9/11 attacks used their real names as they were proud to die for their heinous deeds. Fifteen of the nineteen September 11, 2001 hijackers were Saudi citizens. Three of the nineteen were from a nation bordering Saudi Arabia, the United Arab Emirates (UAE). One hijacker was from Lebanon and one was from Egypt. Here are the names and photos of the jihadists who committed suicide in the execution of the 9/11 attack on America:

Name of Hijacker, Origin and Flight Hijacked

1. Wail al-Shehri   Saudi Arabia   American Airlines Flight 11
2. Abdulaziz al-Omari   Saudi Arabia   American Airlines Flight 11
3. Satam al-Suqami   Saudi Arabia   American Airlines Flight 11
4. Waleed al Shehri   Saudi Arabia   American Airlines Flight 11
5. Mohand al-Shehri   Saudi Arabia   United Airlines Flight 175
6. Hamza al-Ghamdi   Saudi Arabia   United Airlines Flight 175
7. Ahmed al-Ghamdi   Saudi Arabia   United Airlines Flight 175
8. Khalid al-Mihdhar   Saudi Arabia   American Airlines Flight 77
9. Majed Moqed   Saudi Arabia   American Airlines Flight 77
10. Nawaf al-Hazmi   Saudi Arabia   American Airlines Flight 77
11. Salem al-Hazmi   Saudi Arabia   American Airlines Flight 77
12. Hani Hanjour   Saudi Arabia   American Airlines Flight 77
13. Ahmed al-Haznawi   Saudi Arabia   United Airlines Flight 93
14. Ahmed al-Nami   Saudi Arabia   United Airlines Flight 93
15. Saeed al-Ghamdi   Saudi Arabia   United Airlines Flight 93
16. Marwan al-Shehhi   UAE   United Airlines Flight 175
17. Fayez Banihammad   UAE   United Airlines Flight 175
18. Mohammed Atta   Eqypt   American Airlines Flight 11
19. Ziad Jarrah   Lebanon   United Airlines Flight 93

9/11 Jihadist Hijackers Photos

Wail al-Shehri
Saudi Arabia
Flight 11

Abdulaziz al-Omari
Saudi Arabia
Flight 11

Satam al-Suqami
Saudi Arabia
Flight 11

Waleed al-Shehri
Saudi Arabia
Flight 11

Mohand al-Shehri
Saudi Arabia
Flight 175

Hamza al-Ghamdi
Saudi Arabia
Flight 175

Ahmed al-Ghamdi
Saudi Arabia
Flight 175

Khalid al-Mihdhar
Saudi Arabia
Flight 77

Majed Moqed
Saudi Arabia
Flight 77

Nawaf al-Hazmi
Saudi Arabia
Flight 77

Salem al-Hazmi
Saudi Arabia
Flight 77

Hani Hanjour
Saudi Arabia
Flight 77

Ahmed al-Haznawi
Saudi Arabia
Flight 93

Ahmed al-Nami
Saudi Arabia
Flight 93

Saeed al-Ghamdi
Saudi Arabia
Flight 93

Marwan al-Shehhi
UAE
Flight 175

Fayez Banihammad
UAE
Flight 175

Mohammed Atta
Egypt
Flight 11

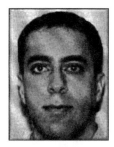

Ziad Jarrah
Lebanon
Flight 93

The Beginning of the War on Terrorism

Within days of the attacks on America, our government informed us that they knew where Osama bin Laden and his followers could be found. The masterminds behind the attacks on America were headquartered in Afghanistan. We were told justice was to be sought in "Operation Enduring Freedom."

The "War on Terrorism" would begin with the invasion of Afghanistan on October 7, 2001. Supported also by Britain, Canada, Australia, Italy, France, Germany, and New Zealand, the mission was to destroy the Taliban and the terrorist training camps located in Afghanistan. Our government promised us that the world would see Osama bin Laden and his followers brought to justice. Young patriotic men and women rushed to join the war on terrorism, and the world supported our efforts. We stood united as a nation with our allies at our side.

Yet behind closed doors in secret meetings in Washington and at Camp David, the Bush Administration plotted. This administration, filled with Neocons, was desperate to fulfill their visions of a Middle Eastern conquest. So after only four months in Afghanistan, we later discovered the U.S. government had already diverted huge resources to Iraq.

Secretary of Defense Donald Rumsfeld announced the formal end of the war in Afghanistan on May 3, 2003. We were told that the Taliban was all but destroyed. Osama bin Laden had escaped along with many of his followers, but bringing bin Laden to justice was no longer a priority. America had to deal with a much greater threat.[41] The Bush Administration insisted we had to deal with the threat of Saddam Hussein and his vast cache of weapons of mass destruction.

NOTES, Chapter 7

1   Ted Thornton, "The Wahhabi Movement, Eighteenth Century Arabia," *History of the Middle East Database*, www.nmhschool.org/tthornton/wahhabi_movement.php.

2   "Women's Rights," *The Center for Democracy and Human Rights in Saudi Arabia*, www.cdhr.info/Issues/WomensRights.

3   Khaleed Waleed, "Is Saudi Arabia Against the Terrorists?" *Faith Freedom International*, May 3, 2006. www.faithfreedom.org/oped/KhaleedWaleed 60503.htm.

4   Ibid.

5   Mufasa Akyol, "Islamocapitalism," *TCS Daily*, www.tcsdaily.com/article.aspx?id=061906C.

6   Md. Abdul Awwal Sarker, "Islamic Business Contracts, Agency Problem and the Theory of the Islamic Firm," *International Journal of Islamic Financial Services* 1, no. 2 (Fall 1999). Available at islamic-finance.net/journals/journal2/art2.pdf. .

7   "Principles of Islamic Banking," *Nida'ul Islam Magazine*, November 1995. Available at www.usc.edu/dept/MSA/economics/nbank1.html.

8   Thornton, "The Wahhabi Movement."

9   Shehzad Saleem, "Islamic Punishments: A Fresh Insight," *Renaissance 12*, no. 9 (Sept 2002). Available at www.renaissance.com.pk/septed2y2.html.

10 Ted Thornton, "Hasan al-Banna," *History of the Middle East Database*, www.nmhschool.org/tthornton/hasan_al.php.

11 Richard Hooker, "Islam: The Caliphate," *Washington State University*, www.wsu.edu/~dee/ISLAM/CALIPH.HTM.

12 Vinod Kumar, "What Is Jihad?" *Kashmir Herald*, January 2004. Available at www.kashmirherald.com/featuredarticle/whatisjihad.html.

13 "Timeline Saudi Arabia," *Timelines of History*, timelines.ws/countries/SAUDI ARABIA.html.

14 Guilain Denoecx, "Hasan al-Banna," *The American Muslim Online* 1, no. 1 (2000). Available at www.americanmuslim.org/1biography1.html.

15 Ibid.

16 Youssef H. Aboul-Enein, "Al-Ikhwan Al-Muslimeen: The Muslim Brotherhood: *Military Review*, July 1, 2003. Available at usacac.army.mil/CAC/milreview/English/JulAug03/JulAug03/abo.pdf.

17 Ibid.

18 Ibid.

19 Ibid.

20 "Muslim Brotherhood," *Wikipedia*, en.wikipedia.org/wiki/Muslim_Brotherhood.

21 Aboul-Enein, "Al-Ikhwan Al-Muslimeen."

22 Col. Jonathan Fighel, "Sheikh Abdullah Azzam: bin Laden's Spiritual Mentor," *The Institute for Counter-Terrorism*, September 27, 2001. www.ict.org.il/articles/articledet.cfm?articleid=388.

23 "Did the US 'Create' Osama bin Laden?" *US Department of State*, usinfo.state.gov/media/Archive/2005/Jan/24-318760.html.

24 *Rambo III*, DVD, directed by Peter MacDonald (1988; Lions Gate, 2004).

25 "Afghanistan's Turbulent History," *BBC*, October 8, 2004. Available at http://news.bbc.co.uk/go/pr/fr/-/1/hi/world/south_asia/1569826.stm.

26 "Create," *US Department of State*.

27 Laura Hayes and Borgna Brunner, "Who Are the Taliban?: Their History and Their Resurgence," *Infoplease*, www.infoplease.com/spot/taliban.html.

28 Alfred McCoy, "Drug Fallout: The CIA's Forty Year Complicity in the Narcotics Trade," *The Progressive*, August 1, 1997.

29 Ibid.

30 Arnie Schifferdecker, "The Taliban-bin Laden-ISI Connection," *American Foreign Service Association*, www.afsa.org/fsj/Dec01/schiff.cfm.

31 The National Commission on Terrorist Attacks Upon the United States, *The 9/11 Commission Report: Final Report* (Washington, DC: GPO, 2004).

32 Michael T. Klare, *Blood and Oil: The Dangers and Consequences of America's Growing Petroleum Dependency (The American Empire Project)* (New York: Metropolitan Books, 2004): 52.

33 Joseph Fitchett and Brian Knowlton, "Bin Laden's Cash Flow to Terrorists Protected U.S. Officials Doubt Pipeline Can Be Cut," *International Herald Tribune*, September 1, 1998. Available at www.highbeam.com/doc/1P1:16972273/ Bin+Ladens+Cash+Flow+To+Terrorists+Protected+U~R~S~R~+ Officials+Doubt+Pipeline+Can+Be+Cut.html?refid=SEO.

34 "Darfur's Real Death Toll," *The Washington Post*, April 24, 2005, B06. Available at www.washingtonpost.com/wp-dyn/articles/A12485-2005Apr23.html.

35 Melissa Boyle Mahle, *Denial and Deception, An Insider's View of the CIA from Iran-Contra to 9/11* (New York: Thunder's Mouth Press, 2005): 99.

36 Andrew McGregor, "Bin Laden's African Folly: Al-Qaeda in Darfur," *The Jamestown Foundation*, jamestown.org/terrorism/news/article.php?articleid= 2369998.

37 Ibid.

38 Ibid.

39 "Hunting Osama bin Laden," *PBS Frontline*, May 1998.

40 Peyman Pejman, "US Suspects Saudi-backed Wahhabis of Role in Attacks," *The Washington Times*, July 14, 2003.

41 a. "Afghanistan: Are We Losing the Peace?" *Council on Foreign Relations*, June 2003, http://www.cfr.org/content/publications/attachments/Afghanistan_TF.pdf.b. Carlotta Gall, "Taliban Threat Is Said to Grow in Afghan South," *New York Times*, May 3, 2006. Available at http://travel2.nytimes.com/2006/05/03/world/asia/ 03afghan.html.

★ 8 ★

Why Do They
Hate America, Mommy?

*"A popular government without popular information,
or the means of acquiring it, is but a prologue
to a farce or a tragedy, or perhaps both."*

James Madison

SHORTLY AFTER THE 9/11 ATTACKS ON AMERICA, my eight-year-old daughter Katie asked me, "Why do they hate America, Mommy?" The question was a really good one, and most people were asking the same thing. George W. Bush made the following statement shortly after the 9/11 attacks: "Americans are asking 'Why do they (terrorists) hate us?' They hate what they see right here in this chamber: a democratically elected government. Their leaders are self-appointed. They hate our freedoms: our freedom of religion, our freedom of speech, our freedom to vote and assemble and disagree with each other."[1] Were the President's comments to the American people candid? Could this be true, or was this a red herring used to distract the American public? Did we simply accept what the President told us because we were busy, patriotic and simply unthinking?

Five years after the 9/11 attacks, while I was sharing lunch with my conservative cousin Rosie, she stated, "I believe they hate us because we are good, kind and compassionate Americans and we know how to enjoy life." I followed up by asking, "Rosie, please tell me how many people hate you because you are good, kind, compassionate and enjoy life?" She looked at me, somewhat bewildered.

127

History has demonstrated that wars are fought because of one of several major reasons: power, land (including the oil, minerals, jewels or water under the land) and ideological or religious differences. Sometimes these reasons are combined to form a basis to go to war. When someone feels threatened, they may attack, run away or retaliate later. According to my research, it appears that the 9/11 attacks on America were retaliation.

Since the majority of the 9/11 attackers were from Saudi Arabia, we must examine the relationship between the U.S. and that nation. What fuels Saudis' and other Muslims' hatred against America and how has this hatred evolved? There are five relevant factors: 1) Perception of American Imperialism; 2) The Unstable, Combustible Marriage; 3) Teaching Hatred; 4) Shame, Humiliation and Retaliation; and 5) The Israeli and Palestinian Question. Each factor will be examined in detail.

1) Perception of American Imperialism

"They rip us of our wealth and of our resources and of our oil...."[2] Saudi Arabia possesses 25 percent of the world's petroleum reserves. While other nations are discovering less oil, Saudi Arabia is actually increasing its percentage of proven reserves as more oil fields are discovered. As an oil-based economy, the petroleum sector accounts for roughly 75 percent of budget revenues, 45 percent of GDP and 90 percent of export earnings. Saudia Arabia ranks as the largest exporter of petroleum, and is a leader in the Organization of Petroleum Exporting Countries (OPEC).[3]

Surprisingly, over the last thirty-five years the per capita income in Saudi Arabia has fallen persistently. It plunged from an average of $23,294 in 1980 to just over $8,000 in 2005. Because of the economic windfalls provided by Saudi Arabia's petroleum products, particularly over the last thirty years, these profits could have been infused into the Saudi Kingdom to provide a rapid assimilation into the twenty-first century global community. However, the Saudis have chosen a very different path, as most mainstream Saudis have no desire to become a part of the global community and are vehemently against becoming "Westernized."

One commenter, Marvin, stated, "Why would we expect them to be like us?" Marvin a computer programmer explained that he believes it is wrong for Americans to "superimpose" our way of life on other nations who may be quite content living their lives in their own way. He said it is fundamentally important to respect differences and not assume our way is superior.

Saudi Arabia has 26 million inhabitants, and estimates of the number of people who make up the Royal Family include approximately 8,000 princes and 40,000 family members.[4] Sally, a nurse who lived and worked in Saudi Arabia for three years in the 1970s, found the culture to be very different from that of the United States.

Sally claimed that the Saudi women were highly honored by their husbands. She found them to be happy and satisfied with their lifestyles. Sally said she felt the Saudi women pitied Western women because the Saudi women did not have to work and were free to take care of their families. Saudi women are discouraged from working except in fields such as nursing.[5] The only exception to the general contentment among women that Sally observed was with the more highly educated Saudi women who wished to participate in government and business but were forbidden to do so by law.

Yet, in an other startling example, the British Broadcasting Company (BBC) reported in a story called "Saudi Police Stop Fire Rescue" a different illustration of how women are treated in Saudi Arabia. In 2002, fifteen young girls died in a fire and fifty others were injured because they were forced to stay inside the burning school building. Since the girls were not dressed with the proper head covering and robes for going out in public, as required by strict interpretation of Islamic laws, they were not allowed to escape. A witness reported "police beating young girls to prevent them from leaving the school . . . ."[6]

The founding ruler, King Ibn Saud, sired forty-four sons by seventeen different wives. (The females are not counted.) According to the Qur'an, a man can have up to four wives at any time. Since divorce is permitted at the whim of any royal family male, he may actually end up with as many wives as he wishes during the course of his life.

Roughly 5.5 million foreign workers are imported to do much of the oil and service-related work, yet by some approximations the unemployment of Saudi Arabian males has skyrocketed to 30 percent.[7] Many young Saudi men with college degrees say finding a job is nearly impossible unless you know the right people. However, possibly the biggest problem is the failure of Saudi schools to prepare its youth to compete in the global market. Two out of three graduating Ph.D.s from within Saudi Arabia are graduating with degrees in Islamic Fundamental Religious Studies taught by the Wahhabis and the Brotherhood.

Islam is currently the second largest religion in the world and it is growing faster than Christianity.[8] There are five essential elements of Islam: declaring faith by reciting the creed (shahadah), "There is no God but God and Muhammad is his Prophet." One must pray five times daily, fast during the month of Ramadan, and, for those who can afford it, make a pilgrimage to Mecca, and give money or gifts to charity. The written teachings of Islam are in the *Qur'an*. Muslims believe that the *Qur'an* contains the word of God as revealed to Muhammad by the archangel Gabriel. Islam has six fundamental beliefs:

1. There is one indivisible God (Allah).
2. God created the angels.
3. Divine scriptures include the *Torah*, the *Psalms*, the original Bible, and the *Qur'an*.
4. The Messengers of God include the prophets Adam, Noah, Abraham, Moses, David, Jesus, John the Baptist, and Muhammad.
5. On the Day of Judgment, people will be held accountable for their deeds on earth. They will either be rewarded in heaven or punished in hell.
6. God's will is supreme.[9]

2) The Unstable, Combustible Marriage

> *"The call to wage war against America was made because America ... support[s an] oppressive, corrupt and tyrannical regime that is in control."* [10]

Osama bin Laden

The U.S. has a long relationship of support for the House of Saud. The U.S. provides such support in exchange for reliable oil trade. Many Saudis believe the House of Saud to be decadent and corrupt. This is a damning indictment that has fueled much hatred against Americans by the Saudi people. The royal family controls the government and the major economic activities within the kingdom. Many of the king's brothers, sons and other close male relatives hold key positions of authority and influence within the government and business sector.[11]

Long before his stroke in 1995, King Fahd appointed his six full brothers—dubbed the "'Sudairi Seven" after their mother's clan—to every major post in the Saudi government, and today the Sudairi still hold the lion's share of power. For instance, Fahd's full brother, Prince Sultan, is both the second deputy prime minister and the defense minister, responsible for overseeing the kingdom's military expansion projects.

Saudi Arabia's wealth is held by members of the royal family and their friends who have made fortunes in construction, real estate, trading, or by acting as agents for foreign companies doing business in the kingdom.

Those who act as agents routinely charge a commission for the goods and services imported to the kingdom. The commission is excessive by most standards, and ranges from 30 percent to 50 percent of the price of the goods or services. These skimmed-off commissions have made the Saudi princes and their families and friends extremely wealthy. It is estimated that Saudis have somewhere between $500 to $700 billion invested in the U.S. economy.[12] Benny, a retired engineer, spent six years living in Saudi Arabia. He said the average Saudi citizen had free housing, free health care, a free vehicle, free education if desired, and a yearly stipend for doing nothing more than showing up to pray five times a day.

Dozens of books and countless articles all point to the dismal problems associated with the Saudi royal family's abuse of power and lack of leadership. The situation worsened after a stroke left King Fahd incapacitated at the age of eighty-one. The Saudi kingdom is said to have floated on a sea of corruption for a full ten-year period from 1995 to 2005.[13]

Accusations have been leveled against many Washington politicians and American corporate executives who are rumored to have sold out by putting Saudi oil interests before those of American citizens.[14] According to former senator Frank Church, U.S. firms "have a 'sweetheart' arrangement with Saudi Arabia . . .", and any change in the Saudi government might eliminate the privileged position of the oil companies.[15]

Charges of corruption against different royal family members are widespread. They include outstanding drug warrants in Florida, exorbitant purchases made on the French Riviera, prostitution and gambling in Morocco, excessive property purchases, drinking, and illegal drug use.[16] At any rate, the difference in lifestyle between the high-rolling royal family and most Saudi citizens provides a dramatic contrast — although the same thing could be said in regards to U.S. corporate executives, a few select political leaders, and the average American.

The crown does not necessarily pass to the eldest son, but rather to the most suitable one chosen by the royal family through a secretive process. Since Ibn Saud's death in 1953, five sons have ruled the nation. This includes King Abdulla, who has no formal education but is well respected within Saudi Arabia and said to be hardworking. The newly crowned king spent many years living in the desert with Bedouin tribes, and is the former head of the National Guard. He has paid solidarity visits to Lebanon, Syria and Egypt. King Abdulla has also shown his support for the Palestine Liberation Organization (PLO) by allowing a charity run by his half-brother, Interior Minister Nayef, to compensate the families of Palestinian "martyrs." Members of the Saudi government have participated in terrorist activities through their monetary contributions.[17] You would think that

Washington officials would find these actions extremely difficult to ignore. Yet, a number of politicians have been quick to defend the Saudis.

3) Teaching Hatred

Studies demonstrate how the Saudi royal family has provided huge levels of funding for Wahhabi schools, temples and teachers who support Islamist extremist efforts in Saudi Arabia, Egypt, Pakistan, Malaysia, Indonesia, Western China, East Africa, and Central Asia. This support has been ongoing for many years.[18]

In the mid-1990s the Wahhabi clerics and the *Mutawi'oon* (the Saudi religious police) were outraged by the continued presence of Americans in Saudi Arabia. The royal family had promised the Saudi nation that the Americans would leave Saudi Arabia the minute the threat from Saddam Hussein was removed. Five years after the first Gulf War, American men and women worked and socialized together publicly in Saudi Arabia. Without wearing the appropriate covering and without male escorts, American women openly drove vehicles. The American behavior was viewed as being in complete disregard of the Saudi culture and the corresponding restrictions imposed on Saudi women. Frustrated because the Americans appeared comfortably settled in Saudia Arabia without any apparent intention of leaving, the Wahhabis began to encourage their brethren to take bolder steps to demonstrate their fury. For example, terrorists bombed the Khobar housing complex of the United States Air Force in Dhahran, Saudi Arabia in 1996.

In 2002, after the 9/11 attacks on America, the United States Congress mandated several agencies to find out more about the attacks. As a result of the findings, several congressional bills such as the Saudi Arabia Accountability Act were introduced. The House Bill 3643 description reads: "To halt Saudi support for institutions that fund, train, incite, encourage, or in any other way aid and abet terrorism, and to secure full Saudi cooperation in the investigation of terrorist incidents." Here are some revealing elements of the bill:

- In October 2002, the Council on Foreign Relations concluded that individuals and charities based in Saudi Arabia had been the most important source of funds and financing for al-Qaeda terrorists for years. Not only have Saudi officials turned a blind eye to this problem, but also some of these very officials are major contributors to al-Qaeda and other terrorist groups.[19]

- The Middle East Media Research Institute concluded on July 3, 2003 that Saudi Arabia has been the main financial supporter of

Palestinian groups fighting against Israel. Over $4 billion has been funneled to finance the Palestinian *intifada* since September 2000.

- A June 2004 report entitled "Update on the Global Campaign Against Terrorist Financing" conducted by the Council on Foreign Relations, reported that "it [remains] regrettable and unacceptable that since September 11, 2001, we know of not a single Saudi donor of funds to terrorist groups who has been publicly punished."

- According to the final report of the National Commission on Terrorist Attacks upon the United States, when asked where terrorist leaders would likely locate their bases, military officers and government officials repeatedly listed Saudi Arabia as a prime location.

- A report released on January 28, 2005 by Freedom House's Center for Religious Freedom found that Saudi Arabia is the state most responsible for the propagation of material promoting hatred, intolerance and violence within United States mosques and Islamic centers, and that these publications are often official publications of a Saudi ministry or distributed by the embassy of Saudi Arabia in Washington, D.C.

- The United States Commission on International Religious Freedom reported Saudi Arabian government-funded textbooks used both in Saudi Arabia and in North American Islamic schools and mosques have been found to encourage incitement to violence against non-Muslims.

- A joint committee of the Select Committee on Intelligence of the Senate and the Permanent Select Committee on Intelligence of the House of Representatives issued a report on July 24, 2003 that quotes various United States government personnel who complained that the Saudis refused to cooperate in the investigation of Osama bin Laden and his network both before and after the September 11, 2001 terrorist attacks.

On March 4, 2004, Senator Charles Schumer (D-NY) said, "When Americans ask why a generation of Muslims hates us, it's because of the way these textbooks and *madrassahs* [Islamic religious schools] promote anti-Americanism and hatred rather than tolerance. It is unwarranted, unacceptable, and needs to be confronted immediately."[20] This statement was made in a press release entitled "Saudi Government Must Eradicate Hate Rhetoric in Textbooks." Another congressional resolution awaiting action, "Expressing the Sense of Congress Regarding the Education Curriculum in the Kingdom of Saudi Arabia," concerns the use of educational curriculum and materials used in schools to promote hatred against non-Muslims.[21] Interestingly enough, the title doesn't give the reader a real sense of what's in the resolution. Here are some of the highlights:

1) Fifteen of the nineteen 9/11 hijackers who launched attacks were Saudi Arabian nationals;

2) Multiple terrorist attacks by Saudi nationals have occurred inside the kingdom of Saudi Arabia;

3) Saudi nationals have joined the insurgency in Iraq, carrying out terrorist activities;

4) The Saudi government has provided financial support to terrorist activities;

5) The Saudi government controls and regulates all forms of education; and

6) Religious education is compulsory at all levels in Saudi Arabia and taught by Wahhabi extremists.

The resolution explains that textbooks in Saudi Arabian schools have been found to foster intolerance and ignorance as well as anti-Semitic, anti-American and anti-Western views in students. This type of educational system could create a new generation of terrorists and other extremist groups. Here are two examples from the Saudi textbooks that may tend to promote violence against Americans:

1) "Jihad in God's cause is the path to victory and to strength in this world, as well as to attaining Paradise in the hereafter (*Qur'an* Commentary, Grade 9 (2000): 90)," and

2) "The abundance of the suicide cases in Western societies is surely because of their [great] distance for the true divine source (Islamic Jurisprudence, Grade 10, (2001): 19)."

In essence, the resolution confronts the Saudi government about the religious curriculum as written and presented, stating that it encourages extremism and hatred of the West. Therefore, it asks the Saudi government to manage the educational practices responsible for creating and enflaming terrorists' activities. Congress urges the government of Saudi Arabia to reform its textbooks and educational curriculum in a manner to promote tolerance and peaceful coexistence with others.

"We defended their country [Saudi Arabia] in Desert Storm and in return they jacked up our gas prices, stopped cooperating in our terror investigations and sent 15 of 19 hijackers to attack us on 9/11. What is this love affair that Republicans have with the Saudis? They are not our allies, they have not behaved like our allies and they should not be treated like allies . . . ."

U.S. Rep. Anthony D. Weiner (D-NY)

In July 2005, the House passed legislation authored by Weiner to halt U.S. aid to the Saudis, but the bill stalled in the U.S. Senate.[22] A poll taken in Saudi Arabia one month after the 9/11 assault on America revealed that 95 percent of educated Saudis between the ages of twenty and forty-one supported bin Laden.[23]

In a statement distributed by the White House on July 21, 2004, President Bush used Saudi Arabia as an example of the positive progress in the War on Terror. This statement was then released in a Fox News report entitled "Saudi Royal Family Faces Troubles." The report declared, "[The Saudi government] is working hard to shut down the facilitators and financial supporters of terrorism . . ." and it propagandized further by specifying, "Today, because Saudi Arabia has seen the danger and joined the war on terror, the American people are safer."[24]

In the spring of 2005, Syrians arrested 300 Saudis before they were able to cross into Iraq to join the jihad against America. In June of 2005, American soldiers found at least two Saudi Arabians in hideouts in northeastern Iraq attempting to cross into Iraq to fight against America.[25]

"We will make no distinction between the terrorists who committed these acts and those who harbor them."

George W. Bush

Recent changes in the Royal Family are worth noting: The ascension of King Abdullah to the throne in August 2005 presented a new opportunity to solve the Saudi school problems, but only time will tell if Saudi Arabia moves in a more tolerant direction. The Saudi government is between a rock and a hard place as they are the keepers of some of the sites considered most sacred to Islam, including Mecca itself. They appear to want to appease a conservative base of followers and still maintain a positive working relationship with the U.S. It is important to note that Saudi Arabia has been a consistent and reliable petroleum partner for the U.S. in recent times. The exception was the 1973 oil embargo. When Iraqi oil production was hindered during the Gulf War, Saudi Arabia increased its daily production to meet U.S. needs. Iraq has not been able to meet its production rates since the first Gulf War and Saudi Arabia has compensated. According to the Saudi government, it has dealt with terrorists in its own private way.

4) Shame, Humiliation and Retaliation

"Power Corrupts and Absolute Power Corrupts Absolutely."

Lord Acton

Scores of Muslims feel that shame and humiliation have been wrought upon them by the U.S., and some of them are seeking revenge. Muslim radicals refer to a time when Islam was great and the nations under their religion thrived. All of these issues are enflamed by the presence of the U.S. in the Middle East and the perceived improper actions taken by the U.S. while conducting the war in Iraq, including torture. Throughout history, attempts have been made to civilize wartime behavior between fighting people. The first Geneva Convention was established in 1864 by Henry Dunant, founder of the Red Cross. It was designed to protect the sick and wounded during times of war. Since then, the Red Cross has been an integral part of creating and enforcing the Geneva Conventions. Treaties include provisions to safeguard citizens and journalists, and another set of provisions to be used when engaging members of the military.[26]

Historically, the United States had been a law-abiding member of the United Nations and signatory to the Geneva Convention. By signing and honoring the Geneva Convention, we made a commitment to the world that America would treat all people with honor and dignity as a rule of law, including the war criminals who committed crimes against us. By doing so, we set a standard so that it would be expected that our own men and women serving in the U.S. Armed Forces would be treated humanely if captured during the course of a military engagement.

Shortly after the 9/11 attacks, the Bush Administration asked the Justice Department and Attorney General John Ashcroft for a written opinion on whether the U.S. could act outside the scope of the Geneva Conventions in order to conduct interrogations to obtain information related to al-Qaeda. Bush was asking for permission to torture people detained for questioning without first establishing their guilt or innocence. Since no due process was followed, we do not know whether these people were innocent, guilty, or just ordinary citizens "in the wrong place at the wrong time."[27]

In response, several documents were provided to the administration. Mr. John Yoo, Deputy Assistant Attorney General, and Mr. Robert J. Delahunty, Special Counsel of the U.S. Department of Justice, concluded that the United States was not beholden to the Geneva Conventions since "these treaties do not protect members of al-Qaeda [and] the Taliban militia."[28] The two justice attorneys and Deputy Attorney General Alberto Gonzales indicated that the President of the United States had the ultimate authority to deal with the detainees held at Guantánamo Bay, however the President deemed appropriate. They said, "As a result, any customary international law of armed conflict in no way binds, as a legal matter, the President or the U.S. Armed Forces concerning the detention or trial of members of al-Qaeda and the Taliban."[29] America was sanctioning torture.

Mr. Yoo was responsible for crafting a series of related documents to include a new interpretation of the international torture convention. These documents became the basis for the legal framework used by President Bush and former Secretary of Defense Donald Rumsfeld to create policies that would encourage the use of torture, a crime against humanity. After more than a dozen investigations, review of FBI emails and hundreds of public interviews, there remains little doubt that the policies, practices and patterns for torture came down from the highest levels of the United States government. They were not only sanctioned by the President, but also advocated by Mr. Rumsfeld.[30]

Kenneth Roth, Executive Director of Human Rights Watch, indicated that Yoo and Delahunty simply ignored the United States' responsibilities and obligations under multiple international agreements. Mr. Roth concluded, "You can't pick or choose what laws you're going to follow," and, "These political lawyers set the nation on a course that permitted the abusive interrogation techniques."[31]

It is important to note that President Bush received written disagreement from the State Department Head of the Legal Office. In response to the interpretation as laid out by the U.S. Justice Department attorneys Yoo and Delahunty, Mr. William Taft IV warned President Bush that if any Presidential actions violated international law, then they would "constitute a breach of an international legal obligation of the United States" and "subject the United States to adverse international consequences in political and legal foray and potentially in the domestic courts of foreign countries."[32]

President Bush and former Secretary Rumsfeld ignored the warnings of the State Department. Later, Americans would be shocked to witness the horrific treatment of the prisoners at Abu Ghraib. In news programs and magazine articles, the stories and photos were explicit in the details of torture. Many of the Abu Ghraib photos are still posted on the Internet for the world to see. The photos clearly depict American soldiers in extremely disturbing graphic scenes. The soldiers have smiles on their faces.[33] Torture by Americans was sanctioned at the highest level of government and military command. As I examined those pictures, tears rushed down my face and pain gripped my heart. Reviewing the photos, I felt as if the wind had been knocked out of me. I cried out in remorse, humiliation and shame for these actions. These acts were condoned and perpetrated in the name of United States of America.

The Geneva Conventions prohibit taking hostages, and they prohibit outrages upon personal dignity, including humiliating and degrading treatment. They also prohibit the passing of sentences and carrying out of executions without a previous judgment by a regularly constituted court affording all judicial guarantees.[34]

America made a conscious decision to defy international standards for justice and the humane treatment of detainees or prisoners. Senator John McCain, a former prisoner of war, spoke against this decision in a press release that called for the President to enact a uniform standard to "prohibit cruel, inhuman, and degrading treatment of persons in the detention of the U.S. government."[35] He explained:

> *The prohibition against cruel, inhumane and degrading treatment has been a longstanding principle in both law and policy in the United States. The Universal Declaration of Human Rights, adopted in 1948, states simply that "No one shall be subject to torture or cruel, inhuman or degrading treatment or punishment . . . ." The binding Convention Against Torture, negotiated by the Reagan administration and ratified by the Senate, prohibits cruel, inhuman, and degrading treatment.*

What all this means is that America is the only country in the world that asserts a legal right to engage in cruel and inhuman treatment. To further exacerbate matters, the prison known as Guantánamo Bay in Cuba remains open, holding detainees, some for more than five years after the 9/11 attacks on America. The detainees at Guantánamo Bay continue to be held without being charged and without representation.[36]

Mr. Yoo is no longer with the U.S. Justice Department. He is a visiting scholar at the conservative think tank, American Enterprise Institute, and Professor of Law at the University of California, Berkeley.[37]

One might ask: Were ordinary Americans concerned about torture? Was the press or the American Civil Liberties Union vocal and outraged? I had never heard of Guantánamo Bay until a retired American nephrologist named Bob and his wife Karen talked about the prison camp in 2003 after coming home from a trip abroad. I discovered that Guantánamo had been active since Castro's takeover of Cuba and that it had played a large role in the 1963 Cuban missile crisis.

In some Middle Eastern nations, much of the male population is growing up in a third-world culture, living with eccentric (to us) taboos regarding women, technology and the global community. They are poor, often illiterate and terribly unskilled. Because of the fundamental extremist Islamic belief in the holy war or struggle, many of these poor young men believe that they will be granted a new life in heaven if they use a suicide bomb against the "infidels" (Americans and their allies). Armed with photos from the Internet of despicable acts perpetrated by Americans against their Muslim brothers in Iraq, al-Qaeda's recruitment for a new generation becomes ever easier. We must also consider the children, grandchildren and surviving Iraqis who have suffered from two wars led by the U.S. Those who lived through the years of brutal sanctions, lost their homes and families, witnessed or were told of horrific prisoner abuse and have watched the aftermath of bitter civil discord unfold will certainly harbor resentment against the U.S.

Thomas Friedman discusses the "curse of oil" that has fallen upon Middle Eastern nations in his book *The World is Flat*.[38] While a small percent of the ruling class of these countries enjoys wealth beyond one's wildest imagination, the masses are subjected to abject poverty with few opportunities to develop their intellectual power. The dictators of these nations have complete power and ability to control every aspect of their citizenry as they monopolize the army, police, intelligence, and school systems. The rulers of these nations never have to introduce any real transparency or be held accountable. Since the officials of these countries are not elected but are monarchies or dictatorships, they can never be voted out of office. They may only be overthrown.

An Analogy of Shame and Humiliation: I'd like to ask you to think about an analogy that might help evaluate this particular factor from another point of view. I am not trying to sidetrack our discussion, but I believe it's one that most Americans can identify with at this particular time. I use it only to make a crucial point.

Recently in the U.S. there has been much intense debate over our nation's immigration policies. Scores of Americans want to build a border fence to keep Mexicans from illegitimately entering the United States. Many of these same Americans protest against any path that might lead towards citizenship for those Mexicans who have come to the United States illegally.

Congressional representatives have been deeply conflicted about this issue. Several of President Bush's core constituents are at conflict with the President's plan to offer illegal immigrants a path to citizenship, saying that it constitutes amnesty, which they are against. Some of the President's base supporters believe the answer is to deport illegal "aliens," even if they have given birth to children in the United States. There are of course, many different sides to this issue. And it is another important subject that citizens wish Congress would tackle and resolve.

Protestors have taken it upon themselves to serve as voluntary border patrollers in my home state of New Mexico and in the adjacent states of Texas and Arizona. These individuals guard the borders between their respective states and Mexico. They call themselves "Minute Men."

Imagine, if you will, that illegal Mexican immigrants started coming into the United States not to work as janitors, housekeepers, gardeners, construction workers, cooks, and migrant workers on America's farms, but instead to build huge military bases all over our country. Imagine that they are mostly members of the Mexican Military. For many years now, they have decided they really like George W. Bush and want him to stay in office for the next twenty years, followed by his brother Jeb Bush. They tell the American people that, by giving Mr. Bush a twenty-eight year reign over the United States, our nation will have a greater chance of increasing technological production, creating a more robust economy and providing us with stronger security. Let's suppose that these Mexican militants believe Canada is under the influence of a madman, and they wish to use our nation as a station from which to launch bombs at Canada. This military and their government insist that the United Nations impose strict sanctions against Canada, after wreaking havoc. These sanctions, over a ten-year period, cause severe financial devastation on the most vulnerable: the working class and poor citizens of Canada.

I can guarantee that few of us would want any outsider occupying our nation, building military bases and telling us how we should run our government or who should run it. Nor would we want any nation using our country as a base from which to shoot bombs at one of our neighboring countries. Would we? This is the vantage point from which Osama bin Laden so often speaks.

The American Minute Men insist that they are deeply patriotic. They are taking personal time and using their own resources to "protect" our borders. Would they become like Osama bin Laden if put in a political pressure cooker? Would they attack in retaliation, even if it wasn't sanctioned by the government?

I asked one of these Minute Men, Mark, how he might react if the conditions were reversed. I laid out the scenario: "What if Muslims had bombed America ten years ago, killing 130,000 or more Americans? And imagine they insisted that the UN impose the harshest sanctions ever forced upon a nation on us because they hoped we would revolt against the President." Then I said, "Continue imagining that after ten years the Muslims conducted another bombing, killing thousands more Americans and demanding the surrender of any Weapons of Mass Destruction." I asked Mark the Minute Man if he would welcome them with open arms. In response, Mark said, "I'd kick their asses to kingdom come and then I'd piss on their *Qur'an.*" And then he explained, "Hey, we are Americans and we would be justified in doing this. But those al-Qaeda, they are just plain evil."

5) *The Palestinian-Israeli* Question

United against a common enemy, many Muslims feel justified in jihad against the United States for its foreign policies that have alienated many Muslims. According to bin Laden:

> *America heads the list of aggressors against Muslims. The recurrence of aggression against Muslims everywhere is proof enough. For over half a century, Muslims in Palestine have been slaughtered and assaulted and robbed of their honor and of their property. Their houses have been blasted, their crops destroyed. And the strange thing is that any act on their part to avenge themselves or to lift the injustice befalling them causes great agitation in the United Nations, which hastens to call for an emergency meeting only to convict the victim and to censure the wronged and the tyrannized whose children have been killed and whose crops have been destroyed and whose farms have been pulverized.*[39]

Osama bin Laden

The Bush Administration has shown unequivocal military support for Israel. Not only has the U.S. sided with Israel but it has also provided the state with U.S. Military arms and financial support. A Pew survey in August of 2006 reported that 69 percent of white evangelical Protestants believe that Israel is God's gift to the Jewish people in fulfillment of biblical prophecies. The survey showed less than one-third of Roman Catholics and mainstream Protestants such as Episcopalians, Presbyterians and Lutherans share these believes. Evangelicals maintain staunch support of military actions initiated by Israel.[40] American politicians are expected to fully back Israel's actions and, according to Dr. John Green, a senior fellow at the Pew Forum, if a politician criticizes or challenges Israel, "[there are] costs to be paid..."[41]

Shaded Areas in West Bank show areas of high Palestinian Populartion

LEBANON SYRIA

Golan Heights

Jenin
Tilkarm Tubas
Naßlus
Qalqilyah
West Bank (Israeli-occupied) JORDAN
Jericho
Jerusalem
Bethlehem
Gaza Strip
Alkhalil

ISRAEL

EGYPT

Failure to wholly and unconditionally support Israel can spell out political suicide for an elected official. But as of late, the U.S. has been charged with jeopardizing its own security in favor of Israel since the Israel-Palestine-Lebanon conflicts of July/August 2006.[42] In mid-2004, a Maryland/Zogby poll of six Arab countries, including Saudi Arabia, reported that rising anti-American attitudes in the Arab world were due mainly to America's foreign policy. Neither of the two surveys of the six Arab countries returned approval ratings of the U.S. above 20 percent. This statistic reflects the fact that America's Iraq policy now equals its Israel-Palestine policy in reaping condemnation.

None of the nations commonly accused of supporting terrorists reported opposing American civilization or values as a major contention against the U.S. In other words, these Arabic nations do not hate Americans because we love freedom as presented by President Bush in 2001.[43] A study conducted by the Defense Science Board in November of 2004 was highly critical of the Bush Administration's efforts in the war on terror and in the wars in Iraq and Afghanistan. The study reported, "Muslims do not hate our freedom, but rather they hate our policies."[44] The study showed that an overwhelming majority of Muslims object to the United States' one-sided support that favors Israel against Palestinian rights. Additionally, Muslims object to the U.S. support of oppressive dictators in the Persian Gulf and in states such as Egypt, Saudi Arabia, Jordan, and Pakistan.[45] So when Americans talk about bringing democracy to Islamic societies, this is seen as self-serving hypocrisy, said a Pentagon Advisory Panel in 2005.[46]

American credibility has been destroyed in the eyes of the international community. By supporting one side over the other, the U.S. is considered partial. Several Middle Eastern nations charge that the U.S. is fighting against Muslims in general and is using Israel as a surrogate. They see the U.S. Military weapons and hear the absolute support for Israel.

How can we expect to be seen as brokers of peace and justice? After a delicate peace fell on the region in late summer of 2006, George W. Bush declared Israel the winner. Is it possible that the President's comment was meant to inflame the public and incite a thirst for bloodshed that was based on false pretenses? Instead of supporting one side over the other, the U.S. might consider being brokers of justice, and do what they can to facilitate a peace plan beneficial to all parties.

Understanding the Real Motivations that Fuel Hatred

In order to stamp out terrorism it is essential that Americans fully understand the true motivations behind the actions of the terrorists. For without a full and comprehensive understanding, U.S. international policies in the Middle East may only serve to further exacerbate an already volatile condition.

According to Miguel, a contractor who worked in Kuwait in the late 1990s and early 2000s, there are a number of anti-American posters, billboards, fliers and signs throughout Middle Eastern countries. These signs show Palestinians in a terrible predicament. Many billboards and posters include photos depicting mothers with sweet but sad looking children pleading for financial support and prayers. Americans must remember that Islam requires a percentage of personal funds be tithed toward the support of charity organizations. The signs provide contact information and beg for help to combat the occupiers of their lands. The embedded message in these signs is that Muslims are being targeted by American and Israeli forces.

We must reexamine the Bush White House policies as they continue to focus on nations outside the scope of the war on terror. Susie, a housewife and mother said, "I am so very sick of hearing about Iraq, I can't stand it." Then she added "Now the President is using the same nuclear weapons allegations about Iran that he used to get us to support the invasion into Iraq and the stupid media mindlessly repeats the President's rhetoric. When on earth are they going to focus on capturing the real terrorists?"

I wholeheartedly agree with Susie. Also, I completely condemn the horrific attacks of 9/11 on our nation. These attacks upon our nation were horrendously wrong as were the perpetrators who executed, planned, financed and continue to support these terrible deeds. I fully back our nation's right to bring specific terrorists groups to justice. But I fear we have lost sight of our objectives in lieu of preplanned Neoconservative global ambitions.

PALESTINE - HELP US - CALL AND DONATE

*The poster shown above reflects an embedded message that states:
"Look at what Israel and America are doing to your fellow Muslims.
Help us fight this aggression." Palestinian charity campaigns distribute
posters like this everywhere across the Middle East.*

NOTES, Chapter 8

1 President Bush, "Address to a Joint Session of Congress and the American People," September 20, 2001. Transcript available at www.whitehouse.gov/news/releases/ 2001/09/20010920-8.html.

2 Osama Bin Laden, interview by John Miller, *PBS Frontline Special*, May 1998. Transcript available at www.pbs.org/wgbh/pages/frontline/shows/binladen/ who/interview.html.

3 "The World Factbook – Saudi Arabia," *Central Intelligence Agency*, https:// www.cia.gov/cia/publications/factbook/geos/sa.html.

4 a. "Saudi Arabia," *Wikipedia*, en.wikipedia.org/wiki/Saudi_Arabia.
   b. "Saudi Royal Family," *Desert Voice*, www.desert-voice.net/new_page_3.htm.

5 "World Report 2001: Saudi Arabia: Human Rights Developments," *Human Rights Watch*, www.hrw.org/wr2k1/mideast/saudi.html.

6 "Saudi Police 'Stopped' Fire Rescue," *BBC*, March 15, 2002.

7 "Saudi Arabia's Unemployment Reaches 30 Percent," *Economics*, May 3, 2003. Available at www.arabicnews.com/ansub/Daily/Day/030305/2003030513.html.

8 a. *ReligiousTolerance.org: Ontario Consultants on Religious Tolerance*, www.religioustolerance.org.
   b. "Islam," *Wikipedia*, en.wikipedia.org/wiki/Islam.

9 Ibid.

10 Osama Bin Laden, interview by Miller.

11 "The World Factbook — Saudi Arabia."

12 Robert G. Kaiser, "Enormous Wealth Spilled Into American Coffers," *The Washington Post*, February 11, 2002, A17.

13 "Saudi Arabia: Country Reports on Human Rights Practices," *U.S. Department of State*, March 8, 2006. Available at www.state.gov/g/drl/rls/hrrpt/2005/61698.htm.

14 a. Robert Baer, *Sleeping with the Devil: How Washington Sold Our Soul for Saudi Crude* (New York: Crown, 2003).
   b. Charles J. Hanley, "Saudi Arabia: Royal Family Gets Quiet Help From U.S. Firm With Connections," *Associated Press*, March 22, 1997. Available at www.corpwatch.org/article.php?id=11176.

15 Frank Church, "The Impotence of Oil Companies," *Foreign Policy* 27 (1977): 49.

16 Brian Ross and Jill Rackmill, "Secrets of the Saudi Royal Family, Critics Call Saudi Rule Hypocritical and Corrupt," *ABC News*, October 15, 2004.

17 Michael Gordon,"Dossier: Abdullah bin Abdel Aziz, Crown Prince of Saudi Arabia," *Middle East Intelligence Bulletin*, 2004.

18 Ted Thornton, "The Wahhabi Movement, Eighteenth Century Arabia," www.nmhschool.org/tthornton/wahhabi_movement.php.

19 Cozen O'Connor, *Civil Action No.: 03 CV 6978*, www.september11terror litigation.com/pdf/Federal_Insurance_Company_First_Amended_Complaint.pdf.

20 "Schumer, Collins Urge State Dept to Add Saudi Arabia to List of Religiously Intolerant Nations," *United States Senate*, June 1, 2006. Press release available at schumer.senate.gov/SchumerWebsite/pressroom/record.cfm?id=259603&&year= 2006&.

21 109th Congress, *House Congressional Resolution 275, 1st Session - Concurrent Resolution* (Washington, DC: The Washington Post Company, 2005).

22 "Weiner Denounces Pro-Saudi Section of 9/11 Bill," *United States House of Representatives*, October 8, 2004. Press release available at www.house.gov/ list/press/ny09_weiner/100804saudisection911.html.

[23] Baer, *Sleeping with the Devil*, pp. 202-203.

[24] Kelley Beaucar Vlahos, "Saudi Royal Family Faces Troubles," *Fox News*, August 9, 2004, www.foxnews.com/printer_friendly_story/0,3566,128348,00.html.

[25] Robert Spencer, "Ending the Saudi Double Game," *FrontPageMagazine.com*, June 23, 2005, www.frontpagemag.com/Articles/ReadArticle.asp?ID=18520.

[26] Society of Professional Journalists, *Reference Guide to the Geneva Conventions*, www.genevaconventions.org/.

[27] PBS Online, "Paper Trail: The Investigations," *Frontline: The Torture Question*, October 18, 2005, www.pbs.org/wgbh/pages/frontline/torture/paper/reports.html.

[28] Patrick F. Philbin, memorandum for William J. Haynes, II, December 28, 2001, www.msnbc.msn.com/id/5022681/site/newsweek/.

[29] Ibid.

[30] a. Steven Strasser, *The Abu Ghraib Investigations: The Official Independent Panel and Pentagon Reports on the Shocking Prisoner Abuse in Iraq*, ed. Karen Greenberg and Joshua Dratel (New York: PublicAffairs, 2004).

b. Anthony Lewis, *The Torture Papers: The Road to Abu Ghraib*, (New York: Cambridge University Press, 2005).

c. *Taguba Report: Iraq Prisoner Abuse Investigation of the U.S. 800th Military Police Brigade*, news.findlaw.com/cnn/docs/iraq/tagubarpt.html.

d. "The Torture Question," *Frontline*.

[31] Philbin, memorandum.

[32] Ibid.

[33] "Abu Ghraib Abuse Photos," *AntiWar.com*, February 17, 2006, www.antiwar.com/news/?articleid=8560.

[34] Jennifer van Bergen, "The New CIA Gulag of Secret Foreign Prisons: Why it Violates Both Domestic and International Law," *FindLaw*, November 7, 2005, writ.news.findlaw.com/commentary/20051107_bergen.html.

[35] John McCain, "Statement on Detainee Amendments on (1) The Army Field Manual and (2) Cruel, Inhumane, Degrading Treatment (Amendment to the Defense Authorization Bill)," *United States Senate* (Capitol, Washington, DC, October 3, 2005). Transcript available at mccain.senate.gov/press_office/view_article.cfm?ID=128.

[36] Seymour M. Hersh, "Torture at Abu Ghraib," *New Yorker*, May 10, 2004.

[37] "John Yoo," *Wikipedia*, en.wikipedia.org/wiki/John_Yoo.

[38] Thomas L. Friedman, *The World is Flat: A Brief History of the Twenty-first Century* (New York: Farrar, Straus and Giroux, 2005): 460.

[39] Osama Bin Laden, interview by Miller.

[40] www.jpost.com/servlet/Satellite?pagename=JPost%2FJPArticle%2FShowFull&cid=1154525949673

[41] Ibid

[42] "The Israel Lobby and U.S. Foreign Policy," *Wikipedia*, en.wikipedia.org/wiki/The_Israel_Lobby_and_U.S._Foreign_Policy

[43] Khaled Dawoud, "Arab Opinions," *Al-Ahram Weekly*, July 30, 2004, yaleglobal.yale.edu/display.article?id=4305.

[44] Tom Regan, "'They hate our policies, not our freedom': Pentagon Report Contains Major Criticisms of Administration," *csmonitor.com*, November 29, 2004, www.csmonitor.com/2004/1129/dailyUpdate.html.

[45] Ibid.

[46] Noam Chomsky, "The Terrorist in the Mirror," *Amnesty International Annual Lecture* (Trinity College, Dublin, Ireland, January 18, 2006).

★ 9 ★

Spin, Baby, Spin

"If you are not with me, you're my enemy."
Anakin Skywalker / Lord Vader

"Only a Sith [Dark Lord] would say such a thing."
Obi-Wan-Kenobi, Revenge of the Sith *(Star Wars III)*

I N LATE 2001, the Italian government claimed to have received letters and documents indicating that Iraqi agents had attempted to buy uranium yellowcake in Niger from government officials. The evidence was shared with both the British and U.S. intelligence services. In February of 2002, the CIA sent former State Department Official Joseph Wilson to investigate these allegations. Wilson was a good choice for the job because he had been a State Department officer in the mid-1970s and was Ambassador to Gabon in the early 1990s. In 1997 and 1998, Wilson was the senior director for Africa at the National Security Council and had spent a fair amount of time dealing with the government of Niger. Finally, Wilson was the last U.S. ambassador in Iraq prior to the first Gulf War.

George W. Bush on Yellowcake Uranium

For Wilson's role in the Gulf War, Rowland Evans wrote that Wilson displayed "the stuff of heroism." President George H. W. Bush also commended Wilson, stating, "Your courageous leadership during this period of great danger for American interests and American citizens has my admiration and respect . . . ."[1]

Ambassador Wilson went to Niger to conduct an investigation regarding the allegations that Iraqi agents had sought uranium. Upon his return,

Mr. Wilson reported to both the CIA and the State Department. He told them he could not confirm the allegations that Iraqi agents had tried to buy yellowcake from Niger. Ambassador Wilson prepared a detailed written memo and sent it directly to State Department Secretary Colin Powell refuting the Italian intelligence.[2]

At this point, the yellowcake story should have been a shut and closed case. Instead, the story was resurrected six months later in a British government dossier published on September 24, 2002. It declared that "Iraq had sought significant quantities of uranium from Africa." Ari Fleisher, the White House Spokesperson, concurred, saying that the U.S. agreed with the British findings.[3]

After receiving Ambassador Wilson's report, Colin Powell refused to use the debunked yellowcake allegations as part of his testimony before the United Nations on the necessity of war in Iraq. CIA Director George Tenet would also forgo the story when he testified before the Senate. George Tenet personally telephoned Deputy National Security Advisor Stephen Hadley in October 2002 to make sure the yellowcake allegations were taken out of a speech George W. Bush was to deliver in Cincinnati. In October, the CIA included a footnote to a 90-page report on the National Intelligence Estimate on Iraqi Weapons Programs, stating that assertions regarding the yellowcake were "highly dubious." In a CIA memo dated October 5, 2002, Stephen Hadley informed chief White House speechwriter Michael Gerson of the CIA's objection to the yellowcake claim that had been placed in a draft of President's State of the Union Address to be delivered in January 2003.[4]

In another memo addressed to Condoleezza Rice and Hadley dated October 6, 2002, the CIA clearly stated there was a "weakness in the evidence."[5] At this point the administration had received one telephone call, a detailed written report and two memos debasing the yellowcake charges. But because the evidence of Iraq's weapons of mass destruction was so scanty, politics trumped truthfulness. This false allegation about the yellowcake uranium was left in the speech by Condoleezza Rice, who would later defend the speech by saying, "if the CIA, the Director of Intelligence, had said, 'Take this out of the speech,' it would have been gone, without question."[6] This yellowcake statement would come back to haunt the administration time and again.

How the War Was Sold to Congress

Never before in the history of our nation have Americans put personalities before the principles upon which our nation was built in such an extraordinary way. We put our trust and support in a President and admin-istration that told us they placed American safety and well being first and foremost. We took them at their word. And since hindsight is always 20/20, we can now say that doing so was probably a big mistake. So how did the Bush Administration obtain the authorization to launch the war on Iraq? The Bush Administration went to Congress asking for permis-sion to launch a war against Saddam Hussein without specifically stating their determined intent to do so. The congressional resolution gave the administration the authority to launch a war against Iraq only if Saddam Hussein refused to allow inspectors back into Iraq and comply with the UN resolutions and only if the administration was able to substantiate a true threat to America's security.

In essence, the purpose of the resolution was to: (1) defend the national security of the United States against the continuing threat posed by Iraq, and (2) enforce all relevant United Nation Security Council resolutions regarding Iraq. The resolution required the President to notify Congress within forty-eight hours of any military action against Iraq and submit, at least every sixty days, a report to Congress on the military cam-paign. It did not tie any U.S. action to a UN resolution.

The administration, while lobbying for the approval, suggested that they sought the authorization mostly as *a threat* to obtain greater coop-eration from Mr. Hussein. On October 22, 2002, the Senate approved the Bush war resolution in a vote of 77-23. Twenty-three senators voted against the resolution. That vote included 22 Democrats and one Repub-lican, Lincoln Chafee (R-RI). Similarly, the House approved the resolu-tion on a vote of 296-133, with six Republicans joining 126 Democrats to vote against it.

I believe some congressional members voted for the resolution out of fear of being portrayed as "weak on security" or "unpatriotic." These members voted for the resolution for political reasons. Others who were more gullible gave the authorization hoping the administration would use it as honest leverage. Few thought the Bush Administration would "rush to war" with it as they did. A majority of Congress, backed by a support-ive public and a virtually unquestioning media, gave President Bush and his administration carte blanche authority to launch the war against Iraq if necessary.

"This resolution amounts to a 'blank check' for the White House. Let us stop, look and listen. Let us not give this President or any President unchecked power. Remember the Constitution."

Senator Robert Byrd (D-WV)

Iraq immediately denied having weapons of mass destruction. They called the Bush allegations "lies." The Iraqi government quickly offered to let U.S. officials inspect any plants suspected of being used to develop nuclear, biological and chemical weapons.[7] Additionally, the Iraqi government encouraged UN weapons inspectors to return for the first time since 1998. The White House was fast to reject the Iraqi offer, saying the matter was not up to Iraq; it was up to the United Nations.[8] The Bush Administration had already begun deploying troops to the Persian Gulf and by March of 2002, Halliburton subsidiaries had already begun building bases in the region.[9]

"You're either with us or against us..." [10]

George W. Bush

George W. Bush told the world, "You're either with us or against us," as he attempted to coerce our allies to join the U.S. in a preemptive strike against Iraq. Americans were put on alert that everyone was expected to cooperate with the administration's newly conceived global War on Terrorism.

Vice President Dick Cheney, Secretary of Defense Donald Rumsfeld and National Security Advisor Condoleezza Rice were featured on virtually every news talk show across the country, parroting the weapons of mass destruction (WMD) theme and peddling fear. While the news media was going nuts selling a war story filled with false information of Iraq's purported stockpiles of weapons of mass destruction, a few Americans were subscribing to other, more comprehensive news sources to find out the truth.

You had to look to find the truth, because mainstream media was not covering this critical information for reasons unknown. What the mainstream media brought into American homes were only the allegations made by the very people Americans hoped to trust to provide the truth: the President, Vice President, and other members of the Bush Administration.

The following examples demonstrate how far from the truth the Bush Administration was willing to place itself in order to advance its war plans against Iraq.

THE HYPE ON IRAQ'S WEAPONS OF MASS DESTRUCTION

March 17, 2002

"We know they have biological and chemical weapons."

Vice President Richard Cheney

"There is no reliable information on whether Iraq is producing and stockpiling chemical weapons or where Iraq has — or will — establish its chemical warfare agent production facilities."

Defense Intelligence Agency[11]

September 8, 2002

"The Czechs say Mohammed Atta met with an Iraqi official.... There's a photo of this meeting...."

Dick Cheney on Meet the Press

The FBI say Mohamed Atta was in Florida at the time this meeting allegedly took place. No one, including the 9/11 Commission, found evidence of any photo.

November 14, 2002

"[In] a week, or a month, Saddam Hussein could give his weapons of mass destruction to al-Qaeda, who could use them to attack the United States and kill 30,000, or 100,000 ... human beings."

Secretary of Defense Donald Rumsfeld

According to the National Intelligence Estimate Report, the intelligence community had "low confidence" regarding whether Iraq would provide al-Qaeda with weapons of mass destruction even if they had them.[12]

January 10, 2003

"The problem here is that there will always be some uncertainty about how quickly he can acquire nuclear weapons. But we don't want the smoking gun to be a mushroom cloud."

Condoleezza Rice

National Security Advisor Rice cleverly alleges Saddam Hussein will soon acquire nuclear weapons and that he will use them to blow up America.[13]

January 29, 2003

"His regime has the design for a nuclear weapon, was working on several different methods of enriching uranium and recently was discovered seeking significant quantities of uranium from Africa."
Secretary of Defense Donald Rumsfeld

State Department intelligence officials and the CIA had previously concluded this claim to be "highly dubious." The Bush Administration had received telephone calls, memos and reports to debunk this fact, but choose to ignore the State Department and the CIA.

March 8, 2003

"We are doing everything we can to avoid war in Iraq. But if Saddam Hussein does not disarm peacefully, he will be disarmed by force."
President George W. Bush

March 30, 2003

"We know where [Iraq's WMDs] are. They're in the area around Tikrit and Baghdad and east, west, south, and north..."[14]
Secretary of Defense Donald Rumsfeld

No WMDs have ever been found in Iraq. The only finds were of aged tubes of degraded sarin and agricultural pesticides that the Bush Administration referred to as biological chemicals.

The U.S. Dog and Pony Show at the UN

Throughout the 1990s, Colin Powell was frequently quoted as referring to Saddam Hussein as "a toothache" or a "kidney stone that would eventually pass."[15] And according to Kenneth Pollack, a former staff member of the National Security Council, it was Colin Powell who determined it would be best to continue a strategy of containment with respect to Saddam Hussein and Iraq.

However, immediately after the 9/11 attacks, Mr. Powell was up against a determined team of Neoconservative war hawks, including Paul Wolfowitz and Vice President Dick Cheney, who wanted to start the "war on terror" first with the elimination of Saddam Hussein in Iraq.[16] The Neocons surrounding President Bush wanted to rush into a preemptive war against Iraq without even bothering to go to the United Nations.[17] Colin Powell knew it would be challenging to conduct a ground war against Iraq, even with international community support, much less for the U.S. to try to go it alone. Powell talked the President into allowing him the opportunity to attempt to convince our allies to support the U.S. war against Iraq through a presentation at the United Nations. The President gave Powell his chance, but made it clear that with or without UN support, the U.S. would strike Iraq.[18]

According to the international community, this would go down in history as one of the more contrived smoke-and-mirrors demonstrations ever put before the United Nations Security Council. And who would have expected it from Collin Powell, probably one of the most highly respected people in the Bush Administration and the U.S. at the time? General Colin Powell, the Secretary of State in 2002, stood before a world audience and attempted to convince the United Nations and the rest of the of us that somehow, after ten years of intense sanctions, Saddam Hussein had obtained weapons of mass destruction.[19] Secretary Powell argued that it was incumbent upon the UN to give the U.S. the authority to launch a preemptive war against Iraq to disarm Hussein as part of America's War on Terrorism.

Mr. Powell engaged in a dog and pony slide show. His presentation was complete with satellite photos of rail cars he alleged produced biological weapons. Other hypothetical accusations were made about additional dark and dangerous weapons moving back and forth across Iraq in rail cars. Mr. Powell stood before the UN Security Council on February 5, 2003 and said, "We have first-hand descriptions of biological weapons factories on wheels and on rails." This theme would be repeated over and over again despite the lack of evidence.[20] Not one solid piece of evidence was put forth to the UN Council or any other rational thinking person in the world.

Mr. Powell claimed a Guantánamo Bay detainee, Mamdouh Habib, had confessed that he and other al-Qaeda members had received training from the Iraqi Government in the use of chemical weaponry and other weapons of mass destruction. It was later discovered that this detainee had been taken to Egypt, tortured and coerced into this confession. Afterwards, detainee Mamdouh Habib recanted his coerced testimony. Most U.S. allies would be no part of another invasion into Iraq and the United Nations refused to sanction the second attack on Iraq.

Dan Rather Gives America a Glimpse

CBS News anchor Dan Rather traveled to Iraq to interview Saddam Hussein on February 27, 2003, less than a month before the U.S.-led attack. Mr. Rather had been a journalist since 1962 and had handled some of the most challenging assignments. Rather earned a reputation for providing substantive, fair and accurate news reports. This, combined with a tough, active style, earned him respect from his peers and the public. He was referred to as "the hardest-working man in broadcast journalism."[21] However, he was targeted because of his tough media evaluations against G.W. Bush and his administration. Powerful Neocons, together with influential conservative right-wing hounds, had long been trying to bring down Mr. Rather.

The Saddam Hussein interview was an attempt to open dialogue between the U.S. and Iraq. It gave the world the chance to evaluate Saddam Hussein and his responses concerning the Bush Administration's allegations of weapons of mass destruction. CBS requested that an official representative from the Bush Administration, such as the President or Vice President, attend the interview. The administration declined the opportunity and the interview was dismissed. White House spokesman Ari Fleischer disregarded the Saddam interview saying it was "60 minutes of lies, deceptions and propaganda."[22] The full interview can be found on the CBS website in a story entitled "Saddam Interview Airs in Iraq." Here are a few key excerpts from the interview:

Dan Rather: "Mr. President, do you expect to be attacked by an American-led invasion?"

Saddam Hussein: ". . . praying to Allah to stop the Americans from going through with it and to spare the Iraqis from the harm that those on the bandwagon of evil want to inflict upon them."

Dan Rather: "Mr. President — do you intend to destroy the al-Samoud missiles that the United Nations prohibits? Will you destroy those missiles?"

Saddam Hussein: ". . . we have committed ourselves to Resolution. It is on this basis that we have conducted ourselves, and it is on this basis that we will continue to behave. As you know, we are allowed to produce land-to-land rockets with a range of up to kilometers, and we are committed to that."

Dan Rather: "I want to make sure that I understand, Mr. President. So, you do not intend to destroy these missiles?"

Saddam Hussein: "Which missiles are you talking about? We do not have missiles that go beyond the prescribed ranges by the UN."

Dan Rather: Mr. President, Americans are very much concerned about anyone's connections to Osama bin Laden. Do you have [or] have you had any connections to al-Qaeda and Osama bin Laden?

Saddam Hussein: "Is this the basis of the anxiety in the minds of U.S. officials? Or is it the basis of anxiety in the minds of the people of the United States?"

Dan Rather: "Mr. President, I believe I can report accurately that it's a major concern in the minds of the people in the United States."

Saddam Hussein: "We have never had any relationship with Mr. Osama bin Laden. And Iraq has never had any relationship with al-Qaeda. And I think that Mr. bin Laden himself has recently, in one of his speeches, given—such an answer, that we have no relation with him."

FORMER CIA SAYS NO WMDS

In recent history, a greater number of former Central Intelligence Agents have begun writing books, producing video programs and providing public forums after they leave the agency to alert the public to the truth.[23] I attended such a forum and was surrounded by several noteworthy individuals who assured everyone at our small, hometown convention center that no such weapons would be found because they never existed. They informed the crowd that it was pure manipulation on the part of the administration to implement something known as the Project for a New American Century.

The Cries of the Innocent

"Truth indeed rather alleviates than hurts, and will always bear up against falsehood, as oil does above water."

Cervantes

The church was packed so I sat on the floor of the front row. It was two weeks before the March 2003 "Shock and Awe" invasion of Iraq led by the U.S. The woman who spoke to our group was a mother and grandmother. Her clothing was simple, her face gaunt with dark circles under her sparkling, warm, compassionate eyes. The most prominent feature was her bald head. While Mary Riseley was not a particularly compelling speaker, her message was simple and forthright. She had just returned from Iraq, forced to leave by both the UN and American soldiers warning that war was imminent. Her message was largely informational and humanitarian in nature. It lacked any real political tendencies.

Mary had been a part of an international peace team whose mission was to open dialogue between volunteers from around the world and the citizens of Iraq. These volunteers took medicines to Iraqis in need and toys for their children. They sought to build a dialogue around compassion and hope that the U.S.-led sanctions on Iraq would be lifted soon. The volunteers went to share the struggle and the difficulties of living life in Iraq under sanctions imposed by the UN.

Mary Riseley captivated us with a beautiful slide show richly illustrating the life of the average Iraqi. On a cold winter night in Santa Fe, New Mexico, over 200 people watched with intrigue as the photos documented an uncensored revelation of life in Baghdad. The photos told the simple stories of humble people who met at coffee shops and bakeries. They showed Iraqis gathered together at the street market. One slide revealed a favorite pastime of Iraqis where they lined up their books each week on a narrow sheet where they would be traded or sold. Another photo showed men attending a theatre program, drinking black espresso, smoking cigarettes, and laughing and crying at their traditions as they were expressed through drama and music. According to Mary, that particular theater program told the story of an arranged marriage, unfulfilled love, sadness, and loneliness that consumed the actors as they portrayed their parts in the play.

There were pictures of young women in uniforms attending school. It was mentioned that while many Iraqis were afraid of Saddam Hussein, they were proud to have one of the best education systems in the Middle East. The Iraqi educational system provided free access to students and encouraged every child, regardless of gender, to receive education from kindergarten through college. Despite the UN sanctions imposed since 1991, Iraqis were proud to be continuing their education and touted the fact that they had one of the highest number of women Ph.D.s of all the Arab Nations.[24]

In one photo in front of a hospital, an Austrian doctor who was a friend and colleague of Mary's was shown volunteering medical service. Free health care was provided for every person in the country under the reign of Saddam Hussein. Other photos showed working women. Despite the fact that many of the Middle Eastern Nations held policies against women working, Iraq upheld policies of equal pay regardless of gender.

The slide show then moved to scenes of destruction, showing portions of Baghdad that had been damaged in the first Gulf War bombings of 1991. In one particular building, several hundred civilians died. They were told they could safely take refuge in the basement of a building, only for it to become their tomb as the walls and roof collapsed above them. Ms. Riseley shared the fears that many Iraqis discussed with her. They were deeply concerned about the health effects their families and friends suffered after the bomb explosions of the first Gulf War. A brief question-and-answer period ensued where for the first time I heard about a substance known as depleted uranium, a by-product used in the bombs that were dropped all over Iraq in the first Gulf War.

We asked why Mary Riseley's head was shaved. She explained that she was terribly distressed and deeply afraid of a second invasion of Iraq. Therefore, she had shaved her head as an act of solidarity for the suffering she knew would be imposed upon the innocent people of Iraq and our American soldiers who also would be drawn into the impending battle.

Mary Riseley served as a volunteer with *Voices in the Wilderness*, an organization that urged for an end to the war and to the UN/U.S. sanctions against Iraq. The meeting ended with people wondering what could be done. A sense of doom loomed throughout the church. People of all denominations bowed heads, said a prayer and went their separate ways.

"Everyone we met in Baghdad talks the Saddam line, including these women. They are Iraq's version of liberated women, the educated elite of Baghdad: teachers, doctors, architects and diplomats who meet once a month at this art gallery and restaurant. They are all Saddam supporters, and they don't trust the American government."

Dan Rather, 2003

THE DANGERS OF DEPLETED URANIUM

Depleted uranium was scattered all over Iraq during the first Gulf War. According to Radiobiologist Dr. Rosalie Bertell, depleted uranium shells retain 60 percent of the radioactivity of unspent "hot" uranium. She warns that if women, children, the sick, the elderly, or anyone else breathes in these elements, it can have severe health repercussions, as even a speck of uranium-238 can cause cancer. The Pentagon admits to firing 320 tons of depleted uranium into Iraq's farms and neighborhoods during Desert Storm. Greenpeace puts the figure closer to 800 tons.[25] Former Basra Dean of Medicine Dr. Alim Abdul-Hamid had a great deal of first-hand experience with Iraq's unprecedented plague of cancers and birth defects after the 1991 Gulf war. The Iraqi physician said he saw unprecedented levels of breast cancer in twenty-year-old women and many increased incidences of colon cancer and thyroid cancer in addition to leukemia and lymphomas.[26] Children are ten to twenty times more sensitive to the effects of radiation than adults.

Today, more than half of all cancers in Iraq are occurring among children under the age of five. Helpless pediatricians in Basra have watched childhood leukemia and cancer rates increase by up to twelve times. Hospitals throughout Iraq have reported as much as a ten-fold increase in birth defects since cities and countryside were bombarded with the radioactive munitions in the first Gulf War.[27]

Shockingly Awful

"I think unleashing 3,000 smart bombs against the city of Baghdad in the first several days of the war...to me, if those were unleashed against the San Francisco Bay Area, I would call that an act of extreme terrorism."

Representative Pete Stark (D-CA)

Like his father, George W. Bush hired the latest media consultants who employed deceptive strategies using consumer-savvy marketers, "information warriors" and "perception managers" to sell the war in Iraq to the American public.

An Army Reserve Officer, Max, did tours in both Afghanistan and in Iraq. He strongly recommended the book *Weapons of Mass Deception* to patriotic citizens regardless of their political persuasion. The book clearly details how the war in Iraq was "sold" to the American public. Sheldon Rampton and John Stauber, authors of the book describe how the Bush Administration paid the world's top advertising agencies and media empires to create the Bush war themes for different aspects of the Iraqi invasion. Consider the phrases "war on terror," "axis of evil" and the "coalition of the willing." For those watching the 2003 attack on Iraq it was packaged like a Fourth of July celebration as the Bush Administration brought this Shock and Awe production into our homes.

Let me digress just for a moment to bring you the reality of the Shock and Awe program. The Air Force had stockpiled 6,000 guidance kits in the Persian Gulf. They converted these ordinary dumb bombs into satellite-guided bombs. These weapons, in addition to 400 cruise missiles, were fired into Baghdad on the first day of the war. This heavy level of bombardment pounded on Iraq every single day until the U.S. ran out of targets.[28]

CBS News Correspondent David Martin reported that more bombs would be dropped on Iraq in the first day of Shock and Awe than were launched during the entire forty days of the first Gulf War. The plan was to take out the city, eliminating power and water, to quickly exhaust the Iraqis physically, emotionally and psychologically.[29] According to an interview provided by Harlan Ullman, the Shock and Awe program would have "...this simultaneous effect, rather like the nuclear weapons at Hiroshima, not taking days or weeks but in minutes."[30] Mr. Ullman was one of the mastermind creators of Shock and Awe, which was developed at the U.S. National Defense University.[31]

The Shock and Awe campaign of war wrought chaos and destruction on the people of Iraq as U.S. Forces bombed electrical grids, water and sewer plants and devastated Baghdad and other parts of Iraq.

We would later discover the errors of this folly. More than three years after the American Shock and Awe production, electricity, water and sewer systems in Iraq are still not fully functional. A May 2006 UN report showed the living conditions in Iraq to be dismal.[32] Even though most Iraqi households are connected to water and electricity, all systems are too unstable to make much difference in people's lives. The Iraqis live with only intermittent water and electricity. For a second time in recent history, the U.S. would be responsible for rampant malnutrition among Iraqi children.[33]

In an interview in June of 2006, a National Guard Reservist named Pete said, "These people don't have chlorinated water systems or ways to purify the water, so they are forced to drink whatever water is in the river beds, and that water is really nasty." Jim, another Reservist, said, "It is so frigging hot in Iraq and there's no reliable electricity, so people don't have refrigeration for their food and that makes life miserable. Air conditioning would be considered a luxury."

Soon we discovered there were no weapons of mass destruction to be found in Iraq, so the Bush Administration shifted its focus. "Operation Iraqi Freedom" became a half-truth story sold to the American people, as if we were to be true liberators of a captive people.

In *Weapons of Mass Deception*, Rampton and Stauber use meticulous research and documentation to deconstruct the "true lies" behind the propaganda created for the purpose of taking us to war. They show how the "weapons of mass destruction" claim was, of course, the biggest deception. The Bush Administration had to first convince Americans that Iraq was a dangerous enemy that had to be stopped immediately. This deceit was discussed in *Watchdogs of Democracy?*, a 2006 book by Helen Thomas, renowned dean of the White House Press Corps. The Bush Administration fully understood that the Iraqi Military had no chance against the U.S. Military. Nonetheless the element of fear was emphasized to convince the American public to support the war, so claims were made regardless of the facts. At the same time, the Bush Administration conducted a "propaganda blitz" to improve the American image in the Muslim world, a strategy everyone, including our troops, saw as an "abject failure."[34]

Other nations have stockpiles of dangerous weapons, but the U.S. government hasn't suggested attacking them. Of course, more recently, we have been hearing similar rattlings as a viable rationale to go after Iran. Iran says it is attempting to increase its nuclear program for energy purposes. The Bush Administration is accusing Iran of attempting to beef up its nuclear program to create weapons of mass destruction. We know for a fact that North Korea has WMDs and has even tested them. Where is the outrage, the fear and the concern regarding the North Korean WMD program? It is so much further along than Iran's.

THE IRAQI SPIN GOES ON

May 1, 2003

"The liberation of Iraq is a crucial advance in the campaign against terror. We've removed an ally of Al Qaeda [sic] and cut off a source of terrorist funding. And this much is certain: No terrorist network will gain weapons of mass destruction from the Iraqi regime, because the regime is no more."

President George W. Bush

The 9/11 Commission reported it found no "collaborative relationship" between Iraq and al-Qaeda, challenging one of the Bush Administration's main justifications for the war in Iraq.

May 1, 2003

"The battle of Iraq is one victory in a war on terror that began on September the 11, 2001—and still goes on...."

President George W. Bush

President Bush later (September 2003) acknowledged, "We've had no evidence that Saddam Hussein was involved with September the 11th."[35]

May 29, 2003

"We found the weapons of mass destruction. We found biological laboratories.... But for those who say we haven't found the banned manufacturing devices or banned weapons, they're wrong, we found them."

President George W. Bush

The Defense Intelligence Agency examined the trailers and concluded that they were most likely used to produce hydrogen for artillery weather balloons.[36]

July 2, 2003

"....Let me finish. There are some who feel like the conditions are such that they can attack us there. My answer is, bring 'em on."
President George W. Bush

The unnecessary bravado demonstrated by the President has been highly criticized as an invitation to al-Qaeda and other terrorists to start attacking Americans in Iraq and Afghanistan.

September 7, 2003

"....we acted in Iraq, where the former regime sponsored terror [and] possessed and used weapons of mass destruction."37
President George W. Bush

> *"Make the lie big, make it simple, keep saying it, and eventually they will believe it."*
>
> Adolf Hitler

Americans who have worked hard at staying informed are extremely upset and others are becoming disgusted as the truth slowly comes to light. Every reason the President gave U.S. citizens for going to war in Iraq has turned out to be bogus. All of the Bush White House allegations have been proven false!

- Saddam Hussein had weapons of mass destruction that threatened the U.S.
- He was reconstituting his nuclear weapons programs.
- He had biological weapons that could be launched quickly in aerial vehicles.
- He had huge stocks of chemical weapons that threatened the U.S.
- He was working with al-Qaeda.
- Iraq had provided training for al-Qaeda in WMD bomb-making, poisons and chemical weapons.
- Hussein was a terrorist and his country harbored terrorists.

Saddam Hussein was executed for some of his crimes, having been found guilty of murder, torture and forced deportation. He was hanged by Iraqi court order on December 30, 2006.

NOTES, Chapter 9

1 David Corn, "A White House Smear," *Nations*, July 17, 2003, www.thenation. com/blogs/capitalgames?bid=3&pid=823.

2 Stefan Halper and Jonathan Clarke, *America Alone: The Neo-Conservatives and the Global Order* (New York: Cambridge University Press, 2005), 214-217.

3 Ibid.

4 Ibid.

5 Halper and Clarke, *America*.

6 Thomas and Lipper, "Condi."

7 "Senate Approves War Resolution," *CNN*, October 11,2002, archives.cnn.com/ 2002/ALLPOLITICS/10/11/iraq.us/.

8 Ibid.

9 PBS Online, *Frontline: Private Warriors*, June 21, 2005, www.pbs.org/wgbh/ pages/frontline/shows/warriors/.

10 George W. Bush, *Press Conference* (Washington, D.C., November 6, 2001).

11 Dick Cheney and his Highness Salam bin Hamad Al Khalifa, *Press Conference* (White House, Washington, D.C., March 17, 2002).

12 Donald Rumsfeld, interview by Steve Croft, *Infinity Radio Connect*, CBS Radio, November 14, 2002. Transcript available at www.defenselink.mil/transcripts/ 2002/t11152002_t1114rum.html.

13 "Condoleeza Rice," *Wikipedia*, en.wikipedia.org/wiki/Condoleezza_Rice.

14 Donald Rumsfeld, interview by George Stephanopoulos, *This Week with George Stephanopoulos*, ABC, March 30, 2003.

15 PBS Online, *Frontline: The War Behind Closed Doors*, February 20, 2003, www.pbs.org/wgbh/pages/frontline/shows/iraq/.

16 Ibid.

17 Ibid.

18 Ibid.

19 Colin Powell, *Address to UN Security Council* (White House, Washington, D.C., February 5, 2003). Transcript available at www.whitehouse.gov/news/releases/ 2003/02/20030205-1.html

20 Agence France Presse, "CIA Officer Claims US Ignored Warnings About WMD Errors," *Agence France Presse*, June 25, 2006.

21 "Biography: Dan Rather," *CBS News*, www.cbsnews.com/stories/2002/02/26/ 60minutes/bios/main502231.shtml.

22 Saddam Hussein, interview by Dan Rather, *CBS News*, CBS, February 27, 2003. Transcript available at www.cbsnews.com/stories/2003/02/21/iraq/ main541427.shtml.

23 *UNCOVERED: The War on Iraq*, Video, directed by Robert Greenwald Culver City, CA, Brave New Films, 2004.

24 There is virtually no documentation to verify this fact. As of May 2006, most sources show a dramatic decline of the educational system in Iraq since 2003.

25 William Thomas, "Invading Hiroshima," *Global Research Canada*, www.global research.ca/articles/THO302A.html.

26 Suren Pillay, "Civilian Bodies: On the Recognition of Death," *Counterpunch*, December 28, 2001, www.counterpunch.org/suren1.html.

27 Ibid.

28 Scott Petersen, "US Mulls Air Strategy in Iraq," *The Christian Science Monitor*, January 30, 2003, www.csmonitor.com/2003/0130/p06s01-woiq.html.

[29] "Iraq Faces Massive U.S. Missile Barrage," CBS News, January 24, 2003, www.cbsnews.com/stories/2003/01/24/eveningnews/main537928.shtml.

[30] Ibid.

[31] "History of the National Defense University," NDU, www.ndu.edu/info/history.cfm.

[32] "Daily Living Conditions in Iraq Dismal, UN Survey Finds," UN News Service, May 12, 2005, www.un.org/apps/news/story.asp?NewsID=14255&Cr=Iraq.

[33] Ibid.

[34] Ibid.

[35] George W. Bush, "Major Combat Operations in Iraq Have Ended, President's Remarks (USS Abraham Lincoln, San Diego, CA, May 1, 2003). Press release available at www.whitehouse.gov/news/releases/2003/05/20030501-15.html.

[36] George W. Bush, interview by TVP, TV Poland, May 29, 2003.

[37] George W. Bush, Presidential Address (White House, Washington, D.C., September 7, 2003). Transcript available at www.pbs.org/newshour/bb/white_house/july-dec03/bush_iraq_speech.html.

★ 10 ★

God Bless the Troops

*"I hate those men who would send into war youth to fight
and die for them; the pride and cowardice of those old men,
making their wars for whom our young boys must die."*

Mary Roberts Rinehart

The Recurring Nightmare

NO, HE DID NOT WITNESS IRAQI FAMILIES with open arms smiling with glee, filled with happiness to see the American troops. Instead he watched Iraqi women and children lining their bodies across the road, blocking the road in hopes of stopping the American convoys from infiltrating their communities. At first the convoys swerved to the side of the road to avoid hitting the women and children, but after an IED exploded the sergeant ordered the convoys to continue driving, running over the women and children. Although he was the driver of the third vehicle within the convoy, the "thumping" sound as he drove over the families would forever haunt him.[1] He woke up screaming in a cold sweat night after night. Was it a dream or had it happened? He wasn't sure. Maybe he was losing his mind.

Our Mission is to Do or Die: We Do Not Question Why

Based upon my research and interviews, I would classify the troops into three categories. The first and by far the largest category I will refer to as the devoted troops. The second, a much smaller category, I will refer to as the questioning troops. The final category, a small but growing number, will be referred to as the resistant troops.

The devoted troops believe they are in Iraq first and foremost to stop terrorism. They believe Saddam Hussein was training al-Qaeda, but they admit it is difficult to prove this allegation. One trooper said the palaces where Saddam Hussein trained the Iraqi Republican Guard were the same places used to train al-Qaeda. According to a National Guard reservist, the proof of this existed in the emblem of a black horse believed to be the symbol of al-Qaeda. The devoted troops think they are in Iraq to preserve the natural resources of Iraq, meaning protection of the oil for the bene-fit of the Iraqis. They feel they are working to provide a stable environment for the Iraqi government to take over and are proud of their work. They say the U.S. is making an important contribution to Iraq and report that the Iraqi people are "incredible." One trooper cited the projects com-pleted, such as the rebuilding of a school. He said most Iraqi children were able to attend school safely while he was in Iraq in 2004. Like others in this category, he believes that as soon as the work is done, the U.S. will pull out of Iraq and leave the government and resources to the Iraqis.

A few questioning troopers had many of the same beliefs as the devoted troops regarding the reasons they were in Iraq. However, they were troubled because they had been advised not to communicate with the Iraqis upon entering Iraq. Based on the rhetoric of President Bush, they felt misled because they expected to be warmly welcomed by the Iraqis. However, their superiors had told them to suspect every Iraqi of being a potential terrorist. These orders conflicted with their expectations.

These troops might be a bit envious because of the compensation difference between themselves and the Kellogg, Brown and Root (KBR) private security people and outside contractors. Troops who were attempting to provide stability referred to the contractors as extremely dangerous "cowboys with no training and a bad attitude."[2] It was felt that the recklessness and arrogance of these contractors compromised the mission of the troops. Rather than blend in, contractors drove around in brand new SUVs and were sitting ducks whenever they left the safety of the Green Zone—the highly fortified bases used to house the U.S. mil-itary and the contractors.

One trooper reported that because promotions and money were "tied" to the number of missions conducted, many missions were sent out at night so as to increase the pay for officers. He said these missions were unnecessary, increased troop risk, and only fueled tensions and added to the instability.

The resistant troops were those who voluntarily joined the National Guard under the impression it would be for a limited scope of service and time. Some of these troops have now been deployed as many as three times and are charging the government with instituting a backdoor draft.[3] They are becoming increasingly bitter and vocal about this situation. The video documentary *The Insurgency* graphically shows an Iraq that has gone from bad to worse to total chaos from 2003 through 2005.[4] By the summer of 2006, soldiers' morale in Iraq was reported to have hit "rock bottom."[5]

> *"Most soldiers would empty their bank accounts just for a plane ticket home," said one recent congressional letter written by an Army soldier now based in Iraq.*[6]

Troop satisfaction or discontent seems to be related to three major factors. One had to do with where the troops had been deployed within Iraq. The second had to do with whether they were reservists or recruits and finally the third had to do with the number of deployments undertaken. For those deployed in Kurdistan or northern Iraq, much more "progress" has been made than in the Sunni Triangle. Those troops who have experienced more such progress appear much less discontented.

Almost every trooper acknowledged the pollution caused by the incessant U.S. bombing of Iraq. They talked about the "air quality monitoring stations" that detected the amount of uranium or, in the words of one trooper, "We checked the radiation levels in the air daily and troops are advised when levels were too high to be outside." He said, "All deployed Americans are very aware of the 'weather stations' used for the purpose of radiation monitoring," and they pay close attention to the reports. Troopers spoke of the polluted water systems and how grateful they were to have bottled water. They mentioned that it was "unfortunate that many Iraqis still [lack] access to consistent clean water sources" three and a half years after the invasion of Iraq.

Some troops blamed the media for the poor perception of what is going on in Iraq, with some saying they wished the media would just stay out of Iraq because they only reported negativity; or, as one trooper reported, he especially "hated Geraldo Rivera of *Fox News* because Geraldo gave the enemy too much information on what we are doing. This made it more dangerous for me and my unit."[7]

Troops felt the Iraqi civil death toll was exaggerated by the media and compared it to the death toll in the state of California. A number of troops said that the military informed them that the California analogy was an accurate comparison. I decided to do some research on this analogy, and found it to be true only if one is solely counting the American casualties and not the Iraqi casualties as well. However, to count only the American casualties would be like only counting a drunk driver when he or she is killed and not all the others that are killed as passengers or victims of a drunk-driving accident. When you include the Iraqis in the death toll and calculate from the start of the war through June of 2006, the average death rate in Iraq is almost 100 times higher than the State of California's rate.[8]

Sadly, no one seems to be thinking about the victims on both sides that are severely injured or impaired for life. Those who have had their limbs blown off or have become blinded or handicapped must be counted in the cost of this war too. According to the HBO video documentary entitled *Baghdad ER*, 17,381 American soldiers had been severely wounded in Iraq as of March 2006. However, another Department of Defense report revealed a much higher tally of 50,508 wounded and diseased veterans as of November 2006.

American Veterans Killed and Wounded – American Contractors Killed in Iraq

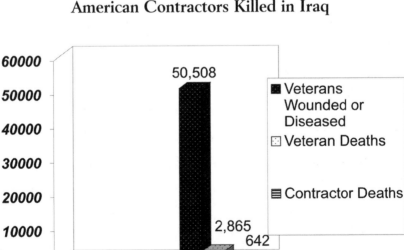

Department of Defense — Nov. 4, 2006 & Associated Press Nov. 20, 2006

No soldiers thought it would be safe to have a surgery performed in any hospital in Iraq because, according to the troops, Iraq is not sanitary enough to provide surgeries nor does it have the needed technology. Injured troops are flown to Germany if they need the services of an acute hospital.[9] The Iraqi hospitals just make do with whatever they can, with many patients dying, according to a 2005 international report entitled "Iraqi Hospitals Ailing under Occupation." The report describes an almost inhumane situation for those who are injured.[10] Those thousands of innocent Iraqi women and children who are victims of the bombings and air strikes are identified by the U.S. as "collateral damage." General Tommy Franks has been quoted as saying, "We don't do body counts," in reference to counting the number of dead Iraqis.[11] Tracking the number of injured Iraqis is even more difficult.

A Flawed Plan

"In the lead up to the Iraq war and its later conduct, I saw, at a minimum, true dereliction, negligence and irresponsibility; at worst, lying, incompetence and corruption."[12]

General Anthony Zinni, retired

Donald Rumsfeld, the former Secretary of the Defense Department, was determined to go to war in Iraq as quickly as possible, with much fewer troops than recommended by the professional military staff. For instance, in March 2003, when asked during two congressional committee meetings, General Eric Shinseki, one of the top ranking generals in the military, said he thought an invasion and occupation of Iraq would require hundreds of thousands of troops. This estimate was echoed throughout the professional military establishment.[13] In fact, the military generals recommended at least 430,000 soldiers and told Donald Rumsfeld that any less would serve as a *"recipe for disaster."*[14] Mr. Rumsfeld dismissed these recommendations, saying publicly that General Shinseki was "far off the mark." Deputy Defense Department Secretary and fellow Neocon Paul Wolfowitz was quoted as saying that General Shinseki was "wildly off the mark," and a senior Pentagon staff member was quoted as stating that military estimates were "bullshit from a Clintonite enamored of using the army for peacekeeping and not winning wars."[15]

One of the most widely respected generals in the military, Anthony Zinni, publicly stated that the war in Iraq was not only the wrong war at the wrong time but also a war with a wrong strategy. General Zinni said the military believed the war in Iraq was unnecessary and that the sanctions imposed upon Saddam Hussein were working effectively to contain him.[16] Another highly respected general, Gregory Newbold, who served as the Joint Chiefs of Staff Director of Operations, left the military in 2002. Before the 2003 invasion of Iraq, he said, "I retired from the military four months before the invasion, in part because of my opposition to those who had used 9/11's tragedy to hijack our security policy."[17]

Generals Zinni, Newbold and Shinseki, as well as other military heavy hitters such as Generals Brent Scowcroft, Norman Schwarzkopf, Wesley Clark, Charles Swannack, John Batiste, and John Riggs have also weighed in. After leaving the military, these highly respected, tenured professionals have gone public regarding their apprehensions related to Iraq and their criticism of Donald Rumsfeld. High-ranking military officers serving under Secretary Rumsfeld have publicly excoriated the former Secretary of Defense for numerous allegations related to multiple leadership failures they found problematic![18] The following charges have been levied against Mr. Rumsfeld by different generals:

The Rush to War and Failure to Plan

- Rumsfeld rushed to war with his own civilian war plan, ignoring the expert, prescribed war plans for Iraq designed by the military. For instance, the professional military staff told Rumsfeld they needed at least seven months to prepare for a war against Iraq. They were given thirty days, and their requests for necessary equipment were ignored or deemed unnecessary.

- There was a lack of sufficiently trained Arabic-speaking Americans who could interpret for the Americans in Iraq. Troops were unable to communicate with Iraqis, causing many fatal mistakes that resulted in anger, fear and distrust on both sides.

- Failure to secure the multiple munitions sites meant that guns and weapons fell into the hands of insurgents and Sunni al-Qaeda. These were later used against U.S. troops.

- The military was at a standstill just after the invasion due to funding shortages for the reconstruction projects. Lack of funding that had been promised to the Iraqis served to create further distrust.

- The shortage of troops continues to be a major problem in the ability of the U.S. to resolve conflicts and maintain any sustainable peace in Iraq.

- Because of the rush to war, the largely publicized body armor required to protect our troops and save American lives was in short supply.

HORRIBLE MISUNDERSTANDING ENSUES

One trooper reported that a tragic incident occurred when a single woman walked out of her village towards the Americans who were sitting in a convoy. The troops started firing their weapons in the air. They yelled at the woman, telling her in English to stop. The woman continued walking towards the troops and a soldier, fearing she might be a suicide bomber, opened fire on her. Within seconds, several other troopers shot at the woman. The troops later discovered that the dead woman had been carrying a white flag.[19]

Alienation of Allies to Rebuild Iraq

- Donald Rumsfeld and the Neocons made it a mission to repudiate the United Nations. They made derogatory allegations and indulged in negative "bashing" designed to discredit the UN when it refused to authorize the preemptive attack on Iraq.
- Rumsfeld and Bush taunted nations with the "You are either with us or against us" remarks, which have now come back to haunt the U.S. when we most need the international community's help to rebuild Iraq.

Having an Outside Agenda

- Former Secretary Rumsfeld and the Neocons had targeted Iraq for invasion before the 9/11 attacks, and thus the war was based upon deception. Remember the 1992 document authored by Wolfowitz that later became the working papers for the Project for a New American Century?
- There were neither connections between Saddam Hussein and al-Qaeda, nor any weapons of mass destruction, leaving the professional military to wonder about the real motives for the invasion of Iraq.

The Shia and Sunni Discord

For many Americans the civil discord in Iraq is hard to understand. Since both Shia and Sunni are branches of Islam, Americans might ask, "Why the conflict?" Recall the conflict between the Catholic and Protestant Irish. Despite the fact that Catholics and Protestants are both Christians, Ireland was torn for years over religious conflicts. Saddam Hussein was a secular Sunni from Iraq, but the Sunni make up only 37 percent of the population (and this includes 17 percent of the Sunni Kurds). It has been reported that the Shia suffered heavy discrimination under Saddam Hussein. After the U.S. toppled Saddam, a predominately Shia government came to power in Iraq, and many Shi'ites apparently took revenge on Sunnis. Not all Shi'ites have been thrilled by the U.S. invasion of Iraq. Moqtada al-Sadr, the young radical Shi'ite cleric, has led a small army in resistance of the U.S. occupation and has proven an influential leader.

Many neighboring countries with Sunni majorities feel obligated to help their fellow Sunnis from attacks by the Shi'ite militias. These countries blame the predominately Shia government for failing to protect the Sunnis. Osama bin Laden and his al-Qaeda followers are Sunnis. Sunni al-Qaeda from Syria and Saudi Arabia have reportedly infiltrated Iraq. Iran was glad to see their long enemy Saddam Hussein banished and the predominately Shi'ites of Iran have a vested interest in seeing a Shia government in Iraq succeed. The Bush Administration singles out Iran for blame. As we will see in subsequent chapters, the U.S. occupation failed to plan for any of these complexities. This chart shows the religious make-up of the countries bordering Iraq:

COUNTRY	PERCENT SUNNI	PERCENT SHIA OR ALEVI	OTHER
Iraq	37%	60%	3%
Syria	75%	14.5%	9.5%
Turkey	74.5%	24.5%	.05%
Iran	10%	85%	5%
Kuwait	58%	33%	9%
Saudia Arabia	76%	13.5%	10.5%
Jordan	80%	15%	5%

Failure to Retain and Reconstitute the Iraqi Military

Since Rumsfeld, along with the Bush Administration, insisted that the U.S. did not need the authorization of the UN, the major burden has fallen on the U.S. to manage the ground conflict after the occupation.[20]

- The "go it alone" attitude, or rather the flimsy "coalition of the willing," has severely impacted the U.S.'s ability to control Iraq.

- Many of the trained Iraqi Military were put into prisons such as Abu Ghraib, leaving the nation in a military vacuum.

- Military experts claim you should create loyalty. The disbanded army of Saddam Hussein should have been used to create peace. Instead of taking over a fully functional and intact Iraqi Military, the U.S. discarded them and in essence armed them with the unsecured caches of weapons. Americans have been forced to organize and retrain the military in addition to defending themselves from "rogue" forces.

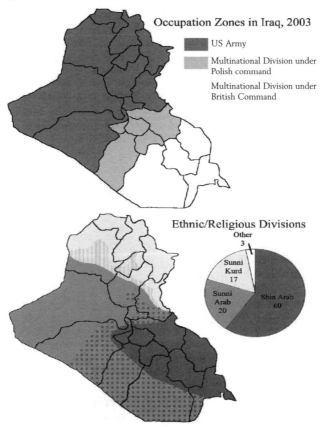

Occupation Zones in Iraq, 2003

US Army

Multinational Division under Polish command

Multinational Division under British Command

Ethnic/Religious Divisions

Other 3

Sunni Kurd 17

Sunni Arab 20

Shia Arab 60

Inability to Quell Civil Disorder

- Mr. Rumsfeld failed to take into consideration the complexity of the citizenry in Iraq. The U.S. Military needed a customized approach for managing the different factions. Instead, Rumsfeld utilized a "one size fits all" approach.

- The inadvertent shooting of innocent civilians by U.S. soldiers and the retaliatory bombing in Fallujah for the murder of American contractors largely exacerbated Iraqi violence.[21]

- The lack of understanding of the cultural differences and the long-held rivalries between segments of Iraqis has fueled anger and distrust of Americans.

- The inability to quickly reinstitute basic services such as water and sewage caused tremendous hardship.

- The "on-and-off" construction, especially of basic services, has inflamed Iraqis who need clean water and electricity for basic living conditions.

- U.S. weapons given to Iraqi security forces are being used against American troops. The U.S. Department of Defense failed to register 97 percent of the weapons handed out in Iraq, and many of those weapons have gone missing. It was reported on October 30, 2006 that insurgents and terrorists may be in possession of thousands of U.S. weapons.

- By 2007 almost all of Iraq is patrolled by U.S. forces solely because virtually all allied forces have been withdrawn. George W. Bush calls for an escalation of American forces in January 2007.

"None of us have seen any good from the Americans.
"Most Americans have a military mindset. They don't
bother to know or learn about our culture or customs.
They have a misinterpretation of Iraqis."[24]

Iraqi citizen

CULTURAL MISUNDERSTANDING
RESULTS IN UNNECESSARY DEATH

An example of not understanding Iraqi customs is exemplified in this incident. It occurred when the U.S. Military set up two zones as checkpoints outside of Baghdad in the spring of 2003. One zone was designated as a green zone and the second as a red zone. When a car arrived at the green zone the first signal made by a trooper was the raising of his fist into the air. This signaled that the driver needed to stop. The second signal was an opened palm sign designed to tell the driver again that he needed to stop. If the driver failed to stop after both hand signals, the troops were ordered to fire arms into the air. If the car reached the red zone, which was only one hundred meters from the green zone, and had still failed to stop, the troops were to shoot inside the vehicle.

A trooper reported that a red Kia did not stop after both hand signals were made and the warning shots given. The troops then fired into the car, killing three of the four occupants. After pulling three dead bodies out of the car, the troops discovered that the driver had somehow miraculously survived. The driver, in shock, cried out at the American soldiers in agony, saying, "Why did you kill my brother? We didn't do anything to you! We're not terrorists! Why did you do this?"[22]

Later the trooper found out that the hand signals the Americans were using had completely different connotations for the Iraqis. The first signal of the raised fist means solidarity and the second signal of the open palm means hello. It is the Iraqi custom to shoot firearms into the air in celebration. The driver of the vehicle thought the Americans were liberators celebrating the new freedom of Iraqis with the signs of solidarity, a hello, and shots of celebration.[23]

Denying that Insurgency Was the Heart of the Opposition to Occupation

- American troops were told that the Iraqis would greet them with open arms, and this did not happen. Secretary Rumsfeld made a grave error in failing to educate the troops in the difference between insurgents and terrorists.[25]

- Insurgents were Iraqi nationals angry over the occupation of Iraq by the U.S. and who have rebelled against U.S. rule.

- Since the U.S. invasion of Iraq, terrorists have infiltrated Iraq from everywhere in the Middle East.

- There was no plan to manage the two different types of problems: the rebellion of the insurgents and the attacks that would later be caused by terrorists entering Iraq via unsecured borders.

MEXICAN FATALITIES SECOND TO AMERICAN TROOPS

It is a little known fact that, besides the death toll of American troops, the next highest number of military fatalities in Iraq is that of Mexican nationals. Despite the fact that Mexico strongly objected to the war in Iraq and is not a member of the coalition forces, Mexicans have been fighting side by side with their American compatriots. In 2002, George W. Bush signed an executive order. He authorized any foreigner who volunteered to fight for the United States in the wars in Iraq and Afghanistan to be given "the fast track towards American citizenship." In spite of that promise, it appears that most Mexican nationals are coming home in body bags.[26]

Failure to Take Recommendations

General Shinseki, along with army officials, was looking to develop a new type of infantry armed with automated and mechanical systems such as the Crusader Mobile Artillery System. This light and easily deployed tank would have saved lives in a ground battle by providing enhanced survivability, lethality and mobility. It would have been much easier to deploy and much more sustainable than current systems.[27] This recommendation was nixed by Rumsfeld. Rumsfeld favored the more expensive but less effective aircraft.

Retaliation

There are numerous accounts of how former Secretary Rumsfeld engaged in retaliation, including one of the most public feuds with former Army Secretary Thomas White. White stood up to Rumsfeld and was adamant about several issues, including the fact that more troops would be needed to stabilize Iraq. When Rumsfeld canceled the Crusader artillery project, White made the debate public. The Army Secretary believed this equipment was critically needed to protect the troops. After the public debate, Rumsfeld asked White to resign.[28]

- Mr. Rumsfeld fired General Baccus from Guantánamo Bay after the general refused to engage in torture practices.

- Lieutenant Commander Charles Swift, a military lawyer, was assigned to defend Salim Hamdan, a Yemeni held in Guantánamo Bay accused of being an al-Qaeda leader. The Bush plan was for Swift to get Salim Hamdan to plead guilty before the Bush military tribunals. Lt. Commander Swift realized the unconstitutionality of his task and how it blatantly violated the Geneva Conventions. For three years he was embroiled in a case that ended up before the Supreme Court. Lt. Commander Swift, a twenty-year veteran, won the court case, but was informed two weeks later that he would not be promoted. Under the Navy's rules, he would be forced to leave the service.

- After coming forth with the photos depicting the prisoner abuse at Abu Ghraib, Donald Rumsfeld unnecessarily broke a pledge of anonymity by divulging the identity of the M.P. who alerted his supervisors to the abuse. Joseph M. Darby's identity was revealed before a congressional committee. Instead of being celebrated for being an American of integrity and honesty, Darby was demonized. A trooper told me that an inside "smear job" was commenced on Darby. The message sent to the troops was if unethical or immoral actions were perpetrated by American soldiers they were to be kept secret amongst the troops. Whistleblowers would be portrayed as traitors and losers. After being "outed" by Rumsfeld, Specialist Darby was dismissed from duty. Following the receipt of numerous death threats, Mr. Darby, his wife and family were forced into secret protective custody.

Replacing Competent Commanders with Less Competent Commanders

In October of 2002, Brigadier General Rick Baccus was relieved from duty as the detention camp commander at Guantánamo Bay because he was "too nice" to the 598 inmates.[29]

Investigations later revealed that General Baccus refused to deviate from both 50 years of U.S. Military practice and the Geneva Conventions to engage in the torture practices foisted upon him by former Secretary Rumsfeld. The consequences for refusing resulted in the firing of General Baccus, and his replacement by Jeffery Miller.[30] Miller, along with behavioral scientists who specialized in human manipulation and exploitation, were brought in to explore cultural phobias, psychological fears and personal vulnerabilities of the prisoners.[31] They would initiate a culture of torture that would infect our troops with violent, non-typical behavior.

Shocked Americans would read newspaper accounts of entire families allegedly murdered in cold blood. They would learn of the rape and murder of an innocent 15 year-old Iraqi girl and the execution of her entire family—a family that most probably witnessed the assault. The body of the girl would be set on fire to hide the hideous deed.

Demanding that Legal Structures Be Stretched

Many legal structures were stretched to accommodate Secretary of Defense Rumsfeld's war in Iraq, but the push for the deviation from the Geneva Conventions will probably be the most problematic.

How a Culture of Torture Was Encouraged

An organizational culture is identified by the shared beliefs, practices and attitudes that characterize an organization. You learn plenty about an organizational culture by how bosses communicate with their employees and in turn how employees communicate with each other and with the public.

Donald Rumsfeld not only sanctioned the use of torture, but he also mandated its use. He created a culture of torture in the U.S. Military. It started in Afghanistan, moved to Guantánamo Bay, and then spread into Iraq. From the beginning, with Rumsfeld at the helm, all signs pointed to Iraq turning into a boiling cauldron of calamity. Rumsfeld personally pushed harder for the institution of torture practices at Guantánamo Bay with prisoners from Afghanistan, and then at Abu Ghraib.

Malcolm Gladwell reminds us in *The Tipping Point* of what can happen when lines become even slightly blurred, as in the example of the early 1970s Stanford University "Power of Context" studies conducted by Philip Zimbardo."[32] In this study it was found that even pacifists who participated in a study emulating guards and prisoners in the basement of the psychology department of the university quickly became more cruel and sadistic as the experiment progressed when they were told to interrogate prisoners. The speed and intensity with which this happened shocked the social scientists observing the experiment. An experiment that was expected to last for two weeks was stopped after only six days because of the rapid escalation of violent behaviors engaged in by the "guards."[33]

Insistence Upon the Use of Torture [34]

- Former Secretary Rumsfeld insisted that military interrogators use more aggressive techniques after the exodus of General Baccus.[35]

- In isolation and far away from public scrutiny, Rumsfeld brought in behavioral scientists to find ways to manipulate the detainees.[36]

- The lines appear to have quickly become blurred as detainees were subjected to long periods of isolation and deprived of food and water.

- The detainees were subjected to twenty-hour interrogations, and individual phobias were exploited as they were humiliated.

- Religious items were removed and the detainees were held shackled in stress positions for four-hour periods.

- During the internal military investigations, a handwritten note by Donald Rumsfeld showed how closely he managed and demanded torture standards; he wrote, "I stand eight to ten hours a day, why only four hours?" The stress positions were then expanded to twenty-four-hour periods.

- Detainees were denied bathroom breaks and left in their excrement for over 24 hours.

- Rumsfeld authorized the use of dogs to terrorize detainees.

- Sexual taunting was used by female officers as they engaged in lap dancing upon the detainees and allegedly touched them inappropriately.[37]

"We are abandoning fifty years of military legal thought.
They [torture policies] are going to get us into trouble.
They are not who we are as a nation."[38]

Senator Lindsay Graham (R-SC)

Rumsfeld misunderstood the nature of al-Qaeda and how each cell oper-ated independently. Most of the prisoners at Guantánamo Bay were indi-viduals swept up in Afghanistan. It appears that the U.S. didn't know if they were legitimate members of al-Qaeda, members of the Taliban, the Muslim Brotherhood, or just people in the wrong place at the wrong time. Supposedly, one of the highest-ranking Guantánamo Bay prisoners was a man who allegedly served as a driver for Osama bin Laden.

Detainees continue to be held at Guantánamo Bay some four and a half years later without being charged and without representation. Only a few have been released. There have been several suicide attempts at Guantánamo Bay. One such attempt in May of 2006 was made by Jumah Dossari, a detainee who spent two years in isolation.[39] Three detainees were successful in their suicide efforts on June 10, 2006 by hanging themselves. In light of the negative publicity, the Department of Defense had long before changed the terminology to classify suicide attempts as "manipulative self-injurious behavior" or SIBs. Prior to changing the terminology, there were forty-one suicide attempts per week. Journalist David Rose noted that six months after the new terminology was insti-tuted, there was an average of two attempts documented per week.[40]

General Swannack is quoted as saying in a telephone interview, "I believe [Rumsfeld] has culpability associated with the Abu Ghraib prison scandal and, so, rather than admitting these mistakes, he continually jus-tifies them to the press..."[41]

George W. Bush was given a choice. He was given two separate legal options — one from the State Department advising against the use of torture, and another from the Justice Department that bent the law to provide a so-called loophole for using torture. The President made his choice. He abandoned international laws and the Geneva Conventions; he chucked valued allies and time-honored treaties. He reversed the effi-cacy of military law and promoted the torture practices instituted within the U.S. Military.

Donald Rumsfeld not only encouraged torture but also insisted upon it by firing those who failed to accommodate his orders. These condi-tions created a culture of torture carried from Guantánamo Bay on to Abu Ghraib. In fact, General Jeffery Miller was sent to the Abu Ghraib prison in Iraq to "Gitmoize" the prison.[42] The findings from one of the twelve investigations, this one led by Army Brig. Gen. Richard P. Formica, found that prisoners had received only bread and water for seventeen days. Other detainees were wedged into cramped cells in huddled positions.

Imagine being hunched over in a cramped and confined space for up to seven days. The cells were so small that the prisoners could neither lie down nor stand up. Loud music played intermittently to disrupt sleep.[43] The investigation found that detainees had been stripped naked, drenched with water and then interrogated in air-conditioned rooms or in cold weather. General Formica reported that members of the Navy Seals had apparently used this specific technique with one detainee who later died after being questioned in a prison in Mosul, Iraq in 2004.[44] However, no specific allegations that the use of the technique was related to that death were documented in the report.[45]

General Formica recommended against personnel discipline, stating that while what occurred was wrong, it was not deliberate abuse. Instead, the general faulted "inadequate policy guidance" rather than "personal failure."

Television broadcast beheadings of coalition forces began shortly after the disclosure of the heinous practices at Abu Ghraib. The culture of terror originating at Guantánamo Bay spread throughout the military, as reported by one official. It was a "wink-wink" atmosphere, according to a number of troops.[46]

Let us never forget the notorious Alberto Gonzales quote that opened the gates leading us to this fetid culture: *"This new paradigm renders obsolete Geneva's strict limitations on questioning enemy prisoners."*[47] This torture culture raised its ugly face in incidents at Haditha, where it was alleged that the U.S. Military, in retaliation for a road bombing, went door to door murdering entire families and then attempted to cover it up.[48] The torture culture once again raised its ugly head when another cover up — of the premeditated rape of a young Iraqi girl and the cold-blooded murder of her entire family — came to light. U.S. citizens and the rest of the world watch in horror on a daily basis as the plight in Iraq continues to unravel.

The Supreme Court ruled on June 29, 2006, with a majority of five justices, that the commissions outlined by Bush in a military order on November 13, 2001 were neither authorized by federal law nor required by military necessity, and ran afoul of the Geneva Conventions.[49] The conventions referred to and defied by the Bush Administration are as follows:[50]

> Persons . . . shall in all circumstances be treated humanely, without any adverse distinction founded on race, color, religion or faith, sex, birth or wealth, or any other similar criteria. To this end, the following acts are and shall remain prohibited at any time and in any place whatsoever with respect to the above-mentioned persons:

1. violence to life and person, in particular murder of all kinds, mutilation, cruel treatment and torture;

2. taking of hostages;

3. outrages upon personal dignity, in particular humiliating and degrading treatment;

4. the passing of sentences and the carrying out of executions without previous judgment pronounced by a regularly constituted court affording all the judicial guarantees which are recognized as indispensable by civilized peoples.

On January 5, 2006, Human Rights First and the ACLU filed a consolidated amended complaint in the civil lawsuit charging Secretary of Defense Donald Rumsfeld with legal responsibility for the torture and abuse of detainees in U.S. Military custody in Afghanistan and Iraq. Unrelenting and repeated calls for Donald Rumsfeld's resignation were made for years. President Bush emphatically insisted to the bitter end that "Secretary Rumsfeld is a really good Secretary of Defense," who has done a "great job."[51] It reminded me of the Enron story shortly before the collapse, when Ken Lay stood by Andy Faust, declaring to the world that Faust was an excellent CFO. Faust later pled guilty to numerous counts of fraud.

> *"I just want to say: Who are we? We are people who have always been for inspections of prisons, for some degree of human rights, and now we're defending neither.... We have now violated everything that we stand for. It is the first time in my life I have been ashamed of my country."*

Nina Totenberg, senior legal correspondent, NPR

Torture Does Not Work

The most important point is the fact that torture as a means to obtain information does not work. Rumsfeld believed that through torture, he would obtain reliable information. Did he? In a special video documentary entitled "The Torture Question" produced by Frontline, it was reported—by individuals including the Republican Senator John McCain from Arizona, a former prisoner of war who was tortured—that torture techniques provided little of value. Senator McCain reported that when he was tortured he provided the enemy with the names of football players from the Green Bay Packers.[52] Several leading experts like Jack Rice, former CIA Special Field Operations, say that torture does not work.[53] Colin Powell, former Secretary of State, wrote a letter to President Bush, explaining, "The world is beginning to doubt the moral basis of our fight against terrorism. To redefine Common Article 3 would add to those doubts. Furthermore it would put our own troops at risk."[54]

Congress Sanctions Torture

"The President wants torture, or a nice euphemism for torture, and all he'll get out of it is made-up information, revenge later against American prisoners, perhaps, and destroying any moral high ground we might still have in the world."

Keith Olbermann, *MSNBC*

Mainstream media paid little attention to the issue of U.S.-sanctioned torture until a split appeared within the Republican Party. Three senators, John McCain (R-AZ), Lindsey Graham (R-SC) and John Warner (R-VA), refused to go along with a 2006 bill proposed by the Bush Administration that included overt violations of the Geneva Conventions.[55] Despite their efforts, these senators failed to break the commitment of the Bush Administration to engage in what it refers to as "alternative methods of interrogation." These methods are deemed "unreliable" and "counterproductive" by virtually all senior officers of the U.S. Military. Most importantly, by engaging in these practices we set a precedent that creates greater danger for Americans who may be captured by hostile combatants.[56]

By caving into the administration's pressure, Republican leaders abandoned their role and duty in government. Since the Republican majority had dominated Congress, they demonstrated a complete inability to provide any counterbalance to the Bush Administration.[57]

The media attempted to distort the caving in by "maverick Republicans" by calling it a compromise. The reality is that there was no compromise. The Republican senators simply gave the Bush Administration the go-ahead to do as it wished with regard to torture.[58]

We Will Not Change Course

The Iraqi government gave the U.S. a deadline for troop withdrawal on June 11, 2006. Jennifer Loven of the Associated Press reported that Iraqi Prime Minister Nouri al-Maliki said Iraqi forces will be capable of controlling security in all of Iraq within eighteen months, meaning that the U.S. can bring our troops home no later than November 2007.[59]

In response, President Bush indicated he would be the decision-maker or, as he prefers to call himself, "the decider" on this matter to determine if it was realistic.[60] In early August of 2006, there were more deaths each day in Iraq than the highly publicized battles between Israel and Hezbollah. Right-wing pundits attempted to put a positive spin on the issue, saying there were fewer U.S. soldiers killed during this period. This was true, but the overall death toll in Iraq, including Iraqi civilians, increased.[61]

The First to Cut and Run

There was a time when those who planned wars were seen at the head of the cavalry, leading the march into battle. This is exactly the opposite of what the Neocon civilian military architects who cooked up the war in Iraq have done. None of these Neocons have been involved in active duty in Iraq. They have called the shots from the safety of their Washington offices and when things began to fall apart, they moved on to bigger and better endeavors. Those in charge of the U.S. Department of Defense, the Pentagon, the Defense Policy Board, and the rebuilding of Iraq are cashing in on this war of choice. For example, Paul Wolfowitz, prime author of the Middle East plan for American imperialism, now heads up the World Bank. The World Bank has a notorious reputation for human rights violations.[62]

The Heritage Foundation's Paul Bremer, who was instrumental in getting the controversial Star Wars program back up and running, was one of the first to cut and run.[63] Military experts charge that Mr. Bremer made a series of poor decisions in Iraq, such as disbanding Saddam's army and imprisoning them, firing thousands of government workers simply because they were members of the Ba'ath Party and shutting down Moqtada al-Sadr's newspaper, thereby making the little known cleric an overnight celebrity. Al-Sadr continues to stir up trouble for the Americans. For these efforts Bremer received the Presidential Medal of Honor and retired in December of 2004.[64]

Other examples include that of John Yoo, who redefined the Geneva Convention torture standards, and Douglas Feith, who have both since "cut and run." Mr. Feith headed the controversial Office of Special Plans at the Pentagon from September 2002 to June of 2003. This defunct intelligence gathering unit stands accused of manipulating intelligence to bolster support for the 2003 U.S. invasion of Iraq. Both Yoo and Feith have taken professorship positions at prestigious universities.

The revolving door at the Bush White House swings both ways. Appointees are supposed to be public servants, but instead they privatize government operations and then leave directly to enjoy the fruits of their efforts.[65] One report revealed that by the summer of 2006, more than ninety Bush appointees had since left the administration for better corporate opportunities. War-mongering Neocons like Richard Perle continue to attempt to cash in on deals they make while sitting on the Defense Policy Board.

Prolific writers from the Project for a New American Century who beat the war drums against Saddam Hussein and Iraq, such as William Kristol and Robert Kagan of the *The Weekly Standard*, are now drumming up support to launch yet another preemptive war against Iran. Again they are using the same scare tactics, "fear of nuclear weapons of mass destruction." Sadly, there still exists a virtually unquestioning media who irresponsibly promulgates such blatant lies every single day by making references to Iran's WMD "program."[66]

The Bush policymakers, men of privilege who never served in the defense of our nation, have been the first to "cut, run and cash in."[67] Dick Cheney, who received five deferments from serving in Vietnam, and George W. Bush, who barely completed his National Guard service, have the audacity to label those who question this war as cowards or as supporters of al-Qaeda. Meanwhile, every aspect of this war has run amok.

"There has been poor strategic thinking... There has been poor operational planning... And to think that we are going to 'stay the course,' the course is headed over Niagara Falls. I think it's time to change course... or at least hold somebody responsible for putting you on this course... because it's been a failure."[68]

General Anthony Zinni

NOTES, Chapter 10

1 Confessions of a trooper suffering from PTSD, on "Iraqi collateral damage." This confession was made with a commitment for complete anonymity.

2 Comment made by a trooper in an interview. The problem was also reported in the 2005 PBS video documentary "Private Warriors."

3 Frank, Nathaniel, "Revolving Door For Troops," July 12, 2004, The Washington Post, www.military-education.org/newsclips/2004_0712_WashPost.pdf.

4 PBS Online, *Frontline: The Insurgency*, www.pbs.org/wgbh/pages/frontline/insurgency/.

5 Scott-Tyson, Ann, "Troop Morale Hits Rock Bottom," *Christian Science Monitor,* August 23, 2006, www.csmonitor.com/2003/0707/p02s01-woiq.html.

6 Ibid.

7 A trooper by the name of Garcia made this statement while we sat in the airport in Las Vegas, NV. While waiting for connections, I asked him if I could interview him. He agreed, as long as I only used one name to identify him.

8 This calculation is made using the absolute lowest number of casualties reported by all entities reporting. At the time it was made, the Iraqi death toll was estimated to be approximately 50,000 since the 2003 invasion. Later, it was discovered that the Iraqi death toll is actually higher.

9 HBO Online, *Baghdad ER*, www.hbo.com/docs/programs/baghdader/index.html.

10 Dahr Jamail, "Iraqi Hospitals Ailing Under Occupation," *Dahr Jamail's MidEast Dispatches*, dahrjamailiraq.com/reports/HealthcareUnderOccupationDahr Jamail.pdf.

11 BBC Online, "Counting the Civilian Cost in Iraq," *BBC News*, June 6, 2005, news.bbc.co.uk/2/hi/middle_east/3672298.stm.

12 CBS Online, "Gen. Zinni: 'They've Screwed Up'," *60 Minutes*, May 21, 2004, www.cbsnews.com/stories/2004/05/21/60minutes/main618896.shtml.

13 Matthew Engel, "Scorned general's tactics proved right, Profile of the army chief sidelined by Rumsfeld," *The Guardian*, March 29, 2003.

14 Ibid.

15 Ibid.

16 CBS Online, "Screwed Up."

17 Thom Shanker, "Third General Wants Rumsfeld Out," *New York Times*, April 10, 2006, www.globalpolicy.org/security/issues/iraq/attack/statement/2006/0410third.htm.

18 CBS Online, "Screwed Up."

19 PBS Online, *Frontline: The Soldier's Heart*, www.pbs.org/wgbh/pages/frontline/shows/heart/.

20 PBS Online, *Frontline: Rumsfeld's War*, www.pbs.org/wgbh/pages/frontline/shows/pentagon/.

21 Andrew Buncombe, "Take them out, dude: pilot toast hit on Iraqi 'civilians'," *The Independent*, October 6, 2004, news.independent.co.uk/world/americas/article27141.ece.

22 Jimmy Massey, "Warrior to War Protestor: From Warriors to Resisters, U.S. Veterans on Terrorism," SOA Watch, 2005 pp. 72-75.

23 Ibid.

24 PBS Online, *Frontline: Beyond Baghdad*, www.pbs.org/wgbh/pages/frontline/shows/beyond.

[25] Ahmed S. Hashim, PhD, "The Sunni Insurgency In Iraq," *Center for Naval Warfare Studies*, August 15, 2003, www.mideasti.org/articles/doc89.html.

[26] John Ross, "Proxy Soldiers in Bush's War: Mexico Fiercely Opposes the Iraq War, But Mexicans Are Dying There Every Week," *La Prensa San Diego*, August 27, 2004, www.laprensa-sandiego.org/archieve/august27-04/proxy.htm.

[27] "Crusader 155mm Self Propelled Howitzer, USA," *Army Technology.com*, www.army-technology.com/projects/crusader/.

[28] USA Online, "Rumsfeld fired Army secretary Thomas White," *USA Today*, April 25, 2003, www.usatoday.com/news/washington/2003-04-25-white-resigns_x.htm.

[29] Julian Borger, " 'Soft' Guantanamo chief ousted," *The Guardian*, October 16, 2002, www.guardian.co.uk/afghanistan/story/0,1284,812647,00.html.

[30] Neil A. Lewis and Eric Schmitt, "Inquiry Finds Abuses at Guantanamo Bay," *New York Times*, May 1, 2005, www.truthout.org/cgi-bin/artman/exec/view.cgi/37/10768.

[31] PBS Online, *Frontline: The Torture Question*, www.pbs.org/wgbh/pages/frontline/torture.

[32] Malcolm Gladwell, *The Tipping Point: How Little Things Can Make a Big Difference* (New York, Little Brown & Co., 2002), pp. 152-3.

[33] Ibid.

[34] "Calls Grow Within American Psychological Association for Ban on Participation in Military Interrogations," *Cageprisoners*, June 17, 2006, www.cageprisoners.com/articles.php?id=14608.

[35] Ibid.

[36] PBS Online, *The Torture Question*.

[37] Lewis and Schmitt, "Inquiry."

[38] Ibid.

[39] Josh White, "Guantanamo Desperation Seen in Suicide Attempts," *The Washington Post*, November 1, 2005, www.washingtonpost.com/wp-dyn/content/article/2005/10/31/AR2005103101987.html.

[40] Ibid.

[41] "Another general joins ranks opposing Rumsfeld," *CNN*, April 14, 2006, www.cnn.com/2006/POLITICS/04/13/iraq.rumsfeld/index.html.

[42] PBS Online, *The Torture Question*.

[43] Eric Schmitt, "Pentagon Study Describes Abuse by Units in Iraq," *New York Times*, June 17, 2006.

[44] Ibid.

[45] Ibid.

[46] Ibid.

[47] Charles Lane, "High Court Rejects Detainee Tribunals," *The Washington Post*, June 30, 2006, www.washingtonpost.com/wp-dyn/content/article/2006/06/29/AR2006062900928.html.

[48] Ellen Knickmeyer, "In Hathida, Memories of a Massacre," *The Washington Post*, May 27, 2006, www.washingtonpost.com/wp-dyn/content/article/2006/05/26/AR2006052602069.html.

[49] Lane, "High Court."

[50] Society of Professional Journalists, *Reference Guide to the Geneva Conventions*, www.genevaconventions.org.

[51] "Bush apologizes for abuse scandal, rejecting call for Rumsfeld's resignation," *People's Daily Online*, May 7, 2004, english.people.com.cn/200405/07/eng20040507_142508.html.

[52] Ibid.

[53] a. MSNBC Online, "Pitfalls of Torture," *Countdown*, www.msnbc.msn.com/id/3036677/.
b. Senator John McCain, "Torture's Terrible Toll," *Newsweek*, November 21, 2005, www.msnbc.msn.com/id/10019179/site/newsweek/.

[54] Frank James, "Gen. Powell opposes Bush tribunals," *Chicago Tribune: The Swamp*, September 14, 2006, newsblogs.chicagotribune.com/ news_the swamp/2006/09/colin_powell_op.html.

[55] Eugene Robinson, "Torture Is Torture: Bush's 'Program' Disgraces All Americans," *The Washington Post*, September 19, 2006, A21, www.washingtonpost.com/wp-dyn/content/article/2006/09/18/AR2006091800995.html.

[56] Dan Froomkin, "Bush Gets His Way," *The Washington Post*, September 22, 2006, www.washingtonpost.com/wp-dyn/content/blog/2006/09/22/BL2006092200703.html.

[57] Ibid.

[58] Ibid.

[59] Jennifer Loven, "Bush Prepares for Summit in Iraq," *Associated Press*, June 11, 2006.

[60] Ibid.

[61] Brent Baker, "NBC's Williams Ignores Declining U.S. Troop Deaths, Highlights Total Iraq 'Death Toll'," *NewsBusters*, August 1, 2006, newsbusters.org/node/6698.

[62] "World Bank support for extractives: complicity in human rights violations," *Mines & Communities*, September 12, 2005, www.minesandcommunities.org/Action/press743.htm.

[63] Bremer served for a short period as the U.S. Ambassador to Iraq.

[64] "Presidential Medal of Freedom Recipient L. Paul Bremer," *Medal of Freedom*, December 2, 2004, www.medaloffreedom.com/PaulBremer.htm.

[65] Kyle Pope, "Goldman Sachs Rules the World," *The Los Angeles Times*, June 4, 2006, www.latimes.com/news/printedition/suncommentary/la-op-pope4jun04,1,3092145.story?coll=la-headlines-suncomment.

[66] a. World Tribune.com, "Syria agrees to hide Iran weapons," *The World Tribune*, December 20, 2005, www.worldtribune.com/worldtribune/WTARC/2005/me_syria_12_19.html.
b. USA Online, "U.S. bans transactions with 4 Chinese companies for aiding Iran weapons programs," *USA Today*, June 13, 2006, www.usatoday.com/news/washington/2006-06-13-sanctions_x.htm
c. FOX Online, "Treasury Head Speaks Out on Terror Funds," *FOX News*, September 18, 2006, www.foxnews.com/wires/2006Sep18/0,4670,Paulson TerrorFinancing,00.html.

[67] With the exception of Donald Rumsfeld, who did serve in the U.S. Military, but appears to have found ways to cash in while in the public service.

[68] CBS Online, "Screwed Up."

★ 11 ★

The Cost of Dissent

"It's the recklessness at the top of our government, not the press'
exposure of it, that has truly aided the enemy, put American lives
at risk and potentially sabotaged national security."

Frank Rich

THE BUSH ADMINISTRATION STRONGLY EMPHASIZED that any dissent to
their policies would be considered as near an act of treason as one
could possibly perpetrate. They sent a message to the American
public emphasizing that to question or oppose the policies of Bush and
Cheney would only aid the enemy. Vice President Dick Cheney has
gone as far as calling politicians who question the administration's policies "supporters of so-called al-Qaeda types."[1] In an August 2006
speech, Mr. Cheney referred to Connecticut voters as terrorists because
they sought a political alternative to "staying the course." Democratic
voters chose anti-war senatorial candidate Ned Lamont over incumbent
Joe Lieberman in the 2006 primary.[2]

The trust that Congress and the American public put in this administration has been manipulated. In a nation fighting for "freedom" abroad,
Americans are witnessing countless casualties of those freedoms at home.
Americans have found themselves in painful positions for speaking out,
writing and making comments of dissent against the Bush Administration.
They have found themselves ridiculed, shamed, humiliated, banned, fired
from their jobs, and voted out of office. Many have been quickly silenced
through a variety of means.

I was shocked to read a 2006 story in *The New Mexican*, our local newspaper, about an area nurse who was under investigation for sedition. Sedition is defined by the *Encarta* dictionary as "actions or words intended to provoke or incite a rebellion against the government."[3] The editor of *The New Mexican* described the incident as one in which the nurse, who worked in the Behavioral Health Unit of the Veterans Administration in Albuquerque, had written an editorial letter to *The Alibi*, an Albuquerque weekly and online newspaper.[4]

The nurse, Laura Berg, worked daily with veterans returning from Iraq. She was upset about the war in Iraq, Hurricane Katrina and the Bush Administration, and she wrote a scathing commentary entitled "Wake Up and Get Real." In the letter, she points out the incompetence of the Bush Administration in its response to Katrina by saying, "Bush and his team partied and delayed while millions of people were displaced, hundreds of thousands were abandoned to a living hell. Thousands more died of drowning, dehydration, hunger, and exposure; most bodies remain unburied and rotting in attics and floodwater."[5] Ms. Berg lamented the sums of money going to Iraq while cities like New Orleans that had long been in need of repair were ignored. Concerning the returning war veterans, she wrote, "As a VA nurse working with returning OIF vets, I know the public has no sense of the additional devastating human and financial costs of post-traumatic stress disorder; now spreading their pain, anger and isolation through family and communities . . . ."[6] Then Ms. Berg wrote, "Bush, Cheney, Chertoff, Brown, and Rice should be tried for criminal negligence. This country needs to get out of Iraq now and return to our original vision and priorities of caring for land and people and resources rather than killing for oil."[7] The letter was critically sharp. However, I question the degree of consternation that followed.

Two weeks after the letter was published, Ms. Berg became the object of a federal investigation. The federal government charged her with sedition. Her computer at work was confiscated by government officials, and the contents of her hard drive were examined. She received a formal letter from the Veterans Administration stating that she was being investigated for her call to overthrow the Bush Administration.[8]

First and foremost, Ms. Berg's letter was an example of an ordinary frustrated U.S. citizen "blowing off some steam" by using one of the great American privileges of freedom of speech. Ms. Berg was exercising her right of free speech to criticize the government. It was not a call to overthrow the government, but rather a call to hold specific members of the Bush Administration accountable. Secondly, Ms. Berg had not written this letter on her work computer, but that seemed to matter little. A terrified Ms. Berg sought legal counsel through the American Civil Liberties Union. The ACLU took the case, which was later dropped.

The shock of the story reverberated throughout the state of New Mexico, and an editorial in my local newspaper said it was hoped that this reaction from the U.S. government was an isolated incident. The editor advocated that those who dissent should not have to face intimidation. However, at a dinner party in May 2006, a physician from Ithaca, New York told us about a priest who had been imprisoned for staging a demonstration at an army camp near his hometown.[9]

It is probably true that we do not know the extent of the government's efforts toward silencing or intimidating average citizens like Laura Berg. We have, however, witnessed what has happened to public figures that have spoken out against the Bush Administration.

Back to the Yellowcake — One of the Most Public Dissenters

Recall the story of the debunked yellowcake uranium allegations discussed in "Spin, Baby, Spin." Former State Department official Ambassador Joseph Wilson had investigated the allegations that Iraq was seeking to purchase uranium from Niger. He provided written reports to both the CIA and the State Department. Ambassador Wilson was concerned because President Bush and the Vice President continued to publicly make these allegations despite the fact that they had been told repeatedly that the allegations were unproven.

Therefore, on July 6, 2003, in an attempt to stop the administration from using false allegations, Ambassador Wilson wrote an opinion editorial that was published by both the *New York Times* and *The Washington Post* entitled "What I Didn't Find in Africa." In the op-ed, Mr. Wilson provided a detailed account of the mission he undertook to determine the validity of the allegations against Iraq. He stated that:

1. Niger's government officials confirmed they knew the allegations;

2. In reports to Washington, the Nigerian government had already debunked the rumors of any uranium sales to Iraq;

3. Through interviews from all parties alleged to have been involved, he had verification that Iraqi agents never attempted to buy yellowcake from government officials in Niger;

4. Any such transaction was most unlikely because of the tight oversight and close-knit nature of the community from which a sale would have transpired.

Mr. Wilson publicly and openly asked:

1. Had his Niger Mission Report been provided to the President? If so, was the report fully understood?
2. Was the information ignored because it did not fit certain preconceptions about Iraq?
3. Did the U.S. go to war under false pretenses?
4. Did the Bush Administration manipulate intelligence concerning Saddam Hussein's weapons of mass destruction program?
5. Did the Bush Administration exaggerate the threat of Iraq?

Mr. Wilson ended his editorial with these words: "America's foreign policy depends on the sanctity of its information. For this reason, questioning the selective use of intelligence to justify the war in Iraq is neither idle sniping nor 'revisionist history' as Mr. Bush has suggested. The act of war is the last option of a democracy, taken when there is a grave threat to our national security. More than 200 American soldiers have lost their lives in Iraq already. We have a duty to ensure that their sacrifice came for the right reasons."[10]

Agent Valerie Plame Pays the Price

In what appeared to be retaliation for the op-ed letter written by Ambassador Wilson, his wife's name appeared in the weekly column by conservative Robert Novak. Two weeks after the op-ed was published, Mr. Novak wrote, "Wilson never worked for the CIA, but his wife, Valerie Plame, is an agency operative on weapons of mass destruction. Two senior administration officials told me Wilson's wife suggested sending him to Niger to investigate the Italian report. The CIA says its counter-proliferation officials selected Wilson and asked his wife to contact him."[11] On Sept. 28, 2003, *The Washington Post* reported, "... two top White House officials called at least six Washington journalists and disclosed the identity and occupation of Wilson's wife."[12]

Three days after the Novak Column appeared, Dave Corn, editor of *The Nation* magazine, asked in an article entitled "A White House Smear," "Did senior Bush officials blow the cover of a U.S. intelligence officer working covertly in a field of vital importance to national security — and break the law—in order to strike at a Bush Administration critic and intimidate others?"[13]

These reports continued *ad nauseam* with more journalists allegedly receiving the same telephone calls from White House officials. A cat-and-mouse game of who-knew-what-and-when and who-told-whom-what went on for months, and then years. The outing itself would become the topic of a national debate.

After many belabored efforts and much pressure from Democrats, a special council was appointed to investigate the leak. The leak came from a close circle around the President. Vice President Dick Cheney had made handwritten notes on the Novak article and his scribbled comments were made public by Special Investigator Patrick Fitzgerald. The "Turd Blossom," White House strategist Karl Rove, was called to testify at least five times before a grand jury.

On October 28, 2005, Scooter Libby, Chief of Staff to Vice President Cheney, was indicted on charges of obstruction of justice, false statement and perjury. The indictment was for lying about how he obtained and disclosed then-classified information concerning the CIA's employment of Valerie Plame to reporters.

Libby was later charged and indicted on five counts by a federal grand jury.[14] To date, no one has been charged with leaking the information on Ms. Plame as a CIA agent, a crime that can include a fine of $50,000, imprisonment of up to ten years, or both.

The Valerie Plame outing served as a distraction from the Wilson report on Niger and the denial of the yellowcake uranium allegations, which the Bush Administration used to justify the war in Iraq. The more important Wilson Report and op-ed story were buried under the CIA outing hoopla.

What Happens to Public Dissenters

There are many brave men and women who have stood up to the Bush Administration to voice dissent. Their actions have had consequences. Here are examples of eight public dissenters. Review the messages they delivered, examine the White House reaction to their messages, and evaluate the price they have paid for their dissent. I have selected two government officials, Paul O'Neill and Richard Clark; two journalists, Dan Rather and Dana Priest; two celebrities, The Dixie Chicks and George Clooney; and two elected officials, Representatives John Murtha and Cynthia McKinney.

Paul O'Neill, Former U.S. Treasury Secretary
Retired Chairman and CEO of Alcoa

Paul O'Neill is the outspoken former U.S. Secretary of the Treasury. It was reported that Mr. O'Neill had been pulled out of retirement by Alan Greenspan, who recruited O'Neill specifically for the Secretary of the Treasury position. Mr. O'Neill had been the competent head of many successful endeavors, including the past CEO of ALCOA Corporation. He was known as a savvy businessman and a fiscal conservative.

Paul O'Neill claimed that within eight days of his taking office in early January 2001, George W. Bush discussed targeting Saddam Hussein and regime change in Iraq. And according to O'Neill, the real discussion lead by Vice President Cheney revolved around the oil contracts in Iraq and who would get the contracts.[15] O'Neill describes the great tension between himself and Vice President Cheney. He charged that Bush's economic policies were irresponsible and would have a negative impact on future generations and programs like social security. He was concerned about the U.S. budget going from a surplus to a deficit, and he warned of the consequences of raising the debt ceiling. According to Mr. O'Neill, his warnings fell on deaf ears because Cheney and Rove were calling the shots. He says Vice President Cheney never cared about budget deficits. O'Neill was against the Bush tax cuts; and he had fiscal concerns about the wars in Iraq and Afghanistan, and their slowing down the economy. But these were concerns the Bush Administration didn't want to hear.

Mr. O'Neill charges that George W. Bush was asleep at the wheel, lacking an inquisitive nature and "like a blind man in a roomful of deaf people." He said George W. Bush's habit of giving people nicknames was a form of bullying.[16]

After being forced out of the Bush White House, Mr. O'Neill became one of the first to criticize President Bush and the administration. More critical details followed in a book by Ron Suskind entitled *The Price of Loyalty: George W. Bush, the White House, and the Education of Paul O'Neill*.[17]

The Bush Administration charged that Secretary O'Neill's allegations were nothing more than sour grapes. They suggested that his ideas were "wacky." Former Republican Senator Bob Dole said that Mr. O'Neill simply wanted to sell books in order to get back at the administration for being fired.[18]

"... at the first National Security Meeting ... they discussed invading Iraq, and two days later they discussed the post-Saddam regime, including who wants oil contracts and where oil might be." [19]

Paul O'Neill

Richard A. Clark, Former Czar on Terrorism
Counter Terrorism Advisor to Presidents Reagan, George H.W. Bush, Bill Clinton, and George W. Bush

Richard A. Clark was the most prominent member of the government involved in overseeing the problems associated with terrorism. For thirty years he was responsible for advising Presidents and top-level cabinet members. Mr. Clark served as a Senior Executive Service Advisor to Presidents Reagan, George H.W. Bush, Bill Clinton, and George W. Bush.[20] He was the only government official to apologize publicly for the failure to keep our nation safe against terrorism. He told the 9/11 Commission that he had failed our nation, and for that he was deeply sorry. He also said that President Bush and the Bush Administration had failed the nation.[21]

Mr. Clark resigned from his position in January of 2003. Subsequently, he wrote the book *Against All Enemies: Inside America's War on Terror.*[22] In his book, Mr. Clark says that the Bush Administration failed to take terrorism and al-Qaeda seriously, and that Condoleezza Rice was skeptical about al-Qaeda threats in early 2001. Rice was so skeptical that she blocked Richard Clark's access to President Bush and other key decision makers. According to Mr. Clark, his requests to the Bush Administration to make terrorism a top priority were met with apathy and procrastination. He says the administration was so in the dark that Deputy Defense Secretary Paul Wolfowitz had asked what "all the fuss was about Osama bin Laden" before the 9/11 attacks.

Mr. Clark reports that after the terrorist attacks on New York and Washington, the Bush Administration turned their attention immediately to Iraq, a nation not involved in the attacks, and that George W. Bush continues to be fixated on Iraq to this day. Clark believes that taking a unilateral approach in Iraq would lead to more attacks on Americans and American interests worldwide in the future.

Both President George H.W. Bush's failure to eliminate Saddam Hussein in 1991 and the American presence in Saudi Arabia increased anti-American sentiment in the Middle East, according to Mr. Clark. He says terrorism was a growing threat under the presidency of George H.W. Bush but it went ignored, despite the best efforts of Clark as the former Czar on Terrorism. And it was those ignored and yet inflamed sentiments that lead to the 9/11 attacks. Mr. Clark charges that the George W. Bush Administration didn't get it before 9/11 and still doesn't get it.

Richard Clark says he believes that President Clinton understood the gravity of terrorism and was obsessed with stopping al-Qaeda. But President Clinton was unable to do so because of political infighting and the sex scandal leading to his impeachment.

Vice President Cheney made the following statements about Richard Clark: "Clark is an uninformed underling.... he wasn't in the loop, frankly, on a lot of this stuff. He was head of counterterrorism for several years...and I didn't notice that they had any great success dealing with the terrorist threat."[23] Scott McClellan, former Press Secretary for the White House, said that Mr. Clark was bitter about not getting a position in the Homeland Security Department, and accused Mr. Clark of playing politics instead of being concerned with terrorism. Soon after Richard Clark's book was released, Condoleezza Rice appeared on almost all the television networks to disparage his work and to question his effectiveness.[24]

> *"I find it outrageous that the President [Bush] is running for re-election on the grounds that he's done such great things about terrorism....He ignored terrorism for months, when maybe we could have done something to stop 9/11."*

Richard Clark[25]

Dan Rather, CBS Evening News Anchor, "60 Minutes Contributor"

Dan Rather was a respected journalist for forty-four years, one whom the public trusted for accurate reporting. When the battle for the Presidency ended in a 2000 Supreme Court ruling, Rather reported, "A sharply split and, some say, politically and ideologically motivated U.S. Supreme Court ended Vice President Gore's contest [in the Florida election]."[26] Americans should remember that when the Supreme Court ordered the Florida vote recount stopped, George W. Bush was ahead by less than 600 votes. Al Gore had won the popular vote across the U.S., and there were numerous questions concerning the validity of the Florida win for George W. Bush. Charges of conflict of interests, poorly designed ballots, disenfranchised voters, and discounted or lost votes were all factors in the election's questionable nature. The fact that George W. Bush's brother, Jeb Bush, was Florida's governor and a controversial and staunchly Republican Florida Secretary of State provided additional fodder for a contentious fight to the bitter end. For many, the view was that George W. Bush did not win the Presidency, but rather the Supreme Court awarded him the Presidency.

Mr. Rather remained critically vigilant as he kept a close eye on the Bush Administration. On the CBS *Evening News* in January 2001, he reported, "Many in the Bush Cabinet and other top posts have two things in common: they're multimillionaires and many hold stock in companies affected by federal action."[27] Mr. Rather tried to expose the controversial appointees of the Bush Administration by pointing out their various conflicts of interests.[28]

When George W. Bush was promoting another round of tax cuts, Mr. Rather stated, "President Bush tonight outlines his cut-federal-programs-to-get-a-tax-cut plan to Congress and the nation. Democrats . . . say Mr. Bush's ideas are risky business, endangering among other things, Social Security and Medicare."[29]

And when the deficit was rising, Mr. Rather reported, "The red ink keeps rising. The Medicare overhaul and prescription drug benefit haven't taken effect yet and President Bush is already upping the ten-year price tag. First pegged at $400 billion, the *Associated Press* says the new estimate is $540 billion."

Mr. Rather provided a frank report on the war in Iraq and the difficulty Americans were having in finding good paying jobs. On the March 31, 2004 evening news, he rhetorically asked, "What drives American civilians to risk death in Iraq? In this economy, it may be, for some, the only job they can find."

Mr. Rather accurately reported on the civil discontent in Iraq, saying, "In Najaf, the militant Shiite cleric al-Sadr echoed the refrain [that] Iraq could become, quote, 'another Vietnam' for America."[30] And, when reporting on torture, Mr. Rather brought the photographic evidence of Iraqi prisoner abuse to the attention of Americans through a special CBS *60 Minutes* investigative documentary. He raised the question to George W. Bush: would he "fire Defense Secretary Rumsfeld?"[31]

When reporting on the 9/11 Commission, Mr. Rather reminded Americans that the families of the 9/11 victims had to pressure the Bush Administration before it finally agreed to form an independent commission. And only under additional duress did the President finally agree to appear before the commission, albeit ". . . under his ground rules, on his ground. At the President's insistence, it was a joint appearance with the Vice President behind the closed doors of the Oval Office and there was no audio or video recording and no full written transcript."[32]

Mr. Rather attempted to depict the abuses of Halliburton, reporting, "The FBI has revealed that it is expanding its investigation into how the Halliburton Company billed taxpayers for its contract work in Iraq. The FBI will now include a criminal investigation of how the Bush Administration awarded Halliburton those no-bid contracts in the first place and whether there was any insider favoritism."[33]

Prior to the 2004 elections, Mr. Rather aired a story that covered what appeared to be the preferential treatment George W. Bush received while in the U.S. National Guard and how he might have neglected his military commitments. The story was factual and corroborated, but forged documents allegedly planted by the "Turd Blossom" derailed the story. The newscast created an enormous brouhaha. Critics of the newscast chose to focus only on a questionable document rather than on the content of the story, which has not yet been proven wrong.

Soon thereafter, Mr. Rather announced his retirement. Marla Maples, the producer of the George W. Bush National Guard story, was fired along with three other employees from CBS.[34] I believe when the Bush White House finally brought down Dan Rather, it sent ripples through the U.S. media. The message sent was that if you criticized this administration, *you would pay a price.* Dan Rather reported the news with precision and accuracy, and for these reasons he was targeted.

"...there was a time, in South Africa, where people would put flaming tires around peoples' necks if they dissented. And in some ways, the fear is that you'll be necklaced here, you'll have the flaming tire of lack of patriotism put around your neck. Now it's that fear that keeps journalists from asking the toughest of the tough questions and to continue to bore in on the tough questions so often. And again, I'm humbled to say, I do not except myself from this criticism."

Dan Rather, *BBC's Newsnight* program, May 16, 2002

Dana Priest
Author and Pulitzer Prize-Winning Journalist
Washington Post Staff Writer

Dana Priest is a writer for *The Washington Post*. In 2003, she authored the book *The Mission: Waging War and Keeping Peace with America's Military*. Ms. Priest has covered news about the U.S. Intelligence community for many years, and she believes in providing analytical judgments supported by facts.

In her 2006 investigative reports, Ms. Priest revealed that a covert U.S. program allowed the CIA to capture al-Qaeda suspects and keep them in secret prisons abroad. She discovered that these secret facilities had been set up by the Bush Administration and had been in operation for four years in eight countries, including Thailand, Afghanistan and others in Eastern Europe.[35] She concluded that nothing was known about these facilities, the interrogation methods used or the length of time detainees were to be held. She further revealed the fact that there appeared to be no congressional oversight of these facilities.[36]

Ms. Priest described the CIA use of torture techniques that are forbidden by international treaties including the Geneva Conventions.[37] She reported that an uncooperative Afghan youth was detained, stripped naked, beaten, and bruised all while he was under the supervision of the CIA. The young man was found frozen to death after he was chained to a concrete floor and left overnight without blankets.[38]

Ms. Priest described the wrongful imprisonment of Khaled Masri, a German citizen who was held for five months. She detailed how a CIA request was made to the German government asking them not to disclose the wrongful imprisonment for fear of potential legal challenges. According to Ms. Priest, detainees may be captured and held on speculative or weak evidence.[39]

Immediately, the Bush Administration reframed the secret prison story, choosing to focus instead on Ms. Priest personally, the *New York Times* and executives of the papers who broke the story. The story was referred to as a "leak" by the administration, and Americans became distracted by a public debate on freedom of the press. This tactic allowed the administration to avoid any legal analysis of the policies of capturing suspects under flimsy circumstances, holding them in secret prisons, using prohibited interrogation tactics, and withholding information from congressional oversight.

The President called the story "disgraceful," and a coordinated White House assault was made on the *New York Times* for publishing it.

Statements made by various journalists included: "The White House escalated what amounts to a shame campaign against one of the nation's most prominent newspapers, the *New York Times...*" and, "The Bush Administration has decided that it's a better political strategy to shoot the messenger."[40] Dick Cheney was quoted as saying, "The *New York Times* has now made it more difficult for us to prevent attacks in the future."[41] President Bush said, "For a newspaper to publish [this story] does great harm to the United States of America." Treasury Secretary John Snow insisted it was "... irresponsible and harmful reporting." And talk show host Scott Hennen referred to the *New York Times* as "a terrorist tip sheet."[42]

Ms. Priest was forced to testify before several congressional committees to determine if she had broken any laws. *The Washington Post* reported on April 21, 2006 that Mary McCarthy, a CIA employee, was fired for allegedly leaking classified information to Ms. Priest and other journalists.[43]

> *"The congressional oversight of intelligence is the weakest leg of the stool. Too many times, in my experience, members either don't want to know, are afraid to push for answers or don't understand the details and implications of programs. Also, of course, the White House has chosen to brief just the chair and ranking members of the committees, without staff, on the most controversial programs."*
>
> Dana Priest[44]

Natalie Maines, Lead Singer, Dixie Chicks
#1 Song and Album in the U.S. in March 2003

Like many in America, I had never heard of the Dixie Chicks before Natalie Maines, their lead singer, made her infamous remarks about George W. Bush. In front of a live London audience on the eve of the U.S.-led invasion of Iraq in March 2003, Ms. Maines said, "Just so you know, we're ashamed the President of the United States is from Texas." The audience went wild, applauding enthusiastically.

The Dixie Chicks are a trio of all-American women who play country music. They were touring overseas in the spring of 2003 but were still following the news accounts of the U.S.'s preemptive attack on Iraq. They watched the anti-American sentiment grow and became concerned. They were quoted as saying they believed that President Bush was "ignoring the opinions of many in the U.S. and alienating the rest of the world." Ms. Maines held that her comments were made in frustration, and she pointed out that "one of the privileges of being an American is you are free to voice your own point of view." The band vowed that they supported the U.S. troops, but were frightened because a war with Iraq meant the loss of innocent lives including those of American soldiers.[45]

Immediately after Natalie Maines made her anti-Bush comment, it was splashed across American newspapers and news programs. An acidic reaction was instant as country radio stations called for a boycott of the Dixie Chicks. Outraged radio DJs and inflamed patrons called for the ban of Dixie Chicks music, and one station sponsored a trash party where people were encouraged to dump Dixie Chicks CDs in the garbage. DJs also invited patrons to a "chicken toss", asking fans to throw away tickets previously purchased for Dixie Chicks concerts. "Natalie Maines is not paid to espouse her ideas on stage," said one DJ, and President George W. Bush called Natalie Maines "dumb."[46] Within days of Ms. Maines' comment, 29 percent of country stations refused to play the Dixie Chicks and their music sales plummeted by 42 percent.[47]

George Clooney
Actor, Academy Award Winner, and Film Director

George Clooney has been an outspoken critic of the Bush Administration for a number of reasons, but his initial criticism was over the war in Iraq. He was quoted, "In 2003, a lot of us were saying, where is the link between Saddam and bin Laden? What does Iraq have to do with 9/11? We knew it was bullshit."[48] He also said, "we moved away from what we were going after, which was the al-Qaeda, and there's no connection between al-Qaeda and Iraq, which we know, but we spent a lot of time trying to prove it...And we're going to go into a war and we're going to kill a lot of innocent people."[49]

Mr. Clooney understood the tactics the Bush Administration was employing and how they were attempting to muzzle dissenters. He said, "Dissent is not disloyalty."[50] He continued by saying, "We have to agree that it's not unpatriotic to hold our leaders accountable and to speak out."[51] He has encouraged Americans to feel free to ask questions and to hold the Bush Administration and Congress accountable for the actions they have taken on behalf of our nation. He further maintains, "One of the things we absolutely need to agree on is the idea that we're all allowed to question authority."[52]

George Clooney has used his talents to bring consciousness to important matters we face in America. His Academy Award-winning film *Good Night and Good Luck* reminds us of the courage of Edward R. Murrow. Mr. Murrow was considered one of the greatest American news journalists. He was noted for his honesty and integrity in delivering the news. In 1954, Mr. Murrow produced a series of television news reports that helped lead to the censure of Senator Joseph McCarthy. Senator McCarthy (R-WI) made reckless, baseless accusations against innocent Americans, charging them as Communists or Soviet spies. After Mr. Murrow exposed Mr. McCarthy, he accused Murrow of being a Communist. Another film by Clooney is *Syriana*, a fictional work that depicts how conflicts arise over the control of oil, arms, money, and loyalties.

Mr. Clooney has been denounced as a traitor and his picture was one in a deck of cards dubbed the *United Nations of Weasels*.[53] An online campaign was launched to boycott Clooney.[54] Bill O'Reilly of *Fox News* charged George Clooney with being "mean-spirited" and a "mudslinger."[55] George Clooney remains a critic of the Bush Administration, challenging the U.S. government to become active in preventing the genocide in Darfur. Clooney brings attention to the ongoing human rights battle in Sudan and the U.S.'s failure to address this battle.

> *"I am a liberal. And I make no apologies for it. Hell,*
> *I'm proud of it. Too many people run away from*
> *the label...like it's a dirty word."*[56]

George Clooney

Representative John Murtha (D-PA)
Retired Marine Corps Reserve Colonel, Decorated Vietnam Veteran

Members of the Bush Administration and some Republican congressional members have attempted to discredit military veteran John Murtha by calling him a "chicken." The Bush Administration has proven its ability to successfully discredit veterans using such tactics.[57] John Murtha proudly served America as a member of the U.S. Marines for thirty-seven years. He is a decorated war veteran who comes from a family of veterans, including his father, brothers and uncles. Representative Murtha was a staunch supporter of George H.W. Bush's Gulf War in 1991, and he has always been considered a hawkish Democrat in military matters.

As a strong supporter of the military, Mr. Murtha visits wounded troops at Bethesda and Walter Reed hospitals regularly, and has been doing so since the beginning of the war in 2003. He says American troops were at a disadvantage because they were rushed into war with insufficient manpower and equipment. Not having the body armor needed for protection against the physical devastation caused by IED explosions has deeply affected troop morale, Mr. Murtha reported. Additionally, troops have returned only to discover their homes ravaged by hurricanes.[58] Many troops have complained to him about being deployed two and three times and the hardships related to leaving their families behind without a solid network of support.[59]

Mr. Murtha discovered that the U.S. armed forces in Iraq lacked body armor. He also revealed the need for "jammers" to help protect U.S. troops against IEDs. He helped to secure funding for needed equipment. He publicized his concerns related to inadequate troop levels in Iraq and brought attention to the fact that the Humvees used in Iraq were not up to par. He emphasized that the situation in Iraq continues to grow worse with the number of incidents climbing higher on a monthly basis. He cited increasing incidents, "from 16 to 19 to 45 to 75 to over 100 per month."[60]

Mr. Murtha pointed out that Donald Rumsfeld, the Former Secretary of Defense, was responsible for the quagmire in Iraq, and he asked where the responsibility and accountability for Iraq lies. He charged that the Bush Administration provides nothing more than political rhetoric to solve the problems in Iraq, failing to come up with "real solutions." Yet, the administration attacks those who come up with alternative resolutions. Mr. Murtha says the American public has long grown weary of supporting the multi-billion dollar war in Iraq. He believes the U.S. cannot win militarily because American troops are caught in the middle of a civil war. He has indicated it is time to begin bringing U.S. troops home.

Larry Bailey, a retired Navy captain, declared he would do his "best to 'swift boat' John Murtha," and Craig Minnick called Representative Murtha "irresponsible and un-American." Vice President Dick Cheney, who never served in the U.S. Military and received five deferments to avoid going to Vietnam, made the following insinuation while referring to John Murtha: "Certain politicians are losing backbone," and "Murtha has lost all perspective."[61] Former Speaker Newt Gingrich said he hoped Congress would censure Murtha for his comments. The conservative *Pittsburgh Tribune Review* wrote, "It is time for Congressman John Murtha to take a time out from criticizing our military, protecting the terrorists and worrying about world opinion."[62]

"Rhetoric does not solve the problem. We need a plan.
It's not enough to say 'stay the course'." [63]

Representative John Murtha

Cynthia McKinney
Former Representative 4th District, Atlanta, Georgia

The former representative from Georgia is known for her feisty and highly critical style. She has been voted out of office twice and she is equally scathing in her criticism of both Democrats and Republicans alike. As with the Dixie Chicks, I had never heard of Representative McKinney until researching this project. I'd like to start the story of Ms. McKinney by describing a radio interview that was conducted on March 25, 2002. Representative McKinney was a guest on *Flashpoints*, an independent radio program produced and hosted by Dennis Bernstein. The program is broadcast from Berkeley, California on Pacifica station KPFA. During the course of the thirty-minute radio interview, Representative McKinney stated that the "American people deserve a full, complete and no-holds-barred investigation of the events involving 9/11, and what the Bush Administration knew and when they knew it."[64]

Shortly, after the radio interview, Juliet Eilperin, a *Washington Post* staff writer, wrote an article entitled, "Democrat Implies Sept. 11 Administration Plot." Immediately after *The Washington Post* article, Ms. McKinney was tagged "crazy" and "treacherous."[65] White House Press Secretary Scott McLellan responded, "The American people know the facts, and they dismiss such ludicrous, baseless views." An article by Jonah Goldberg posted on the *National Review* entitled *Representative Awful* stated, "...the congresswoman is suffering paranoid, America-hating, crypto-Marxist conspiratorial delusions."[66] Mr. Goldberg insulted Ms. McKinney by saying, "[She] is dumber than rock salt and more repugnant than Yasser Arafat's three-week-old underwear."[67] In addition, he called her "dangerous and irresponsible." Cynthia McKinney lost her congressional seat in 2002, but fought back to reclaim it once again in 2004.

Once back in Congress, she continued to ask tough questions and demand answers. She asked about the purported warnings that were received from several foreign governments related to the 9/11 attacks. She asked if it was possible that these warnings were ignored. She called for an investigation of the unusually large profits made on 9/11 involving several airlines, brokerages and insurance firms. She wanted to determine the nature of the relationship between the oil company Unocal and the Taliban rulers of Afghanistan.[65] Ms. McKinney asked for information on the relationship between the Bush Administration and the Carlyle Group. The Carlyle Group is an investment firm with major defense holdings for whom George H.W. Bush worked.

Ms. McKinney wanted to find out if the President and the Vice President hampered the 9/11 investigations. She recommended an investigation of the profits made by those defense corporations with ties to the administration.[69] She also held hearings for disgruntled family members of the victims of 9/11 who felt the Bush-appointed 9/11 task force had failed to perform adequately.

Americans might recall Cynthia McKinney when I remind you of a ruckus that received national attention. On March 29, 2006, Ms. McKinney sidestepped a House office building metal detector, as House and Senate members are allowed to do. She did not have her badge on, but most members of Congress have admitted they rarely wear theirs. She entered the building while rushing to a meeting and simultaneously talking on her cell phone. A house guard failed to recognize her and shouted after her to stop. When she failed to stop, the guard chased after her.

Apparently, Ms. McKinney was unaware of the guard and continued walking and talking on her cell phone. When the guard "grabbed" her she had a "knee-jerk" reaction and allegedly hit him in the chest with her cell phone. From there the situation and story exploded, and the incident was highlighted for months in newspapers and programs throughout the nation. Ms. McKinney charged racial profiling; the guard charged assault.

The situation snowballed and resulted in an extensive and thorough investigation by a Washington, D.C. Superior Court grand jury to determine if Ms. McKinney could possibly be indicted. Ms. McKinney apologized for the incident publicly in the U.S. House of Representatives. No charges were ever filed against her. On June 17, 2006, after the scuffle had been kept in the public limelight for almost three months, the indictment case was rejected.[70] Representative Cynthia McKinney lost her congressional seat for the second time in 2006.

"Now is the time for our elected officials to be held accountable. Now is the time for the media to be held accountable. Why aren't the hard questions being asked?" [71]

Cynthia McKinney

Support our Troops — Bring them Home!
The Mantra of Anti-War Demonstrators

Trying to put my finger on the many different facets of the psychological warfare waged on the American public by the Bush Administration has been challenging. One of the most brilliant yet highly disingenuous and debilitating tactics has been the use of the troops to deflect criticism. While launching the preemptive war against Iraq, the Bush Administration launched another media campaign: the yellow-ribbon, support-the-troops campaign. Early in 2003, whenever a person criticized the Bush Administration or the war in Iraq, it was considered the equivalent to attacking the troops.

With many Vietnam veterans still suffering and wounded from that war, no one in their right mind wished to offend our veterans, patriots who had served our nation on the battlefields of South Asia. By deflecting criticism onto the soldiers, the Bush Administration could distract attention and divert criticism. By insisting that criticizing the war was equivalent to criticizing the soldiers, they successfully blunted or totally muted much of the real criticism and debate over the legitimacy or necessity of the war in Iraq.

A Survey of Anti-War Demonstrators

Every single Friday in my home town, for an hour at noon, protestors stand on all of the corners of one of the busiest intersections in the city. They carry signs protesting the war. They ask drivers to honk as they pass by if they support an end to the war. They have been demonstrating against the war since well before it started, with some protesting since August 2002, some six months before the invasion of Iraq. I decided to interview these protestors to determine their perspectives and so on several different Fridays I questioned them with a clip board in hand.

I asked the question: "Do you support the troops?" "Of course, absolutely, we support the troops. The troops are our children, our brothers, sisters, mothers, fathers, cousins. These troops are our family. That's why we want them to come home quickly and safely." These were the emphatic responses I received from anti-war demonstrators. They made it very clear that their demonstrations were not about the troops.[72] One protestor said, "It's a perfect example of how Bush attempts to manipulate everything people do to make him look good and those who disagree look bad."

I asked a total of eight questions: Why are you here? What do you believe about the war in Iraq? How long have you been doing this? Do you support the troops? Are you against all war or just preemptive wars? I also asked their age, occupation and political affiliation. Almost all of the protestors were over forty years old, and at least half of them were military veterans who had served in Vietnam or the first Gulf War. They were doctors, carpenters, writers, accountants, architects, photographers, housekeepers, waiters, directors of non-profit agencies, and government employees (on their lunch hour).

One of the first demonstrators of whom I asked "Why are you here?" responded by saying, "For four years, I've driven by every Friday and I see the protestors and I honk my horn. A couple of months ago, I asked myself, what would happen if no one showed up?" He decided at that moment to pull over, park his car and join them. It was his third time as an anti-war demonstrator, and he said he felt good about doing it. He said it kept the community aware that while our nation was at war, there were those who believed the war was wrong.

A retired Marine said he was there to "defend the U.S. Constitution." Another retired Marine said he had never before been a part of a protest, but that he had been coming regularly on Fridays for two years. The protestors varied in the amount of time they had been protesting. About half were regulars who had been protesting more than two years. One-fourth protested whenever they were able to protest, and had been since the start of the war; and another fourth had started within the last year.

Here are some of the protesters' responses to the question of "Why are you here?"

- The U.S. has horrendous and unconscionable foreign policies.

- The war in Iraq is about protecting Bush's special interest groups.

- I am opposed to an illegal, unconstitutional, immoral war.

- I am protesting an invasion and the occupation of a country under the guise of freedom.

- I am mad about what is going on in the Middle East and hate the lies Bush keeps telling.

- Young men and women are dying in an unnecessary war.

- Our country has gone in the wrong direction and right-wing Republicans are responsible.

- I find the war very offensive, and we must stop it or otherwise, tomorrow the U.S. will go after Iran. When will it stop?

- Corrupt politicians have become Imperialists seeking world hegemony (domination).
- The war is about controlling Iraq and the Middle East oil.
- I worked the GI hotline in Hawaii and heard first-hand from the vets in Iraq about the situation.

In response to the question "What do you believe about this war in Iraq?" they said:

- It is based on lies, power, greed and oil.
- We need to get out right now.
- The Bush Administration and warhawks should be charged for committing war crimes.
- A responsible government follows laws and treaties, but the U.S. has lost all its morality.
- The Bush Administration and those who lied for the war will be caught, and they will have to face the consequences.
- The war is wrong and it should have never happened.
- It is a huge mistake, costing American lives and running up the federal deficit.
- To continue in Iraq is to continue the mistake.
- It is all about money and power.
- It is an exploitation of American soldiers who will be homeless, spiritually bankrupt, wounded, or dead — never able to come home.
- While our soldiers are out there giving their lives, the government is busy cutting veterans benefits.
- We need to make financial restitution to the citizens of Iraq and bring the troops home.
- I am worried about how the violence is affecting our soldiers.

Only two protestors said they were against all war. Everyone else said they supported wars fought in self-defense or "just" wars. More than half described themselves as Democrats, and the others described themselves as Independents or Green Party members. One person said he had previously been registered a Republican, but he was now registered as an Independent.

It was heartwarming to see the compassion and generosity of the anti-war demonstrators. Four of the protestors, including two Vietnam veterans, said they were concerned with the cuts in veterans' benefits and the lack of resources for those coming home from the wars in Iraq and Afghanistan. Two anti-war demonstrators volunteer regularly at the homeless shelter, assisting returning veterans to re-assimilate back into society. Two licensed mental health practitioners donate counseling services to returning veterans.

In August 2006, on the final day that I was to conduct anti-war demonstrator interviews, I invited my thirteen-year-old daughter to accompany me. After completing the interviews, my daughter began telling me of what she witnessed as we stood in the middle of the busiest intersection in town. She had stood between an elderly couple and talked with them about going back to school in the fall. Since I was interviewing the demonstrators and taking notes, I paid little attention to the cars going by.

Katie said, "Mom, I can't believe how rude some people were." I asked her to tell me more. And she continued by saying, "Some people threw fingers at me and another person in a car pointed at me and mimicked shooting me . . . Mommy, it was really scary." I thought of my precious daughter, sweetly talking to those elderly grandparents who were part of the anti-war demonstration. I reflected on the grandmother holding her sign that read, "Who would Jesus bomb?" and her husband's sign with the message "Support our Troops — Bring them Home!" What kind of an environment causes people to drive by and throw fingers and mimic shooting a gun at the elderly and at youngsters? Perhaps the hostility is caused by a citizenry that has become highly divided and polarized.

Insult, Discredit, Diminish, and Silence Them

The administration and right-wing media mufflers have worked hard to silence dissenters. According to Bush, Cheney and several right-wing pundits, including Ann Coulter and Bill O'Reilly, mothers such as Cindy Sheehan, who have lost their sons in the Iraq war, don't have the right to speak out against the war. Nor do the families who lost loved ones in the 9/11 attacks, such as widows Kristen Breitweiser, Patty Casazza, Lorie Van Auken, and Mindy Kleinberg. And neither do the military men and women who have served in active duty. Anti-war protestors, regardless of whether they are average citizens, politicians, journalists, educators, or entertainers, may not speak out because they are *"dumb," "uniformed,"* *"traitors," "paranoid," "crazy," "chicken," "spineless," "treacherous,"* *"America-hating," "wacky," "bitter," "abettors of terrorists," "aiding al-Qaeda,"* and *"unpatriotic."*

Those who exercise their constitutional freedom of speech by voicing their dissent have suffered consequences. Daring to dissent has been personally and professionally costly. The media's truthful, unbiased reporting was one of the first casualties of 9/11.[73] A more in-depth evaluation of the media and this impact, the scope of the 9/11 Commission's inadequacies and the failures of congressional oversight is considered in greater detail in the chapter, "When Watchdogs Become Lap Dogs."

Government workers who determine that the administration's actions appear illegal can no longer blow the whistle under protection because the Bush Administration went to the Supreme Court to get those protections demolished. The whistleblower protection program for government workers was disbanded in June 2006. And if anyone in the media tries to provide decent news coverage, they are immediately accused of a "liberal bias" and discredited for pointing out the truth.

Also we must keep in mind how divisionary tactics have been used successfully to deflect criticism against the Bush Administration. Some people may remember in June of 2004, Senator Patrick Leahy (D-VT) levied concerns against Vice President Dick Cheney, condemning the amount of war profiteering being made by Halliburton; he questioned the Vice President as to how Halliburton became the sole source contract winner in Iraq. Vice President Cheney, the former CEO of Halliburton, responded to the Senator by telling him "Go f—— yourself."[74] Later, the Vice President appeared on Fox News to discuss the relief he felt after cursing at Senator Leahy. A protracted news blitz took place over the foul language used by the Vice President, thereby deflecting the actual criticisms made by the Senator.

The focus of the story became about the foul language instead of the accusations of war profiting and alleged preferential treatment pertinent to Halliburton.[75] The Bush Administration tactics of distraction, division and polarization proved its effectiveness for at least four and half years after the 9/11 attacks. American citizens, for the most part trusting, loyal and busy, would give the administration a pass, but only for a little bit longer.

NOTES, Chapter 11

1 Vice President Dick Cheney referred to John Murtha, who is calling for redeployment of troops in Iraq, as a "supporter of so-called al-Qaeda." Dick Cheney, interview by Chris Matthews, Hardball, NBC, August, 17, 2006.

2 Cheney is quoted as calling the 146,587 residents of Connecticut who voted for Ned Lamont terrorists. www.tedkennedy.com/apologize.

3 Section 2 of the 1978 Sedition Act defines sedition as "To write, print, utter or publish, or cause it to be done, or assist in it, any false, scandalous, and malicious writing against the government of the United States, or either House of Congress, or the President, with intent to defame, or bring either into contempt or disrepute, or to excite against either the hatred of the people of the United States, or to stir up sedition, or to excite unlawful combinations against the government, or to resist it, or to aid or encourage hostile designs of foreign nations. See www.constitution.org/rf/sedition_1798.htm

4 Steven Robert Allen, "Big Brother is Watching," *Weekly Alibi* 15, no. 6, alibi.com/index.php?story=14092.

5 Ibid.

6 Ibid.

7 Ibid.

8 "V.A. Nurse Accused of Sedition After Publishing Letter Critical of Bush on Katrina, Iraq," *Democracy Now!*, March 2, 2006, www.democracynow.org/article.pl?sid=06/03/02/148237&mode=thread&tid=25.

9 a. Charles Shaw, "Regulated Resistance: Is it possible to change the system when you are the system?," *Newtopia Magazine*, April 26, 2005, www.newtopiamagazine.net/modules.php?op=modload&name=News&file=article&sid=30. .

b. *Grandmothers for Peace International*, June 2003, www.grandmothersforpeace.org/newsletters/gfp-newsletter-2003-06.pdf.

10 Joseph C. Wilson IV, "What I Didn't Find in Africa," *New York Times*, July 6, 2003.

11 Robert Novak, "Mission to Niger," *Washington Post*, July 14, 2003.

12 Chris Suellentrop, "Robert Novak: The Hollow Center of the Plame Affair," *Slate*, October 2, 2003.

13 David Corn, "A White House Smear," *The Nation Blog*, July 16, 2003, www.thenation.com/blogs/capitalgames?bid=3&pid=823.

14 Patrick J. Fitzgerald, *Press Release*, October 28, 2005, www.usdoj.gov/usao/iln/osc/documents/libby_pr_28102005.pdf.

15 Leslie Stahl, "Bush Sought 'Way' To Invade Iraq?," *60 Minutes*, January 11, 2004, www.cbsnews.com/stories/2004/01/09/60minutes/main592330.shtml.

16 Former Treasurer O'Neill provided the author with 19,000 internal documents, including National Security Council meeting documents.

17 Ron Suskind, *The Price of Loyalty: George W. Bush, the White House, and the Education of Paul O'Neill* (New York: Simon & Schuster, 2004).

18 "Cabinet members defend Bush from O'Neill," *CNN*, January 12, 2004, www.cnn.com/2004/ALLPOLITICS/01/11/oneill.bush/.

19 Suskind, *Loyalty*.

20 Richard A. Clarke, *Wikipedia*, en.wikipedia.org/wiki/Richard_A._Clarke.

21 Dylan Avery, *Loose Change*, www.loosechange911.com/.

22 Richard A. Clarke, *Against All Enemies: Inside America's War on Terror* (New York: Free Press, 2004).

23 William Douglas, "Shoot the Messenger, White House Tries to Discredit Counterterrorism Coordinator," *Knight-Ridder*, March 22, 2004.

24 Ibid.

25 Ibid.

26 *The Dan RatherFile*, www.mediaresearch.org/profiles/rather/topic.asp#bush.

27 ratherbiased.com/compare.htm. It was later discovered that the investigations on many of these corporations were suspended on September 11, 2001, when World Trade Center Building 7 collapsed. This is a third building that collapsed within hours of the North and South Towers.

28 Ibid.

29 Ibid.

30 Dan Rather, *CBS Evening News*, April 7, 2004.

31 Dan Rather, *CBS Evening News*, May 6, 2004.

32 Dan Rather, *CBS Evening News*, April 29, 2004.

33 Dan Rather, *CBS Evening News*, October 28, 2004.

34 "CBS ousts four over Bush Guard story," *CNN*, January 11, 2005, www.cnn.com/2005/SHOWBIZ/TV/01/10/cbs.guard/index.html.

35 Dana Priest, "CIA Holds Terror Suspects in Secret Prisons, Debate Is Growing Within Agency About Legality and Morality of Overseas System Set Up After 9/11," *Washington Post*, November 2, 2005, www.washingtonpost.com/wp-dyn/content/article/2005/11/01/AR2005110101644.html.

36 Ibid.

37 Dana Priest, "Covert CIA Program Withstands New Furor, Anti-Terror Effort Continues to Grow," *Washington Post*, December 30, 2005, www.washingtonpost.com/wp-dyn/content/article/2005/12/29/AR2005122901585.html.

38 Dana Priest, "CIA Avoids Scrutiny of Detainee Treatment, Afghan's Death Took Two Years to Come to Light; Agency Says Abuse Claims Are Probed Fully," *Washington Post*, March 3, 2005, www.washingtonpost.com/wp-dyn/content/article/2005/03/24/AR2005032402115.html.

39 Dana Priest, "Wrongful Imprisonment: Anatomy of a CIA Mistake, German Citizen Released After Months in 'Rendition'," *Washington Post*, December 4, 2005 www.washingtonpost.com/wp-dyn/content/article/2005/12/03/AR2005120301476.html.

40 Howard Kurtz, "Piling On the New York Times With a Scoop," *Washington Post*, June 28, 2006, www.washingtonpost.com/wp-dyn/content/article/2006/06/27/AR2006062701708_pf.html.

41 Robert Scheer, "Bush vs. New York Times," *Truthdig*, June 28, 2006, www.alternet.org/mediaculture/38251/.

42 "CyberAlert," *Media Research Center*, June 28, 2006, www.mrc.org/cyberalerts/2006/cyb20060628.asp.

43 Dafna Linzer, "CIA Officer Is Fired for Media Leaks", *Washington Post*, April 22, 2006.

44 Dana Priest, "Live discussion with Post staff writer," *Washington Post*, May 11, 2006, www.washingtonpost.com/wp-dyn/content/discussion/2006/05/04/DI2006050401309.html.

[45] Joe D'Angelo, "Dixie Chicks Backlash Hits Home on Albums Chart," *MTV,* March 26, 2003, www.mtv.com/news/articles/1470769/20030326/50_cent.jhtml? headlines=true.

[46] a. Terry Dorsey, *WBAP/820 AM.*

b. "Dixie Chicks Draw More Controversy," *The New Mexican,* October 29, 2006.

[47] D'Angelo, "Dixie Chicks."

[48] "Actor-activist blasts claims of being misled: 'You were afraid of being called unpatriotic'" *WorldNetDaily,* March 13, 2006, www.worldnetdaily.com/news/ article.asp?ARTICLE_ID=49241.

[49] George Clooney, interview by Larry King, *Larry King Live,* CNN, February 16, 2006, www.clooneyfiles.com/press/interviews/int2006-001.shtml.

[50] Ibid.

[51] Ibid.

[52] Ibid.

[53] a. *NewsMax,* www.newsmax.com/weasels/images/4-hearts.gif.

b. *Libertas,* February 28, 2006, libertyfilmfestival.com/libertas/?p=1356.

[54] "George Clooney," *Boycott Liberalism,* boycottliberalism.com/biographies/ Clooney.htm.

[55] Bill O'Reilly, "The Politics of Hollywood," *The O'Reilly Factor,* FOX News, February 20, 2006, www.billoreilly.com/show?action=viewTVShow&show ID=683&dest=/pg/jsp/community/tvshowprint.jsp.

[56] King, "George Clooney."

[57] Despite never serving in the military, Neocons have successfully launched dirty political campaigns against veterans, such as Max Clelland who lost both his legs in Vietnam. Using unethical campaign tactics, Neocons showed a false connection between Senator Clelland and Osama bin Laden. Senator Clelland lost his seat in 2002.

[58] John Murtha, interview by Chris Matthews, *Hardball,* NBC, August 18, 2006.

[59] John Murtha, "War in Iraq," *John Murtha,* November 17, 2005, www.house.gov/ apps/list/press/pa12_murtha/pr051117iraq.html.

[60] Ibid.

[61] John Nichols, "Cheney Picks a Fight With a Marine," *The Nation Blog,* November 18, 2005, www.thenation.com/blogs/thebeat?bid=1&pid=38198.

[62] Dan Stuthers Churchill, "Murtha's wars," *Pittsburgh Tribune-Review,* October 6, 2006, www.pittsburghlive.com/x/pittsburghtrib/opinion/letters/send/ s_473675.html.

[63] Matthews, "John Murtha."

[64] Michael Davidson, "Kill the Messenger, Public Reaction to Rep. McKinney's Call for 9/11 Investigation Quashes Intended Media Massacre," *From the Wilderness,* May 6, 2002, www.fromthewilderness.com/free/ww3/050702_killthe.html.

[65] Chris Sullentrop, "Cynthia McKinney: The Rep Who Cries Racism," *Slate,* April 19, 2002, www.slate.com/?id=2064530.

[66] Jonathan Goldberg, "Representative Awful, Cynthia McKinney's insanity and hypocrisy," *National Review,* April 12, 2002, www.nationalreview.com/goldberg/ goldberg041202.asp.

[67] Ibid.

[68] Ibid.

[69] Ibid.

[70] Eric M. Weiss and Petula Dvorak, "Indictment Rejected for Rep. McKinney," *Washington Post*, June 17, 2006, www.washingtonpost.com/wp-dyn/content/article/2006/06/16/AR2006061601382_pf.html.

[71] Cynthia A. McKinney, "Thoughts On Our War Against Terrorism," *Counterpunch*, April 13, 2006, www.counterpunch.org/mckinney0413.html.

[72] Only one person responded she could not support the troops: only when they engaged in unethical behaviors or practiced torture.

[73] David Dadge, *Casualty of War: The Bush Administration's Assault on a Free Press* (New York: Prometheus Books, 2004).

[74] Helen Dewar and Dana Milbank, "Cheney Dismisses Critic With Obscenity," *Washington Post*, June 25, 2004, www.washingtonpost.com/wp-dyn/articles/A3699-2004Jun24.html.

[75] "Sources: Cheney curses senator over Halliburton criticism, *CNN*, "June 25, 2004, www.cnn.com/2004/ALLPOLITICS/06/24/cheney.leahy/

★ 12 ★

No WMDs?
It's Terrorism, You Idiot!

*"Political language . . . is designed to make lies sound
truthful and murder respectable, and to give an
appearance of solidity to pure wind."*

George Orwell

The Downing Street Memo

THE "DOWNING STREET MEMO" detailed the actual minutes of a meeting held on July 23, 2002. In attendance were the British Prime Minister, Tony Blair and his top cabinet members. The infamous confidential "Downing Street Memo" highlighted the false allegations used by the U.S. and Great Britain to lead a military invasion into Iraq. It contained several interesting facts but most important is the following statement:

> "Military action was now seen as inevitable. Bush wanted to remove Saddam, through *military action, justified by the conjunction of terrorism and WMD. But the intelligence and facts were being fixed around the policy.* The NSC had no patience with the UN route, and no enthusiasm for publishing material on the Iraqi regime's record. There was little discussion in Washington of the aftermath after military action."[1]

215

The meeting notes provided hard proof that the Bush Administration had planned the war on Iraq three full months prior to the President approaching Congress to seek approval for a potential attack on Iraq.[2] The leaked document further provided evidence that George W. Bush had already made up his mind he was taking America to war and that he would use allegations of Iraqi weapons of mass destruction whether or not they were true. All the while George W. Bush was making statements such as the following to the American public.

"We are doing everything we can to avoid war in Iraq.
But if Saddam Hussein does not disarm peacefully,
he will be disarmed by force."

George W. Bush, March 8, 2003 Radio Address

The Downing Street document leaked to the British public was published in the UK Sunday Times on June 12. 2005.[3] I would have expected Congress to have launched an immediate investigative probe. They did not. This deplorable piece of evidence was all but ignored by the U.S. Congress. I kept asking myself, "Where is Kenneth Starr?" Ken Starr was the U.S. Independent Counsel whose vigilant and thorough investigations led to Bill Clinton's impeachment.

The Truth on the WMD Allegations

What is extremely disturbing is how polarized and confused Americans had become. In 2006, as many as 50 percent of Americans believe there were weapons of mass destruction found in Iraq.[4] This percentage is up from 36 percent in 2005, despite the fact that no real weapons have been found other than those few old tubes of degraded chemicals and pesticides that Fox News and the Bush Administration keep talking about. John Prados, in his book *Hoodwinked: The Documents That Reveal How Bush Sold Us a War*, shows how the Bush Administration used half-truths, exaggerations and outright fabrications to take the U.S. to war against Iraq. They continue to use these same strategies over and over again.[5]

The Iraq Survey Group, made up of American weapons hunters, declared in 2004 that Iraq had dismantled its chemical, biological and nuclear arms programs in 1991 under UN oversight. After a sixteen-month, $900-million-plus investigation, they validated the work of UN inspectors who, in 2002-03, found no trace of banned arsenals in Iraq.[6]

The 9/11 Commission concluded there were no ties between Iraq and al-Qaeda. The Bush Administration insisted that the discovery of agricultural "pesticides" constituted a find of chemical biological weapons because they argued they *could* be converted into those products. In reality the only weapons of mass destruction found in Iraq were 500 tubes of degraded mustard sarin that a senior Defense Department official pointed out were not in useable condition.[7] The tubes were pre-1991.[8] This story, reported by Fox News in June 2006, had already been reported on in 2004 when the tubes were initially found.

To put the degraded sarin tubes in a more proper perspective, during the summer of June 2006, an Army contractor at the U.S. Umatilla, Oregon Army Base was charged with destroying tens of thousands of sarin-filled artillery shells. Members of the Umatilla Tribe have held demonstrations to protest the environmental problems associated with the destruction of these weapons. They are concerned about the environmental effects on their community. The *Global Security Newswire*, the *Tri-City Herald* and the *Oregonian* reported that approximately 91,000 sarin-filled rockets had already been destroyed by the U.S. Army contractor at the Umatilla Base.[9] Imagine the vastness of the U.S. chemical and biological stockpiles of weapons of mass destruction. With literally thousands of U.S. Military bases throughout the U.S. and world,[10] one wonders how many biological chemicals we have stored.

When the Dark Side Becomes the Right Side

One of the most intriguing yet disturbing traits associated with the Bush Administration is its manipulative use of the English language to describe its activities. The English language continues to be hijacked as Americans are indoctrinated with Bush terms that have distinctly different meanings from the norm. Combined with distraction, this practice has been perfected to a fine art.

Consider when Congress attempted to confront the Bush Administration about the fact that no weapons of mass destruction were found in Iraq. The Bush Administration loudly and belligerently shot back an unwavering counter attack of "So what if no weapons of mass destruction were found in Iraq? It's about terrorism!" And when intelligent, concerned U.S. citizens ask, "Why did we attack Iraq in a preemptive war?" or "Why are we still at war in Iraq?" The response the Bush Administration fires back is, "Because we are fighting a global war on terror, (you idiot!)" You hear the "you idiot" in their tone of voice and in the constant assertions made by this administration that the war in Iraq is the same as the war on terror.

The strategy of distraction, combined with Machiavellian terminologies used by the Bush Administration, has proven highly effective. At a public meeting in Washington, D.C. on June 18, 2002, George W. Bush said, "I just want you to know that when we talk about war, we're really talking about peace."[11] In 1948, George Orwell, using the memory of Adolf Hitler and Nazi Germany as a backdrop, writes in his book *1984* about a "big brother" government that spies on its people while telling them that **"War is Peace"** and **"Ignorance is Strength"** and **"Freedom is Slavery."**

The President's statement brought shivers up and down the spines of all cogent thinking Americans. It would serve as a reminder in the years to follow that this President would use language in a most unprecedented manner.

The Yellow Ribbon campaign and the tendency to use the troops to deflect criticism was an important element in making the dark side suddenly appear to be the right side. The Bush Administration launched their Yellow Ribbon and American Flag sticker campaigns that included a strong sentiment of support embedded within them. The words *"Support the Troops"* became synonymous with supporting the war in Iraq. When honest Americans who are paying close attention criticize, ask questions or demand that American troops be brought home, they have been accused of failing to support the troops and they are personally attacked. In Orwell's *1984*, citizens are ordered to "report thought crime." They are told it is their patriotic duty to squash thoughts or comments of dissent. Similarly there was an all-out attack launched on those who attempted to dissent. The fact of the matter is the war in Iraq had nothing to do with the war on terror and everything to do with the Project for a New American Century.

The Power of Words

In my business seminars, I occasionally conduct a simple experiment to demonstrate the impact and power of words in both verbal and written communication. In this experiment, I provide one-half of the participants with a short case study describing an upcoming renovation of their office building. I include five positive words to describe the upcoming renovation. The other half of the group receives the exact same scenario except that five words are changed. These five words have a more negative connotation. Words like exciting, enhancement and opportunity are given to the first group. The others receive words like challenging, demolition and inconvenient.

I ask each participant to write down how they feel about the upcoming renovation and afterwards to prepare a written statement about the renovations. A scribe from each group records the participants' responses. It is fascinating to witness the impact of five simple words on an executive's expectations, emotions and ability to transfer the message to their subordinates and customers. Since conducting this exercise, I am acutely aware of how word choices impact a message. This awareness helps in evaluating newspaper articles and televised programs more critically.

I thought it might be interesting to examine what words George W. Bush uses in his speeches. I copied two speeches President Bush had delivered that were posted on the GOP website in June 2006. In the first speech, he spoke a total of 2,440 words, probably close to a five-minute speech. He used the word "terror" 10 times, the word "war" 9 times, the word "enemy" 7 times, the word "kill" 2 times, and the word "hate" once. In a second speech, he spoke 6,196 words, probably close to a fifteen-minute speech. In this speech he used the word "terror" 62 times, the word "war" 29 times, the word "enemy" 12 times, the word "kill" 7 times and the word "hate" once. These particular word choices used with such frequency are guaranteed to increase fear and anxiety amongst the American public.

A History of Language Manipulation

Since George W. Bush's first days in office when he began promoting legislative changes to our environmental protection laws, I have been surprised to see how successful the administration has been in hiding their disingenuous intentions. The Bush Administration disguises its objectives by naming bills, acts, initiatives, and government interventions with names that have almost the opposite meaning from what they represent.

The first time I became acutely aware of this trend was when the Bush Administration was attempting to gut the Clean Air Act and replace it with a new bill entitled the Clear Skies Act. According to the Sierra Club, "The misnamed 'Clear Skies' weakened many parts of the Clean Air Act and resulted in significantly fewer reductions of air pollutants."[12] For example, the Bush-sponsored Clear Skies Act called for relaxing the cap on NOx pollution. NOx is a mixture of nitrogen monoxide and nitrogen dioxide and is both a pollutant and major contributor to smog. This change may result in an increase of 68 percent more NOx pollution by 2008.[13] Smog is linked to increased asthma and lung disease.[14] Because of these changes, adults will be exposed to higher risks of lung cancer.

The Bush sponsored Clear Skies Act also allowed for a greater increase in the levels of sulphur dioxide ($SO2$) that could be discharged into U.S. streams and lands. Sulphur dioxide is a major contributor to acid rain and soot.[15]

Another Bush authorized change in the Clear Skies Act allowed for a 250-percent increase in the amount of mercury dumped into our environment. The actual amount of the increase rose from the previously allowed five to twenty-six tons of mercury that would now be released into our environment annually.[16] Studies show women with elevated mercury levels give birth to children with neurological impairments and other birth defects.[17] Since the Bush Administration was unable to get the mercury dump increase approved legislatively, they simply bypassed Congress and made the change as part of the Clean Air Mercury Rule in 2005.[18] Additionally, the Bush-sponsored Clear Skies Act contains several loopholes that exempted power plants from reducing pollution.[19]

Another example of language manipulation is the controversial United States PATRIOT Act. (PATRIOT is actually an acronym that stands for Providing Appropriate Tools Required to Intercept and Obstruct Terrorism). This Act was passed within a few weeks of the 9/11 attacks and was signed into law on October 21, 2001. The subtitle of the act states, "Uniting and strengthening America by providing...." The bill authorizing the Act is 342 pages long.

The first controversy was related to how the Bush Administration rushed the bill before Congress. It was issued late in the evening and the vote on the bill was demanded immediately. The Bush Administration indicated a desperate need to get it passed quickly. Many members of Congress admitted they did not have the time to read the Act or thoroughly evaluate it before voting on it.

Only one senator voted against the Act and that was Senator Russ Feingold (D-WI). Senator Feingold has repeated his position as one of "Preserving American's Freedoms While Defending Against Terrorism." It is my belief that congressional representatives and senators supported the Act for fear of being labeled weak on terrorism if they opposed it.

Everyone I know agrees we must have mechanisms in place to allow our government to conduct surveillance and be able to act swiftly against perceived threats. However, such mechanisms must come with the safety of checks and balances against any potential abuse by the government.

Senator Feingold understood what so many others have said since. He believed Americans must not reward the terrorists by weakening our laws to the point of giving up our cherished freedoms. These are the very freedoms the terrorists seek to destroy.[20] We must remember, we have been told the terrorists hate freedom. If Americans are willing to walk away from the tenets of the United States Constitution by surrendering freedoms, then the terrorists have truly won.

One of the controversies over the PATRIOT Act was the provision that allowed the U.S. government to spy on American citizens without a warrant and without oversight. The Bush Administration conducted warrantless surveillance on American citizens in secret for years.[21] When this practice was accidentally discovered, they argued that it was necessary for the global war on terrorism. But the emergency provisions in the FISA (law governing surveillance) give the government the right to initiate surveillance on an American citizen immediately. There is no delay. The government can conduct surveillance for three full days (up to 72 hours) without a warrant; but must initiate a request for a warrant within that time. Warrants are issued within hours of the request once petitioned from the courts. The Bush Administration does not need a warrant for the surveillance of foreigners under FISA. It has the right to place any foreigner suspected under surveillance without a warrant.[22]

What the Bush Administration put into place is a system that allows the administration, and select government employees or contractors, to spy on American citizens without ever obtaining a warrant. There is inherent danger in allowing this precedent to continue. A *New York Times* investigative report revealed a classified FBI memorandum leaked in November of 2003.[23] It showed the Bush Administration using the PATRIOT Act for the purpose of corroborating and coordinating a "nationwide effort to collect intelligence regarding demonstrations."[24]

The federal government, through the offices of the FBI, had begun targeting innocent Americans for engaging in the lawful right of protest and dissent against the war in Iraq.[25] *NBC News* reported in 2006 that the United States Military continued to maintain databases, such as one known as Talon that contains information on anti-war meetings and peaceful protests around the country. Even after government analysts concluded that the people and events on the database posed no threat to our nation, they continue to be targeted. Ben Wizner, a lawyer for the American Civil Liberties Union, is quoted as saying, "There is simply no reason why the United States Military should be monitoring the peaceful activities of American citizens who oppose U.S. war policies."[26]

While many Americans, both Democrats and Republicans, have shown concern about this, others say it does not matter. They say the Bush Administration should be given free rein to monitor whomever they wish, in any manner and for as long as they wish. However, if those who do not believe it matters found themselves wanting to protest or dissent against a controversial matter, say against an abortion clinic, or if they were to be part of an anti-flag burning demonstration, how might they feel if they discovered they were now targeted by their own government? In some respects the PATRIOT Act is incredibly un-American and unpatriotic.

Americans are constantly inundated with Bush terms that have distinctly different meaning from what we normally believe them to mean. As another example, who would question a program called the Healthy Forest Initiative? It sounds like something wonderful for our forests. Environmentalists and conservationists were outraged in 2002 when Bush unveiled the initiative that put the logging industry in charge of thinning our forests.[27] They were free to cut away with no provisions in place for restoration. The Bush Administration ignored a blueprint based on research conducted by the U.S. Forest Service and endorsed by the Wilderness Society, the Sierra Club and several other groups.[28] Additionally, this Bush sponsored action has further aggravated the global warming problem.

Here are other examples of terms defined by the Bush Administration. Their real implications are very different.

Axis of Evil: Originally the "axis of evil" was described as Iraq, Iran and North Korea. According to the Bush Administration, these nations pose a great threat to the United States. Iraq and Iran were nations who at the time of the allegations did not have nuclear weapons but according to experts might have been able to develop them within a five to fifteen year period.[29] Since George W. Bush attacked Iraq, the other two nations, Iran and North Korea, have begun racing to make sure the allegations become truth. Iran and Iraq are nations that the Bush Administration has shown a strong interest in because of their oil resources. In accordance with the plans outlined in the Project for a New American Century and the Bush doctrine, the U.S. will launch preemptive wars against these nations in order to prevent future wars and to promote American hegemony.

Other Axes of Evil: These were nations that George W. Bush added to the original axis list. It now includes Libya, China and Syria. Later, Venezuela and Ecuador were added. According to George W. Bush, these are nations that wish to do us harm. China is one of the U.S.'s largest trading partners. So this term really appears to pertain to any nation who disagrees with U.S. policies. It also applies to nations whose resources the U.S. wishes to better control.

Coalition of the Willing: This was a term made up by the Bush Administration to imply international support of the war in Iraq. It included

Great Britain, Italy and Spain. But to put the coalition in proper prospective, the most troops provided by any nation other than the U.S. was Great Britain. Their contribution was a grand total of 7,500, versus the U.S., who contributed 150,000 at the onset of the war. Others nations gave mostly verbal support. The U.S. has carried close to 100 percent of the burden for this war while pretending to have international support.

Regime Change: This term was used to describe the removal of Saddam Hussein as the dictator of Iraq and has since been used to describe the removal of Mahmoud Ahmadinejad, the President of Iran, and Hugo Chavez of Venezuela. The Bush Administration uses this term to mean the U.S. government will get rid of evil dictators. What it really means is that the U.S. will try to overthrow a government using American taxpayers' dollars for the benefit of corporate capitalists.

Family Values: These are values that support families. They include honesty, integrity, compassion, and ethical practices. The reality is that the Bush-controlled Republican Congress has failed to make families a real priority. Under Tom DeLay, the former Republican representative from Texas, Congress blocked legislation to protect child labor overseas, allowing sweatshops to continue operating that benefited their corporate sponsors.[30] In return, these corporate sponsors made illegal kickbacks to the Republican Party. Several members of Congress who professed to have family values have engaged in money-making schemes that helped them personally all while covering up elicit deals and a lurid sex scandal.[31] The multiple tax breaks given to the wealthiest Americans have failed to trickle down to America's families in the middle and lower classes.[32] More on this topic will be explored in the chapter, "Meanwhile Back at the Ranch."

America's Allies: Our new Allies are nations some with horrific human rights records. Many are nations who have been known to harbor terrorists as well as being major monetary contributors to terrorists groups. These allies include Pakistan, Saudi Arabia, Qatar, Jordan, and Egypt. America's allies are no longer any of our respected traditional allies, like Germany and France. In fact, George W. Bush and members of his administration continually encourage bullying and verbal bashing of nations and their leaders. Verbal abuse is especially sharp when foreign leaders or their people are critical of the U.S.[33]

The Global War on Terror: This was supposed to mean the Taliban and al-Qaeda, terrorists who wish to do us harm. However, under the Bush Administration, it appears to mean Middle Eastern nations like Iraq and more recently Iran.

American Liberators: Told that they would be seen in Iraq as liberators, American troops and private contractors were deployed to Iraq. They were to bring freedom. Instead, a mismanaged war has resulted in chaos, death, prisoner abuse, wasted tax dollars, and a failed Iraqi occupation.

Stay the Course: A term meaning we must stay in Iraq. Americans must sacrifice their children and tax dollars until George W. Bush tells us otherwise. What this really means is that Americans will stay until permanent military bases in Iraq are completely built, security is fully established and the oil is firmly under U.S. corporate control. Those who wish to leave Iraq are referred to as losers who wish to "cut and run."

Liberals: Evil, Godless Americans, wimps, lightweights, naysayers, tree-huggers, and morally deficient individuals. The reality is that liberals have been fighters for middle- and working-class Americans, protectors of the environment and individual rights, seekers of health care reform, and supporters of public education, social security, civil rights, and Medicare. The word "liberal" is defined as "broad and open-minded, tolerant of different views, standards and behaviors, favoring civil liberties; supportive of progressive political and social reforms that extend democracy, distribute wealth more evenly and protect the personal freedom of the individual."

Conservatives: Bush refers to Conservatives as his base. They are God-loving and God-fearing Christians who have broadly supported George W. Bush and his administration. Many Christian conservatives have advocated imposing morality through governmental intervention. "Conservative" used to mean fiscally conservative individuals who advocated limited government and who tended to be pro-business. The word "conservative" is defined as cautious and restrained, in favor of preserving the status quo, reluctant to consider new ideas or accept change, favoring traditional values, views and customs, cautiously moderate and against abrupt change."

The PATRIOT Act: It has been promoted as a tool necessary to fight terrorism. What it really means is unmonitored government surveillance, wiretapping and the infiltration of political groups in the U.S. that are in disagreement with the administration and its policies. The Act has lead to abuses of civil rights and liberties. It has placed restraints on the right to dissent and criticize. With freedom of expression potentially punishable, it has allowed the U.S. executive branch the power to police without any oversight.

Junk Science: Corporations call science about global warming or research that negatively impacts them "junk science." Neocon "Think Tanks" write opinions they call position papers to "debunk true science." These position papers have failed to be vetted, scrutinized or examined by peers for accuracy. The work of any scientist, group, university, or association that is certified, bona fide, credentialed, and legitimate, and any such individual who is authorized and who speaks or writes on scientific matters may be called junk science. This is ludicrous, as the ones calling it junk science are the frauds themselves. A complete in-depth detail of this phenomenon will be discussed in the chapter, "The Fifth Commandment."

In a healthy, functioning democratic society, one recognizes the need for a balance of liberal and conservative ideologies. Neither ideology is, in and of itself, bad. I know people who represent both sides. They are liberals and conservatives in the true senses of the words. They are honest, hard-working and dedicated Americans. They see things from a different perspective and most importantly, they often have more in common than they do not. The challenges arise in how to go about fixing problems within our society, together.

Communication, discussion and recognition of commonalities are good places to start. Unfortunately, in a political climate that advocates "my way or the highway," there is a disadvantage in the approach to problem solving. Bringing people together rather than polarizing them helps the problem-solving process by creating better support and buy-in and a deeper commitment to the final decisions.

There is a principle which is a bar against all information, which is proof against all arguments and which cannot fail to keep a man in everlasting ignorance — that principle is contempt prior to investigation.

Herbert Spencer

NOTES, Chapter 12

[1] "Downing Street Memo," *WikiSource*, en.wikisource.org/wiki/Downing_Street_memo.

[2] *The Downing Street Memo(s)*, downingstreetmemo.com/index.html.

[3] Ibid.

[4] "Belief that Iraq Had Weapons of Mass Destruction Has Increased Substantially," *The Harris Poll* #57, July 21, 2006, www.harrisinteractive.com/harris_poll/index.asp?PID=684.

[5] John Prados, *Hoodwinked: The Documents That Reveal How Bush Sold Us a War* (New York: New Press, 2004).

[6] Charles J. Hanley, "Half of U.S. Still Believes Iraq Had WMD," *The Associated Press*, August 7, 2006, www.washingtonpost.com/wp-dyn/content/article/2006/08/07/AR2006080700189.html.

[7] U.S. Senate, "Hundreds of WMDs Found in Iraq," *FOX News*, June 22, 2006, www.foxnews.com/story/0,2933,200499,00.html.

[8] a. Ibid.

b. John D. Negroponte, fax message to Oeter Hoekstra, June 21, 2006. Available at www.foxnews.com/projects/pdf/Iraq_WMD_Declassified.pdf.

[9] NTI, "Last U.S. Sarin Bomb Destroyed in Oregon," *Global Security Newswire*, June 13, 2006, nti.org/d%5Fnewswire/issues/2006/6/13/1d7d6686%2D35f7%2D4c9a%2Da094%2D8fe524549447.html.

[10] John Lindsay-Poland and Nick Morgan, "Overseas Military Bases and Environment," *Foreign Policy In Focus 3*, no. 15 (1998): 1. Available at www.fpif.org/ pdf/vol3/15ifmil.pdf.

[11] Remarks by the President on Homeownership at the Department of Housing and Urban Development, Washington, D.C., June 18, 2002, www.hud.gov/news/speeches/presremarks.cfm.

[12] "Clear Skies Proposal Weakens the Clean Air Act," *Sierra Club*, www.sierraclub.org/cleanair/clear_skies.asp.

[13] Ibid.

[14] Ibid.

[15] Ibid.

[16] Ibid.

[17] a. "Mercury," *League of Conservation Voters*, www.lcveducation.org/programs/vote-environment/campaigns/ve2004/LCV_AllMercury1in12_0418Final_VP04.pdf.
b. *Our Stolen Future*, www.ourstolenfuture.org/NewScience/human/humepi.htm.

[18] "Clear Skies Proposal."

[19] "Clear Skies Act of 2003," *U.S. Environmental Protection Agency*, www.epa.gov/air/clearskies/fact2003.html.

[20] Sen. Russell Feingold, "On Opposing the U.S.A. Patriot Act," *Associated Press Managing Editors Conference*, Milwaukee Art Museum, Milwaukee, October 12, 2001, www.archipelago.org/vol6-2/feingold.htm.

[21] Edward Epstein, "Bush defends eavesdropping, blasts senators on Patriot Act," *San Francisco Chronicle*, December 19, 2005, www.sfgate.com/cgi-bin/article.cgi?f=/c/a/2005/12/19/MNG9JGAFEV10.DTL.

[22] "Top 12 media myths and falsehoods on the Bush Administration's spying scandal," *Media Matters for America*, mediamatters.org/items/200512240002.

[23] Jim Lobe, "FBI Plans for Antiwar Movement Spur Opposition," *Antiwar.com*, November 26, 2003, www.antiwar.com/ips/lobe112603.html.

[24] Ibid.

[25] a. Ibid.

b. Eric Lichtblau, "Documents Reveal Scope of U.S. Database on Antiwar Protests," *New York Times*, October 13, 2006, www.commondreams.org/cgi-bin/print.cgi?file=/headlines06/1013-01.htm.

[26] Ibid.

[27] CNN Online, "Bush Unveils 'Healthy Forests' Plan," *CNN InsidePolitics*, August 22, 2002, archives.cnn.com/2002/ALLPOLITICS/08/22/bush.timber/index.html.

[28] Ibid.

[29] Richard Falk, "Storm Clouds Over Iran," *The Nation*, January 27, 2006, www.wagingpeace.org/articles/2006/01/27_falk_storm-clouds-over-iran.htm.

[30] "Wal-Mart Breakdown," *The Stakeholder*, October 31, 2005, www.dccc.org/stakeholder/archives/2005_10.html.

[31] Adam Nagourney, "In House Races, More GOP Seats Are Seen at Risk," *New York Times*, October 7, 2006, www.truthout.org/docs_2006/100706Y.shtml.

[32] Mike Whitney, "Bush's Chernobyl Economy; hard times are on the way," *Information Clearing House*, November 8, 2006, www.informationclearinghouse.info/article15545.htm.

[33] *Miquelon*, www.miquelon.org. This website has a list of quotes of American Politicians bashing the French in particular.

★ 13 ★

The Freedom Fight and the Facts

IN A JUNE 2005 REPORT by Patrick Cockburn entitled "From Turning Point to Vanishing Point . . . Iraq: A Bloody Mess," a ruthless, savage, bloody chaos is described.[1] He reports that the only way U.S. troops can travel in Iraq is via heavily armed convoys. Mr. Cockburn depicts waves of murders and assassinations of government officials. His report highlights the fact that there has been a mass exodus of much of the Iraqi population. Middle-class Iraqis have long fled their country in great numbers. It is an increasingly dangerous place to live where conditions just simply continue to deteriorate. Iraqi neighborhoods are nothing more than deadly battle zones pitted one against another.

Iraq — A Chaotic Mess

Tragedies such as this one reported by the *Associated Press* (AP) appear far too often in Iraq. It is the story of a husband rushing his pregnant wife to a hospital in Baghdad in May of 2006. When the husband failed to stop at a roadblock, Iraqi police and witnesses say the "troops gunned down the woman" in the car.[2] Can you imagine the grief of this family to discover a loved one along with her expectant new baby had been killed in this terrible manner? What of the outrage from the family and friends that would normally follow such a dreadful incident?

The AP report stated that the Iraqi civil death toll continues to climb monthly and annually with the prolonged U.S. occupation. More than 3,500 Iraqi civilians were reported killed in July of 2006, but that number would be exacerbated monthly through the fall of 2006 as the U.S. failed to crush the civilian turmoil. Each month the Iraqi civilian death toll increases.[3]

Experts, news reporters, international critics, our own troops, generals, and U.S. congressional representatives all tell us the situation in Iraq is getting worse. These are people who have been in and out of Iraq since the beginning of the U.S. occupation. The findings of a State Department survey reported in September 2006 indicated that 75 percent of Iraqis felt the departure of U.S. forces would lead to greater security and less sectarian violence, and 65 percent wanted an immediate pullout of U.S. troops. The Iraqis who are strongly dependent upon the U.S. for security purposes appear to be the Kurds in Northern Iraq. Interestingly, a huge majority, 77 percent of Iraqis, believe the U.S. will not pull out even after being asked to do so.[4]

Several stories have been written detailing the bombing of Iraq by the Bush Administration during Shock and Awe. However, little focus was placed on the devastating loss of Iraqi civilians by the U.S. media. Again, I remind you of General Tommy Franks when he said nonchalantly that "we don't do body counts" in reference to the fact that the U.S. wasn't tracking the numbers of Iraqi civilian deaths attributable to "collateral damage."[5]

It made me wonder if Saddam Hussein used similar words to describe the deaths of the civilians in his multiple attacks used to suppress uprisings. Since the U.S. government has blatantly admitted that it is not tracking the Iraqi civilian death toll, other organizations have attempted to do so. *The Associated Press* estimated the number of civilian deaths at 50,000. The Iraqi Ministry of Health, an agency that has been under several different administrators in the last three years, estimated the number of Iraqi civilian deaths at 150,000.[6] A medical research study headed by Johns Hopkins University, Bloomberg School of Public Health, released in October of 2006, put the Iraqi civilian death toll due to the war at 654,965.[7] Deaths directly attributable to the American bombing of Iraq during Shock and Awe are estimated at 30 percent of this number. The remaining 70 percent are considered "excess deaths," meaning that if the U.S. had not invaded Iraq, these Iraqis would be alive today.[8] I am curious about how the average Iraqi feels about the price he has paid for freedom.

The outgoing UN Secretary General, Kofi Annan, reported in December of 2006 that life was better for the Iraqis under Saddam Hussein than it is under American occupation. He said although Saddam was a brutal dictator, the Iraqi people had their streets and their safety. According to Annan, the Iraqis could go to work and school and not fear for their lives and those of their loved ones. In a slap-in-the-face comment to the Bush Administration, Annan said the war in Iraq could have prevented with just a little more time and a few more inspectors.[9]

The Cost of Freedom in Iraqi Lives

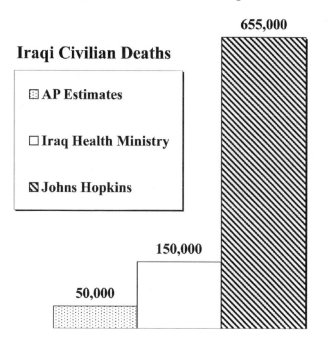

Iraqi Civilian Deaths

☒ AP Estimates

☐ Iraq Health Ministry

☒ Johns Hopkins

655,000

150,000

50,000

Recommendations Ignored

The Iraq Study Group was an appointed bi-partisan group of prestigious Republicans and Democrats who were charged with providing the Bush Administration with an assessment and written recommendations on the war in Iraq. The Group, led by co-chairs former Secretary of State James Baker and former Representative Lee Hamilton, released their report in December 2006. The report defined the situation in Iraq as grave and deteriorating. The report stressed that there was no guarantee for a U.S. success in Iraq and it recommended that U.S. troops be brought home by 2008.[10] The well researched report was all but ignored by George W. Bush who was under intense pressure to accept it. Instead of moving forward with the recommendations, George W. Bush determined to go in the opposite direction. He told the nation in January 2007 that he would instead increase the number of troops deployed to Iraq.

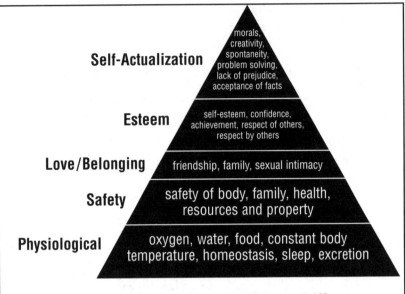

*MASLOWS' HIERARCHY OF NEEDS[12]

LEVEL 1: Physiological Needs
The biological needs are the base of the pyramid and are elements such as oxygen, food, water, and a relatively constant body temperature. They are the strongest needs because survival is dependent upon having these needs met, first and foremost.

LEVEL 2: Safety Needs
When all physiological needs are fully met the need for security is activated. Normally, we forget about the need for security except in emergencies. In times such as war, rioting, natural catastrophic conditions like hurricanes, tornados and fire the human need for safety emerges.

LEVEL 3: Love, Affection and Belongingness
When safety and physiological requirements are met, the need for love, affection and a desire to belong surfaces.

LEVEL 4: Needs for Esteem
When the first three levels are satisfied the need for esteem materializes. At this point human beings seek ways to increase their self-esteem, respect and value. Freedom and democracy might be sought at this level.

LEVEL 5: Needs for Self-Actualization
When levels one through four are fulfilled then the need for self-actualization is triggered. It could be described as a person's need to be and do that which the person was "born to do."

Winning Hearts and Minds

"We're not going to cure terrorism and spread peace and good will in the Middle East by killing innocent people... They [Iraqis] don't have food, they don't have clean water, they don't have electricity. They don't have medicine, they don't have doctors. We need to get our military presence out of there, and that's what's gonna start building good will.... I see Iraq as the base for spreading imperialism...."[13]

Cindy Sheehan

Over the last few years, as I have watched in horror at the decline in Iraq, I've wondered if the U.S. Military really understood the way to "win hearts and minds." In my first year of college, I studied Abraham Maslow, one of the fathers of humanistic psychology. Maslow taught that all humans have needs and that until the first level of need is met, people are unable to move to the next level. As each level is met, they are able to continue moving up the scale towards "self-actualization."

In terms of the American invasion of Iraq, this means that in order to have a successful occupation, the first issue should have been to provide the basic necessities for the Iraqis. This meant food, clean drinking water and fresh air to breathe. Providing safety and security was absolutely essential. After the successful initiation of Shock and Awe, Americans failed to provide even the most basic elements in Level One. The air is foul on many days and the water systems remain contaminated throughout most of the region. Civil discord is rampant and there is a daily deluge of mayhem, violence and murder. After four years of occupation we continue to miss the mark on both Levels One and Two.

Actions Speak Louder Than Words

Another huge U.S. miscalculation was the fact that no one paid attention to the historical treasures of Iraq. Many priceless and sacred archaeological riches were destroyed, damaged or stolen during the Baghdad bombing and the subsequent looting of the museums. The loss of many of Iraq's most treasured artifacts and relics was seen as a travesty.

The U.S. Military's decision not to take care of the most basic Iraqi needs, coupled with the failure to establish peace, compounded problems.

These mistakes, combined with the U.S.'s preoccupation with Iraq's oil resources, sent an important message to the Iraqis. Actions speak louder than words and Americans' actions spoke volumes to Iraqis. What America valued most was all too apparent. The U.S. placed its attention on preserving the oil fields of Iraq.

The Changing Justifications for the War in Iraq

A vast number of Americans, especially our men and women fighting in the armed forces and their families, held the belief that we went to war in Iraq to defend our country from Iraq's "weapons of mass destruction" and its potential security threat to America. This security threat included Saddam Hussein. The Bush Administration called for a regime change to incorporate Hussein's removal. Liberation for Iraqis would be a subsequent outcome. However, the reasoning behind the U.S.'s presence in Iraq shifted again shortly after the U.S. captured Saddam Hussein and it was discovered there were no weapons of mass destruction to be found in Iraq. The U.S. was to provide freedom and "democracy" to the citizens of Iraq. After several different installations of new Iraqi governments and three "democratic" elections, we have provided neither freedom nor democracy. American troops have served honorably, and with great sacrifice to secure safety for *our* nation.

A majority of Americans keep asking, *Why are we still in Iraq?* Wanda, a Republican and a small business owner, says she believes the reason the U.S. attacked Iraq in 2003 was in retaliation for Saddam Hussein's failed executive order to assassinate George H.W. Bush, the President's father.[14] Allegedly, Saddam Hussein developed a plot to assassinate George H.W. Bush when the former President made a visit to Kuwait in June of 2003 after the first Gulf War.

Sam, a Republican and retired electrician, says he believes the U.S. would never have invaded Iraq if it weren't for "that faulty intelligence" given to the President. The President himself has given a wide variety of reasons about why the U.S. is at war in Iraq.

The Real Motivation for Staying the Course

George W. Bush has insisted that we must "stay the course" in Iraq. He has persisted in telling the nation that U.S. troops will remain in Iraq as long as he is President. He has used scare tactics, telling Americans that if we bring our troops home, al-Qaeda will follow them. It's like the boogeyman that might be hiding in the closet or under the bed. So how

THE PRESIDENT'S EVER SHIFTING RHETORIC ON IRAQ

- In September 2002, the President told the United Nations that the U.S. would work collaboratively with the UN to ensure that Iraq was held accountable to the UN for adhering to the imposed sanctions.[15]

- Less than one month later the President's rhetoric shifted dramatically, alleging on October 7, 2002 that if Saddam Hussein "has dangerous weapons," it makes no sense for the world to wait before confronting him.[16]

- After the invasion of Iraq, when it appeared no weapons of mass destruction would be found there, the Presidential rhetoric changed again, with George W. Bush emphasizing that America was on a mission to remove "a grave threat" and to liberate oppressed people. The public was told shortly thereafter that the "mission had been accomplished."[17]

- By 2005, the message on Iraq had shifted yet again. The President informed U.S. citizens that it had become American policy to promote democracy in every nation and culture throughout the world with an ultimate goal of ending tyranny.[18]

- A year and half later, in August of 2006, the President would insist that the War on Terror and the war in Iraq were one and the same, referring to both as Islamic radicalism and Islamic fascism, spread by fundamentalists who wanted to attack "those who love freedom."[19]

- In October 2006, the President strongly tied terrorism to the war in Iraq, saying that the war in Iraq is "a central front" and that Americans must ensure the success of democracy in Iraq to keep the homeland more secure.[20]

- The President has indicated he expects the U.S. to be at war in the Middle East for years to come. He is committed to staying the course in Iraq as long as he continues to be President.[21]

- George W. Bush, in the week preceding the 2006 midterm election, told Americans while campaigning for Republican candidates that the reason the U.S. was in Iraq was to stabilize gasoline prices, ensuring Americans could purchase gasoline for around $2.00 per gallon.[22]

well do the President's scare tactics work? Please refer back to Maslow's chart and you will find that they work incredibly well to achieve his goals.

After all, safety is Level Two on the chart. For Americans and Iraqis alike, we have demonstrated that if it comes to security or freedom, we choose security first. I cringe when the President spouts lines about the importance of freedom and tells America that we are delivering freedom to the Iraqis. He uses manipulative tactics to tap into our emotions, knowing that Americans love freedom. But we must remember that freedom is further up the scale and can only be appreciated after the human needs of Levels One and Two have been satisfied.

According to experts, including members of the now disbanded 9/11 Commission, America is not winning the War on Terrorism, nor are we winning the war in Iraq.[23] The President refuses to seek international assistance or provide the nation with any additional alternatives other than his rhetoric of "we must not cut and run." A number of politicians, Republicans and Democrats alike, have questioned the rhetoric and pointed out that "staying the course" and making cheering statements are empty sound bites. While Americans are preoccupied with their busy lives, they are not stupid. Americans want realistic goals, plans of actions and a definable exit strategy on Iraq.

The Sad Truth

So why, against the advice of so many experts and against the wishes of a majority of Americans, was America destined to "stay the course" in Iraq? The U.S. economy is based upon oil. We are in Iraq to secure oil for America and we have put American security on the line to accomplish this goal.

I believe the statement made by President Bush in October 2006, whereby he stated his rationale for American troops in Iraq was related to the purpose of gasoline price stabilization. It appeared the most honest and forthright answer given to the American public. The U.S. government under the Bush Administration has long been committed to securing the Middle East region for the purpose of obtaining oil resources. In 2003, a consortium of ten oil companies decided it was too risky to use their own funds to build a $3.5 billion petroleum pipeline project in the Middle East.[24] Fear of anti-Western sentiments, coupled with the interests of Middle Eastern countries who want to control their own resources, would make this endeavor extremely challenging. The commercial banks also agreed it was too risky and apparently declined the loan for the thousand-plus mile pipeline that would run from the Caspian Sea through Georgia and on to the Mediterranean coast of Turkey.

Caspian Oil Pipeline

However, the oil industry did find a backer for their project. The project was endorsed by the Bush Administration and they agreed to subsidize the ExxonMobil-BP pipeline deal with American taxpayer dollars. First the U.S. government agreed to pay for the engineering studies in Azerbaijan and then committed to as much as $500 million to help finance the project. We gave the world's wealthiest companies "free public money" according to British Petroleum CEO John Browne.[25]

Later, with Neoconservative and Iraqi war architect Paul Wolfowitz at the helm of the World Bank, an increase in the World Bank's lending limits was authorized by the Bush Administration in order to finance the project.[26] The Bush Administration has said that the assistance to the oil industries was justified because it would help create jobs in 2003. But the facts simply don't substantiate the oil industry's actions. Despite blockbuster revenues and public subsidies, ExxonMobil and ChevronTexaco have actually slashed their work forces by more than twenty thousand in recent years.[27]

America's New Home in Iraq

In 2004, U.S. engineers focused on the construction of 14 "enduring bases," long-term encampments in Iraq.[28] Brigadier General Mark Kimmitt, deputy chief of operations for the coalition in Iraq, said, "This is a blueprint for how we could operate in the Middle East," and the engineering vision is well ahead of the policy vision.[29] In spring of 2006 it was revealed that the U.S. government was building the largest embassy in the world in Baghdad.[30] At the same time, almost all other Iraqi projects were behind schedule, including health clinics, water-treatment facilities and electrical plants. Countless other important projects for the Iraqis have been either downsized or completely eliminated. This is because of the numerous miscaculations about the war and because mismanaged funds purportedly have since vanished.

The U.S. Embassy hidden inside the Green Zone moved according to schedule and was finished in June 2006. The cost to American taxpayers was at least $592 million.[31] The cost for the embassy was approved, as have been almost all of the war expenditures, as part of an "off-the-books" separate emergency appropriation.[32] In order to show lower budgetary projections, the cost for the wars in Iraq and Afghanistan are accounted for and requested through "supplementary spending bills."

Who Wins and How They Win

I was reminded of how influential lobbying money is by one of my clients. Barbara, a lobbyist, told me that a big part of her job was to ensure that funding bills and other legislation affecting her industry made it through both houses of Congress. If, on the other hand, legislation was going to negatively impact her industry, it was her job to make sure these bills were killed. She drives from her home in Virginia to Washington, D.C. to meet with senators and representatives. She explains bills and justifies subsidies for her industry. While I have no idea how much her industry gives to candidates, she indicated that it was quite substantial.

Who influences wars and who benefits from war? By reviewing the benefactors of war and identifying where the big lobbying dollars go, it might help to explain why Congress has asked few questions of the Bush Administration. For six years, the Bush-controlled Congress freely and generously opened U.S. Government coffers for wars in the Middle East. The Republican-controlled Congress has bloodied its hands and hearts, giving the Bush Administration *carte blanche* authority. It demanded no accountability on how tax dollars were used. The charts in the next few pages show the winners of war. Americans must ask how lobbying dollars influence the U.S. Congress. *The Washington Post* reported that in October of 2003, fourteen contractors receiving work in both Iraq and Afghanistan had contributed $23 million to national political campaigns since 1990.[33]

"A blessing in disguise." [In reference to 9/11]

Donald Rumsfeld, Secretary of Defense
Interview with Jim Lehrer 9/11/02

Oil & Gas Contribution Trends by Political Party
Courtesy Center for Responsive Politics

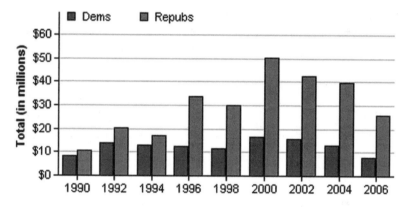

Oil & Gas: Top Eight Senate Recipients
Election Cycle 2006

Rank	Candidate	Office	Amount
1	Hutchison, Kay Bailey (R-TX)	Senate	$258,461
2	Burns, Conrad (R-MT)	Senate	$193,775
3	Santorum, Rick (R-PA)	Senate	$193,120
4	Talent, James M (R-MO)	Senate	$156,470
5	Bode, Denise (R-OK)	House	$156,150
6	Allen, George (R-VA)	Senate	$155,100
7	Cornyn, John (R-TX)	Senate	$141,750
8	Barton, Joe (R-TX)	House	$141,450

Courtesy Center for Responsive Politics

Top 20 Gas and Oil Individual Company Contributions
Election Cycle 2006

Rank	Organization	Amount	Dems	Repubs	Source ■ Indivs ■ PACs ■ Soft $
1	Koch Industries	$731,755	12%	88%	
2	Exxon Mobil	$652,972	11%	89%	
3	Valero Energy	$562,700	13%	87%	
4	Occidental Petroleum	$386,025	25%	75%	
5	Chevron Corp	$376,687	17%	83%	
6	Marathon Oil	$364,903	19%	81%	
7	Independent Petroleum Assn of America	$361,340	5%	95%	
8	American Gas Assn	$265,059	36%	64%	
9	National Propane Gas Assn	$222,600	41%	59%	
10	Sunoco Inc	$205,300	15%	85%	
11	TRT Holdings	$202,900	0%	100%	
12	ConocoPhillips	$197,427	12%	88%	
13	Chesapeake Energy	$195,220	5%	95%	
14	Benson Minerals Group	$182,425	0%	100%	
15	Petroleum Marketers Assn	$174,650	10%	90%	
16	Anadarko Petroleum	$165,700	4%	96%	
17	Bass Brothers Enterprises	$156,300	0%	100%	
18	Hunt Consolidated	$155,150	0%	100%	
19	Halliburton Co	$152,690	7%	93%	
20	Pilot Corp	$151,450	0%	100%	

Courtesy Center for Responsive Politics

Presidential Contributions 2000 & 2004
Election Energy & Natural Resources

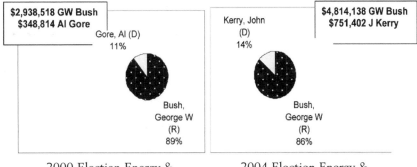

$2,938,518 GW Bush
$348,814 Al Gore

Gore, Al (D)
11%

Bush,
George W
(R)
89%

Kerry, John
(D)
14%

$4,814,138 GW Bush
$751,402 J Kerry

Bush,
George W
(R)
86%

2000 Election Energy &
Natural Resources

2004 Election Energy &
Natural Resources

Energy/Natural Resources:
Long-Term Contribution Trends

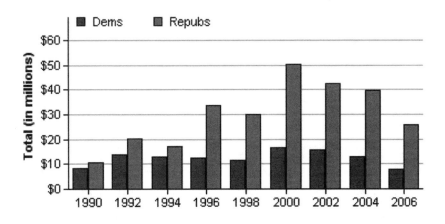

Courtesy Center for Responsive Politics

Energy/Natural Resources: Top Contributors to Federal Candidates and Parties, Election Cycle 2006

Courtesy Center for Responsive Politics

Total contributions: $24,895,190

Democrats
$2,380,812
(17%)

Republicans
$11,847,570
(83%)

Top Eight Congressional Recipients of Energy/Natural Resources, Election Cycle 2006

Courtesy Center for Responsive Politics

Rank	Candidate	Office	Amount
1	Santorum, Rick (R-PA)	Senate	$631,671
2	Allen, George (R-VA)	Senate	$432,640
3	Barton, Joe (R-TX)	House	$432,300
4	Talent, James M (R-MO)	Senate	$393,470
5	Hutchison, Kay Bailey (R-TX)	Senate	$369,186
6	Burns, Conrad (R-MT)	Senate	$357,079
7	Bingaman, Jeff (D-NM)	Senate	$314,351
8	Kyl, Jon (R-AZ)	Senate	$286,522

http://www.opensecrets.org/industries/contrib.asp?Ind=E&cycle=2006

Defense: Top 20 Long-Term Political Party Contribution Trends, Election Cycle 2006

Courtesy Center for Responsive Politics

Rank	Organization	Amount	Dems	Repubs	Source ■ Indivs ■ PACs ■ Soft $
1	Lockheed Martin	$1,483,834	40%	59%	
2	Northrop Grumman	$1,157,601	37%	62%	
3	General Dynamics	$1,073,785	38%	60%	
4	Raytheon Co	$973,304	43%	57%	
5	BAE Systems	$889,889	35%	64%	
6	United Technologies	$631,050	30%	59%	
7	DRS Technologies	$577,799	45%	55%	
8	L-3 Communications	$556,085	34%	66%	
9	Science Applications International Corp	$550,792	41%	58%	
10	Honeywell International	$506,593	37%	63%	
11	Cubic Corp	$219,450	18%	82%	
12	Boeing Co	$205,000	40%	56%	
13	Alliant Techsystems	$197,575	36%	64%	
14	Harris Corp	$191,915	8%	92%	
15	General Electric	$174,200	43%	55%	
16	Sierra Nevada Corp	$169,250	55%	45%	
17	AM General Corp	$146,600	11%	89%	
18	Mantech International	$134,000	52%	48%	
19	Collazo Enterprises	$131,400	0%	100%	
20	Vought Aircraft	$124,000	26%	74%	

Construction Long-Term Political
Party Contribution Trends
Courtesy Center for Responsive Politics

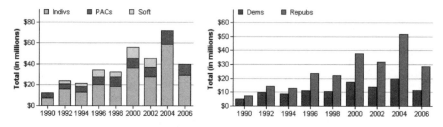

Construction: Top Contributors to
Federal Candidates and Parties, Election Cycle 2006
Courtesy Center for Responsive Politics

Total contributions: **$40,266,484**

Miscellaneous Defense Long-Term Contribution Trends
Courtesy Center for Responsive Politics

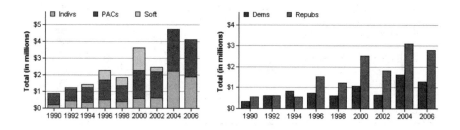

Miscellaneous Defense — Top 20 Contributors to Federal Candidates and Parties
Election Cycle 2006

Courtesy Center for Responsive Politics

Rank	Organization	Amount	Dems	Repubs	Source ■ Indivs ■ PACs ▧ Soft $
1	Northrop Grumman	$1,157,601	37%	62%	
2	BAE Systems Land & Armaments	$303,255	26%	73%	
3	Alliant Techsystems	$197,575	36%	64%	
4	AM General Corp	$146,600	11%	89%	
5	Mantech International	$134,000	52%	48%	
6	Collazo Enterprises	$131,400	0%	100%	
7	Washington Group International	$110,814	20%	80%	
8	Phoenix Management	$103,450	0%	100%	
9	SRA International	$97,289	40%	56%	
10	MZM Inc	$96,125	0%	100%	
11	21st Century Systems	$82,000	86%	14%	
12	AAI Corp	$79,500	38%	62%	
13	General Atomics	$78,400	36%	64%	
14	PMA Group	$78,000	44%	56%	
15	Battelle Memorial Institute	$76,150	25%	75%	
16	Armor Holdings	$66,950	23%	77%	
17	Davidson Technologies	$66,800	0%	100%	
18	Institute for Defense Analyses	$65,612	5%	95%	
19	BEAMHIT	$56,500	55%	45%	
20	Gehr Industries	$53,200	0%	100%	

Are We Really Safer Under Bush?

While the Bush Administration touts its record of keeping America safe, it has failed to implement even the most basic recommendations made by the 9/11 Commission. One of the most essential recommendations was to restructure U.S. intelligence agencies in order to ensure information sharing, reduce redundancy and provide for quick responses to suspected terror threats. The report recommended fresh management and a new direction utilizing competent experts from within the U.S. federal government and the private sector. The recommendations included a consolidation of the many different bureaucratic offices and layers. The goal was to create one powerful agency and remove barriers to information sharing that have existed among the numerous agencies. This would provide for a leaner, smarter and proactive intelligence operation.

The recommendations were completely ignored by the Bush Administration. It has left the extensive bureaucratic muddle intact and untouched, and it has made matters worse by creating yet another bureaucracy. A newly created institution was made up of more than one thousand people in an Office of the Director of National Intelligence, headed by Neoconservative John Negroponte. In 2007, Negroponte was moved to the number two position at the Secretary of State's office and a new Director of National Intelligence, Mike McConnel, took over.

It appears the priority of the United States in Iraq has been the rebuilding of the oil pipelines, a gigantic embassy and permanent military bases. It has failed to make the rebuilding of homes, hospitals and commerce a priority. Iraqi communities sit in rubble without reliable utilities, including water, sewer and electricity. The 9/11 Commission recommendations go unheeded; bin Laden continues to energize al-Qaeda, war industries get richer while America's coffers head towards bankruptcy. Republicans campaign under the guise of vigilant security protection. Despite evidence to the contrary, some Americans swear we are safer under the Bush watch. Others scream in frustration, insisting it just isn't so.

NOTES, Chapter 13

[1] Patrick Cockburn, "From Turning Point to Vanishing Point...Iraq: A Bloody Mess," *Counterpunch*, June 28, 2005.

[2] Hamza Hendawi, "War in Iraq, Police: Troops Kill Pregnant Woman", *The Associated Press*, May 2006.

[3] Ibid.

[4] Amit R. Paley, "Most Iraqis Favor Immediate U.S. Pullout, Polls Show," *The Washington Post*, September 27, 2006, A22, www.washingtonpost.com/wp-dyn/content/article/2006/09/26/AR2006092601721_pf.html.

[5] Andrew J. Bacevich, "What's An Iraqi Life Worth?" *The Washington Post*, July 9, 2006, B01, www.washingtonpost.com/wp-dyn/content/article/2006/07/07/AR2006070701155.html?sub=AR.

[6] Steven R. Hurst, "Official Estimates Civilian Deaths at 150,000," *The New Mexican*, November 10, 2006, A3.

[7] "Updated Iraq Survey Affirms Earlier Mortality Estimates," *Johns Hopkins: Bloomberg School of Public Health*, October 11, 2006, www.jhsph.edu/publichealthnews/press_releases/2006/burnham_iraq_2006.html.

[8] "Minuteman Founder Jim Gilchrist Storms Off *Democracy Now!* Debate With Columbia Student Organizer," *Democracy Now, The War and Peace Report*, October 11, 2006, www.democracynow.org/article.pl?sid=06/10/11/1430231.

[9] www.guardian.co.uk/Iraq/Story/0,,1963612,00.html

[10] A copy of the full Iraq Study Group Report can be found on the internet at www.reliefweb.int/rw/RWB.NSF/db900SID/YSAR-6W8TZ7/$File/Full_Report.pdf

[11] Ben Feller, Bush seeks advice on new course in Iraq, *Associated Press*, December 11, 2006.

[12] Janet A. Simons, Donald B. Irwin and Beverly A. Drinnien, "Maslow's Hierarchy of Needs," in *Psychology - The Search for Understanding* (New York: West Publishing Company, 1987). honolulu.hawaii.edu/intranet/committees/FacDevCom/ guidebk/teachtip/maslow.htm

[13] Chris Matthews and Cindy Sheehan, *Hardball*, MSNBC, August 15, 2005.

[14] Seymour M. Hersh, "A Case Not Closed," *The New Yorker*, November 1, 1993, www.newyorker.com/archive/content/articles/020930fr_archive02?020930fr_archive02.

[15] George W. Bush, *Address to the UN General Assembly*, September 12, 2002, quoted in Tom Saum, "Bush's Ever-changing Justification for War in Iraq," *Associated Press*, October 15, 2006.

[16] George W. Bush, *Presidential Address*, Cincinnati, October 7, 2002, quoted in Tom Saum, "Bush's Ever-changing Justification for War in Iraq," *Associated Press*, October 15, 2006.

[17] George W. Bush, *Address to United States Troops*, Qatar, June 5, 2003, quoted in Tom Saum, "Bush's Ever-changing Justification for War in Iraq," *Associated Press*, October 15, 2006.

[18] George W. Bush, *Second Inaugural Address*, January 20, 2005, quoted in Tom Saum, "Bush's Ever-changing Justification for War in Iraq," *Associated Press*, October 15, 2006.

[19] George W. Bush, *News Conference*, Crawford Texas, August 7, 2006, quoted in Tom Saum, "Bush's Ever-changing Justification for War in Iraq," *Associated Press*, October 15, 2006.

[20] George W. Bush, *GOP Fundraiser*, California, October 3, 2006, quoted in Tom Saum, "Bush's Ever-changing Justification for War in Iraq," *Associated Press*, October 15, 2006.

[21] "Bush on Iraq: 'We're Not Leaving So Long As I'm The President'," *Think Progress*, August 21, 2006, thinkprogress.org/2006/08/21/bush-not-leaving/.

[22] The Countdown with Keith Olbermann, MSNBC, Presidential video footage while campaigning for Republican Candidates, November 2006.

[23] John Lehman, "We're Not Winning This War, Despite Some Notable Achievements, New Thinking Is Needed on the Home Front and Abroad," *The Washington Post*, August, 31, 2006, A25.

[24] Daphne Eviatar, "Public Money in the Pipeline," *Mother Jones*, January/February 2003, www.motherjones.com/news/outfront/2003/01/ma_216_01.html.

[25] Ibid.

[26] Alexandr Shkolnikov and John D. Sullivan, "Conditions for International Lending: Alternatives To Current IMF And World Bank Loan Programs," *Center for International Private Enterprise*, www.cipe.org/pdf/publications/fs/conditionality_final.pdf.

[27] "Why the fuss about Baku's new oil pipeline?" *Money Week*, March 6, 2005, www.moneyweek.com/file/2691/baku-pipeline.html.

[28] Christine Spolar, "Long-term Military Presence Planned," *Chicago Tribune*, March 24, 2004, www.globalsecurity.org/org/news/2004/040323-enduring-bases.htm.

[29] Ibid.

[30] Leila Fadel, "Massive Embassy Rising In Iraq," *Mercury News*, May 25, 2006.

[31] Barbara Slavin, "Giant U.S. Embassy Rising in Baghdad," *USA Today*, April 19, 2006 www.usatoday.com/news/world/iraq/2006-04-19-us-embassy_x.htm.

[32] Susan B. Epstein, "U.S. Embassy In Iraq," *CRS Report to Congress*, April 11, 2005, fas.org/sgp/crs/mideast/RS21867.pdf#search=American%20Embassy%20in%20Iraq%20Construction.

[33] Peter Slevin, "Group Says Iraq Contractors Donated Significantly to Bush's Campaign," *The Washington Post*, October 30, 2003, www.washingtonpost.com/ac2/wp-dyn?pagename=article&node=&contentId=A40708-2003Oct30&notFound=true.

★ 14 ★

Push, Push Back: Distraction, Division and Polarization

"Minds are like parachutes, they only work when they are open."

Anonymous

THIS CHAPTER IS ESPECIALLY DEDICATED to my father, the late Antonio "Nap" Benavidez. Nap was a staunch Democrat, who voted in 2000 for George W. Bush on a single issue. As a devout Catholic and daily mass attendee, Dad did not believe in abortion except in instances of rape, incest or if the mother's life was threatened.

Before dad died, he expressed remorse over his vote, saying, "Bush tricked me; he never intended to change the laws on abortion. [Bush's] goal was to divide families and communities over moral issues as a way to distract Americans." Nap witnessed the Bush Administration, together with a Republican-controlled Congress, as they rolled back laws designed to protect average Americans while "promoting an unnecessary war in Iraq." My father died of prostate cancer in September 2005.

Push, Push Back Creates Conflict and Fails to Solve Problems

In my seminars I frequently conduct an exercise designed to show how conflict works. I ask participants to find a partner and to put their hands up against their partner's hands and push just as hard as they can against their partner's hands. The only thing I ask is that they don't knock each other off their chairs. The participants push for about 30 seconds and then I ask the question, who just won? The answers are usually the same. No one wins. Partner A pushes and Partner B pushes back a little harder and so it goes, back and forth. It's a no-win situation.

Throughout the year since Dad's passing, I've thought about the words he shared with me in the last weeks of his life. And as I've researched, I found that the Bush Administration purposely created distractions, divisions and polarizations using emotionally charged wedge issues. Their first goal was to distract Americans over sizzling moral issues. After citizens were emotionally stirred up, the Bush Administration could divide the American people. When the divisions are deep enough polarization sets in, people stop talking to each other and it becomes difficult to solve problems.

While many Americans have been focused on their most passionate "wedge" issue, we have not had time to concentrate on other important issues that affect us collectively. In other words, while Americans have been engaged in a no-win match of "push, push back," the Bush Administration cut taxes again and again for the wealthy, eliminated laws designed to protect workers and abolished rules and regulations that protect the environment. They rushed us into a no-win war in Iraq and then they gave huge no-bid contracts and subsidies to their corporate friends. Now the administration is gunning for another war against Iran. The impact of these actions on the homeland will be discussed in subsequent chapters.

Dividers of America, including media pundits on both sides, have engaged in the ridiculous divisionary tactic of framing the political debate in terms of Red State versus Blue State and Conservative versus Liberal. At last, some are beginning to see through the veil of such artificially dividing tactics. In reality, there are no truly red states — they all have pockets of blue — and neither are there any completely blue states. Even within the great Lone Star State of Texas there is blue. Just look at Austin and you will find the capital of Texas to be as blue as blue gets. Within blue states such as California you will also find red pockets. My observation after traveling and conducting seminars throughout America is that Americans are neither Red nor Blue. In the words of Senator, Barack Obama, (D-IL), "They are purple!"

The politics of divisiveness is extremely debilitating to our nation and its people. We are always at our best as a people when we can communicate and work together to solve our common problems. But when a nation becomes so polarized that we are unable to dialogue, we all lose.

2004 Presidential Election

Presidential popular votes by county. Created by Michael Gastner,
Cosma Shalizi, and Mark Nudeman of the University of Michigan.
Source: http://www-personal.umich.edu/~mejn/election/

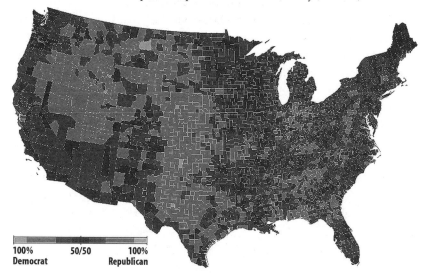

100%	50/50	100%
Democrat		Republican

United We Stand — Divided We Fall

"A house divided against itself cannot stand."

Abraham Lincoln

I would venture to say that abortion is the most polarizing topic for Americans, and the Bush Administration frequently uses it divisively to its advantage. Several experiences have affected my thoughts on abortion. In 1979, on the anniversary of Roe vs. Wade, while working for the New Mexico Public Health Department, I recall several staff members asking permission to attend rallies at the State Capitol. Roe vs. Wade is the Supreme Court decision that legalized abortion. Some staff members were going to attend a rally in support and others were going to march in protest of the decision. The director of the health agency gave permission to staff members to go to the event of their choice. Permission was required since the events were scheduled during working hours. Before several employees left the building, he said, "You cannot outlaw immorality." I pondered that statement for years.

His statement hit me between the eyes when I was in my mid-twenties and discussing abortion with an elderly couple Elsie and Ralph, whom I trusted and loved dearly. Needless to say, I was highly opioniated on the matter at the time. The elderly couple confided the reason they had adopted their three children was because Elsie had chosen to have a "back alley" abortion in 1933. Abortion was illegal at the time. The procedure left her half dead and sterile. Elsie said when she made her decision to have an abortion she was a seventeen year old unmarried girl and scared witless. Ralph died in 1990 and Elsie in 1993. I was proud to know them and would have never considered them radical or immoral. They remained staunch supporters of legalized abortion to their dying days.

Even discussing abortion can divide a family. There is the story of a father who disowned his daughter. He disowned her because she *advocated* an abortion as an option. Leslie, a colleague, told me of how she had provided her daughter with all of the options, after her terrified fifteen-year old confided in her that she was pregnant. The young girl ultimately gave the baby up for adoption. When Leslie saw her father, she told him of the counseling she had provided her daughter, his granddaughter. Leslie's father, a Catholic, did not believe in abortion as a viable option under any circumstances. Leslie said that her father renounced her for nearly two years. She said it was painful when he didn't send her a birthday or Christmas card and even more difficult when he refused to come to her home. But she said she simply could not apologize to her father. Leslie said it was an important decision that her daughter would have to live with for the rest of her life. She felt, as a mother, the obligation to give her child all the options and to trust her child to make the best decision.

Leslie's father became conflicted enough over the situation to seek the counsel of a priest. The priest asked Leslie's father if he was willing to abort his living relationship with his daughter over the matter. The wise priest suggested Leslie's father pray and love Leslie unconditionally. He explained that there is a greater chance for people to become convinced of these matters through the "unconditional love Jesus demonstrated." This was fifteen years ago. Leslie and her dad now have a good relationship, though neither of them has ever changed their minds. She said, "We agreed not to discuss the subject. He tells me he prays for me and I thank him." This powerful story showed me how this painful topic nearly destroyed a family.

Last winter, a high school counselor, Jenna, and her husband were visiting mutual friends in Santa Fe. This couple is from a small town in West Texas. During the course of their visit, Jenna joined me at the local gym for a workout and we discussed her job as a counselor. Jenna indicated she was absolutely heart-wrenched over her work. She explained that large numbers of high school students were engaging in sexual activity. Jenna described her predominately evangelical Protestant community and said it was a place where no one discussed, much less practiced, protected sex. The only discussions taking place were about sexual abstinence.

Jenna said she wasn't supposed to advocate protection because the school district had adopted a strict abstinence policy. Jenna understood it was only a matter of time before a number of young teenage girls would become pregnant as many already had. She said the saddest part of her job was that most of the girls that went home pregnant were disowned by their families. Jenna expressed the emotional devastation of watching it occur. She believed the people in her community would be better off if they used their skills, energy, money, and talents to create truly loving, compassionate support homes for the young, unwed mothers. She wished that homes could be created to help these young girls complete their education and assist them with child rearing or the adoption process. And she wondered whether it would help to eliminate abortions if social attitudes toward single mothers were more kindhearted and accepting. Finally Jenna said the best way to deal with protecting against unwanted pregnancies was by instituting and maintaining strong prevention programs that included information about contraception and condoms for the prevention of sexually transmitted diseases (STDs) and unintended pregnancies. She felt it would be a hard sell in her community.

On the subject of abortion, a 2005 *Harris Poll* survey found that a majority of those polled (55 percent) favored keeping abortion legal but with conditions. And nearly a quarter (23 percent) favored keeping abortion legal in all circumstances. Of those polled by Harris, 21 percent opposed abortion in all situations.[1] The pro-life contingencies of the Religious Right have been diligent to this key value: making abortion illegal. They have been willing to support politicians who will do and say anything to get elected as long as these politicians *"say"* they oppose abortion.

When the Bush Administration brings up the abortion issue, it is more often through the lens of embryonic stem cell research. George W. Bush used his first Presidential veto in 2006 against a bill passed by both Republican-controlled houses that would have provided federal funding for embryonic stem cell research.[2]

According to a 2004 *Harris Poll*, 80 percent of Democrats, 83 percent of Independents and 60 percent of Republicans support embryonic stem cell research. The polling question by Harris was structured as follows: "Stem cells come from embryos left over from *in vitro* fertilization, which are not used and normally destroyed. Many medical researchers want to use them to develop treatments, or to prevent diseases, such as diabetes, Alzheimer's or Parkinson's disease. On balance, do you think this research should or should not be allowed?"[3]

It is a remarkable exercise to examine how Americans feel about abortion, embryonic stem-cell research, assisted suicide, and the death penalty. Here are some typical examples from random interviews I conducted:

Thomas is a teacher who describes himself as a moderate. He is a registered Democrat, married with three children. He says abortion should be made illegal except in life-threatening instances. He is against the death penalty, but supports embryonic stem cell research, and he says he believes in "death with dignity," otherwise known as assisted suicide or euthanasia.

Sandy runs her own business and has a two-year secretarial degree. She is a registered Republican and considers herself "fairly conservative." She is married with one adult child and one teenager. Sandy is against embryonic stem cell research and is pro-life. She supports the death penalty but is against assisted suicide.

Josie is a medical doctor and a registered Democrat. She refers to herself as a moral liberal and a fiscal conservative. Josie is pro-choice, supports embryonic stem cell research and favors assisted sucide when medically necessary. Josie opposes the death penalty.

Margo is a realtor who is divorced with one grown son. She identifies herself as a moderate and is registered as an Independent. She confided that abortions should be limited to no more than two in a lifetime. Margo supports embryonic stem-cell research and she supports the death penalty, but only for "unusual, cruel crimes." She supports assisted suicide, especially for those suffering from painful terminal illnesses or for those who are "clinically brain-dead."

Betty is a graphic artist and is registered as a Republican. She describes herself as a "moderate." Betty thinks abortion should be legal only in cases of rape or incest or if the mother's life is endangered. Betty is undecided about embryonic stem cell research. She favors the death penalty, but opposes suicide assistance under any circumstances.

Jack is a chef at a high-end restaurant and is registered as a member of the Green Party. He is pro-choice with no restrictions. Jack supports embryonic stem cell research and he favors the death penalty. He is supportive of assisted suicide but only with extremely diligently oversight.

George W. Bush, who postures himself as cherishing Christian values, remains one of the staunchest advocates of the death penalty. While he was the governor of Texas, George W. Bush proudly signed the execution orders of 152 inmates on death row.[4] According to the *Catholic News Service*, John Kerry would have been the most anti-death penalty President in over half a century.[5] However, there was virtually no public debate or comparison over the conflicting position regarding the death penalty as held by the two men.

Prior to the U.S.-led invasion of Iraq and before his death, Pope John Paul, one of the world's eminent Christian leaders, provided theological details explaining why America's war on Iraq was not justified on moral grounds. The Pope met with President Bush to explain why the invasion of Iraq would be "immoral, illegal and unjust."[6] Bush's response was to say he would not be influenced by the Pope's appeals.[7]

We live in challenging times and these life issues are important.[8] With respect to life and death questions, there are no clear red/blue distinctions. These are purple questions for most Americans. A 2006 *Pew Study* indicated most Americans don't want to be polarized on these matters. They would prefer to find the middle ground.[9] If you examine the following chart, you may find yourself making choices to the right and to the left. Incidentally, they do not correspond philosophically to either a liberal or a conservative model. Many liberals who support choice in abortion are against the death penalty. Many conservatives who are against abortion support the death penalty. Others, like those in the *Pew Study*, will find themselves with preferences down the middle.

Wedge Issues

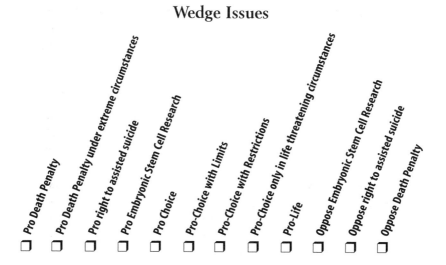

Church, God and Government

Another polarizing issue is the debate over the separation of church and state. Our forefathers fought the American Revolutionary War in part because of the religious persecution they had suffered at the hands of the British government. Our Constitution was written in a manner that guarantees the right of each and every American to practice his or her own religion, or no religion at all. It is among the most fundamental of the freedoms guaranteed by the Bill of Rights.

The Constitution's framers understood that religious liberty can flourish *only* if the people are free from government interference or sponsorship of religion. The blurring of the line can have dire results. When one religious group claims to have derived power from the government, it may be inclined to subjugate or suppress other religions. Or such a group may engage in promoting its religion in an effort to convert others.

History is full of religious groups claiming political power and the abuses that follow are most often egregious. While Christians may be thrilled at having a President who is willing to blur the lines on their behalf, they may want to consider how it might feel if the President were a Muslim who was providing preferential treatment to Muslim groups or making judgments that would benefit Muslims. Having a clear separation of church and state is the best protection for Americans of all faiths and those with no faith at all.

When Did Jesus Become a Republican?

I actually laughed out loud when I read the rhetorical question in the Reverend Jim Wallis's book *God's Politics — Why the Right Gets It Wrong and the Left Doesn't Get It.*[10] For me, as an American with a deep spiritual faith, the issue resounded. Reverend Wallis begged the question, "When did Jesus become a Republican?"

As a woman who has studied scripture, prays daily, and experienced being "born again" over thirty years ago, I ask, "When did Jesus become a war god and ask us to launch wars to prevent war?" When did He become pro-rich, advocating that we turn our back on the poor? When did Jesus preach hate, bigotry, racism and division? The Jesus I know is loving and compassionate.

I do not know when I will die or be called; but I do know that each of us are walking around with a predetermined "expiration date." As such, I don't believe that the God of my understanding will ask me at the end of my life about the abundance of wealth I accumulated, or the number or homes or cars I possessed. Rather, I believe I might be asked how I used the gifts God gave me to make the world a better place. I believe I might be asked, "What did I do for the less fortunate of my brethren?" Did I feed the poor, visit the imprisoned, provide shelter for the homeless and did I take care of the sick? These are the questions those professing Christianity must be prepared to answer. How will those who have a moral conscience regardless of their faith or lack of faith answer these questions?

In the 2004 elections, 78 percent of white evangelical Protestants and "traditional" or conservative Christians, including conservative Catholics, voted for George W. Bush. The religious right accounted for over 40 percent of his total popular vote, according to John Green, a political scientist at the University of Akron. Bush's faith-based social welfare strategy accelerated our nation toward a theocracy.[11] Theocracy is a form of government guided by a religious code. Right-leaning evangelical churches had been promised taxpayer money so they—instead of the federal government—could perform public services. This is in direct violation of the separation of church and state that is so fundamental to the U.S. Constitution. These churches have been found to frequently attack candidates and politicians who favor increasing public services for the poor and needy through established government programs such as Medicaid and state-administered Welfare to Work programs.[12]

Rove's requests to evangelical churches to acquire membership lists for political mailings and to target votes for George W. Bush seem to go largely unnoticed. Evangelical churches throughout the country proudly display the American flag, and many sermons include elements of God, Country and Patriotism.[13] Prior to the 2004 elections, religious right church leaders took out full-page advertisements in major newspapers telling voters it was a sin to support pro-choice candidates, including John Kerry.[14] During this same time, the American Life League, a pro-life organization in Virginia, targeted Catholic bishops in a half a million-dollar media campaign demanding that Catholic priests deny Communion to pro-choice politicians.[15] Deal W. Hudson, the editor of a politically conservative Catholic magazine and a key Bush supporter, recommended that Catholic priests read letters from the pulpit denouncing the senator from Massachusetts.[16]

The Bush Administration turned a blind eye to church activities that benefited their candidates and the Republican Party. However, the fervor shown to stamp out opposition to those entities and individuals who are aligned otherwise is quite another story. Take the matter of the All Saints Episcopal Church and its rector, the Reverend Ed Bacon, in Pasadena. The church and pastor have been accused of improper campaigning. The IRS is threatening the church with the loss of its non-profit status because it alleges the Reverend preached antiwar sermons throughout 2004. The Internal Revenue Service ordered the Church to turn over all the documents and e-mails produced during the 2004 election year with references to political candidates. The All Saints Episcopal Church and Reverend Bacon had until September 29, 2006 to present the sermons, newsletters and electronic communications. The Episcopal Church is referred to as a "liberal" church in articles related to the IRS investigation. One wonders why it would be considered unusual that a Christian church would preach against war. The hypocrisy lies in the fact that no Christian evangelical church or leaders are facing federal probes for any alleged blurring of the lines between church and state.[17]

For example, the Christian Coalition, a conservative political advocacy group founded by evangelical Pat Robertson, distributed over 70 million voter guides in churches all across America, including over 5 million in Spanish, prior to the 2000 Presidential election. In the 2004 Presidential election, the Christian Coalition distributed 30 million voter guides in targeted states and congressional districts, focusing their efforts on races that were considered more politically competitive.[18] After a long battle with the IRS over the Coalition's partisan political activities, the IRS finally agreed in 2005 to allow the Christian Coalition *to keep its tax-exempt status and to distribute voter guides directly in churches.*[19]

Division and Base Building

Instead of dealing with any major critical issues in the spring of 2006, the President and the Republican-controlled Congress chose to focus on gay marriage and flag burning.

According to a poll conducted in June of 2006, 58 percent of Americans say that same-sex marriage should be illegal. However, only 4 in 10 said they support amending the Constitution to ban gay marriage, and a majority said the states should make their own laws on the issue.[20] The Congress in June of 2006 rejected a bill to amend the Constitution to make gay marriage illegal. This subject appears to come up for debate mainly when the Bush Administration needs some distraction from the bad news of its failing policies in Iraq or the economy.

It was clear from the beginning that even with a Republican-controlled Congress, changing the Constitution to ban gay marriage was destined to fail. But because President Bush's approval ratings were hovering in the mid-30s, he put the gay marriage issue back on the front burner to create further divisions and polarize Americans. By using this divisive subject he hoped to drum up support for himself and distract Americans from the many more pressing issues facing our nation.

Members of the President's base, such as the religious right, are beginning to see the rhetoric and timing of the debate on these issues as a manipulative exercise. Gary Glenn, president of the American Family Association, has said that the Association "expect[s] real action, not just politically timed attempts to motivate and organize the base."[21]

In the book *Tempting Faith . . . An Inside Account of the Rise of Christian Conservatives and Their Betrayal by the Bush White House*, author David Kuo reveals how the Bush White House ridiculed, mocked and used the Religious Right for political purposes.[22] David Kuo was second in command in the Office of Faith Based Initiatives in the George W. Bush Administration. He describes how members of the Bush Administration referred to evangelical Christians as "nuts" and "goofy." He says Christians were dismissed as "ridiculous" and "out of control." Mr. Kuo tells what happened to a $1.7 trillion Bush-sponsored tax cut that was suppose to include $6 billion in tax credits for faith-based initiatives. It was eliminated from the budget after the administration decided they were no longer interested in pursuing the faith-based initiative dollars. The reality is that faith-based initiatives and other charities *lost five billion dollars* under the Bush Administration because of tax law changes made to the charitable giving rules.[23]

Using the Faithful

Mr. Kuo describes how the Office of Faith Based Initiatives was used to galvanize votes for Republican candidates through publicly funded tax-payer programs. One program designed as the "Round Table Discussions" included frequent conference calls and a series of face-to-face meetings between Republican candidates and grass roots evangelical leaders from all over the country. The evangelicals and a select group of twenty Republican candidates met frequently to discuss how these Republican candidates could help serve the poor. No Democratic candidates were invited to attend any of the sessions.

The Round Tables proved to be so successful that 19 of the 20 Republicans won targeted seats in 2004, with 76 percent of evangelical Christians voting for Republicans. The White House devised a cover-up scheme to "inoculate against accusations that we were using religion and religious leaders to promote specific candidates."[24] Conference calls with evangelical leaders such as Pat Robertson, James Dawson, Ted Haggard, and Michael Reagan served to keep the base engaged with Republican leaders.

When apprehensive evangelical Christians got concerned about their issues, they were pacified. According to Mr. Kuo, they were given tickets to see George W. Bush when he came to their town. Other tokens of appeasement included front row passes allowing them to shake the President's hand, and trinkets such as cuff links, pens and pads of paper. The Christian base was reminded that the President had instituted a National Day of Prayer. David Kuo affirms that George W. Bush is no different than any other politician. Mr. Kuo left the White House saying the Bush Administration had made a mockery of the millions of faithful Christians who had put their hope and trust in the President.

Analyzing the Walk and Talk of Conservative Politicians

We must make an honest assessment of the walk and talk of conservative politicians. The Bush Administration and many Republican politicians say they are "compassionate conservatives." They speak of the values that matter most to Americans sprinkling their speeches with frequent and warm mentions of "God." However, their actions reflect nothing of God and little of compassion.

According to Frank Thomas, author of *What's Wrong with Kansas*, there is a difference in how politicians talk the line of Jesus Christ on the campaign trail and how they walk it. Once these politicians have secured their office, they walk a very straight corporate line. Their decisions and policies are all geared towards helping corporate America and rich Americans, who supported them financially in their political campaigns. The middle class and the poor haven't contributed much money, so once they have voted they stop mattering to these politicians. All the other "God-like" issues evaporate. Politicians give little more than lip service to these issues.

The goal of these compassionate conservatives has never been to help middle- or working-class Americans. While talking American values, they serve up dishes of corporate complicity instead. The promised values are never delivered: abortion is never stopped and flag burning is never made illegal. It is a classic bait and switch. Here's what's promised and what is delivered instead:

WHAT CONSERVATIVE POLITICIANS PROMISE	WHAT IS DELIVERED
Make the U.S. strong	Increase foreign oil dependency in the Middle East.
Stop government intrusion	Allow polluting companies and auto emissions to ruin the environment.
Stay the Course	Refuse to leave Iraq until American corporate oil interests are secure.
Secure your future	Eliminate Social Security.
Get government off your back	Ignore public school education problems.
Stand up to terrorism	Isolate the U.S. and cut homeland security budget.
Protect the economy	Reject minimum wage increases, give more tax breaks to the rich and drive up the federal deficit.
Protect family values	Discount city needs (like New Orleans), eliminate overtime pay and employee OSHA safety programs. Slash funding for public assistance programs.
Support the troops	Cut VA benefits, deploy reservists several times, and lie to and deceive enlistees.
Protect the Pledge of Allegiance	Spy on American citizens, conduct illegal wire-tapping and outsource more American jobs abroad.
Protect Public Prayer	Torture detainees, void international treaties, resuscitate Star Wars. Increase our own stockpile of WMDs and sell more arms globally.
Protect Stem Cells	Look for ways to provoke more wars aboard with nations like Iran, Syria and North Korea. Fail to provide leadership for peace between Lebanon, Palestine and Israel.
Stop Abortion	Give tax cuts to the rich.
Stop Flag Burning	Deregulate energy companies.
Stop Gay Marriage	Give billion dollar no-bid contracts to their friends.

The Self-Defeating Behavior of
Middle- and Working-Class Americans

The most frightening aspect of this entire debacle is that for years, most Americans have believed we are safer and more secure under this administration. Until 2006, it appeared the majority of Americans had been willing to blindly support the President and the Republican-controlled Congress' agenda. This agenda has done more harm to the American middle-class and working-class than any other political agenda in over a century.

Thomas Frank aptly describes this fiasco when he writes, "Here is a movement (middle- and working-class Americans) whose response to the power structure is to make the rich even richer; whose answer to the inexorable degradation of working-class life is to lash out angrily at labor unions and liberal workplace-safety programs; whose solution to the rise of ignorance in America is to pull the rug out from public education."[25] Hard-right Washington politicians blame everything bad on Bill Clinton, Democrats and liberals. All while stirring the pot of political dissention, they move their Neoconservative agenda further and further along.

Further Alienation of the Center and Left

My research indicates people can normally concentrate on five to seven issues at a time, give or take two different issues. Given that Americans have so much on their plates, how much attention, time and energy can really be dedicated to issues outside our normal lives? During the battle between Israel and Lebanon in July and August of 2006, the United States sat on the sidelines, failing to provide any real leadership or strategy needed to broker a workable peace plan. The U.S. blamed Hezbollah, Iran, and Syria for the conflict.[26] And when a delicate peace finally fell, George W. Bush antagonistically proclaimed that Israel had won. It appears he loves to increase consternation in the Middle East.

Those who are aware of the Neocon plot to dominate and promote American hegemony across the Middle East understand there is no real motivation for the U.S. to broker any true substantial peace plan. The real goal of the Neocons is to find a way to embroil the U.S. in a direct combat alongside Israel against Hezbollah, with the hope of drawing Iran into the conflict more directly.[27] The whispering tactics about Iran being the sponsor of Hezbollah is being used by the Neocons to manipulate

America emotionally. As the whispering turns to murmuring, it may soon turn to shouts. Americans are being bombarded with media messages of how Hezbollah is but "a surrogate of Iran and Syria."[28]

In accordance with the Project for a New American Century and the Neoconservative dictates that are now U.S. policy, Iran and Syria are next on the list for attack. Prolific Neoconservative writers like Charles Krauthammer and William Kristol are at it again, beating for war. They are using the same old worn-out tactics, warning of weapons of mass destruction to incite fear, but this time it's against Iran and Iranian President Mahmoud Ahmadinejad. Their columns fill our daily newspapers and respected magazines. Periodicals on both the left and on the right, find room for their battle cries for more war, never questioning the real bases for their accusations.[29]

Distraction by Color Code

Almost simultaneously, commotion is created to distract Americans from finding out what is really going on. The day after the success of Democrat Ned Lamont's bid over incumbent Joe Lieberman in Connecticut's state primary for one of the Senatorial seats, our nation was suddenly placed under a THREAT ALERT. The color code used was RED, the highest level of alert.[30] Republicans have exercised this tactic so many times one would think Americans should be used to it by now. Immediately after the Democratic National Convention in the summer of 2004, many of our major cities went under threat alert to distract Americans from the convention. It was later discovered that the threat alert was based upon dated materials barely relevant and hardly worth their weight. However, it worked well as a diversionary tactic.

During the 2004 Presidential election, whenever John Kerry's ratings spiked, Bush initiated terror warnings. Also, in 2006, an announcement was made stating planned terrorist attacks had been thwarted. The announcement coincided with the public disclosure and evaluation of the White House tactics related to the illegal domestic wire-tapping scandal.

The Bush/Cheney team whirl fear tactics anytime a spike is needed to improve their ratings. These fear-mongering tactics have gotten under the skin of many Americans. For example, Sally, a consultant from Dallas, said she was sure that if we brought the U.S. troops home from Iraq we would get "hit again" just like 9/11.[31]

The Turd Blossom Factor

George W. Bush's nickname for Karl Rove is the "Turd Blossom." A turd blossom is a Texan term for a flower that grows out from under a pile of cow dung.[32] This is most interesting. I would ask you to pause for a moment and ask yourself what would cause your boss to give you such a nickname. Karl Rove is a college dropout and a political consultant who is frequently referred to as Bush's brain and the architect behind his political wins. Rove has a long history of employing dirty politics and has freely admitted to engaging in foul tactics. He once used a false identity in 1970 to get into the office of Illinois Democrat Alan Dixon. Dixon was running for state treasurer. Rove stole Mr. Dixon's letterhead stationery and sent out 1,000 bogus invitations to the opening of the candidate's headquarters promising "free beer, free food, girls and a good time for nothing."[33] Rove laughs at this early account.

However, with time and experience, Rove's tactics have grown in malice and intensity. Rove's alleged use of "whisper campaigns" against his opponents has proven to be highly damaging. A whisper campaign is a covert method of influencing voters by initiating false and extremely damaging rumors or innuendo about the opposing candidate. The initiator of the rumors works anonymously while still spreading the innuendo. It is a exceptionally unscrupulous practice. There are more than fifty allegations against Karl Rove, the Turd Blossom. These allegations represent unethical, corrupt and disgusting tactics used by Rove against his opponents. Here are a few examples:

According to Marissa, a hair stylist and former Texan, Karl Rove was well known in Texas for taking his opponents' best attributes and turning them against them with "mean-spirited" and "hateful rumors." Marissa said with the George W. Bush versus Ann Richards 1994 gubernatorial race in mind, "Everyone knew Ann Richards was a tolerant person, so when George W. Bush was down in the polls, Rove started a false lesbian rumor.

"In the race for governor against Ann Richards, Rove was accused of using pollsters to call voters to ask if they would be 'more or less likely to vote for Governor Richards if they knew her staff was dominated by lesbians.'" During the race, a regional chairman of the Bush campaign was quoted criticizing Richards for "appointing avowed homosexual activists" to state jobs.[34] Only circumstantial evidence would link Rove to these tactics. They were designed to destroy Richards' creditability. And this rumor worked well, especially in a place as conservative as Texas." Marissa said, "We just watched as Governor Richards kept dropping in the polls as the lesbian allegations kept coming up from every direction."[35]

Annette, a psychologist and another Texan, talked about the "scare tactics" used by Bush and Rove when Bush was running for governor of Texas. Annette said, "I just remember it was all about being afraid because crime was going up. We heard the message over and over again." According to Annette, "It was all about the perception of fear and safety even back then." She said, "In debates, Bush would repeat the word 'crime' over and over again against Ann — just like he used the word terrorism against Kerry — it always came back to that."

In 1999 John McCain defeated George W. Bush in the 2000 Republican Presidential primary in New Hampshire. It is alleged that in response Bush's campaign conducted a push poll asking voters, "Would you be more likely or less likely to vote for John McCain for President if you knew he had fathered an illegitimate black child?"[36] The authors of the 2003 book and subsequent film *Bush's Brain: How Karl Rove Made George W. Bush Presidential* allege that Rove was involved in the poll. John McCain's poll numbers would continue to drop as other unscrupulous tactics like these were used against him.

A former Rove staffer reported that in a bitter battle for a seat on the Alabama Supreme Court between incumbent Mark Kennedy and Harold See, the Turd Blossom engaged in vicious campaign tactics. It was reported that Rove, who was running See's campaign against the Democrat Mark Kennedy, was dissatisfied with the effectiveness of his efforts to push See ahead, despite the repulsive tactics he employed. The Turd Blossom was determined to win at all costs. Mark Kennedy had served on a board of directors for a youth agency, donating his time, money and expertise. Rove initiated a whisper campaign against Mr. Kennedy, charging that he was a pedophile.[37] That despicable lie did the trick and Karl Rove's candidate Harold See won by less than one percentage point.

One of the most infamous methods of the Turd Blossom is to plant damaging evidence against his own political clients. After which Karl Rove and his candidate then turn around and accuse their opponent of planting the evidence. *Bush's Brain* provides several instances where Rove has been accused of this particular tactic. In one race in Texas, Rove alleged that someone had placed a camera inside his office to spy on him during the campaign. Rove called both the police and the media, and he accused the opposition. Later, after an investigation was launched it was discovered that the camera was literally brand new and no film had ever been shot from it. But by the time this fact was discovered, the damage to the opposing candidate had already been done. The day after Senator

Joseph Lieberman lost the Connecticut Democratic primary to Ned Lamont, the Lieberman campaign accused the Lamont campaign of tinkering with Lieberman's website in an effort to bring it down. The Bush White House encouraged Lieberman to run as an Independent. The website allegation appeared to be a typical Turd Blossom strategy. There remains little doubt in the minds of those familiar with Rove that the accusations against the Lamont camp were nothing more than a standard depraved Turd Blossom line of attack.

Rove chaired the White House Iraq Group (WHIG), a secretive internal working group established in August 2002, eight months prior to the 2003 invasion of Iraq. According to *CNN* and *Newsweek*, WHIG was "charged with developing a strategy for publicizing the White House's assertion that Saddam Hussein posed a threat to the United States."

Critics alleged that Rove had professional ties to the producers of the Swift Boat Veterans for Truth television ads that criticized John F. Kerry's Vietnam military service. Later it turned out that the assertions made by these swift boaters were based on lies, but again by the time this was proven the damage was already done once again.

A few months after the 2004 election, Representative Maurice Hinchey (D-NY) publicly alleged that Rove engineered the Killian documents controversy by planting fake anti-Bush documents with *CBS News* to deflect attention from Bush's service record during the Vietnam War. Rove denied any involvement.[38] What the media focused on was a single dummied document, and the whole report got blackballed along with Dan Rather, Mary Maples, and three of her staffers. Contrast the media hoopla and outrage over one dummied document with an entire fabrication of lies and documents used to overthrow a country, bomb it to smithereens, kill thousands of people, and spend billions of American taxpayer dollars. Go figure!

These are only a few examples of an operative deliberately spreading disgusting lies against political opponents to win elections or eliminate critics. They have been done in a most vile and sleazy manner.

According to Kerwin Swint, the author of *Mudslingers: The Top 25 Negative Political Campaigns of All Time*, George W. Bush and his father George H.W. Bush hold the dubious distinction of running three of the top twenty-five negative campaigns since the beginning of American politics.[39]

Sick of Divisionary Tactics and Exploitation

Much of the political climate has been sabotaged and hijacked by the divisive Neoconservative agenda combined with the manipulative tactics of the Turd Blossom. But this too is shifting. Michael Gerson, the evangelical speech writer for George W. Bush who resigned from the Bush White House in June of 2006, explained that many evangelicals want to expand their focus to include more global issues such as fighting poverty, eliminating human trafficking and dealing with the AIDS crisis in Africa. This presents a change from the narrower values of abortion and gay marriage. Mr. Gerson said he found American evangelical Christians were more and more likely to request a meeting with the President to discuss their concerns over the problems of genocide in Darfur than to discuss gay marriage.[40]

A new group called the Red Letter Christians urges Christians to "vote their values" by taking into consideration the war in Iraq, the Bush-sanctioned torture, environmental destruction, and the failure to take care of the poor. This coalition reminds Americans that these, too, are vital religious concerns. By the end of 2006, a tidal wave of disenchanted voters began moving away from the politics of division and polarization. Voters fed up with George W. Bush's stubborn stance on Iraq, the endorsement of torture, congressional rubber-stamping, and the cover up of sex scandals and other political improprieties helped pave the way.

In an effort to help restore balance to our nation, evangelical pastors in the fall of 2006 assisted in writing Minnesota's Democratic state preamble, saying, "Democrats in this state are seeking the Common Good— the best life for each person of this state, the orphan, the family, the sick, the healthy, the wealthy, the poor, the citizen, the stranger, the first, and the last."[41]

Bush has a history of finding divisionary tactics that have worked to his benefit. When he won by a mere one percent against John Kerry in the 2004 election, he immediately afterwards declared that he now had a "mandate" to move forward with his agenda. This ploy of calling a slim one percent margin win a mandate undeniably further alienated much of the nation who felt their voices increasingly ignored by this President. Our nation became more divided.

Yet for all the diverseness, this is coming to be one of the most critical eras for Americans to come together collectively for the sake of democracy as we know it, and to ensure the survival of the middle class.

"Whenever the people are well informed, they can be trusted with their own government; that whenever things get so far wrong as to attract their notice, they may be relied on to set them right."

Thomas Jefferson

NOTES, Chapter 14

1 "Only a Small Majority Still Supports Roe v. Wade and Opposition is at its Highest in 20 Years," *The Harris Poll*, March 3, 2005, www.harrisinteractive.com/harris_poll/index.asp?PID=547.

2 Richard Benedetto and Andrea Stone, "Bush rejects stem cell bill with his first veto," *USA Today*, July 7, 2006, www.usatoday.com/news/washington/2006-07-19-stemcells_x.htm?POE=NEWISVA.

3 "Public Support for Stem Cell Research Increases to a 73 to 11 Percent Majority, According to Harris Interactive," *Harris Interactive*, September 7, 2004, www.harrisinteractive.com/news/allnewsbydate.asp?NewsID=839.

4 Patricia Zapor, "Campaign '04: Kerry, Bush at near-opposite extremes on death penalty," *Catholic News Service*, September 3, 2004, www.catholicnews.com/data/stories/cns/0404872.htm.

5 Ibid.

6 "Signs of the Times: Papal Envoy Meets Bush," *America: The National Catholic Weekly*, March 17, 2003, www.catholicpeacefellowship.org/nextpage.asp?m=2278/

7 Pasquale Maria Aliberti, "The Pope's Resistance to the "Unjust War" on Iraq The Vatican's Divisions at the Beginning of World War IV," *Global Research*, April 2, 2005, www.globalresearch.ca/index.php?context=viewArticle&code=MAR20050402&articleId=481,

8 *The Holy See*, www.vatican.va/phome_en.htm.

9 "Pragmatic Americans."

10 Jim Wallis, *God's Politics: Why the Right Gets It Wrong and the Left Doesn't Get It* (New York: HarperCollins, 2006).

11 Barbara Ehrenreich, "The Faith Factor," *The Nation*, November 29, 2004, www.thenation.com/doc/20041129/ehrenreich.

12 Ibid.

13 "Profile: Silent Evangelical Support of Bush's Proposed War Against Iraq," *Morning Edition*, National Public Radio, February 26, 2003, www.npr.org/programs/morning/transcripts/2003/feb/030226.hagerty.html.

14 Ray Suarez, *Holy Vote* (New York: HarperCollins, 2006).

15 Alan Cooperman, "Ad Assails D.C. Cardinal for Stance on Communion," *Washington Post*, May 7, 2004, Page A03.

16 Ibid.

17 "Evangelical Support."

18 "The Christian Coalition," *Wikipedia*, en.wikipedia.org/wiki/Christian_Coalition.

19 Ibid.

20 Deb Riechmann, "Bush Voices Support for Same-Sex-Marriage Ban," *Associated Press*, June 6, 2006.

21 Mara Reynold and Janet Hook, "Bush Stance Fails to Sway Base," *Los Angeles Times*, June 4, 2006.

22 David Kuo, *Tempting Fate: An Inside Story of Political Seduction*, (Free Press, 2006).

23 Ibid.

24 Ibid.

25 Thomas Frank, *What's the Matter With Kansas?* (New York: Metropolitan Books, 2004), 6-7.

26 Caren Bohan, "U.S. accuses Syria, Iran, Hezbollah on Lebanon," *Reuters*, November 1, 2006 www.news.yahoo.com/s/nm/20061101/ts_nm/mideast_lebanon_usa_dc.

27 PNAC, *Rebuilding America's Defenses: Strategy, Forces, and Resources for a New Century* (PNAC: Washington, 2000), www.newamericancentury.org/RebuildingAmericasDefenses.pdf.

28 Martin Fletcher, "Regional tensions fuel Lebanon-Israel clashes," *NBC News*, July 12, 2006, msnbc.msn.com/id/13827858/.

29 a. Charles Krauthammer, "Counterpoint: Actually the Middle East Is Our Crisis Too, The war is now part of the global conflict between the U.S. and radical Islam," *Time*, August 7, 2006 pg. 31.
b. William Kristol, "It's Our War, Bush should go to Jerusalem—and the U.S. should confront Iran," *The Weekly Standard*, Volume 011, Issue 42, July 24, 2006.

30 Ellen Knickmeyer and Fred Barbash, "Britain Thwarts Airline Terror Plot, UK, U.S. Raise Security Threat Levels," *The Washington Post*, August 10, 2006.

31 Ned Lamont, interview by Chris Matthews, *Hardball*, MSNBC, August 10, 2006.

32 "Turd Blossom," *Wikipedia*, en.wikipedia.org/wiki/Turd_Blossom.

33 Dan Balz, "Karl Rove The Strategist," *The Washington Post*, July 23, 1999, www.washingtonpost.com/wp-srv/politics/campaigns/wh2000/stories/rove072399.htm.

34 *Bush's Brain*, DVD, directed by Michael Paradies Shoob and Joseph Mealey (2004; Los Angeles: Tartan Video, 2004), www.sundancechannel.com/film/?ixFilmID=5972.

35 Joshua Green, "Karl Rove in a Corner," *The Atlantic Monthly*, November 2004, www.theatlantic.com/doc/200411/green.

36 Richard H. Davis, "The Anatomy of a Smear," *Boston Globe*, March 21, 2004.

37 Green, "Karl Rove."

38 "Bush's Military Record," Lies of Bush, liesofbush.com/bushmilitary.shtml.

39 Kerwin C. Swint, *Mudslingers: The Top 25 Negative Political Campaigns of All Time Countdown from No. 25 to No. 1* (Westport, CT: Praeger Publishers, 2005).

40 Michael Gerson, "A New Social Gospel: Many evangelicals are chafing at the narrowness of the religious right. A new faith-based agenda," *Newsweek*, November 13, 2006.

41 Alan Cooperman, "GOP's Hold on Evangelicals Weakening, Party's Showing in Midterm Elections May Be Hurt as Polls Indicate Support Dropping in Base," *The Washington Post*, October 6, 2006, A06.

★ 15 ★

Meanwhile, Back at the Ranch

*"Where justice is denied, where poverty is enforced,
where ignorance prevails, and where any one class is made
to feel that society is in an organized conspiracy to oppress, rob,
and degrade them, neither persons nor property will be safe."*

Fredrick Douglas

The Rich Get Richer—
The Middle Class Stagnates—The Poor Lose

I F YOU ARE A BILLIONAIRE OR EVEN A MILLIONAIRE, you have done incredibly well during the George W. Bush era. You have paid a smaller percentage of taxes than any other class of people in our nation. The Bush Tax Plan disproportionately provided $50,000+ to those making over $1 million a year while only purporting to provide $350 to 80 percent of America's families by some estimates and as little as $80 by others.[1] Taxpayers with an income of $26 million paid about the same amount in taxes as those in the $200,000 to $500,000 income bracket because of the lowered rates on investment income.[2] Under the Bush Plan, the tax benefits will continue increasing for the richest Americans while the purported tax relief will completely disappear for the middle class and less fortunate.[3] Cutting additional taxes for the wealthiest among us while the U.S. treasury coffers are running a deficit is considered irresponsible by most financial experts.[4]

According to Billionaires for Bush, an ironic "political advocacy group," the wealthiest Americans will receive $1.1 trillion dollars in tax cuts under the Bush Tax Plan.[5] The group declares that the average "Joe taxpayer" will be stuck paying for these tax cuts over the next thirty years.[6] The Billionaires for Bush group boasts of how their bounty will be paid for by way of the Bush Administration's cuts to social security, health care and other "terrible New Deal programs." Program cuts will be required to rein in the budget deficit.[7] Many critics charge the Bush Administration with practicing reverse Robin Hood tactics, stealing from America's children, the poor and the middle-class to give generous tax cuts to the most affluent. George W. Bush has done this in a number of ways. For example, middle-class families who set up college savings funds for their teenagers discovered that in May of 2006, he signed a tax bill that tripled the tax rates on these accounts.[8]

America's Budget Priorities

The pie chart clearly illustrates the U.S.'s national priorities. Americans busy working to make ends meet have trusted Congress and the administration to make wise investments. The U.S. government has jeopardized our future by spending obscene amounts on futile wars paid for with borrowed money. Instead of investing in our nation to make the U.S. more

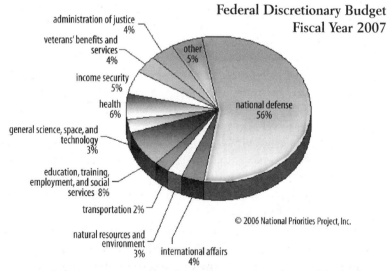

Federal Discretionary Budget Fiscal Year 2007

- administration of justice 4%
- veterans' benefits and services 4%
- income security 5%
- health 6%
- general science, space, and technology 3%
- education, training, employment, and social services 8%
- transportation 2%
- natural resources and environment 3%
- international affairs 4%
- other 5%
- national defense 56%

© 2006 National Priorities Project, Inc.

Other energy, agriculture, commerce and housing credit, community and regional development, general government, and the administration of Social Security and Medicare. National defense does include $50 billion in anticipated funding for the wars in Iraq and Afghanistan. However, it is likely that the wars will cost around $100-$125 billion.

educated, productive, competitive, and healthy, we invest in weapons of mass destruction and no-bid contracts to rebuild countries we have pre-emptively attacked and destroyed. The Bush Administration crows about keeping us safe while America foreign policies and actions infuriate much of the world, making the job of keeping us safe all the more difficult.[9]

The Working Class Get Laid Off or Penalized

As the rich benefit from the Bush tax cuts, the other 98 percent of Americans have found their buying power has decreased as personal debt has climbed upwards.[10] Middle-class Americans have lost ground during the Bush era and the lower working classes and poor have been at a terrible disadvantage. Several studies show the poorest working Americans received no tax relief from the Bush tax cuts.

Additionally, the working poor—many who are single mothers that work as secretaries, cooks, laborers, clerks, caretakers, and health aides—lost important government services they relied upon to help make ends meet.[11] Several government-sponsored programs that served the working poor were reduced or eliminated as the Bush deficit grew. Childcare, financial aid, rent subsidies, utility assistance programs particularly for the elderly, and the public housing crime prevention program have largely been abolished. Critical job-training programs designed to provide skills for the unskilled or unemployed and federal financial aid grants for college have been frozen or eliminated.[12]

A 2006 Bureau of the Census report indicated that U.S. domestic profits are up by a whopping 72 percent. Business worker productivity is also up substantially by 18.4 percent. On the other hand, median household income in the United States is down by half a point.[13] In fact, a *Time Magazine* report revealed that 80 percent of earners, those making less than $90,000 a year, lost ground.[14] So while scores of corporations are enjoying phenomenal profits, they do so on the backs of the working class. Many of these same corporations are at the same time cutting health care benefits programs or shifting more of the costs to their employees and/or cutting retirement programs.[15]

It could be worse. If you are one of the unfortunate American workers who have been laid off because your company went bankrupt or because your company has now decided to offshore your job, you may be feeling considerably more vulnerable. According to a recent report entitled "Do you believe your lying eyes," the economy is not improving. A few headlines serve as reminders.[16]

- **Ford lays off 25,000[17]**
- **Kraft cuts 8000 jobs**
- **Dell hires 5000 in India**
- **GM trims $4B from budget**
- **Visteon shifts resources offshore**
- **OfficeMax closes 110 stores**
- **Toys R Us closes 75 stores, lays off 3000**

In October of 2006, Edward, a CEO of a financial services company, bristled as we discussed the U.S. economy. He said, "My God, the economy is going blockbuster. Haven't you seen the stock market? It's off the Richter scale!" He seemed to be unaware that almost half of U.S. households, 47 percent, have wealth valued at less than $10,000, and that 17 percent of those families had zero valued assets.[18] More importantly, countless numbers of these households are responsible for greater amounts of debt than valued assets, much less stocks. How well the stock market performs fails to impact these families' fiscal bottom line.

If you are one of the millions of American families that live from paycheck to paycheck, you are probably more aware of the brutal changes made by Congress as it whittled away at the mandatory overtime provisions of the 1938 Fair Labor Standards Act. In 2004 Bush led the fight to end overtime pay for eight million middle-class income workers, including nurses. The bill passed Congress successfully despite widespread public disapproval.[19] The Bush-declared triumph saved employers from paying out an estimated $1.9 billion a year in overtime pay. Billionaires for Bush proudly proclaim this to mean "longer hours with less pay" for scores of working Americans.[20] Many of these families desperately needed the overtime compensation just to stay afloat financially.

The Bush federal budgets have focused on *reducing* the government's commitment to protecting workers' safety and health. Every year while in office, the Bush Administration's priorities and policies favor employers over workers.[21] This administration cut significant funds for the Occupational Safety and Health Administration (OSHA) and the National Institute for Occupational Safety and Health (NIOSH).[22] The Bush Administration killed dozens of worker protection measures under development at OSHA and the Mine, Safety and Health Administration (MSHA), including rules on cancer-causing substances, reactive chemicals and infectious diseases such as TB. They have refused to issue rules requiring employers to pay for personal protective equipment. Disastrous mining accidents that have occurred in the last few years are deemed to be a direct result of relaxing safety regulations and monitoring.[23] According to the International Brotherhood of Teamsters, the George W. Bush Administration has the worst record on safety rules in OSHA's entire history.[24]

Social Security Becomes Ever More Vulnerable

The Bush Administration was determined to dismantle the Social Security program, stripping retirement protection from millions of Americans, even though there is overwhelming opposition from a majority of Americans.[25] Republican congressional representatives, including the House Majority Leader Bill Frist (R-TN), made pledges to get serious about privatizing Social Security after the 2006 mid-term elections. Baby boomers getting ready to retire in the near future will find the federal government unable to fulfill its long-term promise to provide for retirement. Because of failures to safeguard, protect and wisely invest our social security funds, masses of Americans will be penalized.

Vice President Cheney recommended that families living from paycheck to paycheck should save more money.[26] His out-of-touch commentary is equal to Marie Antoinette's infamous remark, "Let them eat cake." Marie Antoinette, the Queen of France, purportedly made the comment just before starving French citizens stormed Versailles, instigating the French revolution. (Later she, King Louis XVI and their children were beheaded.)

Wage Gap Grows — The Poor Grow Poorer

Democrats tried unsuccessfully to raise the minimum wage for the lowest paid Americans for several congressional sessions. The Republican-controlled Congress had effectively frozen the minimum wage at $5.15 per hour since 1997 and they successfully blocked all efforts to raise it. George W. Bush, who campaigned as a compassionate Conservative and a champion of family values, has refused to back any efforts to raise wages for America's working poor, stating he did not want to do anything that might potentially hurt business.

Sixteen percent of all earners, or 11.2 million workers, earn only the minimum wage. Studies indicate a majority of these low wage earners — 62.3 percent — are women, many single with children.[27] These women are desperately trying to raise families. While George W. Bush puts more money in the pockets of wealthy Americans, poverty in America has increased since 2000 by 4.4 million to 35.9 million people in 2003.[28] According to a study conducted by a U.S. conference of mayors, many working poor become homeless because of low wages and the inability to pay rent.[29]

My biggest concern over the Bush policy changes is that the middle class is becoming increasingly susceptible of falling into poverty. I am a rabid proponent of keeping America's middle class strong, healthy and highly productive. I have seen how government assistance programs can help the improvised and working poor to become successful members of America's middle class. For fourteen years, I worked for New Mexico state government in both the Health and Human Services departments. I saw first hand the vulnerability of the working poor and how easy it is for them to become homeless, drug or alcohol addicted or criminals. It is much better to give these people training, education and a chance to become contributing taxpayers. When we turn our backs on these citizens and they lack the resources to crawl out of poverty, they become a huge drain on our society. Crime rates spike, homelessness increases, child abuse and neglect result, and it takes a toll on our communities.

During the summer of 2006, Republicans in Congress finally agreed to raise the minimum wage from $5.15 to $7.25, but very slowly over time, and the raise was tied to a series of substantial tax cuts for wealthy Americans. A majority of Democrats and a few Republican senators rejected the wage increase, bill fondly named by Republicans as the "trifecta." According to estimates, just one element of the "trifecta," the reduction in amount paid in estate taxes, would have decreased federal tax revenue by $268 billion over ten years.[30] Even workers' unions were against this minimum wage initiative, with Gerald W. McEntee, the president of the American Federation of State, County and Municipal Employees (AFSCME), saying, "This was a transparent attempt to dangle a minimum-wage increase for families struggling to make ends meet [in order] to secure yet another Texas-sized tax handout for the wealthiest."[31] Those voting against the bill cited the massive tax cuts tied to the bill as the primary rationale. Congressional representatives pointed out the current U.S. fiscal deficit, the escalating cost of wars in Iraq and Afghanistan and reconstruction efforts in the U.S. Gulf Coast as additional reasons for voting against slashing future federal revenue sources.

Despite the fact that a majority of Americans have supported a minimum wage increase, Majority Leader Bill Frist (R-TN) cautioned he would block the minimum wage proposal from surfacing again in the future if the 2006 Republican "trifecta" failed to pass.[32] Tying the wage increase for the working poor to tax breaks appeared to be a manipulative ploy to derail the badly needed wage increase.

While the Bush Administration doesn't believe it important to raise the minimum wage they did find it necessary to better compensate their political appointees by reinstating cash bonuses for those in the executive branch of the U.S. Government.[33] Bill Clinton prohibited the payment of such cash bonuses. The administration provided five tax cuts benefiting a very small percentage of Americans, and the Republican-controlled Congress gave itself three raises in this same ten-year period while refusing to increase the minimum wage. It became one of the first priorities of the Democrats. Once empowered in 2007, they sought and approved a bill to finally raise the minimum wage.

Razing Welfare Reform

The Welfare Reform Act of 1996, initiated during the Clinton Administration, provided dramatic results. States reported an impressive 60 percent decline in the number of needy families requiring benefits.[34] State-administered programs under block grants allowed for assistance to beneficiaries, giving them opportunities to obtain education, eliminate addictions and get vocational training. Previously, individual states had the flexibility to design programs to work with their specific populations. Federally funded yet state-designed programs miraculously provided some of the most disadvantaged people a chance to become productive, tax paying citizens. The state welfare programs provided a ticket out of poverty for many recipients.

Democrats wanted a slight increase in funding to help working parents with the cost of childcare. These parents were participating in welfare-to-work programs. Republicans argued the state-operated programs were already too generous. The Bush Administration won again.

New rules written by the Republican-controlled Congress became effective on October 1, 2006. Changes required states to concentrate on making more poor people work and at the same time discourage other activities that help ensure the long-term success of recipients. So for example, welfare recipients are now required to work 30 hours instead of 20 hours per week. They receive only six weeks of training and must eliminate drug addictions with less help. These are unrealistic and harsh requirements because the populations in this category suffer from multiple adversities besides poverty, such as physical and mental handicaps, inadequate education or training, insufficient support systems, and drug and alcohol addictions. The federal government will strictly monitor the states, and federal enforcement includes stiff monetary penalties for failure to comply with the new rules.

Congress ignored the gross mismanagement of Dick Cheney's Halliburton war corporation whose incompetence has cost the taxpayers billions of dollars. Yet, the Bush-controlled Congress showed through 2006 its contempt for American families by turning its back on the most vulnerable in our society; those unfortunates who, with a little assistance, could be turned into successful taxpayers and productive employees.

Wild Spending — Hidden and Deferred Debt

In a 2004 *USA Today* report entitled "One Nation under Debt," researchers Dennis Cauchon and John Waggoner revealed that the nation's hidden debt is more than five times the estimated $84,454 each household owes in personal debt.

AMERICAN TAXPAYERS SADDLED WITH BUSH DEBT FAR INTO THE FUTURE

American taxpayers are financially obligated to pay the debts hidden in the U.S. federal deficits that were equal to $473,456 per household in 2004.[35] The Bush Administration has demonstrated little regard for driving up the federal deficit. Perhaps they recognize they will be long gone by the time serious deficit repayments are required in 2008.

Since George W. Bush took office, federal spending has jumped the most since World War II.[36] According to C-SPAN reports, the Bush Administration has increased the U.S. federal deficit spending limit five times since 2002. Here are the increases:

June 2002	$450 billion increase
May 2003	$984 billion increase
Nov. 2004	$800 billion increase
Mar. 2006	$780 billion increase
FY 2007	Request debt limit increase to $11.3 trillion[37]

The U.S. government cannot continue borrowing without a viable repayment plan. Every single year that repayment plans are delayed, the deficit grows by $1 trillion, according to experts at the U.S. Treasury Department.[38] In 2006, 406 billion taxpayer dollars were spent on interest payments alone to the holders of the U.S. national debt.

Borrowing is an extremely expensive endeavor, especially when you compare those interest payment dollars to the measly $61 billion that the U.S. is spending on education or the $56 billion spent on the Department of Transportation.[39] Imagine overrunning your household budget on credit cards every single month and then barely making the minimum interest payments. You can monitor the national debt at the Treasury Department's website found on the internet at http://www.publicdebt.treas.gov/opd/opdpenny.htm. A daily update is provided for the public on the growing debt.

National Debt (to the Penny) as of November 18, 2006:
$8,606,686,309,802.15[40]

Smoke and Mirrors Budgetary Tactics

Recall the smoke and mirrors schemes of Enron and the deceptive tactics used by the Houston-based energy corporation to make it look financially vibrant and healthy. It used these tactics to hide its anemic reality. It fizzled overnight once its antics were exposed. Those tricks are similar to those engaged in by the Bush Administration. The administration's practice of funding war activities and other projects through supplemental requests hides the true budgetary costs. For example, in early 2006, Congress approved an additional $72.4 billion for the wars in Iraq and Afghanistan, and another $19.8 billion for reconstruction efforts in the Gulf States affected by Katrina, through supplemental spending.[41]

The Bush Administration has not only abused supplemental spending, it has also engaged in scavenging from regularly budgeted items for its wars in the Middle East. For example, Representative James Walsh (R-NY) sponsored an amendment to shift funds earmarked for the U.S. Veterans Administration hospitals to pump into the wars in Iraq and Afghanistan.[42] These strategies harm American veterans who, when they return home, find shortfalls in the necessary services they seek to secure.

Fiscal conservatives are deeply concerned with the huge deficit overruns and the hidden costs of these wars. The *New York Times* reported evidence of the smoke-and-mirrors policies we have feared most in an article entitled "Audit Finds U.S. Hid Cost of Iraq Projects." The Bush

Administration persists in using dishonest accounting methods to fund the wars in Iraq and Afghanistan.

The U.S. federal government keeps two sets of books, just like Enron. The public set of books shows a false bottom line. For instance, in 2005, the U.S. government showed $318 billion in federal deficit spending. The real books, however, the ones using standard accounting rules and audited, reveal a much more alarming financial picture for the U.S. The true picture uncovers $760 billion in deficit spending for 2005. This $760 billon deficit does not even include the financial obligations for the Social Security and Medicare programs. When the obligations of these programs are included and appropriate accounting rules applied, the federal deficit as of August 2006 loomed at a shocking $8.4 trillion.[43] By keeping two sets of books, one that is publicly presented and another that is hidden, the administration can pretend to be keeping the U.S. fiscally sound and secure.

My Republican grandfather, the late Frank S. Ortiz, a fiscal conservative who served as the mayor of Santa Fe, New Mexico in the late 1940s, is rolling over in his grave as he watches this new breed of Republicans drive up the federal deficit today.

Where Do our Tax Dollars Go?

"Cutting the military budgets back by ten percent and using that money to basically solve the real, serious poverty problems in the world would be a much better investment in fighting terrorism…you don't stop terrorism with tanks, you stop it with giving people hope so they won't want to blow themselves up."[44]

Ted Turner

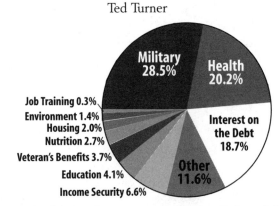

Source: Breakdown of income taxes is based on Budget of the United States Government. View sources and methodology, at http://www.nationalpriorities.org/auxiliary/interactivetaxchart/taxchart.html#

Courtesy National Priorities

America Loses its Competitive Advantage

According to global trends, U.S. companies requiring scientific and engineering expertise will face a drastic shortage of employees in the next three years, with many baby boomers retiring. A Hay Study estimated 43 percent of electrical shift supervisors and another 40 percent of senior electrical engineers in the utilities business will be eligible for retirement within the next three years. The U.S. will be unable to hire enough American engineers to fill these vacancies.[45] In 2001, the U.S. graduated 59,536 engineers to China's 219,563.[46] Of course, getting updated information from many of the U.S. government websites is nearly impossible. For instance the National Science Foundation provided website updates every year from 1995 through 2001. But this website has not been updated since 2001. Perhaps it is because in 2001 the U.S. was at a 14-year low in its recruitment efforts for the engineering programs. As a matter of fact, in 2005, Asian schools were graduating more than ten engineering students for every one U.S. student.[47] Marvin, a scientist at the Los Alamos National Laboratory, said, "The low priority of science and education in general is indicative of the Bush Administration's fundamental interest in religion as opposed to a legitimate interest in teaching our nation's students math and science."

A 2006 *Time* study revealed that an alarming number of American high school students have been dropping out of school. The ten-year trend disclosed that up to *33 percent*, or *one-third* of American children will be left behind. Vocational technical school program cuts to cover other budgetary priorities under the Bush Administration, coupled with a flawed No Child Left Behind initiative, are considered prime reasons for the high dropout rates.

A strong investment in America's educational system for U.S. children promises a bright and competitive future, but the Bush Administration has refused to examine any alternatives to fixing the public school problem. Their only suggestion has been to promote a voucher initiative whereby money is taken from the public education budget and given out in the form of vouchers for private schools.[48] As a mother of two children who I have sent to attend both private and public schools, I would love to have some financial support for my daughters to help pay for their attendance at the private schools, but I would refuse to accept such support if it means financially gutting public school programs.

The U.S. urgently needs to fix the problems with our public school system. Each year's delay means America loses further ground to other nations. A number of public school organizations charge that the federal government has deliberately attempted to sabotage the public educational system by short-changing schools in assorted ways. There are so many accusations it would be challenging to list them all. But here is one example, as summarized by a letter written by the Reading First Program. The non-profit group Reading Recovery Council of North America, Inc. is a professional association that provides early intervention to help first and second grade children who are struggling with reading and writing.[49] The letter was sent to the Inspector General for the U.S. Department of Education.

The letter charged that the federal government had not implemented the Reading First Program in good faith, had not honored congressional intent and had impeded and interfered with the program. The organization outlined four major areas of concern:

1. It charged that the federal government supported a quiet yet pervasive misinformation campaign against the Reading First Program despite a large body of research demonstrating Reading Recovery's effectiveness and long-term results.[50]

2. It alleged that the federal government restricted state and local authorities from selecting scientifically based reading programs.

3. It indicated that during the implementation of Reading First, the federal government systematically favored curriculum developed by friends of the administration while excluding scientifically based programs with proven track records.

4. It specified that the federal government excluded one-to-one instruction in the Reading First program, contradicting the statute, congressional intent and scientific research findings of effectiveness for the lowest-achieving children.

The Neocon Perspective

Ann Coulter, hailed as one of the most highly respected Neoconservative intellectuals, is a syndicated columnist, author and self-professed Christian. She frequently appears on national television and radio programs. Ms. Coulter's answers to the problems of education in the U.S. were made public in an interview posted on a Neoconservative website, the Cybercast News Service:

> **Cybercast News Service:** In your book *[Godless: The Church of Liberalism]*, you state: "*If you gave all the money in the United States to the public schools, they would not improve; they would*

simply cost more." Can you envision any federal attempt to improve education at the local level that would be effective?

Ann Coulter: "Yes, abolish the Department of Education and bring RICO [Racketeer Influenced and Corrupt Organizations Act] suits against the teachers' unions."[51]

For many Neocons, the answer to America's failing schools is to simply shut them down and give parents a miserly tax credit so they can either home-school their children or send them to a private school. Neocons cite the lack of prayer in schools, the failure to teach creationism and the lack of disciplinary options as reasons for the demise of the U.S. public school system. These Neocons also blame what they refer to as the liberal teachers' unions for the decline in American education. Nick and Jim, two very conservatives Republicans from different parts of the country, clearly echoed this sentiment. Both men said their wives were stay-at-home mothers who were home-schooling their children. Many Americans would neither wish for nor be able to entertain the option voiced by Nick and Jim.

The American educational system needs a total and complete overhaul. Setting smart standards, integrating the latest understanding of learning styles, curriculum, and technologies would be a good start. Accelerated teaching programs, smaller class sizes and an adequate budget to re-establish important vocational technical programs would go a long way towards fixing the problem. It is a shame that America falls further and further behind while the government ignores the problem or actively promotes policies that further damage our public education system.

Rising College Costs

Last spring, I sat and listened to one of my dearest friends as she commiserated about the high cost of college for her daughter. Both Michelle and her husband Ted had diligently saved for their children's college fund. However, the costs of college were much higher than they anticipated. Being dutiful parents they had promised their daughter that if she graduated with a 4.0 average, they would pay for the college of her choice. Their daughter, Lisa, achieved the 4.0 grade average and chose a college that cost $42,000 per year, plus additional fees. I watched silently and sadly as Michelle and Ted refinanced their home to pull out $100,000 in equity loans to pay for the increased cost of college.

Michelle and Ted are not alone. More and more Americans have pulled equity out of their homes to pay for the increased cost of college, credit card debt, vacations, and unexpected health care bills. With over 25 percent of home loans financed as adjustable-rate mortgages and interest-only loans, Americans are fiscally vulnerable to rising interest rates and declining home values. If the economy takes even a slight turn and interest rates are raised, many American homeowners could face higher payments and even foreclosure.[52]

American Cities Perish
While Taxpayer Dollars Rebuild Baghdad

*"For years, we have cut our taxes and let the infrastructure
throughout the country go, and this [Katrina] is just
the first of a number of other crumbling things that
are going to happen to us."*[53]

Nina Totenberg

One of the worst natural disasters in American history hit New Orleans and much of the Gulf Coast in late August 2005. In the days immediately after, our nation discovered that thousands of poor, primarily African American people lacked the resources to protect themselves and their families from the destruction. Images of the dead and the impoverished Americans who suffered through the ordeal reminded Americans of numerous failed policies. New Orleans officials testified that for years they made the levee deficiencies well known to the federal government. The problems were largely ignored.

Other warnings came as well, including the apprehension over the incompetence of FEMA. Pleasant Mann, a sixteen-year FEMA veteran, told Congress the FEMA professional staff had been systematically replaced by Bush. The replacements were political appointees and contractors with little or no experience in emergency services.[54] Warnings to the Bush Administration about the dangers of a Katrina-like hurricane went unheeded and came from numerous sources including Senator Joseph Lieberman (D-CT).[55] In 2004, the Bush Administration provided significantly less funding than requested by New Orleans officials to provide minimum hurricane safety protections for the city. Funds originally earmarked for fixing the levees were instead diverted to the war in Iraq. A Louisiana reporter named Sheila Grissett, writing for the *Times-Picayune* newspaper in New Orleans, predicted, "Shifting federal budget erodes protection from levees; Because of cuts, hurricane risk grows." This article appeared on June 8, 2004. Sadly, due to the fixation on Iraq, the necessary work to the levees in 2004 and 2005 was never performed.

According to the Spike Lee documentary, *When the Levees Broke: A Requiem in Four Acts,* the slow response to Katrina was "a criminal act."[56] This act resulted in more than 1,300 American deaths and at least half a million displaced or homeless people. The mayor of New Orleans and the governor of Louisiana certainly need to shoulder some of the responsibility as they fall short issuing timely mandatory evacuation orders and utilizing local transportation resources to assist in the evacuation.[57]

However, the magnitude of the Katrina catastrophe required a concerted and well-coordinated federal response. Days after the hurricane, while the Bush Administration accused the media of exaggerating the aftermath of Katrina, tens of thousands of poor Americans were crowded into the Morial Convention Center without food or water. Dead Americans floated in the gutters of the streets or lay abandoned in their homes. Armed police officers turned back hurricane evacuees as they attempted to cross a Mississippi River bridge. They were desperately trying to escape the mayhem of the city.[58]

The cost of the New Orleans cleanup of the debris is estimated to have been at least 25 times more than that of the 9/11 World Trade Center collapses.[59] The Associated Press reported that only $117 million out of the $25 billion in federal aid had gone back to New Orleans one year after Katrina. Terrible federal mismanagement continues to plague the reconstruction of New Orleans. According to federal investigators, $2 billion in taxpayer money has been lost because of fraud and no-bid contracts.[60] The examples of mismanagement are plentiful; for instance, $7.9 million was spent on the renovation of Fort McClellan Army Base in Anniston, Alabama to house displaced New Orleans citizens. By the time the renovations were finally completed and the shelter opened it was no longer needed. FEMA closed it after only one month.[61]

In another example, the federal government purchased 20,000 mobile homes, each costing $34,500. These homes were to provide temporary housing to hurricane victims. According to reports, Louisiana officials cringed at installing them. Since FEMA had not discussed how they were to be used and how many were needed, approximately half of these mobile homes, or 10,000 of the $860 million worth of units, were stored in Arkansas, at a taxpayer cost of $250,000 a month.[62] In November 2006, it was reported that more than half of these had been weather damaged because they had not been properly protected while in storage.[63]

THE PRESIDENT'S RESPONSE TO KATRINA

The President was informed of the potential dangers associated with the breaching of the levees in New Orleans days before Katrina hit. Televised excerpts are available on the MSNBC website. The actual televised conversation between George W. Bush and FEMA staff prior to the hurricane's approach can be seen and heard.[64] The President does not ask a single question during the "confidential telephone conversation," but instead George W. Bush ensures officials that "we are prepared."[65] What America witnessed in the administration could be construed as either indifference or a total lack of understanding of how to protect vulnerable Americans.

Reverend Jesse Jackson said, "Many black people feel that their race, their property conditions and their voting patterns have been a factor in the response." He then said, "I'll say it: If the majority of the hardest hit victims of Hurricane Katrina in New Orleans were white people, they would not have gone for days without food and water, forcing many to steal for mere survival. Their bodies would not have been left to float in putrid water. They would have been rescued and relocated a hell of a lot faster than this, period... The President has put himself at risk by visiting the troops in Iraq, but didn't venture anywhere near the Superdome or the Convention Center, where thousands of victims, mostly black and poor, needed to see that he gave a damn."[66]

Cutting Security at Home

An undisclosed government panel determined that New York City and Washington D.C. faced significant Homeland Security budget cuts in June of 2006.[67] Both cities will have to do with 40 percent less in federal funding to secure their cities in the future. Additionally, vulnerable cities such as New Orleans received only half of the grant money expected for security and disaster preparedness. Comedians across the nation joked about how the Homeland Security grant funding was to be distributed nationally. Attention focused on the fact that a petting zoo in

Iowa was to receive Homeland Security funds while ports and enforcement officers took hefty cuts. Homeland Security became the butt of jokes on national television.[68] While many laughed at such stupidity, others were outraged.

A Broken Health Care System

I watched my daughter play soccer with great pride on a beautiful fall day in mid-September 2006. Playing on the Junior Varsity team for her school, she had just scored her third goal. Suddenly one of the opposing team's players collided with our goalie. Luckily, the injuries were not too serious. However, both girls needed stitches. One of our team mothers is a physician who offered to provide the services. The young girl from the opposing team went into a panic. She began to cry. She said her family had no medical insurance and lacked the financial resources to pay for any medical bills. I too found myself in tears, saddened that even youngsters in our society were more afraid of the medical debt their family might incur than from a painful injury.

Millions of Americans lack health care insurance and millions more are underinsured. We have a health care system that is heavily dependent upon the private sector. Treatment, tests and health care are based upon the ability to pay. In the richest country in the world, treating the sick is one of the largest moneymaking schemes. The goal of the private sector is to make a profit regardless of the requirements of our neediest citizens.

For those with health care coverage, the cost has skyrocketed out of control. Every year, health care insurance premiums, co-payments and deductibles increase at alarming rates.[69] As these increase, more employers find it necessary to pass more of the costs onto employees, effectively shrinking paychecks or causing some employees to opt out of insurance programs or reduce coverage when they feel they can no longer afford to pay. The broken health care system is especially cumbersome and expensive for America's middle class. For the working poor, health insurance is a luxury they cannot afford.

Eliminate, Hide or Change Bad Data

The Bush Administration eliminates or changes reports that do not bear the same conclusions the administration wishes Americans to see. They have successfully concealed, manipulated and withheld evidence for political gain time after time. For example, in 2002, the Bush Administration stopped issuing a monthly Bureau of Labor Statistics report, saying it cost too much to produce and was therefore subjected to budget cuts. This report tracked factory closing throughout the country. In order to bury critical data that showed massive job loss, the information was hidden in a footnote of the department's purported final report. The details of the mass layoff statistics were revealed on Christmas Eve. Nearly a quarter-million workers' jobs had been cut and lost. After the *Washington Post* called the administration on this blatant data censoring, the report was reinstated.

The Bush Administration has a habit of waiting to make major news announcements by releasing the information late on Friday afternoons when most reporters have gone for the weekend. More detrimental notices are released immediately before a major holiday such as Thanksgiving, Christmas and New Year's Eve.

In 2003, a report by the Environmental Protection Agency's Inspector General found that the White House directed the agency to alter a report regarding the health risks from debris in the air after the World Trade Center collapse. According to the report, the White House "convinced the EPA to add reassuring statements and delete cautionary ones."[70]

In another example, the administration nixed a study by former Treasury Secretary Paul O'Neill that predicted huge budget deficits well into the future. The survey, which stated the baby-boom generation's future health care and retirement costs would swamp U.S. coffers, was dropped from a 2004 budget summary published in February 2003. This happened at the same time the administration was lobbying for a tax-cut package that critics warned would greatly expand future deficits. Several respected financial experts, including those from the *Financial Times*, affirmed this study. A Bush Administration spokesperson alleged that the study was merely a thought exercise.

One of the most egregious examples is the Bush appointed official who rewrote multiple environmental impact studies. Phillip Cooney, the White House Environmental Quality Chief of Staff and a fomer lobbyist, repeatedly altered government climate reports related to global warming and climate change. After being caught red-handed, he resigned and went to work the *very next day* for ExxonMobil.[71]

The report on terrorism conducted by sixteen governmental agencies entitled "Trends in Global Terrorism: Implications for the United States" was completed in the spring of 2006.[72] The report was purposely hidden from the public because it confirmed that the war in Iraq and U.S. foreign policies were exacerbating terrorism. The Bush Administration made strong attempts to distract the public from the report's findings by turning the focus instead to the fact that it became public through a "leak." The American public was told that Democrats were responsible for a politically motivated leak. A media brouhaha stormed over the "leak," as opposed to the more important fact that sixteen different agencies were telling the Bush White House we were increasingly less safe.

After it was discovered that a gay Republican member of Congress, Mark Foley, had been soliciting young male pages in Congress, Republicans, who had long been aware of Mr. Foley's indiscretions, charged Democrats with revealing these charges for politically motivated purposes. Rather than taking any responsibility, this particular Republican-controlled Congress and administration showed its preference for blaming, denying, and hiding the facts.

Americans Are Swayed

Fiscal conservatives, along with many other Americans, are horrified to see our nation's financial security squandered away. Under the Bush Administration and the Republican-controlled Congress, Americans witnessed an ever-expanding government, out-of-control spending, an embroiled Middle East entrapment, government incompetence, cronyism, corruption, and a failure to take care of our needs at home.[73]

A majority of Americans, from all political parties together with Independents, had had enough, and in November 2006 the plug was pulled on the Republican-controlled Congress. Both the Senate and House of Representatives went to the Democrats. The message was sent to these politicians and the President: the U.S. needs to pull together to solve the many critical issues facing our nation.

I bring up a few of the issues facing Americans today and I think about my conservative friend Darlene. She recently told me, "Bernadette, I don't understand why you are so worried about this 'stuff'...for heaven's sake, you have a wonderful life, healthy children and a husband who loves you dearly. Perhaps you should just relax and let it go."

I asked myself, "How could I ever live with myself if I just let it go?" I think of my precious little granddaughter, Summer Elizabeth Brown, and wonder if she will ask me someday, "Grandma, why didn't you do anything...didn't you care about the world your generation was leaving behind?"

NOTES, Chapter 15

1 "Tax Cuts, the Deficit, and Destroying Public Services," *Billionaires for Bush*, www.billionairesforbush.com/candidate_taxcuts.php#taxcuts.

2 "Study: Bush tax cuts making rich richer, Report: The wealthiest Americans are reaping huge gains from reduced taxes on investment income," *CNN Money*, April 5, 2006, money.cnn.com/2006/04/05/news/tax_cuts/index.htm?cnn=yes.

3 a. "Tax Cuts."
b. Bob McIntyre, "Most Tax Payers Get Little Help from Bush's Latest Tax Plan," *Citizens for Tax Justice*, May 2003,

4 "Straus Military Reform Project," *Center for Defense Information*, www.cdi.org/news/mrp/Unified-Security-Budget-flier.pdf.

5 "Tax Cuts."

6 Ibid.

7 Ibid.

8 David Cay Johnston, "Despite Pledge, Taxes Increase For Teenagers," *New York Times*, May 21, 2006.

9 Robert W. Tucker and David C. Hendrickson, "The Sources of American Legitimacy," *Foreign Affairs*, November/December 2004, www.foreignaffairs.org/20041101faessay83603/robert-w-tucker-david-c-hendrickson/the-sources-of-american-legitimacy.html.

10 "Report: State's wages not keeping pace despite productivity gains," *The Day*, September 5, 2006.

11 Melvin Claxton and Ronald J. Hansen, "Working poor suffer under Bush tax cuts," *The Detroit News*, September 26, 2004, www.detnews.com/2004/specialreport/0409/26/a01-284666.htm.

12 Ibid.

13 Mike Allen, "Why Bush's Security Pitch May Not Work This Time, Why Voters (and Politicians) are Anxious," *Time Magazine*, September 18, 2006, p. 36.

14 Ibid.

15 a. "Congress Hears of Duke's Pension," *Duke Energy Employee Advocate*, September 23, 2004, www.dukeemployees.com/cash1.shtml.
b. "Broken Promises: Retirement," *Workplace Fairness*, www.workplacefairness.org/sc/retirement.php.

16 "Why believe your LYING eyes," *The Truth Will Set You Free*, February 5, 2006, wakeupfromyourslumber.blogspot.com/2006/02/why-believe-your-lying-eye_113912330468729378.html.

17 Bill Koenig and John Lippert, "Ford Motor May Eliminate 25,000 Jobs to Stem Losses," *Bloomberg.com*, January 20, 2006, www.truthout.org/cgi-bin/artman/view.cgi/36/17112.

18 "Wealth Flows to the Wealthiest as the Percentage of Americans Who Own Stock Falls," *Economic Policy Institute*, August 29, 2006, www.epinet.org/newsroom/releases/2006/08/SWApr-wealth-200608-final.pdf.

19 "U.S. Federal Overtime Law," *PayMyOvertime.com*, www.paymyovertime.com/federal.php.

20 "Workers' Overtime Coverage," *Billionaires for Bush*, www.billionairesforbush.com/candidate_overtime.php#overtime.

21 "Bush Administration Fails Workers on Safety and Health," *International Brotherhood of Teamsters*, April 24, 2006, www.teamster.org/06news/hn_060424_1.asp.

22 Brett Crawford, "Bush Ups and Cuts OSHA Budget," *Summit Training Source, Inc.*, www.summit-training.com/Blog/default.asp?baID=17.

23 "Mining Accidents," Woomer & Friday, Attorneys at Law, www.woomerand friday.com/html/mining-accidents.html.

24 "Administration Fails Workers."

25 "Keep the Heat on the Privatizers," Americans United, www.americansunited forchange.org/augustads.

26 "Cheney urges Americans to save more," USA Today, www.usatoday.com/news/ washington/2006-03-02-cheney-saving_x.htm.

27 Mark D. Turner, "Does the Minimum Wage Help or Hurt Low-Wage Workers?", The Low-Wage Labor Market: Challenges and Opportunities for Economic Self-Sufficiency, aspe.hhs.gov/hsp/lwlm99/turner.htm.

28 WorkingPoor.org, www.workingpoor.org/do/Home.

29 Homeless, www.homeless.org/do/Home.

30 Jeffrey H. Birnbaum, "An Estate Tax Twist Reverses Party Roles On Minimum Wage," Washington Post, August 3, 2006, A01.

31 Charles Babington, "GOP Bid On Wages, Estate Tax Is Blocked, Democrats Prevent Vote on Senate Bill," Washington Post, August 4, 2006, A01.

32 Ibid.

33 "Government News," HavenWorks, havenworks.com/gov/.

34 Amy Goldstein, "Welfare Changes A Burden To States, Work Rules Also Threaten Study, Health Programs," Washington Post, August 7, 2006, A01.

35 Dennis Cauchon and John Waggoner, "The Looming National Benefit Crisis," USA Today, October 3, 2004, www.usatoday.com/news/nation/2004-10-03-debt-cover_x.htm.

36 a. Edwin J. Feulner, Ph.D., "Mourning in America for Reagan's often-forgotten ideas," The Heritage Foundation, www.heritage.org/Press/Commentary/ ed012106a.cfm.
b. "Ford Motor May Eliminate 25,000 Jobs to Stem Losses," Bloomberg.com, January 20, 2006, www.bloomberg.com/apps/news?pid=10000087&sid=a7Ew_ AppY5k4&refer=top_world_news.

37 a. Hon. John M. Spratt Jr., "Frequently Asked Questions About the Federal Budget," House Budget Committee, June 29, 2006, www.house.gov/budget_ democrats/budget_facts/Faq_june07.pdf.
b. Dennis Cauchon and John Waggoner, "The Looming National Benefit Crisis," USA Today, October 3, 2004.

38 "The Debt to the Penny," Bureau of the Public Debt, www.publicdebt.treas. gov/opd/ opdpenny.htm.

39 Federal Budget Spending and the National Debt, www.federalbudget.com/.

40 "Debt to the Penny."

41 Paul M. Irwin and Larry Nowels, "FY2006 Supplemental Appropriations: Iraq and Other International Activities; Additional Katrina Hurricane Relief," Center for Defense Information, March 10, 2006 www.cdi.org/pdfs/CRS%20RL33298% 20FY2006%20War%20and%20Katrina%20Supps%203-10-06.pdf.

42 Mike Ferner and Jeff Leys, "Antiwar activists arrested at House Appropriations Committee meeting," Free Press, March 10, 2006, www.freepress.org/ departments/display/13/2006/1846.

43 Dennis Cauchon, "What's the real federal deficit?," USA Today, August 4, 2006, www.usatoday.com/news/washington/2006-08-02-deficit-usat_x.htm.

44 David Letterman, The Late Show, CBS, September 16, 2005.

45 "Global Trends," International Programming and Systems Inc., www.ipsamerica .com /global_trends.html.

[46] National Science Foundation, *2004 Science and Technology Indicators*, May 2004, Appendix 2-33.

[47] Domenico Grasso, "Is It Time to Shut Down Engineering Colleges?," *Inside Higher Education*, September 23, 2005, insidehighered.com/views/2005/09/23/grasso.

[48] "Tell Lawmakers: 'Public Schools First!'," *People For the American Way*, www.pfaw.org/pfaw/general/default.aspx?oid=7030.

[49] Connie Briggs, Ph.D. and Jady Johnson, letter to John P. Higgins Jr., *Reading Recovery Council of North America*, August 4, 2005, www.readingrecovery.org/pdfs/RRCNAOIGrequest.pdf.

[50] Ibid.

[51] "Coulter: Abortion is Dems' Version of 'Virgin Sacrifice'," *CNS News*, June 6, 2006, www.cnsnews.com/ViewSpecialReports.asp?Page=/SpecialReports/archive/200606/SPE20060606a.html.

[52] Mike Allen, "Why Bush's Security Pitch May Not Work This Time, Why Voter (and Politicians) are Anxious," *Time Magazine*, September 18, 2006, p. 36.

[53] *Inside Washington*, Sept. 3, 2005.

[54] Jon Elliston, "The disaster that shouldn't have been, Warnings about problems at FEMA were sounded soon after Bush put a political appointee in charge—including in the Indy," *Indy Week*, September 7, 2005, www.indyweek.com/gyrobase/Content?oid=oid%3A25117.

[55] "Government 'blocks' Katrina probe," *BBC News*, January 25, 2006, news.bbc.co.uk/2/hi/americas/4645448.stm.

[56] Alex P. Kellogg, "Worth A View: Spike Lee's Katrina Film, American Prospect: Documentary Is A Poignant Examination Of What Went Wrong," *CBS News*, August 22, 2006, www.cbsnews.com/stories/2006/08/22/opinion/main1923876.shtml.

[57] Ibid.

[58] Associated Press, "Feds To Probe Katrina Evacuee Blockade, Why Did Police Turn Back Fleeing New Orleans Residents?," *CBS News*, Aug. 5, 2006, www.cbsnews.com/stories/2006/08/05/katrina/main1868140.shtml.

[59] Spike Lee, "When the Levees Broke: A Requiem in Four Acts", *HBO*, August 21, 2006.

[60] Eric Lipton, "Breathtaking Waste and Fraud in Hurricane Aid," *New York Times*, June 27, 2006.

[61] Ibid.

[62] Ibid.

[63] Richard Skinner, letter to R. David Paulison, *Department of Homeland Security*, October 18, 2006, www.dhs.gov/xoig/assets/mgmtrpts/OIG_07-03_Oct06.pdf.

[64] "Video shows Bush got explicit Katrina warning: President, Chertoff were clearly told of storm's dangers numerous times," *MSNBC*, March 2, 2006, www.msnbc.msn.com/id/11627394/.

[65] Ibid.

[66] "The Send Bush to Abu Ghraib Award," *The DisHonors Awards*, March 30, 3006, www.mrc.org/notablequotables/dishonor/06/award3.asp.

[67] Dan Eggen and Mary Beth Sheridan, "Anti-Terror Funding Cut In D.C. and New York, Homeland Security Criticized Over Grants," *Washington Post*, Thursday, June 1, 2006, A011.

[68] A. "DHS 'Critical Infrastructure': Amish Popcorn, Trees of Mystery," *DefenseTech.org*, July 13, 2006, www.defensetech.org/archives/002580.html.

[69] "Addressing the Health Care Crisis," *United Steelworkers*, www.usw.org/usw/program/content/289.php.

[70] "The Bush Wall of Secrecy," *Joe Lieberman for President 2004*, .www.fas.org/sgp/news/2004/01/lieb-wall010904.html

[71] "Bush's Environment Chief: From the Oil Lobby to the White House to Exxon Mobil," *Democracy Now!*, June 20, 2005, www.democracynow.org/article.pl?sid=05/06/20/1328225.

[72] Mark Mazzetti, "Spy Agencies Say Iraq War Worsens Terrorism Threat," *New York Times*, September 24, 2006, www.nytimes.com/2006/09/24/world/middleeast/24terror.html?_r=1&n=Top%2fReference%2fTimes%20Topics%2fPeople%2fM%2fMazzetti%2c%20Mark&oref=slogin.

[73] "Time For Us To Go, Conservatives on why the GOP should lose in 2006," *Washington Monthly*, October 2006, www.washingtonmonthly.com/features/2006/0610.forum.html.

★ 16 ★

The Fifth Commandment

The Fifth (Protestant and Jewish) or
Fourth (Catholic and Luthern) Commandment is

"Honor Thy Mother and Father."

N ATIONAL AERONAUTICS AND SPACE ADMINISTRATION (NASA) scientists have been warning Americans that climate change will affect our world sooner rather than later. James Hansen, NASA's top climate scientist and one of the world's leading experts on global warming, has been struggling to alert the American public. After studying global warming for over thirty years, he has been sounding alarms that we must take action, as our world is close to reaching the tipping point.[1]

Dr. Hansen and other scientists have charged the Bush Administration with repeatedly meddling, gagging and silencing federal scientists who have tried to publicly publish research or address the impacts of global warming. Dr. Hansen was told to stop speaking out after he called for swift cuts in emissions of the greenhouse gases linked to global warming.[2] His emails were scrutinized and politicians within the Bush Administration have gone as far as tampering with and rewriting his reports and studies.[3] Rick Piltz of the federal Climate Change Science Program reported that his annual report was altered by a former lobbyist for the American Petroleum Institute. The former lobbyist was none other than the Bush-appointed Environmental Quality Chief, Phil Cooney, who made global warming appear less threatening, revising reports before they went to Congress or were published.[4]

*"In my more than three decades in the government
I've never witnessed such restrictions on the ability
of scientists to communicate with the public."*

James Hansen on the Bush Administration

Warmer Temperatures

Our earth is getting warmer because of an increase in greenhouse gases
that are being trapped in the earth's atmosphere. This trapped warmer
air is causing our glaciers to melt at a much faster rate than anyone
believed possible. You might think of it as the earth losing her natural air
conditioning system.

According to a study released in September of 2006, the earth is now
reaching and passing through the warmest levels in nearly 12,000 years
and is within 1.8 degrees F of its hottest temperature levels in the past
million years.[5] There are countless examples throughout the world of how
global warming is influencing weather patterns, wildlife and our global
life-support system.

*"The science is in.... the facts are man has created
a self-inflicted wound through global warming."*

Arnold Schwarzenegger

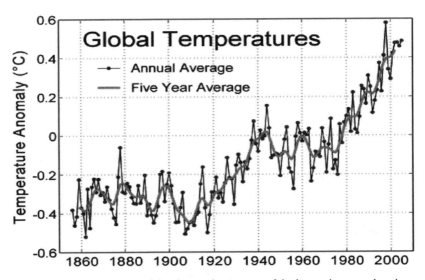

GLOBAL WARMING FACTS

• In 2005, the Union of Concerned Scientists reported that nine of the ten hottest years ever recorded have been in just the last ten years. Twenty of the hottest recorded years have been since 1980.[7]

• Twenty percent of the polar ice has melted since 1979.[8]

• The number of Category 4 and 5 hurricanes has almost doubled in the last thirty years and they are becoming much stronger in velocity.[9] The wind speeds of hurricanes are becoming increasingly fierce, such as in the Category 4 storm that blasted through northeastern Australia at 125 miles per hour in March of 2006. Faster and fiercer speeds increase the damage produced by such storms.

• Malaria has spread to higher altitudes and is now found in places like Nairobi at 5,500 feet and the Colombian Andes at 7,000 feet above sea level.

• Scores of flora and wildlife have already gone extinct, such as 70 species of frogs. Many more are facing extinction with experts predicting they will be gone by 2050.[10] These include polar bears, penguins, the African elephant, the Red-Breasted Goose, the Pinon Mouse, several classes of butterflies, and one-third of the known frogs.[11]

• Much of the United States, has been experiencing drought conditions recently.[12] In 2006 Michael Rounds, governor of South Dakota, requested that 51 of 66 counties be designated a federal agricultural disaster area because of drought.[13] A 2006 *Time Report* indicated that the amount of land devastated by drought has more than doubled globally since 1970. Places such as Ethiopia have been more severely impacted. In California and in other parts of the United States, drought-fueled fires have been on the increase.[14]

• The once lush tropical peat lands of Indonesia are now vulnerable to flooding because of multiple wildfires in the last three years.[15]

GLOBAL WARMING FACTS (continued)

• **Wildfires increase the amount of greenhouse gas carbon dioxide (CO2) in the atmosphere, thus stimulating faster global warming.**

• **Scientists report that greenhouse gases are at their highest levels in 65,000 years. Elevated heat temperatures claimed the lives of 35,000 Europeans in 2003 alone.**[16]

• **The World Health Organization attributes 150,000 deaths a year to climate change.**[17]

• **Poorer nations such as India are losing small villages because of flood storms; the Philippines lost nearly 3,000 lives in 2006 storms and mudslides.**

• **Sea coral is dying at an unprecedented pace because of the increased warm waters. A 2005 scientific report indicated that one-fourth of the seas coral had already died.**[18]

Higher Levels of Greenhouse Gases Including Carbon Dioxide

There is a direct correlation between the warmer temperatures and the increased levels of carbon dioxide gas (CO_2) and other "greenhouse gases" found in the earth's atmosphere.[19] Carbon is the essential ingredient of all fossil fuels. Carbon dioxide (CO_2) is dumped into the earth's atmosphere when coal, gas and oil are burned to provide energy.

Developing nations all over the globe are rapidly becoming more dependent on carbon-based fuels for improving their lifestyle. As fossil fuel dependency increases, more concentrations of CO_2 are pushed into the earth's atmosphere, according to the British Petroleum (BP).[20] Experts say CO_2 has increased from approximately 280 parts per million (ppm) before the Industrial Revolution, to 370 ppm by mid 2005.[21] This represents a 33 percent increase of CO_2 in a very short span of time. If dependencies on fossil fuel continue, the concentration of CO_2 is likely to exceed 700 ppm by the end of this century.[22]

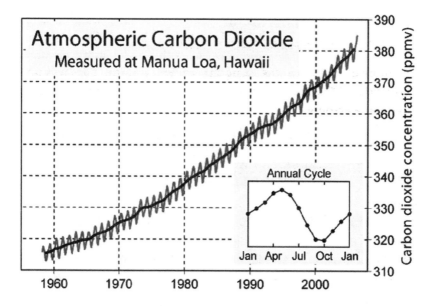

Atmospheric Carbon Dioxide
Measured at Manua Loa, Hawaii

Annual Cycle

Jan Apr Jul Oct Jan

Carbon dioxide concentration (ppmv)

390 380 370 360 350 340 330 320 310

1960 1970 1980 1990 2000

http://www.globalwarmingart.com/wiki/Image:Mauna_Loa_Carbon_Dioxide_png

Glacier Loss Translates to Rapidy Rising Seas

Scientists are concerned that rapidly melting sea ice from the Arctic, Antarctica and Greenland will swiftly unload enough fresh water to disrupt sea currents.[23] Freshwater increases are coming from two sources, from the ice-melt itself and from increased rain and snow. Diminishing ice cover exposes more of the ocean surface, thus causing more moisture to evaporate into the atmosphere. This leads to higher amounts of rainfall.

Greenland ice is melting at a rate three times faster than it was only five years ago.[24] Scientists attribute the loss to warmer climate temperatures. One recent article showed how Greenland is losing the equivalent of half a football stadium of ice *every single day.*[25] Scientists say it is normal for the ice to melt and then regenerate itself. However, those who have been closely monitoring Greenland's ice caps say greater overall regeneration losses are not being regained. Climate experts are becoming alarmed because ice caps are disappearing in ways that computer models had not predicted.[26] According to Robert Gagosian, the president and director of the Woods Hole Oceanographic Institution, major shifts in ocean currents could come as quickly as twenty years.[27] Dr. Gagosian sounded this alert in 2004.

Temperature changes affect the balance between saltwater, which is denser and heavier, and the lighter freshwater. These changes will probably produce major problems in how the earth's ocean waters circulate. Many scientists are now predicting that these transformations will have a dramatic impact on the earth's climate.[28]

Loss in Glacier Thickness

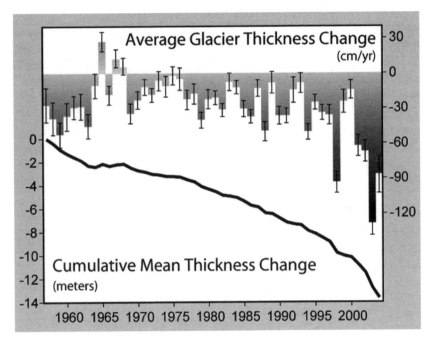

http://www.globalwarmingart.com/wiki/Image:Glacier_Mass_Balance_png

Americans in Denial

According to a 2006 Time/ABC/Stanford University Poll, 85 percent of Americans believe the earth is indeed warming, but only 31 percent believe it is attributable to human influence.[29] Documented studies conducted by scientific experts reveal that temperature changes since 1970 are "far above natural variations."[30]

Bruce, an executive and part-time farmer I met in Denver in 2006, said he had planted several almond trees last year at his small family farm in the heart of California's Central Valley. However, shortly after planting his little orchard, the expected rainy season never materialized. With the help of family and friends, his newly planted trees survived by hand-watering. Bruce does not believe in global warming, he thinks it was just an "off year."

Amy is a conservative from South Carolina. While she says she has noticed climate changes in her community, she believes the environment is "a political issue." Amy told me a story about how a group of environmentalists had destroyed an apple producer in her community. The protesters had publicized the fact that the apple farmer had used some sort of pesticide on his apples. According to Amy, the pesticide did not hurt anyone and the apple issue became political. Amy then gave me another example of people who use politics to gain support for "animal rights causes." Amy does not believe global warming to be a real threat. She said it was her understanding that climate changes were cyclical. I asked Amy if she had seen the documentary film *An Inconvenient Truth*. She laughed and said there was no way she would go see a movie if it had Al Gore in it.

On the other hand, Roger Ebert, movie critic for the *Chicago Sun-Times*, wrote this commentary regarding **An Inconvenient Truth:** "In 39 years, I have never written these words in a movie review, but here they are: You owe it to yourself to see this film. If you do not, and you have grandchildren, you should explain to them why you decided not to."[31]

The Neocon Attack on Mother Earth

While campaigning for the Presidency in 1999, George W. Bush promised to "establish mandatory reduction targets" for carbon dioxide emissions, saying he would make the issue a top priority. However, his promise to reduce carbon emissions was broken after he became President. Two months after assuming the Presidency, Mr. Bush withdrew from the Kyoto Protocol, the global treaty that the United States signed in 1997 to set strict limits on greenhouse emissions.[32] He then placed the inter-agency group that monitors climate change into the Commerce Department. Ironically, Don Evans, a former oil and gas executive, is the Secretary of the Commerce Department.

Instead of establishing mandatory reduction targets of carbon dioxide, Bush instituted a voluntary emissions plan. Experts describe this plan as an abject failure.[33] Only fourteen companies pledged to curb their CO_2 output.[34] To add further insult, President Bush determined that additional climate research was required before he would consider making any public policy changes.[35] The result meant a decade of delay before important changes in regulation and policy could or would be implemented. Bush declared, "We do not know how much our climate could or will change in the future."[36] This speech prompted a public outcry. A letter signed by twenty Nobel laureates, highly respected for their work in the field, accused the Bush Administration of having consistently sought to undermine "public understanding of man's role in global warming."[37]

Similar strategies of inflicting doubt and confusion were successfully used by American cigarette companies for decades to deny the link between cigarette smoking and cancer. In fact, at a recent business meeting, I spoke with a banker who provides investment funding to the tobacco industry and he said he still wasn't sure there is a link between cigarette smoking and lung cancer.

ExxonMobil, one of the world's largest oil corporations, has devised strategies to defer action on global warming.[38] It has created several methodologies for inspiring doubt in the minds of average citizens. Using the media, ExxonMobil funds pseudo-scientific think tanks and scientists to develop materials and articles to "debunk" global warming. Their artificial arguments attempt to quash scientific fact. This has caused confusion and uncertainty in the minds of many people.[39]

Massive attacks are regularly launched by these Neoconservative think tanks to distort and minimize the impact of global warming on the environment. The goal of these opinion papers is to instill reservations in the American public by claiming that global warming is not a fact, but only a theory.[40] The National Academy of Sciences, NAS, has been stating that for more than ten years the scientific community has been closely aligned and in agreement about what the causes and consequences of global warming are for our planet.[41] NASA scientists say that greenhouse skeptics sabotage the scientific process when they fail to act as objective scientists. Ethical and legitimate scientists charge global warming skeptics of presenting only one side of the argument, saying these skeptics act "as if they were lawyers hired to defend a particular viewpoint."[42]

On a Fox News special on global warming, Sterling Burnett, a senior fellow at the National Center for Policy Analysis, an organization that has received over $390,000 from ExxonMobil since 1998, compared watching the blockbuster movie on global warming, *An Inconvenient Truth,* to watching a movie by Nazi propagandist Joseph Goebbels.[43] Fox News programs frequently feature individuals with close ties to oil, coal, mining and other related industries as global warming experts.[44] Most are not scientists in the field. Unfortunately for us, Fox News does not disclose this information. These individuals carry honorary titles of distinction from their Neoconservative think tanks such as *adjunct scholar*, thus providing a sense of legitimacy.[45]

For instance, Steven J. Milloy is a commentator and columnist for Fox News. His clients include tobacco companies Phillip Morris and R.J. Reynolds and oil giant ExxonMobil, among others.[46] Mr. Milloy is neither a scientist nor a bona fide researcher. He is a self-proclaimed public health expert who has created a stream of anti-environmental, anti-public health commentary. He maintains a website appropriately tagged "Junk Science." He is frequently found on Fox News, posing as a legitimate scientist with knowledge on global warming.[47] He has published a book on "junk science" that was never vetted through the traditional academic scientific review process.[48] Mr. Milloy holds a law degree and is an adjunct scholar with the Cato Institute. The institute also receives huge contributions from Conservative foundations and big gas and oil business.[49]

Patrick J. Michaels is referred to as a "global warming skeptic" and is another frequent contributor to Fox News. Mr. Michaels has received over $115,000 in funding from coal and other energy interests. His colleagues in the scientific community have repeatedly criticized his limited scientific work, saying it is filled with "misrepresentation and misinterpretation."[50] Mr. Michaels is also Senior Fellow at the Cato Institute and is associated with several anti-global warming Neoconservative think tanks such as the George C. Marshall Institute. Mr. Michaels takes a position that global warming models are fatally flawed and there is no need to take action because new technologies will soon replace those that emit greenhouse gases. Mr. Michaels has engaged in disingenuous actions, such as presenting global warming position papers that have no global warming data research after 1996.[51] He is a professor at the University of Virginia and one of a very small number of individuals who, despite the evidence, say either nothing can be done about global warming or it is not a problem.

The Washington-based "think tank" Competitive Enterprise Institute states that it is "... a non-profit public policy organization dedicated to advancing the principles of free enterprise and limited government." Their mission statement says, "We believe that individuals are best helped not by government intervention, but by making their own choices in a free marketplace." Since its founding in 1984, CEI has grown into a $3,000,000 institution with a team of over twenty "policy experts" and other staff.[52] It is important to note that of the $3,000,000 this institution boasts, it received enormous contributions of $1,380,000 from ExxonMobil from 2000 to 2003.[53]

These "policy experts" lobby Congress on environmental issues as well as provide opinions at public forums. In 2006 CEI began running their "life" commercials where they call CO_2 *life* and advocate against the potential designation of CO_2 as a pollutant.[54] Using highly sophisticated imagery and psychological manipulation, these commercials are designed to promote CO_2 as safe and healthy, despite carbon dioxide's contribution to global warming. The CEI sponsors advertisements telling the American public that glacier melting is not happening despite widespread evidence to the contrary.[55] CEI stifles public protection against global warming through its powerful lobbying efforts, filing lawsuits against the government, presenting opinion papers, testifying before government agencies, writing op-ed pieces and sponsoring paid advertising to disseminate false claims about global warming.[56]

The National Center for Public Policy and Research or NCPPR is yet another example of the many conservative organizations with a website dedicated to creating confusion on global warming. It, too, receives ExxonMobil funding.[57] There are numerous articles available on NCPPR's website. Again, none of the articles are written by scientists or accredited professionals in the environmental field or the field of global warming. Amy Ridenou, who is pro-tobacco and demonstrably anti-environment, is the president of NCPPR and David Ridenou, her husband, is the vice president.[58] Dana Joel Gattuso is a freelance writer on public policy and a senior fellow at the NCPPR. Tim Graham is the Director of Media Analysis at the Media Research Center, another Neoconservative think tank. This closely knit community of non-scientists takes turns writing articles for each other's websites. Take a close look at their article titles:

Summer Heat is Normal, Not Proof of "Global Warming"[59]
by David Ridenou, The National Center for Public Policy Research
August 4, 2005

Some Global Warming Scare Tactics are So Dumb, They're Funny[60]
by Tim Graham, The National Center for Public Policy Research
June 21, 2006

Kyoto's Anniversary: Little Reason to Celebrate[61]
by Dana Joel Gattuso, The National Center for Public Policy Research
February 2006

Peyton Knight, who runs another Neoconservative organization, the American Policy Center, recently wrote an article for the NCPPR entitled "Save the Planet: Drive an SUV."[62] In a short 110-word article posted on the NCPPR website, Mr. Knight stated that a two-year study "revealed *hybrid vehicles are more 'energy expensive' than even a Hummer H3.*"[63] He concludes his article by insulting environmentally conscious celebrities who drive hybrids.

Mr. Knight provides an annotation to the study from which he quotes. However, following the links back to the study does not provide the reader with the necessary evidence to support Mr. Knight's conclusion. The alleged study was not conducted by a research firm but was conducted by CNW Marketing Research. CNW Marketing Research is a company designed to assist the American automotive industry with marketing and positioning strategies. The CNW Marketing Research website appears to have some detailed reports. However, the reports are only available to members with passwords.

The data presented by CNW used to justify the outrageous statements by Mr. Knight are simply unavailable.[64] A report "draft" does exist on the CNW Marketing website that lists the following:

- Ten most energy efficient automobiles over their lifetime,
- Ten least energy efficient automobiles over their lifetime, and
- Five Hybrid Energy Efficient Cars rates over a lifetime.[65]

CNW Marketing Research declares that the Toyota Prius and the Honda Civic cost more than several American-made cars over the life of the vehicle. This information conflicts with data available by *Consumer Reports*, which asserts that the Toyota Prius and Honda Civic Hybrid provide savings of about $400 and $300 respectively.[66]

Meanwhile, the National Center for Public Policy and Research was in the news in late June of 2006. The NCPPR was reported as being one of the tax-exempt organizations receiving huge sums of money from Jack Abramoff, the indicted Washington lobbyist.[67] According to an article entitled "E-mails link tax-exempt organizations to scandal," investigative reporters Schmidt and Grimaldi allege that the National Center for Public Policy and Research (NCPPR) was used as a pass-through agency to provide illegal funds to sponsor trips for congressional representatives. The Neoconservative think tank was also accused of peddling policies related to specific business purposes to Congress.[68] This is a violation of the tax-exemption for such agencies.[69]

"I applaud the NCPPR staff and supporters for your commitment to educating Americans on... issues that are essential to our nation's prosperity and security. For twenty years, you have remained steadfast in your efforts to advance the cause of individual freedom in the United States."

President George W. Bush[70]

There seem to be countless numbers of these anti-environmental, "keep America stupid about global warming" think tanks. The deceitfully named think tanks promote discord and confusion in the face of sound environmental research. The list that follows illustrates only a few of the many Neoconservative think tanks receiving funding from Exxon/Mobil for their anti-environment rhetoric:

NEOCON THINK TANKS ON CLIMATE CHANGE AND GLOBAL WARMING

Acton Institute for the Study of Religious Liberty[71]

- **"While some environmental concerns are well founded and serious, others are without foundation or greatly exaggerated..."**
- **"Global warming... remains speculative and based on incomplete computer models rather than on demonstrated science."**

ExxonMobil Contributions $155,000

Advancement of Sound Science Center

Run by Steven Milloy, a frequent Fox News commentator.

- **"...reveals there is significant uncertainty about the surface temperature record."**

ExxonMobil Contributions $40,000[72]

American Council for Capital Formation[73]

Focuses on the economics of climate control policies and provides extremely one-sided presentations to Congress.

- "Despite the lack of scientific consensus over global warming, there are factual economic conclusions that can be drawn from government mandates to curb greenhouse gases."[74]
- "Can We Afford to Heed Gore?" "... The other choice is to follow Mr. Gore and tinker with failed policy that would lead to sharp increases in already high energy prices, lost jobs and reduced revenue. That's an inconvenient truth that we cannot afford."[75]
- "The most prudent course of action for the next several decades, he argues, is a 'hedging strategy' that delays taking strong measures to reduce CO_2 emissions until more is known about specific risks to the environment."[76]

ExxonMobil Contributions $909,523

American Council on Science and Health[77]

S. Fred Singer and Patrick J Michaels are listed as scientific advisers. S. Fred Singer is a global warming skeptic who also runs yet another think tank and is an adjunct scholar of the Cato Institute.

- "There is no scientific consensus concerning global warming. The climate change predictions are based on computer models that have not been validated and are far from perfect."

ExxonMobil Contributions $215,000

American Enterprise Institute

The AEI provides pundits specializing in global warming. These skeptics include Sallie Baliunas, David Legates, James Glassman, and Steven F. Hayward. AEI's fellows have repeatedly challenged mainstream climate change science. Sallie Baliunas is an astrophysicist who is well known for her criticism of global warming. Mr. Hayward holds a Ph.D. in American Studies and is not a scientist but is referred to as a conservative environmentalism pundit.[78] Mr. Glassman is a journalist who has been accused of reinventing journalism by turning it into lobbying.[79]

- "The global-warming hype is running out of gas, as it very much deserves."[80]

- **"Scientific facts gathered in the past ten years do not support the notion of catastrophic human-made warming as a basis for drastic carbon dioxide emission cuts."[81]**
- **"No evidence can be found in the temperature measurements to support the theory of catastrophic global warming caused by human activities."[82]**
- **"Importantly, much of the scientific evidence contradicts assertions that substantial global warming is likely to occur soon and that the predicted warming will harm the Earth's biosphere"[83]**

ExxonMobil Contributions $1,600,000

American Legislative Exchange Council[84]

ExxonMobil supports the American Legislative Exchange Council (ALEC) as it pushes conservative policies focusing on fighting greenhouse gas emission controls at the state level. ALEC draws on "skeptic" global warming characters such as Patrick J. Michaels to counter global warming concerns.

ExxonMobil Contributions $712,200

Annapolis Center for Science-Based Public Policy[85]

- **"One major unanswered question is how much of the observed warming of about 1 degree Fahrenheit during the past century may be caused by human activities and how much by natural climate variations..."**

ExxonMobil Contributions $697,500

Atlas Economic Research Foundation[86]

On behalf of Atlas Economic Research Foundation, syndicated columnist and paid speaker Deroy Murdock has repeatedly attempted to discredit the scientific basis of global warming concerns over the years.[87] Mr. Murdock is not a scientist.

- **"As the science behind global warming becomes increasingly sketchy, many environmentalists clutch even harder to their views..."**

ExxonMobil Contributions $440,000

> **Center for the Study of Carbon Dioxide and Global Change** [88]
> • **"There is also little doubt the earth has warmed slightly over the same period; but there is no compelling reason to believe that the rise in temperature was caused by the rise in CO_2."**
> *ExxonMobil Contributions $ 55,000*

A Call to Stop Spreading Misinformation!

The Royal Society, Britain's premier scientific academy, wrote an open letter to ExxonMobil in 2006 demanding that the company stop supporting dozens of groups who have "misrepresented the science of climate change by outright denial of the evidence."[89] The Royal Society cites a survey it conducted which found that ExxonMobil distributed $2.9 million dollars to 39 groups in one year. The scientists allege that ExxonMobil funded the groups to deliberately misrepresent the science of climate change.

Upon release of the six-year scientific UN report on global warming, the American Enterprise Institute began offering ExxonMobil funded cash payments. A $10,000 payment was offered to any scientist who was willing to write an article highlighting a weakness, or criticizing the climate change report. AEI offers were sent to scientists in the U.S., Great Britain and elsewhere.[90]

The Consequences

An article entitled "Lake Becomes Bay as Arctic melts" was buried in the middle of page A3 of my local newspaper.[91] It was reported in September of 2006. The article describes a phenomenon never seen before by scientists. Amazingly, in a six-week period a massive lake the size of the state of Indiana melted out of what was once a humongous glacier in a remote part of the Arctic polar ice cap.[92] Chris Rapley, Director of the British Antarctic Survey, warned of the momentous consequences due to the rise in global sea levels. This is yet another affirmation of polar ice caps melting and sea waters warming at a much faster rate than glaciologists thought possible.[93] This means earth is quickly losing its cooling system as our planet continues to heat up.

But when the detailed six-year UN scientific report on global warming was released in 2007, the Neoconservative talking heads that control

74 percent of America's radio stations dismissed it. The report concluded overwhelming evidence that global warming is man made. Make no mistake: Americans will face the dire consequences of climate change on our planet in the near future. But, in order to build support for more war, these same talking heads rattle on like Chicken Little, instilling fear about Iran and imagined nuclear weapons while the real and most important threat to our nation is ignored. Why would patriotic Americans want to continue to contribute to the financial well being of terrorist nations who hate us while we simultaneously endanger our planet and future generations?

While slashing the budget at National Academy of Sciences, the agency that studies global warming and makes policy recommendations, the Bush White House demands billions of more dollars for the war in Iraq.

We have accomplished great things in the U.S. We have championed democracy, we have made great advances in science and medicine and we have advanced religious freedom and tolerance. The United States is the richest country globally. Yet we have become a consumer society. Our riches and consumerism come with an environmental debt that will have to be paid by our children and grandchildren. We produce billions of tons of CO_2 and more pollutants than any other country in the world. While the U.S. represents five percent of the global population, we are responsible for 25 percent of CO_2 emissions. We must act as a world leader to stop this global poisoning before it's too late. Imagine if the media tracked all of the phenomenal climate changes occurring due to global warming like we track the stock market. America's consciousness of the problem would be greatly enhanced.

Humankind at a Tipping Point
Data from Stewart Udall, November 12, 2006

Total Carbon Emission — CO_2 output by nations:

▨▨▨ Spain
▨▨▨ Saudi Arabia
▨▨▨ Indonesia
▨▨▨ Iran
▨▨▨ Brazil
▨▨▨ Mexico
▨▨▨ Ukraine
▨▨▨ Australia
▨▨▨▨ South Africa
▨▨▨ France
▨▨▨▨ S. Korea
▨▨▨▨ Italy
▨▨▨▨▨ Britian
▨▨▨▨▨ Canada
▨▨▨▨▨▨ Germany
▨▨▨▨▨▨▨ India
▨▨▨▨▨▨▨ Japan
▨▨▨▨▨▨▨▨▨ Russia
▨▨▨▨▨▨▨▨▨▨▨▨▨▨▨▨▨▨▨▨▨ China
▨▨▨▨▨▨▨▨▨▨▨▨▨▨▨▨▨▨▨▨▨▨▨▨▨▨▨▨▨▨▨▨▨▨▨▨ U.S.

▨ Emissions

Our Excesses

Last spring I counted sixteen girls who participated in a soccer tournament sixty to eighty-five miles each way from the girls' homes. One would think that this might mean sixteen cars drove to the tournament. But on this particular weekend I discovered that because of conflicting family member schedules and work variations, there were a total of 22 vehicles that had driven to the tournament. This meant that a child and parent rode together, and that eight other parents or older siblings drove separately to the tournament as well. When I took an average of miles driven to this tournament and multiplied it times the number of vehicles, I discovered that a cumulative total of 3,168 miles were driven each day of the tournament. This is the equivalent of a round trip cross-country drive over the course of the two-day tournament.

We must examine our excessive consumerism in the U.S. We drink water from France and Fiji; we drive vehicles that are jointly produced by Japan and the U.S. Many of us have two cars, some have a boat. A typical "soccer family" will normally own at least one large four-wheel drive SUV. In the U.S. we take for granted the fresh apples we eat in the spring from New Zealand, the white pears from China we enjoy during the holidays, and the best Colombia coffee beans we grind every morning for a delicious cup of coffee. And because we are busy, overworked and tired, we will probably drive into a fast-food establishment at least one night a week where we know we can be eating food out of containers within ten minutes or less. Orange-clothed prisoners pick up garbage along our roads, filling a bag full of trash every 100 feet. We build 2,500-square-foot homes that on average might house four people. These homes are heated and cooled to comfort year round yet most of the time we aren't even there. We keep our work buildings too cool in the summer and too warm in the winter. Lights are left on at night to the degree that we suffer from light pollution in all but the smallest towns. How many readers can relate to this description of our American lifestyle? Awareness is the first step. Taking action to make environmentally considerate choices is the second step.

Countless budding opportunities and initiatives exist. They need only a bit of nurturing and support to succeed. For example, we need to ask the American automobile industry for the cars of the future; they have already been paid to develop them with taxpayer dollars over the last 35 years. Many Americans want to know what happened to the EV1 electric vehicles created by General Motors in the 1990s. They were among the quickest, most efficient cars ever built. The EV1 ran on electricity,

produced no emissions and propelled American technology to the forefront of the automotive industry. According to the recent film documentary, *Who Killed the Electric Car,* the few who drove the EVls never
wanted to relinquish them. General Motors leased all the EVls and then
demanded their return when the lease was up. EVls were destroyed by
shredding them in the Arizona desert. It was reported that the last
remaining EV1 was removed from the Smithsonian shortly before the
début of the film in the summer of 2006.

"What Would Jesus Drive?"
Reverend Jim Ball

According to a 2006 poll conducted by *Time*/ABC News and Stanford
University, 87 percent of Americans believe one of the best ways to fight
global warming is to provide tax breaks to companies that are developing
alternative energy sources. Instead of the U.S. government subsidizing
tobacco farmers and rich oil companies, why not subsidize alternative
energy farms? Farms that are helping to produce solar, wind, and geothermal energy and smart, efficient ethanol, bio-diesel and methanol
fuels should immediately receive huge tax credits.

The billion-dollar tax credits for new exploration and other subsidies
given to the gas and oil industry should be immediately ended. These tax
credits should be directed to the American public for the purchase of
smart energy-conserving innovations and new hybrid vehicles.

Promising organizations and collaborations are cropping up, such as
the Apollo Alliance. The Apollo Alliance is a coalition of labor and environmental groups with a plan to "develop alternative fuels and increase
energy efficiency." They plan to rebuild and expand public transportation
networks and develop other initiatives to reduce fossil fuel use. They
believe they will create more than three million jobs in the process.[94]

It is interesting to remember Dick Cheney's words when he referred
to the possibility that Saddam Hussein might have weapons of mass
destruction. Quoting from Ron Suskin's book, *One Percent Doctrine,*[95]
Dick Cheney said, "We have to deal with this new type of threat in a way
we haven't yet defined.... With a low-probability, high-impact event
like this... If there's a one percent chance that Pakistani scientists are
helping al-Qaeda build or develop a nuclear weapon, we have to treat it
as a certainty in terms of our response."[96] This "one percent chance" was
Dick Cheney's justification for a war in Iraq.

It breaks my heart because we know, with ninety percent certainty,
that global warming is threatening our world. Conscious Americans are

crying out, asking: Why are we not treating this terrible threat as a certainty, Mr. Cheney? Why are we instead stalling? Why did we rush into a war and spend billions upon billions without more study as advocated by George W. Bush on global warming?

The American public must not wait for our politically elected officials to lead the way. It is incumbent on each and every American to do his or her part.

"As we stand at the brink of a second nuclear age and a period of unprecedented climate change, scientists have a special responsibility once again to inform the public and advise leaders about the perils that humanity faces. We foresee great perils if governments and society do not take action now to render nuclear weapons obsolete and prevent further climate change."

Stephen Hawking

What You Can Do about Global Warming

Here's where we can start:

- Learn more about the problem.
- Watch videos and read books about global warming, but make sure they are from credible sources that have been through a scientific peer review.
- Talk about the global warming problem with your friends and family members.
- Get rid of all oversized SUVs or other gas-guzzling motor vehicles.
- Buy fuel-efficient vehicles.
- Reduce driving. One gallon of gas burned creates 20 pounds of CO_2.
- Fill your gas tank with ethanol and bio-diesel products.
- Contact the sponsors, the TV station, your congressional representatives, and the FCC about any news programs featuring Neoconservative global warming skeptics and complain that propaganda is being broadcast as legitimate news.
- Replace appliances with high-energy-efficient appliances.
- Replace light bulbs with low-wattage, long-lasting compact fluorescent bulbs.

- Increase your home insulation, making sure cracks in windows and doors are sealed. Think energy conservation when remodeling.
- Buy wind and solar energy through your power company.
- Talk to your boss at work to see how your organization can better conserve energy, especially fossil fuel. Find out if telecommuting from home is an option and save yourself time and energy.
- Become a smart shopper—buy locally.
- Stop taking bags from the grocery store and throwing them away; instead, recycle your bags.
- Start recycling newspapers, plastic and glass; buy products from recycled materials.
- Vote for civic leaders who are willing to take a stand on the environment, especially global warming and encourage your friends and neighbors to do likewise.
- Organize neighborhood and town meetings to discuss how to increase local energy efficiency.
- If you live out of town, consider moving closer to your job.
- Walk or ride your bike instead of driving; consider arranging car pools whenever possible.
- Build new homes and buildings with increased energy efficiency and solar power.
- Support sustainable farming, fisheries and forestry.
- Endorse farming or start your own farm for products to create ethanol and bio-fuels.
- Demand the government invest in efficient energy policies instead of wars for oil.
- Avoid flying when possible (air travel contributes *huge* amounts of greenhouse gases). Use video conferencing, email, and teleconferencing instead. Consider train or bus travel (reduces emissions by 3 to 7 times that of air travel).
- Support collaborations to export new energy technologies.
- Start these actions now!

"I don't think God is going to ask us how He created the earth, but He will ask us what we did with what He created."

Reverend Rich Cizik

NOTES, Chapter 16

[1] "A Science Adviser Unmuzzled," *Time Magazine*, April 3, 2006 www.time.com/time/magazine/article/0,9171,1176828,00.html.

[2] CBS Online, "Rewriting the Science," *60 Minutes*, July 30, 2006, www.cbsnews.com/stories/2006/03/17/60minutes/main1415985.shtml.

[3] Ibid.

[4] Ibid.

[5] NASA Online, "NASA Study Finds World Warmth Edging Ancient Levels," *Goddard Space Flight Center: News*, September 25, 2006, www.nasa.gov/centers/goddard/news/topstory/2006/world_warmth.html

[6] "Instrumental Temperature Record," *Global Warming Art*, www.globalwarmingart.com/wiki/Image:Instrumental_Temperature_Record.png.

[7] Dr. Marcia Baker, "2005 Vies for Hottest Year on Record," *Union of Concerned Scientists*, www.ucsusa.org/global_warming/science/recordtemp2005.html.

[8] "Global Warming Puts the Polar Bear at Risk of Extinction," *NRDC's BioGems*, www.savebiogems.org/polar/.

[9] "Number of Category 4 and 5 Hurricanes Has Doubled Over the Past 35 Years," *National Science Foundation*, September 15, 2005, www.nsf.gov/news/news_summ.jsp?cntn_id=104428&org=NSF&from=news.

[10] Seth Borenstein, "Pace of Global Warming Causes Alarm 'Very different and frightening world' coming faster than expected, scientists warn," *Associated Press*, November 21, 2006.

[11] ABC News Online, *Hot Zone: Global Warming*, abcnews.go.com/Technology/GlobalWarming/.

[12] Monica Davey, "Blistering Drought Ravages Farmland on Plains," *New York Times*, August 29, 2006,

[13] Ibid.

[14] Jeffrey Kluger, "Polar Ice Caps Are Melting Faster Than Ever... More And More Land Is Being Devastated By Drought... Rising Waters Are Drowning Low-Lying Communities... By Any Measure, Earth Is At ... The Tipping Point," *Time Magazine*, March 26, 2006, www.time.com/time/magazine/article/0,9171,1176980,00.html.

[15] Ibid.

[16] Alister Doyle, "UN Climate Panel to Project Wrenching Change," *Reuters*, January 23, 2007.

[17] Ibid.

[18] Geoffrey Lean, "Global Warming Approaching Point of No Return, Warns Leading Climate Expert," *Independent/UK*, January 23, 2005.

[19] "It's Time to Go on a Low Carbon Diet," *BP Global* www.bp.com/section genericarticle.do?categoryId=4533&contentId=7015199.

[20] Ibid.

[21] Ibid.

[22] Ibid.

[23] Ibid.

[24] David Perlman, "Greenland's ice cap is melting at a frighteningly fast rate," *San Francisco Chronicle*, Friday, August 11, 2006.

[25] Robert Lee Hotz, "As Greenland Melts," *Cyber Diver News Network*, June 25, 2006, www.cdnn.info/news/science/sc060625.html.

[26] National Science Teachers Association, Subcategory Environment and Nature www.nsta.org/sciencenews/&category_ID=277

[27] "A Chilling Possibility," *Science @ NASA*, March 5, 2004, science.nasa.gov/headlines/y2004/05mar_arctic.htm.

[28] Perlman, "Greenland."

[29] "TIME Poll: Global Warming," *Time Magazine*, March 26, 2006, www.time.com/time/magazine/article/0,9171,1176975,00.html.

[30] Paleoclimatic Data for the Last 2000 Years, Peer Reviewed Paper, Last updated, November 16, 2006 *National Climatic Data Center*, www.ncdc.noaa.gov/paleo/globalwarming/paleolast.html.

[31] Roger Ebert, "An Inconvenient Truth," *Chicago Sun-Times*, June 2, 2006.

[32] National Environmental Trust, *"Global Warming, Energy, and the Bush Administration*, United Nations Framework Convention on Climate Change, Bonn, Germany, July 16-27, 2001, www.environet.org/warming/bonn-book.pdf.

[33] Brandon Wu, "Lethal Legacy: A Comprehensive Look at America's Dirtiest Power Plants," *U.S. Public Interest Research Group Education Fund*, October 2003, www.cleartheair.org/reports/lethal_legacy_report.pdf.

[34] "Attorney General Lockyer Challenges Federal Fuel Standards for Failing to Increase Fuel Efficiency, Curb Global Warming Emissions," *Office of the Attorney General, State of California*, May 2, 2006, ag.ca.gov/newsalerts/release.php?id=1299.

[35] National Environmental Trust, "Global Warming."

[36] Ibid.

[37] Drunvalo Melchizedek, "Dry/Ice: Global Warming Revealed," *The Spirit of Ma'at*, July 19, 2004, netmar.com/~maat/announce/ann_dryice.htm.

[38] Stephen Lendman, "The Corporate Control Of Society and Human Life," *LendmanBlog* April 25, 2006, sjlendman.blogspot.com/2006/04/hostile-takeover-corporate-control-of.html.

[39] Ibid.

[40] *An Inconvenient Truth*, DVD, directed by Davis Guggenheim (2006; Culver City, CA: Paramount Home Video, 2006).

[41] Committee on the Science of Climate Change, National Research Council, *Climate Change Science: An Analysis of Some Key Questions* (Washington, DC: National Academy Press, 2001), newton.nap.edu/html/climatechange/.

[42] James Hansen, *The Global Warming Debate*, January 1999, www.giss.nasa.gov/edu/gwdebate/.

[43] "Fox guest likened Al Gore's *An Inconvenient Truth* to Nazi propaganda films," *MediaMatters*, May 24, 2006, mediamatters.org/items/200605240009.

[44] Steven Milloy, "New York City Bans Science," *FOX News*, December 7, 2006, www.foxnews.com/junkscience.

[45] Steven Milloy, "Top Ten Junk Science Stories of the Past Decade," *FOX News*, April 6, 2006, www.foxnews.com/story/0,2933,189706,00.html.

[46] "Steven J. Milloy: The 'Junkman' Exposed," *Americans For Nonsmokers' Rights*, February 2006, www.no-smoke.org/pdf/stevenmilloy.pdf.

[47] Milloy, "Top Ten."

[48] Steven Milloy, "Wilma is Not Global Warming," *FOX News*, October 20, 2005, www.foxnews.com/story/0,2933,172949,00.html.

[49] "Cato Institute," *Media Transparency*, www.mediatransparency.org/recipient profile.php?recipientID=51.

[50] The Center for Media & Democracy, "Patrick J. Michaels," *SourceWatch,* www.sourcewatch.org/index.php?title=Patrick_Michaels.

[51] Ibid.

[52] "About CEI," *Competitive Enterprise Institute,* www.cei.org/pages/about.cfm.

[53] prorev.com/2005/12/money-behind-think-tanks-that-media.htm. Defunct, December 14.

[54] "We Call It Life," *Competitive Enterprise Institute,* www.cei.org/pages/co2.cfm.

[55] Ibid.

[56] The Center for Media & Democracy, "Competitive Enterprise Institute," *SourceWatch,* www.sourcewatch.org/index.php?title=Competitive_Enterprise_Institute.

[57] "About Us," *The National Center for Public Policy Research,* www.national center.org/NCPPRHist.html.

[58] "Amy Ridenour," *Wikipedia,* en.wikipedia.org/wiki/Amy_Ridenour.

[59] David Ridenour, "Summer Heat is Normal, Not Proof of 'Global Warming'." *The National Center for Public Policy Research,* August 4, 2005, www.national center.org/TSR080405.html.

[60] Amy Ridenour, "Some Global Warming Scare Tactics Are So Dumb, They're Funny," *Amy Ridenour's National Center Blog,* June 21, 2006, www.national center.org/2006/06/some-global-warming-scare-tactics-are.html.

[61] Dana Joel Gattuso, "Kyoto's Anniversary: Little Reason to Celebrate," *National Policy Analysis,* February 2006, www.nationalcenter.org/NPA537EuropeKyoto 206.html.

[62] Amy Ridenour, "Save the Planet: Drive an SUV," *Amy Ridenour's National Center Blog,* April 6, 2006, www.nationalcenter.org/2006/04/save-planet-drive-suv.html.

[63] Ibid.

[64] "Efficiency is More Than Just Fuel Economy," *CNW Marketing Research,* www.nvo.com/cnwmr/nss-folder/cnwbywebcontents/Energy Efficiency. Defunct (December 9, 2006).

[65] Ibid.

[66] "The Dollars & Sense of Hybrid Cars," *Consumer Reports Online,* September 2006, www.consumerreports.org/cro/cars/new-cars/high-cost-of-hybrid-vehicles-406/overview/index.htm.

[67] Susan Schmidt and James V. Grimaldi, "Emails Link Tax-Exempt Organizations to Scandal," *The Washington Post,* June 25, 2006.

[68] Ibid.

[69] Ibid.

[70] "About Us," NCPPR.

[71] A survey of ExxonMobil-supported organizations challenging the scientific basis for concern about global climate change. "Put a Tiger in your Think Tank," www.motherjones.com/news/featurex/2005/05/exxon_more.html

[72] www.exxonsecrets.org/html/orgfactsheet.php?id=105.

[73] "Put a Tiger in your Think Tank." *MotherJones.*

[74] *American Council for Capital Formation,* www.accf.org.

[75] Margo Thorning, "Can We Afford to Heed Gore?," *The Baltimore Sun,* May 30, 2006, www.accf.org/publications/articles/baltsun053006.html.

[76] Alan S. Manne, Ph.D., "Global Carbon Dioxide Reductions — Domestic and International Consequences," *American Council for Capital Formation,* April 1995, www.accf.org/publications/reports/sr-globalco2reductions95.html.

[77] "Put a Tiger in your Think Tank." *MotherJones.*

[78] "Steven Hayward," *NNDB*, www.nndb.com/people/867/000118513.

[79] Nicholas Confessore, "Meet the Press: How James Glassman reinvented journalism — as lobbying," *Washington Monthly*, December 2003, www.washingtonmonthly.com/features/2003/0312.confessore.html.

[80] Steven F. Hayward, "Cooled Down," *National Review Online*, January 25, 2005, www.nationalreview.com/issue/hayward200501250748.asp.

[81] Sallie Baliunas, Ph.D., "Warming Up to the Truth: The Real Story About Climate Change," *The Heritage Foundation*, August 22, 2002, author.heritage.org/Research/EnergyandEnvironment/HL758.cfm.

[82] "Sallie Baliunas," *ExxonSecrets*, www.exxonsecrets.org/html/personfactsheet.php?id=3.

[83] "David R. Legates," *ExxonSecrets*, www.exxonsecrets.org/html/personfactsheet.php?id=18.

[84] "Put a Tiger in your Think Tank." *MotherJones*.

[85] Ibid

[86] Ibid

[87] "Deroy Murdock," *The American Conservative Union*, www.conservative.org/pressroom/speakers/murdock.asp.

[88] "Put a Tiger in your Think Tank." *MotherJones*.

[89] David Adam, "Royal Society Tells Exxon: Stop Funding Climate Change Denial," *The Guardian*, September 20, 2006.

[90] Ian Sample, Scientists Offered Cash to Dispute Climate Study, *The Guardian*, Feburary 2, 2007.

[91] Frank D. Roylance, "Lake Becomes Bay as Arctic Melts," *Baltimore Sun*, September 23, 2006.

[92] Ibid.

[93] Ibid.

[94] "New Ads Funded by Big Oil Portray Global Warming Science as Smear Campaign Against Carbon Dioxide," *Think Progress*, May 18, 2006, thinkprogress.org/2006/05/18/new-ads-funded-by-big-oil-portray-global-warming-science-as-smear-campaign-against-carbon-dioxide/.

[95] Ron Suskin, *One Percent Doctrine* (New York: Simon & Schuster Adult Publishing Group, June 2006).

[96] "The One Percent Doctrine," *The Faculty Blog: The Law School at the University of Chicago*, June 27, 2006, uchicagolaw.typepad.com/faculty/2006/06/the_one_percent.html.

★ 17 ★

When Watchdogs
Become Lap Dogs

*"Information is to the democratic system
what blood is to the human body."*

Rep. David Obey (D-WI)

SO WE THINK THERE ARE INHERENT CHECKS AND BALANCES in our American democratic system. The media and Congress are two mechanisms that are supposed to provide safeguards and alert us if public policies and practices become corrupt and self-serving. I will repeat the question posed in the first chapter: what if one or both of these mechanisms becomes unduly influential, infected by partisan politics or is outright corrupt? What becomes of our system of checks and balances?

In this chapter, I would like to examine the roles of the media, the 9/11 Commission and Congress. How has each of these entities contributed to our lack of knowledge and understanding on essential political issues? Have they spread propaganda or even pure disinformation? Do these bodies bear responsibility for failing to report unethical and immoral actions perpetrated in the name of fighting terrorism? Moreover, have they then covered up this failure to report under the guise of patriotism?

Lap Dog — Number One
The Federal Communication Commission

Until 1996, the U.S. government provided safeguards against the formation of media monopolies. In fact, the Supreme Court ruled in 1945 that any media mergers narrowing the dissemination of information were unconstitutional.

A change demanded by a Republican-controlled Congress and signed into law by Bill Clinton deregulated the media industry in 1996. It was supposed to result in more media options for the American public but instead what the U.S. witnessed was the beginning of mass media mergers and consolidations. With the 2001 arrival of George W. Bush and his appointees to the Federal Communications Commission (FCC) began the largest erosion of free speech in the U.S. media ever observed. The Bush-appointed FCC has shown its contempt for the American public. The FCC continually sides with the industry it is supposed to be regulating and providing oversight upon. In 2003, FCC Chairman Michael Powell (son of former Secretary of State Colin Powell) approved a proposal to further deregulate the telecommunications industry, giving the media greater opportunities for additional consolidation. The proposal was blocked only because of the incredible public outcry of three million consumers who disagreed with the ruling. This public response did not change the initial vote by the FCC. Rather, it influenced Congress, who ultimately stopped the FCC proposal.[1]

A whole host of rule changes by the FCC has resulted in public fury and bipartisan congressional battles. The congressional debate related to media ownership in 2004 amended the frequency of periodic ownership reviews from once every two years to once every four years. Some FCC changes have been legally overturned, but only because of public awareness and demand from Congress to intervene on behalf of the American people.

Lap Dog Number Two:
The Media, Television and Radio Monopolies

There is a media monopoly in America. I was shocked when I saw the statistics. I doubted them. Most Americans do not realize that five corporations own 80 percent of the media in America according to a documentary entitled *Independent Intervention.*[2] The chart below shows the top five corporations and illustrates the percentage of American media outlets owned by each. These top five are: News Corporation (Fox News); Viacom (CBS); General Electric (NBC); Walt Disney (ABC); and Tribune. Three corporations own 74 percent of all radio stations in the U.S. Eight others share the remaining 26 percent of the radio stations:

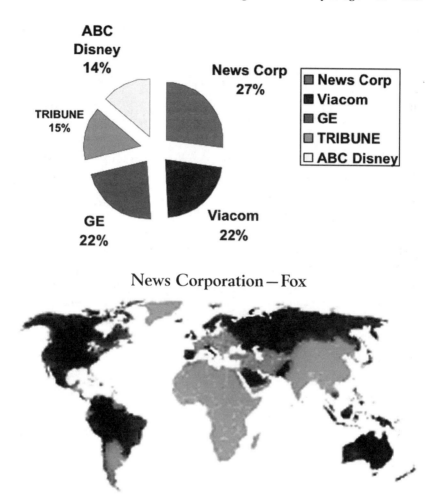

News Corporation — Fox

News Corporation describes itself as an international media and entertainment company with operations in eight industry segments: filmed entertainment; television; cable network programming; direct broadcast satellite television, including DirectTV; magazines including *The Weekly Standard;* magazine inserts; newspapers including the *New York Post;* and at least eight book publishing companies.[3] The Fox station group possesses 35 to 40 owned-and-operated stations and duo-monopolies in the nation's largest television markets.[4] A duo-monopoly means that a corporation has two monopolies serving a single community. For example if a corporation has sole ownership of the only television station within a community in addition to the major newspaper serving the same population, the corporation thus virtually controls all the media the public accesses through those two segments.

As of September 30, 2004, Fox boasted approximately $52 billion in assets and approximately $22 billion in total annual revenues.[5] Local news coverage is aired more than 850 hours per week, and it can be accessed in every U.S. household that has a cable television. In 2003, 70 percent of all households in America had cable television.[6] News Corporation recently signed an agreement with Google that will help push its entities to the forefront of web searches.[7] The map on the previous page illustrates News Corporation's vast worldwide media network and its enormous influential capacity. The dark areas highlight the influence of News Corporation. The listing on the next page gives you an idea of the width and depth of the influential impact of the News Corporation.

The Other Giants

Other media conglomerates in addition to the News Corporation are CNN, HBO, AOL, and Time Warner Corporation. Time Warner completed a mammoth $165 billion mega-merger in January of 2001.

The Viacom and CBS Corporation $50 billion merger in May 2000 made Viacom one of the-largest media conglomerates in the world. Before the merger they claimed combined sales in 1999 of over $12 billion.

The Tribune, whose major stockholders include former Secretary of Defense Donald Rumsfeld and Defense Policy Board Member Richard Perle, boasts operations in twenty-five major markets throughout the nation, including nine of the top ten major markets in the United States. Through newspapers, television, radio, and the Internet, the company brags of its ability to reach more than 80 percent of households in America.[8]

The Walt Disney Company is yet another global media conglomerate. Its fiscal year (FY) 2000 revenues topped $25 billion, with 17 percent from media networks.

The News Corporation's Vast Empire of Influence

DIRECTV	**The History Channel**	HarperCollins
Fox News	*National Geographic*	Rotten Tomatoes
myspace	GEMSTAR TV GUIDE	Reagan Books
American Idol	*THE NEW YORK POST*	Fox Studios
20th Century Fox		ALPHA
Donna Hay	**The Weekly Standard**	BROADSYSTEM
FOX Sports	News Digital Media	FX
STAR	*BIG* LEAGUE	INSIDE OUT

The News Corporation—A Media Conglomerate

Fox Television Stations (partial list)

WNYW – 5 New York
- WWOR TV – 9 New York
- KTTV – 11 Los Angeles
- KCOP – 13 Los Angeles
- WFLD – 32 Chicago
- WPWR TV – 50 Chicago
- WTXF-TV – 29 Philadelphia
- WFXT – 25 Boston
- KDFW – 4 Dallas
- WTTG – 5 Washington DC
- WDCA – 20 Washington DC
- KMSP TV – 9 Minneapolis
- WFTC – 29 Minneapolis
- WJBK – 2 Detroit
- WAGA – 5 Atlanta
- WUTB – 24 Baltimore
- KRIV – 27 Houston
- KTXH – 20 Houston
- WTVT – 13 Tampa Bay
- WRBW – 65 Orlando
- WOFL – 35 Orlando
- WJW – 8 Cleveland
- KSAZ-TV – 10 Phoenix
- KUTP – 45 Phoenix
- KDVR – 31 Denver
- KTVI – 2 St. Louis
- WITI – 6 Milwaukee
- WDAF-TV – 4 Kansas City
- KSTU – 13 Salt Lake City
- WBRC – 6 Birmingham
- WHBQ – TV – 13 Memphis
- WGHP – 8 Greensboro
- KTBC – 7 Austin
- WOGX – 51 Ocala
- KASA – 2 Albuquerque
- KASY – 50 Albuquerque
- KKRA – 24 Rapid City
- KTTD – 58 Twin Falls
- KBTZ – 24 Butte
- KCPM – 27 Fargo

Movie Production Studios

- 20th Century Fox
- 20th Century Fox Espanola
- 20th Century Fox Home Entertainment
- 20th Century Fox International
- 20th Century Fox Television
- Blue Sky Studios
- Fox Studios Australia
- Fox Studios Baja
- Fox Studios LA
- Fox News Stations
- Fox Searchlight Pictures

Cable Networks

- Fox Broadcasting Company
- Fox Sports Australia
- Fox Movie Channel
- Fox College Sports
- Fox Sports Enterprises
- Fox Sports En Espanol
- Fox Sports Net
- Fox Soccer Channel
- Fox Reality
- FUEL TV
- FX
- National Geographic Channel
- SPEED
- STATS, Inc.

Book Publishing and other Media (partial list)

- Harper- Collins
- American Idol

Newspapers (at least 27 International papers)
- New York Post

Satellite

- BSkyB
- DIRECTTV
- FOXTel
- SKY Italia

Star Subsidiaries (partial list)

- National Geographic Channel
- The History Channel
- Star Movies
- Star Gold
- Star One

Magazines (partial list)

- Big League
- InsideOut
- The Weekly Standard
- Gemstar – TV Guide Intl.
- News American Marketing

How Media Coverage Affects Campaigns

In the 2000 Presidential campaign, *Pittsburgh Tribune-Review* publisher Richard Mellon Scaife, the same Scaife that provided the funds for Paula Jones' lawsuit against Bill Clinton, ordered all Al Gore photographs and important mentions removed from the front page of his newspaper. The paper's pre-election Sunday edition featured George W. Bush in every campaign-related headline and photograph. A story about an Al Gore rally held in Pittsburgh that was originally scheduled to run alongside a Bush piece on the front page was moved to the inside of the paper. According to an explanation in the *Pittsburgh Post-Gazette*, the *Tribune-Review* managing editor Robert Fryer said he "tried to dissuade Scaife but was overruled" in his attempts to publicize both candidates equally.[9]

As the "commander and chief" of the United States, George W. Bush has exercised his tremendous power to use the media to his benefit. The Bush Administration has shown its intense obsession with "staying on message." Prior to 2006, George W. Bush was most reluctant to hold press conferences. The ones he did hold were widely seen as tightly scripted.

Activist and journalist Russell Mokhiber says the news conference held in 2003 just prior to the attack on Iraq, "might have been the most controlled Presidential news conference in recent memory. The President disclosed during the press conference that 'this is a scripted' press conference." The President had a list of seventeen reporters upon whom he was going to call. He didn't take any questions from reporters raising their hands. And he refused to call on Helen Thomas, the dean of the White House press corps, who traditionally asks the first question.[10]

During the run-up to the 2004 elections, Americans watched carefully orchestrated media events produced in Hollywood fashion, which portrayed George W. Bush as the confident Commander-in-Chief. These events provided strong images. The producers of these events paid special attention to the venue selection. Every venue was patriotically themed, with American flag backdrops. Only Bush-friendly audience guests were invited. Many Bush Presidential productions were filmed in front of military families or bases to reinforce his subliminal image as the "War President."

Michelle, a friend of mine who is a registered Democrat, had hoped to see the President when he came to Albuquerque, New Mexico in 2003. Michelle was denied access at the door because she did not have a pass and was not on the list. Michelle tried arguing about it, but to no avail; she was denied entrance to the event.

No dissenters were allowed access to any of the President's or Vice President's campaign visits prior to the 2004 elections. I believe it was feared that if Americans witnessed dissent it could potentially trigger questions as to why so many Americans were protesting the President. Before the televised Ohio debate with John Kerry, the Bush caravan went seventeen miles out of the way in order to avoid throngs of sign-carrying protesters; and again, prior to the Florida debate, colleagues who lived in the area reported the Presidential caravan made long detours to avoid dissenters.

I recall the image of John Kerry attempting to have a good old fashioned neighborhood discussion on the porch of a middle class family. He had no script, no flags, and no pretenses: Kerry was just doing old fashioned, door-to-door political campaigning. This event was derailed by a Bush detractor who sat outside the home heckling and yelling throughout the duration of the Kerry visit. Asked if she should be removed, John Kerry said no, indicating it was her right and privilege as an American to dissent. Unfortunately, tolerance was not what was emphasized by the news pundits; instead the media focus was on the hateful words of this sole detractor. Had the media been providing equal coverage, more emphasis would have been placed on the thousands of protestors who appeared outside of every single event attended by George W. Bush, along with an intelligent discussion about what these protestors had to say about President Bush and his policies.

> *"We have an ideological press that's interested in the election of Republicans, and a mainstream press that's interested in the bottom line. Therefore, we don't have a vigilant, independent press whose interest is the American people."*
>
> Bill Moyers

The Media — No Longer Makes News

Access to ethical and honest reporting is all but gone. There seemed to be no one left to provide vigilant, independent press to the American people. Keith Olbermann of the *Countdown* at MSNBC stood as the sole exception, showing a willingness to ask tough questions and deliver confrontational news programs aimed at the Bush Administration on a regular basis. According to a 2005 Columbia University study, even though a overwhelming majority of the American public want independent unbiased news it can trust, there has been a trend towards the delivery of highly "partisan" news that is heavily exaggerated.[11] These news programs are more geared toward affirming the political ideologies of a particular group than to providing independent news coverage. Slowly, however, pundits appear to be finding their spines as the tough questions are finally coming forth.

Sitting at a forum for Literacy of New Mexico, I listened to Ray Suarez, the senior correspondent for the PBS *News Hour*. He was talking about his book *Holy Vote*.[12] After his talk, he took questions from the audience. I took the opportunity to ask Mr. Suarez where the media outrage was over George W. Bush's push to get congressional approval for the use of torture. Mr. Suarez said it was not the media's job to show outrage. It was simply the job of the media to report stories. He said it was up to the public to show the outrage. He told the audience that the *News Hour* had featured two generals who had debated the torture issue. What concerned me was that PBS's *Frontline* produced the best video documentaries on the war in Iraq, some of which focused specifically on how America came to embrace torture as an interrogation technique. I had thought PBS would lead the public debate on the topic of torture. I was wrong in this assumption.

Growing up in the 1960s, we only had access to four television stations: ABC, NBC, CBS, and PBS. I considered PBS the nerdy station. PBS has been under constant and severe attack, accused of having a liberal slant by Senate and House Republicans. Every couple of months, Congress threatened PBS's funding.[13] In order to rein in the fiercely nonpartisan broadcasting company and to exert greater control over PBS programming, the federal government forced the Corporation for Public Broadcasting to sign a "National Programming Service Agreement." This agreement provided the GOP-dominated CPB board with unprecedented influence and power over PBS's programming schedule.[14] Through 2004, PBS attempted to provide in-depth, unbiased, and accurate war coverage.

News Bias

In his book, *Casualty of War: The Bush Administration's Assault on the Free Press*, author David Dadge delivers a chilling account of how the Bush Administration, together with a war-scared nation, stamped out the questioning that would normally occur after an attack. Reporters who dared to ask questions in the days, weeks, months and years after the 9/11 attacks were fired, demoted, characterized as unpatriotic, and promptly silenced.[15]

In 2000, the Pew Center conducted a survey of the media. Approximately one-third of the reporters, editors and news executives polled stated that news that would "hurt the financial interests" of the media organization or their advertisers is simply not reported. Close to half of the reporters said they have avoided stories, or at least toned them down, to benefit their media company's interests. It would be interesting to find out how much greater sponsor influence is today.

Among investigative reporters and editors at TV stations, nearly three-quarters of respondents reported that advertisers had "tried to influence the content" of news at their stations; a 1997 survey published by FAIR discovered that 60 percent of reporters polled said that advertisers had attempted to kill their stories. The survey further found 56 percent of respondents felt pressure from within the station to produce positive news stories beneficial to their advertisers.

Several important websites, studies, reports, and video documentaries have surfaced over the last few years to expose how far the media has gone in order to cater to its sponsors.[16] Americans are only now beginning to realize the truth. News program producers appear to care more about keeping their sponsors happy than about reporting valid information. The focus on keeping media sponsors and owners appeased threatens truth and integrity in American news.

For years, the right wing has accused the media of a liberal bias. A recent *Harris Poll* shed some interesting light on this matter. CNN and Fox viewers were asked if they perceived a liberal bias in the media. Approximately 33 percent of CNN viewers said yes, they perceived a *liberal bias*. However, almost an equal number, 32 percent of CNN viewers said they believed there is a *conservative bias;* and the remaining CNN viewers generally thought the news was delivered in a fair and unbiased mode.

Fox viewers, however, held substantially different views. More than twice as many respondents — 69 percent — perceived a liberal media bias; and only 12 percent believed a conservative bias exists.[17] The Fox viewers considered themselves heavy viewers of the Fox News Channel. Their view is consistent with my research. After watching several Fox News broadcasts during a three-month period, I heard frequent remarks made by Fox News pundits about other news programs' alleged liberal biases. This sentiment about the perceived liberal bias is made with great repetition by conservative talk show hosts as well. In fact, conservative talk show host Sean Hannity goes as far as to provide his listening audience with disparaging names for each of the major television stations. For instance, he referred to ABC as standing for *Anything But Conservative* and so on with each of the major network stations.[18]

In a Gallup poll conducted of "general Americans," 41 percent of respondents believe there is a conservative bias in the media and 18 percent believe there is liberal bias.[19] However, in a poll conducted by the Pew Research Center, twice as many respondents (51 percent) said news organizations had a liberal bias, while 26 percent of respondents perceived a conservative media bias. Fourteen percent said neither label applied.[20] It becomes quickly apparent that the perceived bias is heavily influenced by the news station one is watching, listening to or the publication one reads.

Who Pays for News Production?

So who sponsors American news programs? Watch the news on any station on any day of the week and you will find the usual sponsors of news programming tend to be the same. Companies within the gas and oil industry, such as Exxon/Mobile, Chevron/Texaco and BP sponsor quite a number of news programs. You will quickly realize that several automotive corporations utilize commercial breaks during the news to display their latest and sleekest gas-guzzling models. Boeing, as well as other war profiteering companies, sponsor Fox News and other network news programs as well.[21]

Therefore, do not ever expect to see any real news of substance concerning global warming or the realities of an Iraqi oil-war gone wrong. In addition, continue to expect to hear a great deal of clatter about Iran's nuclear program, instability in the Middle East between Israel, Lebanon and Palestine, and North Korea's test bombs. War is good business for these companies. Keeping Americans in a state of angst is important, and the best way to do this is to spin the news in a manner precisely geared towards increasing anxiety. Here are few titles from the Fox News Reports:

"All-out Civil War in Iraq: Could It Be a Good Thing?"

"Escalating Threat — Can North Korean Nuke Crisis be Solved Diplomatically?"

"Bush: U.S. 'Reserves All Options Against North Korea"

"House Approves of Shipping Nuclear Technology to India"

Let me briefly comment on these titles:

1) If I was a U.S. Military arms dealer or contractor, an all-out civil war in Iraq might be considered a good thing for my pocketbook.

2) The North Korean threat appears difficult to solve diplomatically, especially since George W. Bush has consistently refused to have any direct discussion or negotiations with Kim Jong-il, the leader of North Korea. I suppose when George W. Bush speaks of reserving all options against North Korea he must be speaking militarily and not diplomatically.

3) The U.S. is to begin shipping nuclear technology to India. India is our ally today but will that still be the case tomorrow? The future holds such great uncertainty, as we have seen with Iraq and Saddam Hussein.

Other sponsors influence our news, like the many mining and drilling companies and, of course, the pharmaceutical and health care companies that take advantage of prime time news to tout their newest for-profit products and services.

The Big Cover-Up in Iraq

Right-wingers like former Secretary of Defense Donald Rumsfeld believe the media has deliberately put forth negative reporting on the war in Iraq. On the other hand, the left believes the media has provided a whitewash job on Iraq. Constantly battered by the Bush Administration to put a happy face on Iraq, the U.S. media has only haphazardly attempted to give Americans the story that the rest of the world has been watching for the last four years, not only in words, but also in graphic images.

Recall Tommy Franks' callous comments about Iraqi casualties, saying the U.S. did not do body counts of dead Iraqis. Within a few days after the Shock and Awe attacks on Iraq, I lost my web connection to Voices in the Wilderness, a group of concerned citizens and international physicians who had stayed behind to care for the Iraqis. The physicians had been sending horrific photos via email of bloodied, battered and bombed bodies of dead babies, children, mothers, grandmothers, and grandfathers as well as young men and women. Those photos were blocked as many U.S. computers were censored from receiving websites that contained graphic war images. However, the rest of the world continued to receive those photos on a daily basis. We must remember how far the Bush Administration has gone to "sanitize" the war in Iraq, even placing a ban on photographs of American soldiers' coffins coming back from Iraq.

In a *Wall Street Journal* article entitled "Dealing with Hatred: How the Torrent of Anti-Americanism Affects Teenagers," journalist Jeffrey Zaslow describes how one youngster blames the media for the global anti-American sentiments.[22] The youngster is quoted saying, "Our media feeds off of our failures, broadcasting them all over the world." The ultimate message in this article is that it would be much better to hide or deny our nation's mistakes, instead of owning up to and promptly rectifying them. What the journalist fails to point out is that most of the world knows us by the actions our government engages in while abroad. A good number of these actions are being reported by foreign journalists with greater precision.

According to a 2004 CNN report conducted by British health officials, 100,000 Iraqis had died from the bombing that occurred within the first days of Shock and Awe and in subsequent months thereafter.[23] Pictures of bombed-out communities, homes, cultural centers, water and electrical facilities have been regularly depicted in global news outlets. My friend Margaret, a local realtor, said after traveling abroad, "Most of the world believes the American government is the terrorist and they blame the citizens, since we are supposed to have a democracy and such great freedom of speech. They believe Americans are overworked, over-consuming, and just plain stupid. They can't understand how we elected him [Bush] again in 2004." Margaret said the anger towards Americans in the Muslim countries she visited was so thick you could almost "taste it."

Mainstream television media has participated in one of the biggest news coverups in Iraq. The reconstruction funds that were supposed to be used to rebuild Iraq for the Iraqis was used instead to build permanent military cities all across Iraq for Americans. These include six super-sized bases that range from fifteen to twenty square miles and are the size of small cities and home to several thousand American troops and contractors. One such super-sized base is Balad, 50 miles north of Baghdad. Balad houses 20,000 American troops and has an extended airstrip and airport for 250 planes, two post offices, a hospital and a dump for used Humvees. There is a Pizza Hut, Burger King and Subway restaurant in Balad as well as a miniature golf course.[24]

At another one of these super sized military bases, Al Asad in the Western Anbar Providence, you will discover a football field, a swimming pool, a movie theater, two bus routes, and even a Hertz rental car agency.[25] It is reportedly the biggest American Marine Camp. In 2005, the U.S. was described as having 106 bases ranging in size from "macro to micro" by Bradley Graham, a journalist for *The Washington Post.*

All of the sites scream the intention of a long term U.S. occupation of Iraq. Why, with our seemingly unlimited choice of U.S. programming, have we not seen with our own eyes these super-sized bases? Why have we not seen the images of the bombed out, burned down homes and buildings still strewn across Iraq? I think of Denise, a long-time, staunch conservative, comfortable in her home, who said to me, "I just don't understand why these Iraqis want to keep an insurgency alive and why on earth they keep blowing themselves up!" I thought in response, maybe it's because it is the only way they can get into our daily news?

Controlling and Silencing Free Speech

The U.S. Military publicly denied that assaults on foreign news agencies were intentional. Yet, on at least three separate occasions, foreign media services and staff have been targeted. The offices of Al Jazeera, the Arab broadcasting company with news bureaus in Doha, Kabul and Baghdad, have been bombed twice by the U.S. Military. The Palestine Hotel in Baghdad, home to several international journalists, was besieged by U.S. troops in 2003. The attack resulted in the death of two journalists and injury to others.[26]

On November 13, 2001, the Al Jazeera office in Kabul, Afghanistan, was destroyed by a U.S. missile. Luckily, none of the news staff were in the office at the time the missile was deployed. U.S. officials claimed they thought the news office was a terrorist site.[27]

On April 8, 2003, an Al Jazeera journalist died when the Baghdad bureau was targeted in a bombing campaign by the U.S. Military. A spokesperson for the State Department issued a statement later explaining that the air strike was a mistake.[28] However, Neocon Frank Gaffney, a signatory of the Project for a New American Century, who heads the Neoconservative think tank Center for Security Policy *and* sits on the Defense Policy Board, accused Al Jazeera on Fox News of actually paying for attacks that they later broadcast. He said Al Jazeera was masquerading as a news program while being nothing more than an arm of the enemy spreading anti-American propaganda.[29] Al Jazeera frequently broadcasts live photos of the death and destruction wrought by the war. Mr. Gaffney called for Al Jazeera to be silenced in an article entitled "Take Out Al Jazeera."[30]

International outrage and condemnation ensued after the attack on the Palestine Hotel during the U.S. bombing operation in 2003. The hotel was filled with international journalists who were supposed to be protected from assault under the Geneva Conventions. The U.S. Military response to the criticism was to plead ignorance stating they could not keep track of where journalists were located. An investigation later revealed that the U.S. denied any responsibility because journalists had been previously advised to leave the country due to the dangerous conditions. The U.S. Military explained it could only provide protection for those journalists who were "embedded" (traveling with the U.S. Military). The international community charged the U.S. with deliberately intimidating and discouraging any diversity of reporting on the war in Iraq.[31]

In 2005, the British reported a leaked transcript, detailing a 2004 conversation between Tony Blair and George W. Bush. The transcript alleges that Mr. Blair advised against George W. Bush launching air strikes at Al Jazeera. A twenty-five year tenured British government civil servant David Keogh and a research assistant, Leo O'Connor, were charged with the unathorized disclosure of a damaging document, an offense under Section 3 of the British Official Secrets Act. Tony Blair refused to respond when confronted by these reports.[32] A BBC correspondent later said, that George W. Bush had only been joking during the discussion. The Whitehouse refused to comment saying the allegations were "ludicrous."[33]

Ninety-two journalists have died in Iraq since 2003 while attempting to cover the stories of the war.[34] Iraq is a dangerous place for anyone beyond the safety of the "green zones." An English version of Al Jazeera was launched in 2006 with bureaus in Doha, Kuala Lumpur, London and Washington DC. Their purpose is to shed light on aspects of the world news that the U.S. mainstream media is failing to cover.

The Bush Administration's response to bad news in Iraq is to use American tax dollars to create good news. In August of 2006, the U.S. government allocated $20 million for a public relations contract to promote a positive spin on the war in Iraq. This is in addition to the $100 million that has already been used to purportedly create a "world-class" media operation in Iraq in 2004.[35] It is hard to keep track of all the taxpayer money being used to spin the media, but another $75 million was requested by Condoleezza Rice for 2007, to "promote democracy" in the Middle East through media campaigns.[36]

In a special news report on CNN's *Situation Room* on October 30, 2006, it was revealed that former Defense Secretary Rumsfeld planned to take the media battle to the Internet in an attempt to put a positive spin on Iraq. I feared what this might mean, since no specifics were given in the report.

Reading Headlines

It is important to recognize that many Americans skim what they read. A skimmer is a reader who may read the headline of an article, but not the entire article. The skimming reader thinks he or she understands the essence of the article based upon its title. Like the Bush hijacking of the English language described in the chapter, "No WMDs, It's Terrorism You Idiot," the media does something similar in print articles. Here is an example to illustrate my point:

"Are Some Liberal Elitists Sneaking Into Wal-Mart?"

Wall Street Journal

The author of this article concludes that because bumper stickers on cars are anti-war or anti-Bush, they must belong to "liberal elitists." The writer has no evidence to support this conclusion, but the article is inflammatory, and it provides the *Wall Street Journal* with a cheap shot to denigrate liberal-minded Americans and shoppers at Wal-Mart.

Radio Monopoly
Three Corporations Own 74% of all Stations in USA

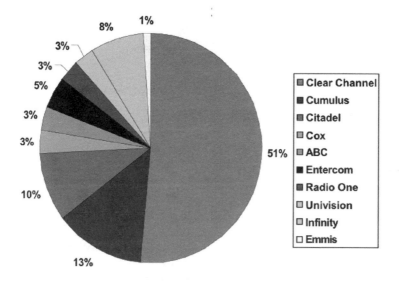

Legend
Clear Channel
Cumulus
Citadel
Cox
ABC
Entercom
Radio One
Univision
Infinity
Emmis

Pie chart values: 51%, 13%, 10%, 3%, 3%, 5%, 3%, 3%, 8%, 1%

Conservative Talk Show Radio

I listened to conservative talk show radio Sean Hannity as he discussed his upcoming guest, former New Jersey Governor James McGreevey. Mr. McGreevy resigned as governor after revealing that he was gay. He was scheduled to discuss his book on Mr. Hannity's talk show program. In anticipation of his guest, Mr. Hannity led a discussion that quickly regressed into one full of contempt, judgment and intolerance towards homosexuals, alcoholics, drug addicts, and street people.

It appears that talk show hosts understand the politics of divisiveness, and use them to increase the polarization in our country. Like with his comments about the "liberal media," Mr. Hannity holds onto his audience through tactics of fear, division and ignorance. One of my conservative friends, Irene, a professional public speaker who talks about women in leadership roles, says she can no longer listen to Rush Limbaugh, another conservative talk show host, because she says, "he has pushed many of his listeners over the edge with his extreme one-sidedness."

Neoconservative radio talk show hosts such as Hannity, Limbaugh and Savage daily launch malicious attacks on those who disagree with the Bush doctrine. They have turned on a majority of the American public with a rash of name calling. Those who disagree are labeled Democrats or liberals and the words are spoken in a manner as to infer a huge insult. Frequently, after calling a disagreeing commenter a Democrat or a liberal, these Neocon pundits will then refer to those differing American citizens as terrorists or terrorist supporters.

Lap Dog Number Three:
A Republican Conrolled Congress

Some pundits referred to the 109th Congress as the do-nothing Congress. It might be more accurate to say the 109th Congress did nothing to benefit the American public. What they did do before adjourning was to make sure they passed a bill to protect the President and those who engaged in breaking international laws. The Military Commissions Act of 2006 was successfully passed after much arm-twisting as discussed earlier. This act was a desperate attempt to provide a safeguard for those who had engaged, authorized and sanctioned the torture of detainees. In its final hours this Congress managed to pass laws benefiting big oil, the pharmaceutical industry, and tax cuts for America's most wealthy citizens were once again extended. This Congress failed to pass nine of the eleven appropriation bills including a critical bill authorizing health care provisions for returning soldiers.

The level of greed and corruption that had infiltrated the 109th Congress had reached alarming levels. It appears that conducting business in the best interest of the American public was the farthest concern of many congressional representatives.

In 2006, several congressional members had been indicted, imprisoned and forced to step down because of major corruption and disgusting scandals. Tom DeLay, the Republican Majority Leader from Texas, was forced to resign after he was indicted in the Jack Abramoff scandal. Randy "Duke" Cunningham, the Republican representative from California, commenced serving an eight-year jail term for bribery. The federal probe into Cunningham's activities may further implicate other members of Congress. Bob Ney, the Republican representative from Ohio, pled guilty to conspiracy to commit fraud and to making false statements; he was imprisoned in 2007.

Mark Foley, the Republican representative from Florida, resigned in September 2006 once it was discovered that he had been sexually approaching young, underage male pages. The former House Majority Leader, John Boehner, the Republican representative from Ohio, told *The Washington Post* that he had been aware of Representative Foley's illegal indiscretions for several months prior to their becoming public; he had even notified House Speaker Hastert (R-IL).

Citizens for Responsibility and Ethics in Washington (CREW) track congressional members' unethical actions and activities. Currently, fourteen Republican representatives, three Democratic representatives and three Republican senators are at the top of its list. Six of those on the CREW list lost their seats in the November 2006 mid-term election. Several other members, including, Republican representative Jerry Lewis from California; Democratic representative William Jefferson from Louisiana; Democratic representative Alan Mollohan from West Virginia; Republican senator Conrad Burns from Montana; and the former Senate Majority Leader, Republican Bill Frist from Tennessee are all under federal investigation for a variety of alleged wrongdoings.

The politically frightened and fractured Democrats sitting in Washington had long been neutered by a Rove-manipulated media that portrayed them as soft on terrorism, flip-floppers, spineless, and without plans. Any efforts by Democrats were minimized, recharacterized and reframed by the Neoconservative controlled media.

Busy with their greedy endeavors, the Republican-controlled Congress forfeit its most fiduciary responsibility. It failed to provide any oversight of the Executive branch as it became a rubber stamp for the Bush White House.

Lap Dog Number Four:
The 9/11 Commission

Independent investigations began within weeks of both Pearl Harbor and the Kennedy assassination. However, the formation of the 9/11 Commission was strongly opposed and blocked for well over a year by the Bush Administration. After sixteen months of political badgering, particularly by the families of the victims of the 9/11 attack, the 9/11 Commission was finally established in December of 2002. It was made up of political appointees, and its mission was to conduct a thorough and comprehensive investigation of the circumstances surrounding the 9/11 attacks on America.

It was destined for failure. The commission stalled repeatedly for a variety of controversial reasons, including the resignation of its first chairperson, Henry Kissinger. Mr. Kissinger was forced to abandon the commission because of his questionable connections and biases, according to family members of the victims of the 9/11 attacks.[37] George Mitchell, a former senator from Maine, also resigned, as did former Georgia senator Max Cleland, an American war hero who lost both legs and his right arm during his Vietnam service. Former Senator Cleland resigned, calling the 9/11 Commission a "sham."[38]

The commission was plagued by a number of obstacles, including an inadequate budget. There were countless allegations of being "stonewalled" by bureaucratic agencies.[39] Commissioners reported numerous hurdles they had to "jump" in order to access data the Bush Administration considered "classified." They described delays in getting requested reports. And when such reports were finally received, they were frequently found to be in conflict with other government reports. The commissioners also reported that there were demands from a variety of interested parties whose objectives often appeared to be at cross purposes.[40]

One of the most significant concerns arose over the appointment of Philip D. Zelikow as the Executive Director of the 9/11 Commission. Mr. Zelikow was a well known Neoconservative who had been appointed to several committees by George W. Bush. He had previously headed the Neoconservative think tank The Aspen Strategy Group. Philip Zelikow had many connections inside the Bush Administration, and it was reported that he maintained close contact with Karl Rove for the duration of the Commission.[41]

Additionally, Mr. Zelikow and Condoleezza Rice had previously worked together, and they had also co-authored a book. Ms. Rice was the National Security Advisor at the time. Kristen Breitweiser, a 9/11 widow, insisted Zelikow had a "clear conflict of interest."[42] And many family members charged that Mr. Zelikow strongly influenced the 9/11 Commission's ability to provide a comprehensive and unbiased report.[43]

Thomas Kean, Chairman of the 9/11 Commission and a former Republican Governor of New Jersey, said the 9/11 attack should have been prevented.[44] In CBS televised interview, Mr. Kean said that appointees inside the Bush Administration had failed to do their jobs properly, yet those same appointees continued to hold positions despite their failures.[45] The 9/11 Commission completed its work in August 2004, yet so many questions and concerns remain unanswered. Critics charge the Bush Administration with the following:

1. failure to immediately launch an independent investigative task force within days of the 9/11 attack;
2. creating a commission made up of politicians instead of impartial specialists in the area of national security;
3. appointing individuals who did not have the necessary expertise to ask the right questions to get to the bottom of matters;
4. political pressure on the committee to make the administration "look good"
5. failure to provide access to records and interviews in a timely manner;
6. attempts to cover up what really happened on 9/11/2001;
7. blatant discrepancies in reporting by various federal agencies, including official reports provided by the FAA and NORAD;[46]
8. false accounts and deception put forth by the FAA and NORAD, which resulted in the commission filing complaints with inspectors general at both the Pentagon and Transportation Department;[47] and
9. failure to act upon the recommendations made by the commission after it completed its work.

A truly non-partisan independent task force was needed immediately to conduct comprehensive research, and ask tough questions that still remain unanswered. Several books and video documentaries have been published about the inadequacies of the 9/11 Commission, including *The 9/11 Commission's Omissions and Distortions: A Critique of the Zelikow Report* by Professor David Ray Griffin, and the 2006 video documentary *9/11: PRESS FOR TRUTH*. Interestingly, after completing his role with the 9/11 Commission, Philip Zelikow was appointed as counsel to the State Department, reporting to Condoleezza Rice.[48]

Family members of the 9/11 victims, together with well-respected professionals, provide powerful arguments that America needs a much deeper investigation into the attacks perpetrated on 9/11. Unanswered questions and accusations have lead to numerous conspiracy theories floating around today.[49]

While attending a conference in Orlando in July 2006, I was stunned by a group of Europeans who stated that many people outside our borders believe the U.S. Military was responsible for 9/11. Speechless, I left the conference to do more research. Even Bill O'Reilly from Fox News addressed these accusations in a report entitled "Sept. 11 Conspiracy Theories Persist," which aired on August 7, 2006.[50] The most disturbing fact is that many people abroad and some at home believe there was a conspiracy behind 9/11. The documentary *Loose Change* suggests the 9/11 attacks were an "inside job" perpetrated by our own military. Since the video can be freely accessed from the Internet, it has been downloaded over twenty-four million times since its inception.[51] Additionally, the film is available for free to the family members of the 9/11 victims in a DVD format. Viewers are encouraged to make free copies to disseminate the film's message. Finally, *Loose Change* has been shown at local movie houses for months. It showed in my home town during the summer for over a month at select times. While some of the documentary points appear farfetched, it also makes some very powerful and convincing points. It asks compelling questions such as:

- How is it possible that the physical implosions of the Twin Towers and Building 7 of the World Trade Center collapse match precisely the characteristics of a planned demolition, and why did all three buildings come directly down so quickly?[52]

- How is it possible that World Trade Building 7, which was two buildings away from the explosion, became "weakened" and was destroyed *within hours* of the Twin Towers *in an identical manner?*[59]

- Why do experts from several fields, including architecture, engineering, physics and demolition, say the buildings appear to have been imploded through a controlled demolition as opposed to falling over?[53]

- How is it possible that jet-fueled fire melted the UL-certified steel in the buildings when jet fuel allegedly burns at such a low intensity?[54]

- Why do specialists say a fire of this nature could not have caused the steel to melt this quickly and dramatically?[55]

- Why do experts say the UL-certified steel in the buildings would have had to burn up to six hours before becoming even significantly weakened,[56] and how is it that a fire has never before or since knocked down a steel-framed high-rise building?[57]

- Why do experts say the impact of the planes hitting the Twin Towers could not have caused enough damage to bring the buildings down, since the buildings were specifically designed to withstand this type of impact?[58]

- What truth is there in the allegations that World Trade Building 7 contained several active Securities Exchange Commission investigations on thousands of corporations, which were totally lost and destroyed?[60]

- What truth is there to the allegations that bomb-sniffing dogs were removed from the World Trade Tower Buildings just two weeks prior to the 9/11 attacks?

- Why did numerous witnesses report multiple "bombs" going off in the World Trade Centers before the collapse?[61]

- Did members of the Bush family, specifically Neil Bush, benefit financially in any way from the 9/11 attacks for their alleged role in the insurance company that insured the World Trade Center? Neil is the brother of President George W. Bush.[62]

- Why was there so much confusion at NORAD and why were most of the fighter jets that were supposed to protect our nation all absent on the day of the 9/11 attacks?[63]

- Doesn't it seem strange that with all the damage done by the attacks at the WTC, the passport of one of the hijackers was found in perfect condition at the scene of the crime? Conspiratists believe it was planted.

- What truth is there behind the allegations that at least one of the suicide bomber families claim: it is that their son, accused of the 9/11 attacks and whose photo appears in this book, is in fact alive and well, purportedly living in Saudi Arabia?

- Why has there been such resistence to fully investigate the claims that unusual stock market trading occurred immediately before and after the 9/11 attacks?

How strange is it that John O'Neill, the former director of the FBI counter terrorism unit and renowned expert on Osama bin Laden, died on 9/11 in the World Trade Center within days of taking the job as the WTC top security chief? It is alleged that Mr. O'Neill left his government employment after the Bush Administration refused to arrest Osama bin Laden early in 2001. John O'Neill had publicly declared that the biggest obstacle to fighting terrorism was the U.S. oil corporate interests and the role the Saudi government played in furthering those interests.[64]

This list represents only a small fraction of the unanswered questions and concerns. According to a 2006 poll conducted by Zogby and reported in *Vanity Fair,* 42 percent of Americans now believe portions of these conspiracy theories to be true, and some believers think that 9/11 was an inside job.[65] A 2006 poll conducted by Scripps Howard/Ohio University revealed that 36 percent of Americans suspect federal officials of assisting in the terrorist attacks and 54 percent say they feel more alienation, resentment and anger towards the government.[66] Others believe the Bush Administration simply sat back and allowed it to happen. These people believe the administration then used the attacks to further their goals of corporate globalization in the Middle East, and as an excuse to launch yet another war against Iraq.[67]

On the fifth anniversary of the 9/11 attacks on America, demonstrations were held in London and elsewhere. The movement, called the *British 9/11 Truth Campaign in London,* carried signs in front of the United States Embassy and the British Broadcasting Company. The signs read *"9/11 was an inside job."*

The tardiness in establishing a truly independent commission free from the tentacles of Karl Rove combined with the apparent failure of government agencies to safeguard the U.S. from such an attack has left the Bush Administration vulnerable to the numerous conspiracy charges. To date the Bush Administration has expressed a complete lack of responsibility for the disaster that occurred on 9/11. It has instead sought to blame previous administrations. Perhaps it was the procrastination to investigate plus the lack of accountability and the shifting of blame that increases and inflames the multitude of conspiracy theories.

NOTES, Chapter 17

[1] Federa; Communications Commission, *FCC's Review of the Broadcast Ownership Rules*, www.fcc.gov/cgb/consumerfacts/reviewrules.html.

[2] a. *Independent Intervention*, Video Documentary.
b. News Corporation map, commons.wikimedia.org/wiki/Image:Fox_News_world_providers.PNG.

[3] "Jack Abernethy Named CEO of Fox Television Stations Inc.," *News Corporation*, December 7, 2004, www.newscorp.com/news/news_235.html.

[4] Ibid.

[5] Ibid.

[6] Center for Digital Democracy, memo to Congressional Black Caucus, "Cable TV: Monopoly Power Over Programmers and the Public," September 26, 2003, www.democraticmedia.org/resources/filings/caucusMemo.html.

[7] "Fox Interactive Media Enters Into Landmark Agreement with Google Inc.," *News Corporation*, August 7, 2006, www.newscorp.com/news/news_309.html.

[8] *Tribune at a Glance*, Tribune Corporation, www.tribune.com/media/pdf/glance_06.pdf.

[9] Janine Jackson and Peter Hart, "How Power Shapes the News," *FAIR*, May/June 2001, www.fair.org/index.php?page=2013.

[10] Peter Johnson, Bush Has Media Walking a Fine Line, March 9, 2003, *USA Today*, www.usatoday.com/life/television/news/2003-03-09-media-mix_x.htm.

[11] The Project for Excellence in Journalism, "Five Major Trends," *Journalism.org: The State of the News Media*, www.stateofthemedia.org/2005/narrative_overview_eight.asp?cat=10&media=1.

[12] Ray Suarez, *Holy Vote: The Politics of Faith in America* (New York: HarperCollins, 2006).

[13] a. MediaCitizen, "Bush Budget Pumps Propaganda, Slashes PBS," *MoveOn.org, February 7, 2006, www.moveon.org/r?r=1865&id=7967-2528421-kYw6UMS60RIC3NHxfisLrg&t=5.*
b. Rick Klein, "GOP takes aim at PBS funding," *The Boston Globe*, June 8, 2006.

[14] "CPB Takes Out a 'Contract'on PBS: How the GOP-led CPB Wants to Control Programming," *The Center for Digital Democracy*, May 10, 2005, www.democraticmedia.org/news/washingtonwatch/CPBNPS.html.

[15] David Dadge, *Casualty of War: The Bush Administration's Assault on a Free Press* (Amherst, NY: Prometheus Books, 2004).

[16] a. *Columbia Journalism Review*, www.cjr.org/.
b. *Outfoxed: Rupert Murdoch's War on Journalism*, DVD, directed by Robert Greenwald (2004; Culver City, CA: BraveNew Films, 2004).

[17] "News Reporting is Perceived as Biased, though Less Agreement on Whether it is Liberal or Conservative Bias," *The Harris Poll* 52, June 30, 2006.

[18] Sean Hannity, *Talk Show Radio*, December 1, 2006.

[19] "Media Bias Basics," *Media Research Center*, www.mediaresearch.org/biasbasics/biasbasics1.asp.

[20] "Strong Opposition to Media Cross-Ownership Emerges: Public Wants Neutrality and Pro-American Point of View," *The Pew Research Center*, July 13, 2003, people-press.org/reports/display.php3?ReportID=188.

[21] "Fox News: The Sponsors: Stop Fox," *SkinTheFox*, January 15, 2005, skinthefox.com/sponsors_001.htm.

[22] Jeffrey Zaslow, "Moving On, Dealing with Hatred: How the Torrent of Anti-Americanism Affects Teenagers," *The Wall Street Journal*, October 5, 2006.

23 "Study puts Iraqi Death Toll at 100,000," *CNN*, October 29, 2004, www.cnn.com/2004/WORLD/meast/10/29/iraq.deaths/

24 Thomas E. Ricks, *Fiasco, The American Military Adventure in Iraq* (New York: Penguin Press, 2006).

25 Oliver Poole, "Football and pizza point to US staying for long haul," *The Telegraph*, February 11, 2006, www.telegraph.co.uk/news/main.jhtml?xml=/news/2006/02/11/wirq11.xml&sSheet=/news/2006/02/11/ixworld.ht.

26 www.truthout.org/docs_2005/022505A.shtml.

27 www.usatoday.com/news/world/2005-11-22-bush-al-jazeera_x.htm.

28 www.editorandpublisher.com/eandp/news/article_display.jsp?vnu_content_id=1859614.

29 www.foxnews.com/story/0,2933,98621,00.html.

30 Ibid.

31 www.truthout.org/docs_2005/022505A.shtml.

32 http://en.wikipedia.org/wiki/Al_Jazeera_bombing_memo.

33 Ibid.

34 http://cpj.org/Briefings/Iraq/Iraq_danger.html.

35 *The Blogiston Post*, October 29, 2003, blogistonpost.blogspot.com/2003_10_01_blogistonpost_archive.html.

36 "Should the US Fund Iranian TV and Opposition Groups?," *NIAC*, February 16, 2006, www.niacouncil.org/pressreleases/press.asp.

37 *9/11 Press for Truth*, DVD, directed by Ray Nowosielski (2006; Culver City, CA: BraveNew Films, 2006).

38 Bill Christison, "Stop Belittling the Theories About September 11," *Dissident Voice*, August 14, 2006, www.dissidentvoice.org.

39 Thomas H. Kean, *The Daily Show*, August 16, 2006.

40 Thomas H. Kean and Lee H. Hamilton, *Without Precedent: The Inside Story of the 9-11 Commission* (New York: Random House, 2006).

41 Morgan Reynolds, "9/11 Skepticism," *LewRockwell*, www.lewrockwell.com/reynolds/reynolds7.html.

42 The Center for Media & Democracy, "Philip D. Zelikow," *SourceWatch*, www.sourcewatch.org/index.php?title=Philip_D._Zelikow.

43 Ibid.

44 Joe Conason, "What's Bush hiding from 9/11 commission? Administration doesn't want truth out before the election," *The New York Observer*, January 21, 2004, www.workingforchange.com/article.cfm?ItemID=16315.

45 Ibid.

46 Kean and Hamilton, *Without Precedent*.

47 Ibid.

48 "Philip D. Zelikow," *Wikipedia*, en.wikipedia.org/wiki/Philip_D._Zelikow.

49 Michael Powell, "The Disbelievers," *Washington Post*, September 8, 2006, C1, www.washingtonpost.com/wp-dyn/content/article/2006/09/07/AR2006090701669.html.

50 "Sept. 11 Conspiracy Theories Persist," *Associated Press*, August 7, 2006, www.foxnews.com/story/0,2933,207279,00.html.

51 *Loose Change*, DVD, directed by Dylan Avery (2005; Oenonta, NY: Louder Than Words, Ilc., 2005).

[52] a."Who Are We?," *Scholars for 9/11 Truth*, www.scholarsfor911truth.org/ WhoAreWe.html.
b. *Loose Change.*

[53] Rodger Herbst, "Mysteries of the Twin Towers," *9-11 Visibility Project*, september eleventh.org/documents/rodgwtcpdf.pdf.

[54] Ibid.

[55] Ibid.

[56] *Scholars for 9/11 Truth.*

[57] *Loose Change.*

[58] a. Ibid.
b. "9-11 The Explosive Truth Revealed - Controlled Demos at WTC," *Let's Roll Forums*, letsroll911.org/ipw-web/bulletin/bb/viewtopic.php?t=887.

[59] a. "'Pulling' Building 7," *WTC7*, www.wtc7.net/pullit.html.
b. "Date, Time, Location," *The National 9/11 Debate*, teamliberty.net/id278.html.

[60] *Loose Change.*

[61] "9/11 Timelines," *9/11 CitizensWatch*, www.911citizenswatch.org/modules.php? op=modload&name=Web_Links&file=index&req=viewlink&cid=3.

[62] *Loose Change.*

[63] Ibid.

[64] Cheryl Seal, "Smoking Gun: The Evidence that May Hang G.W. Bush," *Unknown News: Cheryl's Daily Diatribe*, May 24, 2002, www.unknownnews.net/ cdd052402.html.

[65] Nancy Jo Sales, "Click Here for Conspiracy," *Vanity Fair*, August 2006, www.vanityfair.com/ontheweb/features/2006/08/loosechange200608.

[66] Scripps Howard News Service, "36 percent believe feds conspired in 9/11," *Albuquerque Tribune*, August 3, 2006, www.abqtrib.com/albq/nw_national_ government/article/0,2564,ALBQ_19861_4894025,00.html.

[67] Thomas Hargrove and Guido H. Stempel III, "Was 9/11 an 'inside job'?," *Seattle Post-Intelligencer*, August 3, 2006, seattlepi.nwsource.com/national/279827_ conspiracy02ww.html?source=mypi.

★ 18 ★

Dr. Jekyll and Mr. Hyde — The Double Standard

"The direct use of force is such a poor solution to any problem. It is generally employed only by small children and large nations."

David Friedman

THE STORY OF HOW THE U.S. SUPPORTED Saddam Hussein from the early 1960s through the early 1990s is only one of many examples of the double standard applied historically in U.S. foreign policies. What most Americans fail to realize is that the types of policies practiced beyond our borders are very different from those applied at home. Our government has willingly made pacts with dictators who serve U.S. needs, despite claims of human rights violations and other atrocities. The U.S. government has done so in order to obtain a competitive advantage on behalf of some American corporations.

The Iranian Coup of 1953

Few Americans know that the U.S. government overthrew the democratically elected government of Iran in a 1953 clandestine coup. The Central Intelligence Agency (CIA), together with the British Secret Intelligence Service (SIS), jointly conducted a takeover of the Iranian government and replaced the popular, democratically elected Prime Minister of Iran, Mohammad Mossadeq, in order to maintain control of Iran's oil.

In the 1950s the British controlled Iran's oil through a company named the Anglo-Iranian Oil Company (AIOC) — later it was renamed British Petroleum (BP). Dr. Mohammed Mossadegh, head of the Nationalist Party, galvanized the Iranian Parliament to vote to nationalize Iran's oil fields. The Iranians wished to control their own resources and voted unanimously to do so in 1951. One month later, Dr. Mossadegh was elected as the Prime Minister of Iran.[1] The British, understanding the economic consequences of this action, realized they were going to lose their Iranian oil grip. The loss of the immensely profitable AIOC would have a disastrous economic effect upon Britain.

Prime Minister Mossadegh was replaced by Mohammed Reza Pahlavi, who had previously been ousted and whose father was a former Shah of Iran. The new Shah promised a continued alliance to the British and American governments as he would allow their persistent domination of Iranian oil resources.[2] The CIA went public in 2000 about the 1953 U.S. and British-led coup against Iran, and the *New York Times* published a report about it.[3] The U.S. and British governments turned a blind eye to the Shah's notorious use of widespread repression and torture of Iranian citizens. His dictatorship lasted until the late 1970s when the Islamic revolution started. The U.S. embassy in Tehran was stormed, and American hostages were seized. Before the Iranian Islamic revolution against the Shah, the United States provided Iran's main economic and military support. The relationship changed drastically when the Ayatollah Khomeni came into power.

In 1986 the Reagan Administration facilitated the illegal sale of weapons to Iran. This action was done covertly and against very specific laws created by Congress in the Iran/Contra scandal. It was alleged that the weapons sale was in exchange for American hostages. However, no American hostages were ever released as a result of this "exchange."

The U.S. Trains and Supports Militants

Father Roy Bourgeois captured his audience's rapt attention with his personal testimony as he talked of his work in South America. He is an American Catholic priest with a degree in Geology. Father Bourgeois is also the recipient of a Purple Heart that he received while serving with the U.S. Navy in Vietnam. He spoke before a live audience in Santa Fe in June 2006.

After fulfilling his military service and becoming a Roman Catholic missionary priest, Father Bourgeois spent several years helping the poor in Bolivia in the 1970s. While in South America, he became acutely aware of the many human rights violations that were being perpetrated. In 1980, Father Roy became an opponent of oppressive U.S. foreign policies that were being practiced in Latin America.

San Salvador's Archbishop Oscar Arnulfo Romero was murdered during a religious service because he had criticized the tyrannical military government. Besides the archbishop, several Christian Democratic leaders were assassinated. Three U.S. Catholic nuns and a seventeen year-old girl were raped and killed.[4] Five members of the Salvadoran National Guard were later convicted of murdering the churchwomen. Upon further investigation it was discovered that these cold-blooded murders had been committed by soldiers who had received training in the U.S. at a facility known as the School of the Americas (SOA). It is estimated that this school has trained more than 60,000 Latin American soldiers. Later the school was renamed the Western Hemisphere Institute for Security Cooperation (WHINSC).

In 1996, the Pentagon released training manuals that were used at the school. These manuals taught torture, extortion and execution techniques.[5] The school and its graduates have admitted to teaching and learning terrorist tactics. There are hundreds of documented human rights abuses scattered all over South America that are directly linked to soldiers who have been trained at this school over the last sixty years.[6]

Father Bourgeois indicated that many of the soldiers trained by the U.S. help keep brutal dictatorships in power. These dictators have loyalties to American corporations that hire their citizens in violation of human rights. According to Father Roy, when citizens of Latin American countries have attempted to organize themselves to get better working conditions or wages, the leaders who engaged in organizing workers and their key followers would soon be found dead. Here are examples of incidents perpetrated by U.S.-trained militia:

- In the 1980s, hundreds of people in Honduras were kidnapped, tortured and killed. The killers have been referred to as the infamous Battalion 316. The Battalion 316 human rights violations occurred under the watch of Neoconservative John Negroponte, who was the U.S. Ambassador to Honduras during this period.[7] The militia responsible for these acts was trained by the CIA and Argentine military.

- Negroponte was accused of supporting and carrying out a U.S.-sponsored policy of violations against human rights and international law. Negroponte supervised the creation of the El Aguacate air base. The U.S. trained Nicaraguan Contras during the 1980s on this base, and it was also used as a secret detention and torture center.[8]

- The CIA has over 1,400 documented human rights abuse cases that occurred in Latin America from 1964 to 1995. These cases include violations in El Salvador, Guatemala, Brazil, Nicaragua, Honduras, Chile, and Peru.[9]
- CIA records reveal cases of kidnapping, murder and other human rights abuse cases perpetrated by U.S.-trained fighters.[10]

Father Roy Bourgeois has been a peace activist for over twenty-five years, teaching techniques of nonviolent civil disobedience. He calls for an end to oppressive U.S. foreign policies. He heads the SOA Watch, a non-profit organization that has asked Congress to close down the WHINSC. Every year in November, SOA Watch organizes a demonstration at the Western Hemisphere Institute for Security Cooperation at Fort Benning, in memory of the innocent Latin American victims who have been murdered.

U.S. officials have ignored human rights violations and have not only negotiated with, but also supported terrorist leaders for the sake of allowing a U.S. corporation to turn a profit. The SOA video documentary entitled *SOA: Guns and Greed* provides a list of the many American corporations engaged in sweatshop practices and the exploitation of South America's people and resources.[11]

Just like people, there are great corporate citizens who demonstrate consciousness and care in their decision making and they are critical to our economy. I am reminded of my friend Steve who has worked for three major corporations in his career. Steve bears witness to the fact that these corporations have provided him with good wages and excellent benefits. There are many examples of corporations who maintain integrity and ethical standards. Unfortunately, there are a number of corporations that stand accused of exploitive actions, human rights violations, environmental destruction and caring only about maintaining a highly profitable bottom line.

Will, a registered Republican from Oklahoma and a college professor, said, "People wonder why Cuba is so influential in Latin America." The reason, he said, ". . . is while Americans have been training right wing militias to uphold puppet governments in Latin America, Cuba has been training doctors to help these countries."

Muammar Al-Qaddafi of Libya, Omar al-Bashir of Sudan, Robert Mugabe of Zimbabwe and King Abdullah of Saudi Arabia are all well known for their outrageous human rights violations. These dictators along with at least twenty other dictators exploit, repress, and abuse citizen rights year after year according to an annual Parade Report complied by David Wallechinsky.[12] Failure to adhere to the rules set up by these notorious dictators easily results in execution without trial. Uprisings are quickly and firmly put down. Yet, the U.S. government appears to be obsessed primarily with the human rights violations of those nations who possess abundant resources and who decide they will no longer succumb to U.S. control. We witnessed how the U.S. ignored the human rights violations perpetrated by Saddam Hussein for years. It was only after Saddam Hussein threatened American oil interests by invading Kuwait that he became an enemy of the U.S.

The U.S. — Arms Dealer of the World

The Bush Administration had pledged to weed out terrorism in our world. However, one of the major policies contradicting this statement is the United States' role as the world's leading exporter of arms. American arms sales are often given in return for favors or as a reward. Favors include giving the U.S. access to overseas military bases or facilities. For example, weapons were given as a reward to those nations who helped fight the wars in Iraq and Afghanistan. These purported favors come with a high price tag, threatening both U.S. and global security.[13] Frequently, U.S. arms end up in the hands of unstable, undemocratic or terrorist groups.[14]

The last year for which a full report was available was 2003. In that year the United States transported arms to eighteen of twenty-five countries that were involved in active military disputes. Angola, Chad, Ethiopia, Colombia, Pakistan, and the Philippines all received transfers through U.S. arms sales programs.[15] The U.S. frequently provides weapons and arms to both sides embroiled in a conflict.[16]

More than half of the top 25 nations described as "undemocratic" by the U.S. State Department's Human Rights Report were recipients of U.S. arms transfers.[17] The citizens of these "undemocratic" nations do not have the right to vote out their own government, or their right is seriously limited. These nations received over $2.7 billion in U.S. arms transfers under the Foreign Military Sales and Commercial Sales programs in 2003. The top recipients included Saudi Arabia ($1.1 billion), Egypt ($1.0 billion), Kuwait ($153 million), the United Arab Emirates ($110 million), and Uzbekistan ($33 million).[18]

One wonders how many of these arms and weapons sold to Middle Eastern governments have fallen into the hands of terrorists who wish to do harm to U.S. soldiers? And how many of these arms have Iraqi insurgents obtained? In October of 2006, the nations of the world believed it had come time to limit the sales of arms, and the UN sponsored such a resolution. Every nation on the planet either agreed or abstained from the vote except the U.S., who was the sole nation to vote against the resolution.[19]

The United States Becomes a Rogue Nation

During George W. Bush's first few years in office, he pulled the U.S. out of several important international treaties and began working to undermine the United Nations. Here are four prime examples:

1. *The Anti-Ballistic Missile Treaty.* A treaty between the U.S. and the Soviet Union to limit anti-ballistic missile production (ABM) had been in force for 30 years, from 1972 until 2002. On June 13, 2002, six months after giving the required notice of intent, the Bush Administration withdrew the U.S. from the treaty.[20]

2. *International Campaign to Ban Landmines.* President Clinton committed to "aggressively pursue an international agreement to ban the use, stockpiling, production, and transfer of anti-personnel landmines."[21] However, President Clinton failed to join the majority of the world's nations in signing the Ottawa Mine Ban Treaty in 1996. In 2004, the Bush Administration flat out renounced the Ottawa Treaty. The Pentagon has a stockpile of over ten million anti-personnel mines and says it reserves the right to use these weapons anywhere in the world.[22] The Bush Administration has subsequently moved toward the production of a new anti-personnel landmine prototype.[23]

3. *The Kyoto Protocol.* Australia and the United States were signatories to the Kyoto Treaty but have refused to ratify it. The signature alone is symbolic, as the Kyoto Protocol is non-binding on the United States unless it is ratified. The Kyoto Protocol was an international agreement to limit greenhouse gas emissions signed during the Clinton Administration. This issue was discussed in-depth in the chapter "The Fifth Commandment."

4. *The Comprehensive Nuclear Test Ban Treaty.* The United States and 187 nations signed the Nuclear Non-proliferation Treaty in 1968. The non-proliferation treaty was a negotiation between "nuclear weapons states" that possessed nuclear weapons and those who did not. In this agreement, the non-nuclear weapons states were to forego the development of nuclear weapons. In return, the nuclear weapons states, including the United States, agreed to share civilian nuclear technologies. In Article VI of the agreement, nations were to pursue deliberations toward nuclear disarmament under strict and effective international control.[24] The U.S. has backed out of the 31 year old treaty, threatening world security. The Republican-controlled Senate rejected the Comprehensive Nuclear Test Ban Treaty signed by Clinton in 1999.

Shortly after the 9/11 attacks on America, the Bush Administration unveiled its new "Nuclear Posture."[25] This new policy of preemption identified seven specific nations that the United States would consider striking first with nuclear weapons, including Iraq. *All of the nations identified were signatories to the Nuclear Non-proliferation Treaty.*[26]

While the United States threatens other nations for attempting to acquire nuclear weapons for their defense, the Bush Administration's new preemption policies cleared the way for the development of a new generation of strategic nuclear weapons.[27] Terrified nations that were targeted in the new Bush doctrine began scrambling. I believe the confrontational approach used by George W. Bush led to the decision by North Korea to reactivate their nuclear weapon program which they have aggressively pursued. North Korea has gone as far as testing their nuclear weapons, and the fission materials used to build their weapons was produced during the administrations of George H.W Bush and George W. Bush.[28]

Iran has submitted eight proposals complete with provisions since 2003 concerning their plans to develop nuclear technology for peaceful purposes only. The Bush Administration has dismissed these proposals, refused to communicate with the Iranians and has continually accused them of developing nuclear technology for weapons.[29]

As the months of war drag into years of war in Iraq and the multitude of mistakes and mismanagement come to the light of day, the Bush White House desperately attempts to distract our nation. With belligerent accusations and wild actions such as the storming of the Iranian Embassy in Iraq and the arrest of Iranians, Mr. Bush attempts to provoke another war — with Iran.[31]

Nuclear Nations Listing[30]

Country	Warheads Active/ total*	Year of First Test
Five "Nuclear Weapons States" from the NPT		
United States	5,735/9,960[2]	1945 ("Trinity")
Russia (formerly the Soviet Union)	5,830/16,000[3]	1949 ("RDS-1")
United Kingdom	<200[4]	1952 ("Hurricane")
France	350[5]	1960 ("Gerboise Bleue")
China	130[6]	1964 ("596")
Other Known Nuclear Powers		
India	4-50[7]	1974 ("Smiling Buddha")
Pakistan	30-52[8]	1998 ("Chagai-I")
North Korea	1-10[9]	2006[10]
Undeclared Nuclear Weapons States		
Israel	75-200[11]	1979 (see Vela Incident)

Reframing Democracies

How is it that Venezuela became a part of the axis of evil? The controversial, democratically elected Hugo Chavez, became the President of Venezuela in 1999. He is either well-loved and admired, or hated, detested and seen as a threat. The democratic socialist leader's agenda has included empowering the poor, stimulating economic growth for his nation, combating disease, and eliminating illiteracy, malnutrition, poverty, and other social problems.

Hugo Chavez acted against the Bush White House by supporting alternative models of economic development. He has rallied cooperation among the world's poor nations, especially in Latin America, by advocating what he refers to as "fair bilateral trade and aid agreements" among countries. He has been a staunch critic of what he calls U.S. imperialism and globalization of the inequities he perceives in the Free Trade Area of the Americas, an extension of the North American Free Trade Agreement (NAFTA).[32]

One of Chavez's more controversial positions has been his advocacy in OPEC to enforce strict oil production quotas and to target higher oil prices. He has been critical of U.S. foreign policies, especially those related to the invasion of Iraq. He has publicly embraced Cuban President Fidel Castro, which has caused further alienation. The U.S. has held rigid and sustained economic sanctions against Cuba. George W. Bush and Hugo Chavez have engaged in name calling though the years. Chavez has called President George W. Bush *"pendejo"* (stupid) and in 2006 before the UN he referred to George W. Bush as *"El Diablo"* (the devil). The Bush Administration has frequently referred to Hugo Chavez as *"a dangerous threat"* and as part of *"the axis of evil."*[33]

Born-again evangelical leader Pat Robertson publicly called for the assassination of Venezuelan President Hugo Chavez, saying, ". . . without question this is a dangerous enemy to our south, controlling a huge pool of oil . . . We have the ability to take him out, and I think the time has come that we exercise that ability."[34]

As American citizens we might want to reflect on how the 2001 Neoconservative foreign policies are affecting us abroad, especially with respect to George W. Bush's War on Terrorism. In an early 2007 global poll taken across twenty-five countries, a majority of people said the U.S. was "mainly a negative" influence in the world.[35] Seventy-three percent of respondents reported they disapproved of the war in Iraq and large majorities voiced fear and concern over the Bush White House Middle East policies and their handling of Iran and North Korea.[36]

The U.S. is similar to Doctor Jekyll and Mr. Hyde. At home we attempt to live the values of the good Doctor Jekyll, honoring human rights and personal dignity. However, once beyond our borders, the madness of Mr. Hyde emerges and we engage in either teaching atrocities or committing them ourselves with our CIA and military.

NOTES, Chapter 18

1 "Mohammed Reza Pahlavi," *Reference.com*, www.reference.com/browse/wiki/ Mohammad_Reza_Pahlavi.

2 "Overthrow of Premier Mossadeq of Iran: Preliminary Steps," *Iran Online Archives*, www.iranonline.com/newsroom/Archive/Mossadeq/Preliminary-steps.html.

3 a. James Risen, "Secrets of History: The CIA in Iran," *New York Times*, April 16, 2000, www.nytimes.com/library/world/mideast/041600iran-cia-index.html.
b. Jessica Moore, "Governing Iran: Key Events in Iran Since 1921," *The NewsHour with Jim Lehrer*, PBS, February 20, 2004, www.pbs.org/newshour/indepth_ coverage/middle_east/iran/timeline.html.
c. "Mohammed Mossadegh," *Wikipedia*, en.wikipedia.org/wiki/Mohammed_ Mossadegh.
d. Sylvia Edwards, "Sly's Twentieth Century Time Line," *Litopia*, June 2003, www.edwardsly.com/1900-1999.html.

4 Galen R. Frysinger, "San Salvador, El Salvador," www.galenfrysinger.com/san_ salvador_el_salvador.htm.

5 "SOA/WHINSEC Background," *School of the Americas Watch*, www.soaw.org/ new/sub.php?id=24.

6 Ibid.

7 "John Dimitri Negroponte," *Equipo Nixkor*, www.derechos.org/nizkor/ negroponte/eng.html.

8 Ibid.

9 "Latin America Human Rights Abuses CIA Files," *Paperless Archives*, www.paper lessarchives.com/hrla.html.

10 Ibid.

11 *SOA: Guns and Greed*, VHS, directed by Robert Richter (2000; New York: Maryknoll World Productions, 2001).

12 David Wallechinsky contributing editor, "Who Is the World's Worst Dictator?" *Parade Annual Report*, February 17, 2007, www.parade.com/articles/editions/ 2007/edition_02-11-2007/Dictators.

13 Frida Berrigan and William D. Hartung with Leslie Heffel, "U.S. Weapons at War 2005: Promoting Freedom or Fueling Conflict? U.S. Military Aid and Arms Transfers Since September 11," *World Policy Institute*, June 2005, worldpolicy.org/ projects/arms/reports/wawjune2005.html.

14 Ibid.

15 Ibid.

16 Ibid.

17 Ibid.

18 Ibid.

19 a. Rachel Stohl, "UN to consider arms trade treaty - US opposes," *International Relations and Security Network*, November 16, 2006, www.isn.ethz.ch/news /sw/details.cfm?id=16928.
b. Lisl Brunner, "UN votes to begin work on global arms trade treaty despite US opposition," *Paper Chase Newsburst*, October 27, 2006, jurist.law.pitt.edu/ paperchase/2006/10/un-votes-to-begin-work-on-global-arms.php.

20 Martin D. Fleck and James P. Thomas, "Nuclear Treaty: U.S. Undermines Non-Nuclear treaty," *Seattle Post-Intelligencer*, April 29, 2004, seattlepi.nwsource .com/opinion/171065_nuclear29.html.

[21] *United States Campaign to Ban Landmines*, www.banminesusa.org/index.php? http://www.banminesusa.org/news/879_noCloser.html.

[22] "Events and Campaigns: Land Mines," *Institute for Global Communications*, http://disarm.igc.org/landmine.html.

[23] "U.S. Programs to Develop Alternatives to Antipersonnel Mines," *Human Rights Watch*, April 2000, www.hrw.org/press/2000/04/us-landmines.htm.

[24] Fleck and Thomas, "Nuclear Treaty."

[25] Ibid.

[26] Ibid.

[27] Ibid.

[28] "North Korea's Nuclear Weapons Program," *The Nuclear Weapon Archive*, nuclear-weaponarchive.org/DPRK/index.html.

[29] Paul Kerr, "Iranian, P5+1 Proposals to Resolve Iranian Nuclear Issue," *Arms Control Association*, September 13, 2006, www.armscontrol.org/factsheets/Iran_Nuclear_Proposals.asp.

[30] "List of states with nuclear weapons: Estimated worldwide nuclear stockpiles," *Wikipedia*, en.wikipedia.org/wiki/List_of_states_with_nuclear_weapons#Estimated_worldwide_nuclear_stockpiles.

[31] David E. Sanger and Michael R. Gordon, "Rice Says Bush Authorized Iranians Arrest in Iraq," *New York Times*, January 13, 2007.

[32] "Hugo Chavez," *Wikipedia*, en.wikipedia.org/wiki/Hugo_Chavez.

[33] Tim Padgett, "Hugo Chavez: Leading the Left-Wing Charge," *Time Magazine*, April 30, 2006, www.time.com/time/magazine/article/0,9171,1187165,00.html.

[34] Cort Greene, "The Monroe Doctrine, US Imperialism and Venezuela, *Hands Off Venezuela*, November 8, 2005, www.handsoffvenezuela.org/monroe_doc.

[35] Jim Lobe, "Bush Continues to Unite the World . . . Against Him," *Interpress*, January 23, 2007.

[36] Ibid.

★ 19 ★

A House of Cards

"He that never changes his opinions, never corrects his mistakes ... will never be wiser on the morrow than he is today."

Tyrone Edwards

AN IMPORTANT CONCEPT I discuss in my business seminars is how to deal with mistakes. According to seminar attendees, there is a tendency to deny, hide, bury, or blame someone else for mistakes when they are made. Tom Peters, management guru and best selling author, says that if you aren't making any mistakes then you probably aren't doing anything at all. People will make mistakes. How we acknowledge, handle and fix mistakes is critically important.

What happens when someone makes a mistake yet refuses to acknowledge it? What happens when we are told about a mistake proactively? Consider how we feel about a mistake when someone apologizes for a mistake, takes the time to explain the circumstances and then tells us how they have fixed the mistake, versus someone trying to hide or deny a mistake. We all have an anger barometer and when responsible people deal with mistakes proactively our anger barometers don't have a chance to rise. But when a mistake is made and the responsible party engages in blaming, denying or hiding the facts, it causes the anger barometer to rise. Let us evaluate the first issue in our house of cards: the 9/11 attack on the U.S.

Incompetence Hidden and Denied

"I don't think anybody could have predicted that these people would take an airplane and slam it into the World Trade Center that they would try to use an airplane as a missile — a hijacked airplane as a missile." [1]
May 17, 2002, Condoleezza Rice

"[There] wasn't any way then we could have anticipated what was about to happen, of course, on 9/11." [2]
September 7, 2004, Dick Cheney

"They struck in a way that was unimaginable." [3]
January 26, 2002, George W. Bush

How do you win a relay race? In order to win a relay race each runner on the team must be ready to receive the baton within a specific zone. Every runner must run as fast as they can to deliver the baton to the next receiver in the relay. However, if there is no one to receive the baton or if the baton is dropped, the team loses the race.

What happened to America is that the designated Bush runners for the U.S. national security team failed to show up for their posts. As hard as they tried, U.S. government agencies, congressional leaders and professional staff tried to pass the baton to the new Bush Administration but they were simply not receptive to information about al-Qaeda and the real impending threats to our nation.

In their own words, as quoted above, members of the administration have freely revealed their own total lack of understanding, awareness and preparedness for the events of 9/11.

Had the Bush Administration been up-to-date on the security issues facing the U.S., they would have known that a 1993 Pentagon commissioned expert panel had warned that an airplane could be used as a missile to bomb U.S. national landmarks. [4] The Bush Administration might have known that in 1994 France disrupted a pilot's attempt to fly a jet into the Eiffel Tower. Had the Bush security team interfaced with anti-terrorism experts such as Richard Clark, they would have discovered that during the Clinton Administration the U.S., by way of the Philippines, had uncovered a similar plot to fly planes into the Pentagon and WTC once before in 1995 and had successfully stopped that attack. Had they done their homework, the Bush Administration would have realized that in September of 1999 yet another study had warned that al-Qaeda might crash planes into the Pentagon.[5]

If the agencies under the Bush Administration had been coordinating activities, they would have known that in July 2001 the FBI was concerned with Zacarias Moussaoui's interest in flying jumbo jets. Had this administration been paying attention, they would have taken seriously a subsequent FBI memo that warned Moussaoui could "fly something into the World Trade Center." On September 10, 2001, Senator Dianne Feinstein (D-CA) requested a meeting with Vice President Cheney requesting aggressive counterterrorism measures be enacted to protect our nation. The Senator was told that the Vice President would need six months to prepare for such a meeting.[6]

Not only did the Bush Administration receive several notices but they were also provided with in-depth reports. At least one full year before the 9/11 attacks, government officials had tracked and identified Mohammed Atta, along with three of the other hijackers. They were known to be connected to al-Qaeda.[7] Members of the team that assembled the *Able Danger* report assert they were blocked from sharing information by government lawyers.

Several claims have been made that important documents were destroyed by Bush-appointed attorneys at the Justice Department.[8] Members of the Able Danger team say the Department of Defense not only mismanaged the critical information, but also engaged in retaliation against one of the key team members — Army Intelligence officer Anthony Shaffer — when he stepped forward to shed light on the report.[9] There were notices given to the Bush Administration by the FBI, CIA and other agencies prior to the 9/11 attacks including one intercepted by the National Security Agency (NSA) from Afghanistan to Saudi Arabia stating, "tomorrow is zero hour."[10] The Bush Administration and the Department of Defense under the direction of former Secretary Donald Rumsfeld were completely negligent. They allowed the North American Aerospace Defense Command (NORAD), the U.S. government agency responsible for maintaining the air space protection of our nation to send off every single fighter plane on some innocuous training exercises on 9/11 leaving our nation totally and completely vulnerable to the attacks.[11]

Instead of taking any responsibility for their negligence or dereliction of duty, the Bush Administration blamed Bill Clinton for the 9/11 attacks on the U.S. An ABC five-hour dramatization entitled "The Path to 9/11," produced by the Walt Disney Company and allegedly encouraged by Karl Rove, included several misrepresentations of the facts related to the 9/11 attacks. While many enjoyed the film, it was labeled as inaccurate and irresponsible by numerous groups and individuals including American Airlines and former President Clinton.[12] A colleague, Yolanda, who is a psychologist and the executive director of a non-profit organization, believes that lies and cover-ups eventually are exposed; she says, "it's only a matter of time."

"However, the failure or 'surprise' was not lack of warning but in the lack of any engagement with the warnings at the top."[13]

Joseph D. Douglass, Jr.

Keeping the Lid on Leaks

Desperate to keep leaks from revealing a wide range of activities that have been considered everything from secret to unethical, immoral, and illegal, the Bush Administration has used every conceivable means to clamp down on information that might be damaging to the administration. In June of 2006, the United States Supreme Court struck down the Whistle Blower provisions for government employees. The Whistle Blower provisions provided for protection against acts of retaliation for those government employees who identified wrongdoings. This protection was an important tool that encouraged employees to report government fraud, abuse and illegal activities while safeguarding government employees.

In July of 2006, a Navy lawyer was charged because he disclosed information regarding prisoners held at Guantánamo Bay.[14] The officer, Lieutenant Commander Matthew M. Diaz, an attorney who was stationed at Guantánamo Bay for a six-month period, is facing up to thirty years in prison, forfeiture of pay and allowances and dismissal from the Navy if convicted on all the charges against him. The charges appear extremely disproportional and unduly harsh; when comparing his actions of sending a copy of a printout weighted against the charges for those caught torturing the detainees. The consequences for most of those either responsible or found torturing amounted to nothing more than a verbal reprimand.

More leaks have sprung up regarding the Bush Administration including the alleged illegal awarding of no-bid contracts, the failures to provide oversight on contractors, the incompetence in managing the Katrina calamity, illegal spying on Americans without a warrant, secret prisons, and the rewarding of incompetent contractors with even bigger contracts. Yet the administration continues to operate, intact, unscathed, and unaccountable.

Blatant Political Pay Backs

Using the war in Iraq, the Bush Administration was able to reward some of their most loyal campaign contributors. The CIA's top administrator Kyle "Dusty" Foggo together with a well known Republican fundraiser and defense contractor, Brent R. Wilkes were indicted in February of 2007 on charges of conspiracy, wire fraud and money-laundering. The eleven count indictment against Foggo alleged that several illegal, secretive, and lucrative pay-back schemes had occurred between Foggo and Wilkes. The twenty-five count indictment against Wilkes charged that a series of Defense contracts had been granted to him through illegal means including bribery. Foggo and Wilkes purportedly defrauded tax payers using "shell companies and straw men."

Carol C. Lam and other federal prosecutors overseeing the case against Foggo were fired by the Justice Department after the indictments were announced. Not only had U.S. Attorney Carol Lam and her team exposed the illegal activities of Foggo and Wilkes, she had been instrumental in putting Congressman Randy "Duke" Cunningham (R-CA) in prison for his criminal activities. The planned investigations into other malfeasance perpetrated by Bush appointees and members of Congress are now at a standstill. Honest and ethical government officials whose job it is to uncover wrong doings and bring justice against crooks are fired. Our very democracy is threatened under such conditions of retaliation and revenge.

In another example, Blackwater, founded by twenty-seven year-old Christian conservative and billionaire Erik Prince, was just about to go under before the beginning of the war in Iraq. However, because of the Bush rush to war, Prince's company was identified as a source for paid military mercenaries. This privatized military company employs thousands of mercenary troops for tactical operations, training, logistics, intelligence, and engineering. Companies such as Blackwater have become key components in the U.S. Military operations in Iraq at an astronomical cost to the taxpayer. Compared to the cost of employing one U.S. soldier, Blackwater's cost is anywhere from three to eight times more. Prince donated $1.7 million to the Republican National Committee (RNC) prior to the 2004 elections. The Blackwater weekly newsletter highlighted the 2004 Presidential win with these headlines "Bush Wins!! — Four More Years Hooyah!!"[15]

Four contract employees of Blackwater were killed by an angry civilian Iraqi mob as they drove through the highly volatile city of Fallujah in Iraq on March 31, 2004.[16] These men had been enlisted by Blackwater and told they would be guarding Paul Bremer and out of harm's way according to family members.[17] Apparently the men were sent on a mission in an unguarded vehicle without a rear gunner and without armor as called for by company protocol.

On April 13, 2004, Senator Christopher Dodd (D-CT) called for an investigation to determine what had happened in the Fallujah attack of these American contractors. The proposed investigation was stopped by Senator John Warner (R-VA), who stood to oppose any amendment that included an investigation of Blackwater.[18] It was reported that Blackwater had hired a media firm to help defuse the tragedy. Immediately after the murders of the contractors, meetings with key Republican legislators such as John Warner, Dunkin Hunter and Rick Santorum were held to gain support for insulating Blackwater from any repercussions. Blackwater was not only protected from an investigation, but it was also rewarded in 2005 with a $73 million dollar no-bid FEMA contract.

According to Thomas Ricks, author of *Fiasco,* 300,00 residents of Fallujah were caught up in a military hailstorm of retaliation ordered by Donald Rumsfeld and the Bush White House. In a military operation called "Vigilant Resolve," thousands of Marines stormed Fallujah with orders to "go in and clobber people." The retaliatory operation launched by the U.S. was met with fierce resistance and Fallujah rapidly spun out of control.

Blackwater Contracts

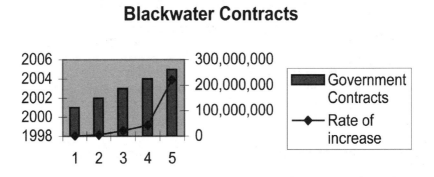

Incompetent Contractors Facilitate Torture

It has become widely evident that the contractors used at Abu Ghraib were responsible for much of the prisoner abuse that occurred at the facility. Interrogators hired by a company known as CACI were supposed to obtain reliable security information. But according to military interrogator Anthony Lagouranis, CACI interrogators were questioning "taxicab drivers" and "pizza delivery guys" who had been picked up off the streets of Baghdad. It was reported that CACI's method of interrogation included many cruel tactics such as urinating on detainees and tying the penises of several detainees together and then pushing one of the men forward, causing all of them to fall.

Senators Christopher Dodd (D- CT) and Senator Carl Levin (D-MI) tried to attach an amendment to a Senate bill that would have prohibited private contractors from conducting interrogations, but it was rejected by the Republican-controlled Senate.

Months after the Taguba Report detailing prisoner abuse was released, none of the CACI interrogators had been terminated. They were still employed and working under minimal supervision in Iraq.[19] CACI continued to enjoy increased government contract work even after the abuses were exposed.

"I felt heartbroken when I saw what I believed to be the American dream destroyed and disgraced at Abu Ghraib."

Aidian Delgado, American Solider

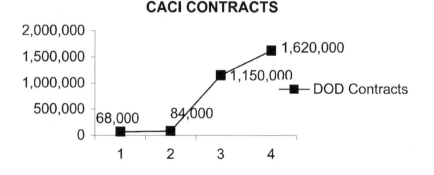

CACI CONTRACTS

Incompetence Rewarded Over and Again

Titan, another government contractor, was hired to provide linguists to support the military. It was widely reported that no test, evaluation or any clearance was required for employment with Titan. American soldiers report that Titan employees were not trained or supervised. Most were incompetent, being unable to read and write as needed and barely fluent in one or the other language. There were huge concerns with the accuracy and quality of the translations. It mattered little as Titan contracts grew astronomically in a four year period from $920,000 to $2.05 billion.[20]

Masters of Gross Mismanagement and Incompetence

The list of grievances concerning the alleged fraud and abuse perpetuated by Halliburton would require its own book to detail the various charges. Here are some of the more obvious allegations. One government audit revealed that Halliburton mismanaged $8.8 billion in Iraqi funds between March 2003 and June 2004.[21] Another government audit found that Halliburton lost about one-third of the property it was given to manage in Iraq, and another audit found $1.8 billion in unsupported charges.

Additionally, it was found that Halliburton had overcharged the taxpayers $61 million for gasoline in addition to overcharging for meals by $67 million.[22] Others, egregious billing examples include:

- Charging U.S. taxpayers $100 for each load of laundry.

- Charging $140 to $145 for a six-pack of coke (purchased from the Saudis).[23]

Henry Bunting, a former procurement specialist for Kellogg, Brown & Root (KBR), subsidary of Halliburton, charged the company with destroying equipment and writing it off as a loss. He gives the example of KBR destroying a brand new $80,000 vehicle because it had a flat tire. In another instance he says new computers still in their boxes were destroyed because they had been ordered incorrectly.[24] Mr. Bunting said Halliburton set these items on fire in a burn pit and then claimed them as a loss.

Halliburton has been charged with excessive spending on unnecessary items. For instance, Halliburton purchased brand new fully loaded SUVs that were rarely used and much more extravagant than necessary for the job at hand. The company conducted training programs at high end luxury hotels and billed American taxpayers for the costs. In another illustration, KBR leased vehicles at a cost of $45,000 or more per year. Instead of purchasing the vehicles outright, the cost to the taxpayer was in several examples $250,000 over a three-year period.[25]

In 2005 Jeff Alex Mazon, an employee of KBR, the Halliburton subsidiary, was indicted for attempting to defraud the U.S. Government of more than $5 million by falsifying paperwork and inflating the price of fuel tankers for military operations. He is accused of taking $1 million from a subcontractor. Another employee, Glenn Allen Powell, pled guilty to taking as much as $1.25 million in kickbacks and defrauding the U.S. government while employed by KBR in Iraq from October 2003 through January 2005.[26]

No Oversight Despite Repeated Demands

Democratic Senator Frank Lautenberg from New Jersey charged that "Halliburton's record of overcharging, bribery, and accounting fraud recites like a textbook example of corporate irresponsibility," and he further stated, "Halliburton has a virtual monopoly on contracts in Iraq and has collected over $9 billion through its subsidiaries." Yet neither KBR nor Halliburton has been investigated. An international watchdog group, Transparency International, detailed in their 2005 Global Corruption Report that the profiteering by U.S.-based corporations threatened to undermine the reconstruction of Iraq.[27]

Bunnatine Greenhouse, a former Chief Contracting Officer with the U.S. government, charged that Halliburton was awarded a $7 billion no-bid contract that had been pre-selected and the terms predetermined. Ms. Greenhouse maintains that never before in her professional career with the U.S. government had she witnessed such blatant corruption and abuse.[28] Of the many reconstruction projects that Halliburton was responsible for in Iraq, few were actually completed because of their high overhead costs. One-third of the amount designated for rebuilding projects went to pay Halliburton's administrative costs according to a 2006 audit report.[29]

A highly disturbing report was made by Ben Carter, a water purification specialist hired by Halliburton. Mr. Carter claimed that sixty-three of sixty-seven water treatment plants that were supposed to be maintained by Halliburton were contaminated and that Halliburton officials refused to alert the military. Despite a Halliburton gag order, Mr. Carter blew the whistle.[30] He said numerous pathogenic organisms such as E coli, salmonella, shigella, giardia, cryptosporidium, and other parasites were in the Iraqi water treatment systems. Carter charges Halliburton with incompetence and willful negligence in their obligation to provide a clean water supply in Iraq. According to Mr. Carter, Halliburton didn't even bother to post signs informing troops they should avoid drinking the shower water.[31] Wil Granger, a quality manager for Halliburton's KBR subsidiary, reported in 2005 that American military troops throughout Iraq suffered from problems associated with water deficiencies.[32]

In an executive order signed by George W. Bush, the President deemed that government contractors would not be held accountable for illegal or inappropriate actions taken in Iraq, thus clearing the way for potential fraud and abuse.[33] In a publicly televised news conference at Johns Hopkins University, George W. Bush was queried on why the U.S. Government was failing to hold contractors accountable. The President responded by saying it was a good question but he didn't know the answer and would have to ask Donald Rumsfeld, former Secretary of Defense. It appears that President Bush either failed to realize or forgot that he had signed an executive order providing immunity to government contractors in Iraq.[34]

Senator Byron Dorgan (D-ND) and Representative Henry Waxman (D-CA) attempted to pass the Hyde amendment calling for congressional oversight on Halliburton and Senator Patrick Leahy (D-VT) asked for an investigation into the many abuses. Senator Jeff Sessions (R-AL) chastised Senators Dorgan and Leahy, suggesting that the Senators should focus on "what is going on that is right in Iraq." The House of Representatives' efforts were publicly dismissed as unnecessary and voted down 53 to 44. Only a fraction of House of Representatives actually voted. The record revealed that 200 Republicans and 179 Democrats abstained from the vote in 2005.

The Bush/Cheney/Rumsfeld practice of arbitrarily marking files "Confidential" or "Secret" has made it challenging to provide the appropriate level of oversight. The Government Accountability Office found that between 2000 and 2004, the Pentagon had designated 20 percent of all documents as top secret, and an audit report revealed that the Pentagon was misclassifying reports.[35]

Private corporations working for profit deeply influence the course of national and international security. They were supposed to assist the troops, help reduce the conflict and complete certain projects. Now these companies, just like the many Bush Administration appointees, are proclaiming mission accomplished and are walking off the job.

After gross mismanagement and negligence, the funds for this expensive endeavor have been frittered away. There is no security in Iraq nor are the already-paid-for projects completed. To stay the course or continue the George W. Bush mission in Iraq will mean only more red ink for American coffers, more dead soldiers and dead Iraqis, more aggression in the Middle East, and greater discord throughout the international community.

The Real Denigration of the Troops

I wish there was another way to describe this situation, but unfortunately this title accurately describes it best. While patriotic, devoted Americans offer their lives in the Middle East, the Bush Administration and Congress have failed to budget adequately for their families while they have been gone.[36] Military families have had to make adjustments because of lower incomes, loss of health care insurance for extended family members, multiple deployments, and unexpected challenges arising in single-parent homes.[37]

The U.S. has failed to provide proper medical compensation and attention for veterans upon their return. Severely wounded veterans who have lost limbs and are in need of physical rehabilitation and care are discharged with a $21,000 disbursement. Failing to read the fine print, many believe it's their compensation for injuries. But in reality, the $21,000 is only a deposit for their medical care and it must be used before they can draw on Veteran's Administration benefits.[38]

Permanently disabled veterans complain they are unable to live on the amount of disability payments received from the government. Scores of these are former middle class Americans who are now falling into poverty and homelessness.[39] A recent report revealed that up to 80 percent of new veterans diagnosed with Post-Traumatic Stress Disorder (PTSD) are not given a referral for treatment.[40] It is a common known fact that PTSD is just like any other wound and will not go away without treatment.

Hypocrites, Cheats, Liars, Thieves and Incompetents

The Bush-created Counterintelligence Field Activity of the Defense Department is under investigation by federal prosecutors. Few Americans have heard of this agency whose actual budget and size are considered top secret. What is known is that the agency spent more than $1 billion in a four year period primarily in outsourced services. The unit came under fire when it was discovered that it was yet another government agency that was keeping records on peaceful American protestors who are against the war in Iraq.[41] Two Bush appointees resigned in August of 2006: David A. Burtt II, the director, and his deputy Joseph Hefferon.

In March 2006, Claude A. Allen, the assistant to George W. Bush for domestic policy, was charged and arrested after Montgomery police accused him of stealing merchandise through a refund scheme and conspiracy to commit theft, both of which are felonies.[42] Mr. Allen thereafter resigned his position with the Bush Administration.

David Safavian, a Bush chief of staff at the General Services Administration, was found guilty of lying and obstructing justice.[43] Mr. Safavian was linked to lobbyist Jack Abramoff through a real estate transaction that involved government property. As Abramoff's guest, Mr. Safavian had enjoyed a week-long vacation at the luxurious St. Andrews resort in Scotland along with Representative Bob Ney, who was later convicted for a number of illegal activities. Two of Ney's aids and the former Christian Coalition executive Ralph Reed were also on the St. Andrews vacation.

Ralph Reed became the executive director of the Christian Coalition after the failed Presidential bid by Pat Robertson, who founded the organization in 1988. Reed left to start his own consulting firm after the Christian Coalition came under fire by IRS for allegedly violating federal campaign laws in 1996.

Ralph Reed, operating on behalf of the infamous Jack Abramoff, manipulated evangelical Christians for the benefit of Abramoff's casino clients.[44] The story was widely publicized in 2004. Mr. Reed was paid in excess of $1 million for his advocacy benefiting Abramoff's patrons.[45] In one case Mr. Reed contacted a church member who convinced his pastor to ask a key legislator to intervene in a casino bill. And in two other instances, Reed was tied to evangelical leaders James Dobson, Tony Perkins, Jerry Falwell, and Pat Robertson, who made pre-recorded telephone calls to Louisiana Christians as well as making radio announcements that benefited Abramoff casino clients.

In an email to Jack Abramoff, Ralph Reed boasted, "We are in overdrive and all pistons are firing." And in another email he claims, "We have over fifty pastors mobilized, with a total membership in those churches of over 40,000."[46] Mr. Reed's association with convicted lobbyist Abramoff, combined with the fact that he received at least $4.2 million from Jack Abramoff for questionable practices involving his influence with evangelical Christians, and then lying to prominent Republicans about his relationship with Abramoff, brought Reed to his political demise.[47]

Evangelical leader Ted Haggard, considered by *Time Magazine* as one of the most influential evangelicals in the U.S., was accused of having a three-year relationship with a gay man. The Reverend Haggard had allegedly paid to have sex with the gay man who publicly exposed him, because he felt that it was hypocritical for the Reverend to preach against homosexuality while secretly engaging in it. Mr. Haggard was also accused of using illegal drugs. The Reverend Haggard, the founder and senior leader of a 14,000-member church in Colorado Springs and the president of the National Association of Evangelicals (NAE), had sermonized against homosexuality, believing that "God's best plan is for people to be heterosexual." Ted Haggard was a staunch advocate of the marriage amendment and it was reported that he spoke weekly with George W. Bush. He was dismissed from his church and forced to resign his position as the president of NAE after publicly confessing to "sexual immorality" in November of 2006. Mr. Haggard is married and has five children. He indicated he was ashamed and embarrassed by the revelation.

In November of 2006, George W. Bush appointed Erik Keroack, a conservative obstetrician and gynecologist to head the nation's family planning programs at the Department of Health and Human Services. Dr. Keroack is responsible for $283 million dollars in federal grant money for family planning services. The family planning program was designed to provide persons with information and contraceptive supplies, especially needy low-income citizens. The ironic part of this appointment is that Dr. Keroack was the medical director of a Christian pregnancy-counseling agency called A Woman's Concern. The agency advocates sexual abstinence until after a person is married. It opposes contraception and does not distribute information promoting birth control. In fact, his organization believes that distributing contraceptives is "demeaning to women." Dr. Keroack has stated that the use of condoms does not provide protection from HIV or other sexually transmitted diseases. This is in direct opposition to the findings of the National Institute of Health that have reported that the use of condoms helps reduce the risk of HIV transmission by 85 percent.[48] Dr. Keroack holds positions on sexuality that are out of step from in his profession.[49] Many concerned citizens are worried that this important component of family planning will be reduced to blatant favoritism, whereby conservative family planning agencies will be given huge contracts to hand out abstinence pamphlets.

It has become evident that retaliatory tactics, lies and the illegal exposing of a CIA undercover agent were crafted at the highest levels of the Bush White House. Mr. Libby, former chief of staff to Vice President Dick Cheney, together with the Vice President and Karl Rove, appear to have been heavily involved. The Scooter Libby trial revealed that trusted servants in our government planted evidence with the media to expose CIA Agent Valerie Plame. Ms. Plame is the wife of Iraq war and Bush critic, Ambassador Joseph Wilson, discussed in earlier chapters.

What can be said about the fact that the former Ambassador to Iraq, Paul Bremer to whom George W. Bush awarded the Presidential Medal of Freedom cannot account for more than $8 billion of the $12 billion dollars earmarked for the Iraqi reconstruction? Paul Bremer was ordered to testify before the House Oversight and Government Reform Committee hearing on waste, fraud and abuse in Iraq headed by Representative Henry Waxman, (D-CA.). American money (freshly printed and shrink-wrapped in $100 bills) that were supposed to be used for humanitarian aid and reconstruction purposes in Iraq simply disappeared under the watch of Mr. Bremer. The cold, hard cash weighing 363 tons was flown into Baghdad according to the testimony provided in February 2007. The former Ambassador said he knew 90 percent of the Iraqi government payrolls were bogus but that he ordered the money be given out to the Iraqis anyway.[50] It is feared that much of that missing money went into the pockets of Shiite militias; militias who may be guilty of attacking and killing American soldiers.

Praying for Armageddon

Two interrelated issues should concern mainstream Americans. The first is the fact that many Evangelical Christians believe we are living in the end times as prophesied in the Book of Revelations of the Bible.[51] These Christians are praying for the second coming of Jesus Christ and for the chance to be saved, which they believe will happen during the "Rapture." In order for the Rapture to occur, the prophecy states that the Messiah will return to the Promised Land (Israel). Evangelical Christians believe they have a biblical responsibility to support Israel.[52]

During an informal discussion at a business women's dinner, Karen, an investment banker who professed to be Jewish, described how American Evangelical Christians are using their credit card points to donate to "Jewish charity causes." Another woman, Joan, who also said she is Jewish, was aware of such donations and said she was shocked by the intensity of such support. Several women at our dinner table talked about the fear of "self-fulfilling prophecies." Self-fulfilling prophecies come true when people believe in something so intently that they appear to actually make it happen. Christians with such forceful faith might actually help facilitate the destruction of our planet through active ignorance of global warming or through supporting wars in the Middle East. Because George W. Bush professes to be a Christian, scores of believers willingly follow his lead.

The second factor is the influence of the Neocons, several of whom are Jewish with strong ties to the arms industry. They have shown a willingness to use aggressive U.S. policies and resources in addition to going to any military lengths to protect Israel.[53] However, many critics, including some prominent scholars, say such fervent support is compromising U.S. security.[54]

The Stack Begins to Fall

As the layers of corruption are peeled away, the American people wake up out of their patriotic slumber to demand accountability. They no longer wish to stay the course in Iraq. They demand to know what job it is that Americans are supposed to be doing and what George W. Bush alludes to when he talks of the U.S. mission in Iraq. They no longer believe that al-Qaeda and Saddam are connected. They don't want to hear of Red Alerts and they don't believe that electing Democrats will cause the terrorists to win. Since both the House of Representatives and the Senate were soundly placed in the hands of the Democrats, a majority of Americans are hopeful that some semblance of balance, respect and decency can be restored to our nation.

NOTES, Chapter 19

1 "Are you safer NOW? Palatable Lie #6," *Tri-City Forum*, September 28, 2006, www.community.tri-cityherald.com/?q=node/297.

2 Ibid.

3 Ibid.

4 "Context of '1993'," *Cooperative Research: History Commons*, www.cooperative research.org/context.jsp?item=a93planesasweapons.

5 "'99 Report Warned Of Suicide Hijacking," *CBS News*, May 17, 2002, www.cbsnews.com/stories/2002/05/17/attack/main509471.shtml.

6 "Are you safer NOW?"

7 Kimberly Hefling, "Report: Military Didn't Identify Hijackers," *The New Mexican*, September 22, 2006, A-3.

8 Paul Thompson, "Complete 9/11 Timeline," *Cooperative Research: History Commons*, www.cooperativeresearch.org/timeline.jsp?timeline= complete911_timeline&startpos=600.

9 *Able Danger Blog*, www.abledangerblog.com/.

10 MSNBC, "Special investigation: Leading up to 9/11," *Countdown with Keith Olbermann*, September 28, 2006, www.msnbc.msn.com/id/15046240/.

11 "Complete 9/11 Timeline," *Cooperative Research: History Commons*, www.cooperativeresearch.org/project.jsp?project=911_project.

12 The Center for Media & Democracy, "The Path to 9/11 (2006 Docudrama)," *SourceWatch*, www.sourcewatch.org/index.php?title=%22The_Path_ to_9/11%22_(2006_Docudrama).

13 Joseph D. Douglass, Jr, "The 9/11 Commission Report: An Appraisal," *Financial Sense Online*, September 7, 2004, www.financialsense.com/editorials/ douglass/2004/0907.html.

14 "Navy Lawyer Charged with Sharing Secret Information from Gitmo," *FOX News*, August 26, 2006.

15 "The Tale of Prince – A War Profiteer," *Iraq for Sale*, DVD, directed by Robert Greenwald (2006; Culver City, CA: BraveNew Films, 2006), youtube.com/watch? v=qfgt3kmv-Hg.

16 Callahan & Blaine, Attorneys at Law, *News & Articles*, 64.8.124.86/ publications.php.

17 *Iraq for Sale: The War Profiteers*, DVD, directed by Robert Greenwald (2006; Culver City, CA: BraveNew Films, 2006).

18 Ibid.

19 Kevin Drum, "Can't we at least send them home?," *Washington Monthly: Political Animal*, May 5, 2004, www.washingtonmonthly.com/archives/monthly/ 2004_05.php.

20 *Iraq for Sale*.

21 "U.S. mismanaged $8.8 billion in Iraqi funds: 'Ghost employees' hired for nonexistent work," *Halliburton Watch*, August 19, 2004, www.halliburton watch.org/news/audit_hackworth.html.

22 "Halliburton," *Harper's Magazine*, harpers.org/Halliburton.html.

23 "Halliburton Fleecing America...," *Rush Limbaugh Online*, www.rushlimbaugh online.com/articles/halliburton.htm.

24 *Iraq for Sale*.

25 Ibid.

[26] Griff Witte, "Former KBR Worker Admits to Fraud in Iraq," *The Washington Post*, August 23, 2005, A11, www.washingtonpost.com/wp-dyn/content/article/2005/08/22/AR2005082201435.html.

[27] Emad Mekay, "Is Iraq Becoming the World's Biggest Cash Cow?," *AntiWar.com*, March 18, 2005, www.antiwar.com/ips/mekay.php?articleid=5255.

[28] Ibid.

[29] Lolita C. Baldor, "Administrative Costs High in Iraq," *ABC News*, October 25, 2006, abcnews.go.com/Politics/wireStory?id=2604253&CMP=OTC-RSS-Feeds0312.

[30] Ibid.

[31] "Whistleblowers' stomach-curdling story: Halliburton serves contaminated water to troops," *Halliburton Watch*, September 20, 2005, www.halliburtonwatch.org/news/contamination.html.

[32] MSNBC, "Memo: Halliburton failed to purify GIs' water," *NBC News*, March 16, 2006, www.msnbc.msn.com/id/11854311/.

[33] The White House, *Executive Order Protecting the Development Fund for Iraq and Certain Other Property in Which Iraq Has An Interest*, 2003 (Washington, DC: Office of the Press Secretary, 2003), www.whitehouse.gov/news/releases/2003/05/20030522-15.html.

[34] *Iraq for Sale.*

[35] Walter Pincus, "GAO Finds Pentagon Erratic In Wielding Secrecy Stamp," *The Washington Post*, July 14, 2006, A19.

[36] Joseph Briseno Sr., interview by Susan Dentzer, *NewsHour with Jim Lehrer*, Public Broadcasting System, April 26, 2005, www.pbs.org/newshour/bb/health/jan-june05/briseno.html.

[37] "Military Families Speak About the Back Door Draft," *Military Families Speak Out*, www.mfso.org/article.php?list=type&type=50.

[38] Natalie Storey, "Hearts of war: The color of sacrifice, part 1: Sacrifice: For Injured Veterans, Coming Home Can be Bigger Challenge," *The New Mexican*, November 11, 2006, A4.

[39] Ibid.

[40] Joseph Briseno Sr. interview.

[41] Walter Pincus, "Counterintelligence Officials Resign," *The Washington Post*, August 10, 1006, A4, www.washingtonpost.com/wp-dyn/content/article/2006/08/09/AR2006080901700_pf.html.

[42] Ernesto Londoño, "Ex-Bush Aide Makes Plea Deal in Thefts – Claude Allen Might Avoid Jail, Files Show," *The Washington Post*, August 3, 2006.

[43] "Ex-Bush aide convicted in D.C. corruption case, Safavian found guilty on 4 counts of obstruction, making false statements," *NBC News*, June 20, 2006.

[44] Thomas B. Edsall, "Reed Confirms Fees From Indian Casino Lobbyists," *The Washington Post*, August 30, 2004, A3, www.washingtonpost.com/wp-dyn/articles/A45348-2004Aug29.html.

[45] Ibid.

[46] Marvin Olasky, "Abramoff/Reed Scandal," *World Magazine*, February 17, 2006, www.worldmag.com/webextra/11574.

[47] Thomas B. Edsall, "In GA, Abramoff Scandal Threatens a Political Ascendancy," *The Washington Post*, January 16, 2006, A1, www.washingtonpost.com/wp-dyn/content/article/2006/01/15/AR2006011500915_pf.html.

[48] "US government censured on family planning policies," *ObGynCenter Online*, November 20, 2006, obgyn.healthcentersonline.com/newsstories/usgovernment censuredonfamilyplanning.cfm.

[49] www.planetwire.org/details/6818?PHPSESSID=42c68cdb978f3262 aad0a7afcc1f7fae

[50] Ex-Iraq civilian chief defends doling out of cash, *Associated Press*, Feb. 6, 2007, www.msnbc.msn.com/id/17007333/.

[51] *The Book of Revelation* (also called *Revelation to John* or *Apocalypse of John*).

[52] John C. Hagee, "Why Christians must support Israel," *The Jerusalem Post*, July 23, 2006, www.jpost.com/servlet/Satellite?cid=1153291980490& pagename=JPost%2FJPArticle%2FShowFull.

[53] Tom Regan, "US Neocons hoped Israel would attack Syria," *The Christian Science Monitor*, August 9, 2006, www.csmonitor.com/2006/0809/dailyUpdate.html.

[54] a. David Gregory, "America's support for Israel under fire, Critics say U.S. policy alienates the rest of the world," *NBC News*, August 2, 2006, www.msnbc.msn.com/id/14157270/.

b. L. Carl Brown, "Book Review: *The Israel Lobby and U.S. Foreign Policy* by John J. Mearsheimer and Stephen M. Walt," *Foreign Affairs*, September/October 2006, www.foreignaffairs.org/20060901fabook85549/john-j-mearsheimer-stephen-m-walt/the-israel-lobby-and-u-s-foreign-policy.html.

★ 20 ★

World Redemption

"I apologize for what my government has done to the world."

Joan Baez

WHERE DO WE BEGIN TO REDEEM the good name and honor of our nation? What are the steps that need to be taken to preserve democracy and ensure the future for a strong middle-class? How can we as a nation best protect ourselves from future attacks? There are a number of issues Americans must not only face, but also be willing to embrace. These are critical matters that need to be fixed to safeguard our survival:

1. We must stop wasting our resources and people and expeditiously find a way out of the botched mess in Iraq. Our security policies must be geared towards the elimination of real sources of threat such as al Qaeda.

2. Leaders and trusted public servants who have lied and misled us must be held accountable to the fullest extent allowed by law.

3. In order to secure true safety we must recognize and deal with the ever-growing feelings of anti-Americanism around the world. We need to live our values as responsible and respectful citizens of the most powerful nation on the planet by striving to engage in admirable policies. We must stop exploitive,

manipulative, unethical foreign policies that cause us to be despised and start making amends.

4. We must reform campaign laws to make certain the U.S. government represents the American public first and foremost instead of special interest groups.

5. We must be assured that U.S. elections are secure and honest and that every vote is counted.

6. It is essential that we break up the media consolidation that has occurred in the last decade so that Americans can receive accurate, honest, thorough and timely news reports.

7. We must find clean renewable alternative energy sources to fuel our vehicles, homes and buildings, and Americans must take the lead in stemming the global warming problem.

8. We must find ways to rein in skyrocketing health care costs and make health care affordable and accessible to all Americans.

9. We must fix the American educational system to ensure our competitive advantage is maintained globally.

10. We must reel in spending to bring down the largest deficit in U.S. history.

My hope is that you will select at least one of these concerns and make it your personal campaign issue. In order to safeguard democracy, middle-class America and our planet, we must become educated and active.

On Iraq and National Security

The war in Iraq was lost the moment it was launched because it was based upon exaggeration, lies, deceit, and false expectations. When the prisoner abuse at Abu Ghraib became public, all hope for achieving a U.S. victory in Iraq was forever doomed. The lack of leadership combined with the U.S.'s hypocrisy and inability to arbitrate a peace plan in the 2006 Israel, Lebanon and Palestine crisis has cost the U.S. The last shred of international credibility available to the U.S. has been lost and will continue to be lost. As long as the Neocons remain in power, the U.S. will be seen as a greater threat to the security of the Middle East than any other threat.

The only chance for bringing peace to the region lies in the U.S.'s ability to form a true international collaboration of support. With closely monitored dollars and Americans taking a back seat, perhaps other nations will be able to assist us in cleaning up the mess we have created in the Middle East. Only more death, pain, resentment, and retaliation will come to the U.S if we continue to go it alone. The faster we can get a true international coalition, including getting help from those in the region, the more quickly we can extricate the U.S. from the bloody quicksand gripping us there.

American politicians must honestly and intelligently assess world threats, instead of parroting popular myths. The Neocon attempt to plant fear around allegations of Iranian weapons of mass destruction and the media's enthusiastic promotion of such lies is wrong. Politicians such as Senator Hillary Clinton (D-NY) who try to capitalize on such claims by echoing false charges of an Iranian threat do so in order to gain popular support and project a tough political image. I believe politicians who blatantly pander in false claims will be quickly dumped by their supporters. They will find their political posturing has been wasted because the groups to whom they desperately pander would most likely not support them anyway.

On May 6, 2006, Iranian President Ahmadinejad wrote a detailed sixteen page letter to George W. Bush asking for help in deciphering the actions of the United States. It begs the question of how a nation guided by a man of professed faith (George W. Bush) could sponsor inequities and injustices in the Middle East, South America and poor countries of the world through repressive foreign policies and preemptive attacks. It asks for a chance to sit down, talk and problem-solve the issues. This letter is posted on the Internet and is available to anyone interested in reading it for themselves.[1] The Bush White House reaction was that they could not be bothered to dignify the letter with *any* type of response.[2]

Imagine if that had been the reaction of the late Ronald Reagan, who with his magnanimous charm and persuasive statesmanship, helped end the Cold War with the Soviet Union. Ronald Reagan showed us that, as the number one military superpower in the world, we must seek to resolve all issues whenever possible, exhausting every single diplomatic means available. Through the willingness to talk and negotiate with Mikhail Gorbachev, the possibility of a nuclear war was minimized and peace was reborn between our nations.

Accountability Demanded

I believe in accountability at every level in government. If lies and deceit were purposely used to win America's approval for a preemptive war in Iraq, then those who perpetrated such lies must be held accountable for their egregious actions. If international laws were ignored and bypassed in order to facilitate secret programs or engage in practices that violated international laws, then those who engaged in the rewriting of the laws and who authorized and sanctioned the breaking of these laws must face the consequences for their decisions. These individuals must be impeached and imprisoned if and when found guilty.

War profiteering companies who have shamefully gouged American taxpayers through illegal and inappropriate billing practices must be held culpable, and every nickel must be accounted for and paid back to the public treasury. Projects that were paid for must be completed.

Amends

As a nation we must make amends to those nations, countries and people that we have harmed because of our greedy ambitions and dependence upon resources that do not belong to the U.S. We must provide compensation to those we have damaged and strive to live as a role model of democracy, freedom and respect.

We are not dictators and we have never adhered to a philosophy of preemptive strikes. We must eliminate our need for foreign oil and other polluting substances. It is only when a strong nation — like a strong person — can stand up and say, "I was wrong and I am sorry," that true freedom, healing and redemption can occur!

Protecting the American Vote

Protecting the integrity of the American vote is fundamental to the survival of democracy. One of the biggest concerns is that votes have been stolen in the past and may continue to be in the future. Eighty percent of America's votes are counted by one of three electronic voting machines. These machines are made by Diebold, ES&S and Sequoia. There is no governmental oversight on how well these machines perform or how secure the software operates within the machines.

The HBO documentary *Hacking Democracy* describes one of many anomalies that occurred in the 2000 Presidential election. In just one example, an electronic voting machine in Volusia County, Florida, registered more than 16,022 negative votes for democratic candidate Al Gore. How is it that a voting machine is recording negative votes?

In 2003 Walden O'Dell, chief executive of Diebold, wrote a campaign letter stating he was "committed to helping Ohio deliver its electoral votes to [President Bush]..."[1] Despite huge security concerns over Diebold voting equipment and the ease with which the machines can be tampered, the state of Ohio chose Diebold electronic voting equipment in time for the 2004 election. A security analysis conducted at Princeton University showed how quick and easy it is to activate a virus in a Diebold machine that will switch the outcome of the votes for any election.[4]

It was discovered that Diebold placed malicious software inside of their machines that allows for vote tampering. Despite public assurances by top Diebold officials that their machines are thoroughly protected from such security threats, it has been discovered that their machines are never tested. Further analysis by independent groups found the malicious software to still be active in Diebold voting equipment. Seattle grandmother and writer Bev Harris, founder of the nonprofit Consumer Protection for Elections: Black Box Voting, found that Diebold machines could be hacked in seconds and votes changed even after obtaining public testimony from top Diebold officials that it wasn't possible.[5] The state of California forced Diebold into compliance by rejecting their machines after the company attempted to foist voting equipment with uncertified software and acknowledged security problems upon the State.[6]

Campaign Reform

There are two insidious factors working to ruin American politics: the first is the amount of money that must be raised to launch a campaign. I always thought that American democracy was by the people for the people. This is no longer the case; the American public is no longer the primary constituent. For many congressional senators and representatives, their primary constituents are those who have paid to put them into power.

With the costs of running a campaign now in the multi-million dollar range and with it reoccurring every two years, it appears the major concern of our elected officials is how they are to be elected again. Because of the hefty contributions made by corporations and special interest groups, our elected officials become beholden to these entities. The paybacks required to these entities are immensely expensive to the taxpayer. The reality is those heavy-moneyed special interest groups become the primary concern of our elected officials. The matters of most importance to the majority of Americans unfortunately have fallen to the bottom of the totem pole.

The second factor that is ruining American democracy is the blatant use of unscrupulous tactics in campaign politics to attack one's opponent. Unfortunately, it appears that candidates are unable to run strictly on the issues. It seems that candidates believe personal attacks must be waged against one's opponent in order to win. While it may have been a clever strategy used by crooked political consultants, Americans have quickly grown weary of the despicable nature of baseless character assassinations that have taken place in lieu of meaningful political discussions.

Americans must demand campaign reform and penalize any politician who engages in unethical personal smearing tactics by not voting for them.

Protecting Free Speech and the Media

The American media has demonstrated how fast it could consolidate for the purpose of maximizing profits and controlling information. The ability to garner timely, fair, reliable, and accurate information has been compromised by the conglomeration of American media corporations.

It is unfathomable to believe that the American public is better served when 74 percent of all radio stations are owned by only three corporations. Because media ownership has become so concentrated and controlled, it has become a detriment to our nation. The ability to safeguard journalistic integrity has been compromised. Media companies are more committed to ensuring a healthy bottom line than to safeguard a healthy democracy. Their habit of delivering profitable news programs that benefit their corporate sponsors at the cost of eliminating, distorting or slanting the news is a liability to democracy. Televised news media has especially failed in its most fundamental responsibility.

The media has a fiduciary responsibility to provide the American public with timely, honest and accurate information and reporting. The majority of mainstream Americans want unbiased, honest media and we must demand it or democracy is surely doomed.

One of the prime examples is the U.S. media's failure to provide high-level attention to the scientific data that exists concerning global warming. Oil, gas and automotive companies such as ExxonMobil and Ford, which are reliant upon oil for their welfare, sponsor regular news programs. These companies care little to ensure the spread of knowledge and information about the detrimental impact of how CO_2 burned from foreign oil is threatening life on our planet.

The news media has sold its soul and potentially our global future for a few dollars. If the news media cared primarily about the American public and the world at large, regular scrolling marquees would be emphasized daily to show significant climate and weather pattern changes. These shifts in our global world are much more important to our future than the daily emphasis placed on the stock market.

Laws must be enacted immediately to break up the media monopoly and this must be insisted upon by the American public. It is undemocratic to have the power of the media so largely concentrated.

Stop Global Warming

The U.S. must become a role model and leader in fighting global warming, the biggest threat to humankind. Cutting back on the use of oil and managing the quickly arriving climate changes due to global warming will be the greatest challenge we face in our lifetime.

We must immediately launch creative means to shift U.S. dependence from foreign oil and begin utilizing new energy sources. Aggressive tax incentives and a variety of innovative programs must be offered. How we deal with this matter will have consequences upon future generations and the very survival of Planet Earth as we know it.

A True Patriotic Act

As citizens of the most powerful nation on earth, we must never be blindsided or misled by patriotism. We have an obligation to stay informed. Democracy requires a public of fully informed and knowledgeable citizens. We must always ask questions of our elected public officials and expect answers that make sense. When answers do not make sense, we must reflect, research and think, and we must demand change when necessary.

Our nation has much work to do. We have amends to make, budgets reflective of true American values to draft, children to teach, and a planet to preserve. Alas, we have made mistakes and we have failed at endeavors. We may, in our ignorance, busyness or naivety, have allowed ourselves to be misled. We are but human beings; nevertheless, we are also proud Americans.

As I have worked across America, the one thing I am sure of is the understanding and faith I have in my fellow citizens, that when they are called upon to act they will respond. Americans are the most creative, innovative, resilient, and positive people on this planet. There simply isn't anything they can't do when they set their minds to it. I believe this with every cell in my being. Let us come together collectively with true humility and honesty. Let us pool our brainpower and resources in concert to reinstate our nation to its place of pride. Let us work to restore our reputation and dignity as one nation under God, indivisible, with liberty and justice for all!

"The pen is mightier than the sword."

Edward Bulwer-Lytton

NOTES Chapter 20

[1] Text of Iranian President Ahmadinejad's letter to President George W. Bush. *Iranian Republic News Agency*, May 9, 2006, www.finalcall.com/artman/publish/article_2607.shtml.

[2] "Iran letter calls on Americans to change Bush policies," www.cnn.com/2006/WORLD/meast/11/29/iran.letter/index.html.

[3] Julie Carr Smyth, "Voting Machine Controversy," *The Cleveland Plain Dealer*, August 28, 2003, www.commondreams.org/headlines03/0828-08.htm.

[4] Ariel J Feldman, J. Alex Halderman, and Edward W. Felten, "Security Analysis of the Diebold AccuVote-TS Voting Machine," *Princeton University: Center for Information Technology Policy*, September 13, 2006, itpolicy.princeton.edu/voting/.

[5] HBO Online, *Hacking Democracy*, www.hbo.com/docs/programs/hacking democracy/index.html.

[6] Andrew Orlowski, "California set to reject Diebold e-voting machines," *The Register*, April 24, 2004, www.theregister.co.uk/2004/04/24/diebold_california/

About the Author

BERNADETTE T. VADURRO is the granddaughter of the late Frank S. Ortiz and the daughter of Nap Benavidez. She grew up in a political household; her maternal grandfather was a prominent member of the Republican Party who served as the mayor of Santa Fe in 1948, before she was born. Her father, Nap Benavidez, was a staunch Democrat who helped run local campaigns and who also served as a precinct chairman. As a child she was commissioned with small political projects like stuffing envelopes, passing out bumper stickers and making telephone calls in the days before an election to remind people to get out and vote. Later when she could drive she took election days off to either work the polls or give elderly people rides to vote.

Bernadette has been registered as both a Republican and a Democrat at different times in her life. In the mid-1980s she worked on the Republican gubernatorial campaign for Gary Carruthers. He won that race in 1987. She believes that while there may be philosophical differences in each party, candidates should be selected based upon their principles and commitments to the issues rather than on a strict party affiliation.

Mrs. Vadurro is the wife of architect Robert Vadurro and the mother of two daughters, Christy and Kate. She is also the grandmother of Summer Elizabeth Brown. Bernadette is a professional business speaker who has traveled across the U.S. conducting seminars on the topics of communication, leadership and customer service. She is a passionate leader who has volunteered her time and service to several nonprofit organizations in her community.

In the spring of 2006, Mrs. Vadurro sensed a shift particularly with her conservative clients. There were becoming disenchanted with the policies of George W. Bush, with some saying they felt betrayed and others saying they felt bewildered and confused. She knew that several seemed to be getting only one side of the story. These were people who were reading a "Donald Rumsfeld" *Tribune* and worked in a predominately Republican setting. After work these good Americans went home to watch Fox News. On Sundays many of them attended an evangelical church. While good, kind and compassionate citizens, they were being totally blindsided by their patriotism. It was time to write this book!

Recommended Resources

BOOKS

Baer, Robert. *Sleeping with the Devil*. New York: Crown Publishers, 2003.

Carter, Jimmy. *Palestine: Peace Not Apartheid*. New York: Simon & Schuster, 2006.

Clarke, Richard A. *Against All Enemies: Inside America's War on Terror*. New York: Free Press, 2004.

Chandrasekaron, Rajiv. *Imperial Life in the Emerald City: Inside Iraq's Green Zone*. New York: Alfred A. Knopf, 2006.

Dadge, David. *Casualty of War*. Amherst, NY: Prometheus Books, 2004.

Danner, Mark. *Torture and Truth: America, Abu Ghraib, and the War on Terror*. New York: The New York Review of Books, 2004

Dean, John. *Conservatives Without Conscience*. New York: Viking Adult, 2006.

de la Vega, Elizabeth. *United States v. George W. Bush et al*. New York: Seven Stories Press, 2006.

Flannery, Tim. *The Weather Makers: How Man Is Changing the Climate and What It Means for Life on Earth*. New York: Atlantic Monthly Press, 2006

Frank, Thomas. *What's the Matter with Kansas?* New York: Henry Holt and Company, 2004.

Galbraith, Peter W. *The End of Iraq: How American Incompetence Created a War Without End*. New York: Simon & Schuster. 2006

Hall, Jamieson, Kathleen and Paul Waldman. *The Press Effect: Politicians, Journalists, and the Stories That Shape the Political World*. New York: Oxford University Press, 2004.

Halper, Stefan and Jonathan Clarke. *America Alone*. New York: Cambridge University Press, 2004.

Kean, Thomas H. and Lee H. Hamilton, eds. *9/11 Commission Report: Final Report of the National Commission on Terrorist Attacks upon the U.S.* Darby, PA: DIANE Publishing, 2004.

——. *Without Precedent: The Inside Story of the 9/11 Commission*. New York: Alfred A. Knopf, 2006.

Kinzer, Stephen. *All the Shah's Men*. Hoboken, NJ: John Wiley & Sons Inc., 2003.

Kolbert, Elizabeth. *Field Notes from a Catastrophe: Man, Nature, and Climate Change*. USA: Bloomsbury Publishing, 2006

Kuo, David. *Tempting Faith: An Inside Story of Political Seduction*. New York: Free Press, 2006.

Lewis, Bernard. *The Crisis of Islam*. New York: Random House Trade, 2004.

Linker, Damon. *The TheoCons: Secular America Under Siege*. New York: Doubleday.

Loo, Dennis and Peter Phillips. *Impeach the President: The Case Against Bush and Cheney*. New York: Seven Stories Press, 2006.

Mahle, Melissa Boyle. *Denial and Deception*. New York: Nation Books, 2004.

McCoy, Alfred W. *A Question of Torture: CIA Interrogation, from the Cold War to the War on Terror*. New York: Metropolitan Books, 2006

Michael, Klare T. *Blood and Oil*. New York: Henry Holt and Company, 2004.

Phillips, Kevin. *American Theocracy*. New York: Penguin Group, 2006.

Prestowitz, Clyde. *Rogue Nation*. New York: Basic Books, 2003.

Priest, Dana. *The Mission: Waging War and Keeping Peace with America's Military*. New York: W.W. Norton & Co., 2003.

Rai, Milan. *Regime Uncharged*. London: Pluto Press, 2003.

Rampton, Sheldon and Stauber John. *Weapons of Mass Deception*. New York: Penguin Group, 2003.

Rich, Frank. *The Greatest Story Ever Sold: The Decline and Fall of Truth from 9/11 to Katrina*. New York: Penguin Group, 2006.

Ricks, Thomas E. *Fiasco: The American Military Adventure in Iraq*. New York: Penguin Press, 2006.

Roberts, Paul. *The End of Oil: On the Edge of a Perilous New World*. New York: Mariner Books, 2005.

Stone, R. Geoffrey. *Perilous Times*. New York: W.W. Norton & Company, 2004.

Suarez, Ray. *The Holy Vote: The Politics of Faith in America*. New York: HarperCollins, 2006.

Suskind, Ron. *The One Percent Doctrine*. New York: Simon & Schuster, 2006.

Wallis, Jim. *God's Politics: Why the Right Gets It Wrong and the Left Doesn't Get It*. New York: HarperCollins, 2006.

MOVIES AND DOCUMENTARIES

Baghdad ER. Directed by Jon Alpert and Matthew O'Neill. 2006; New York: HBO Home Video, 2006.

Frontline. al-Qaeda's New Front. PBS, January 25, 2005.
www.pbs.org/wgbh/pages/frontline/shows/front/

——. *Beyond Baghdad*. PBS, February 14, 2004.
www.pbs.org/wgbh/pages/frontline/shows/beyond/

——. *The Enemy Within*. PBS, October 10, 2006.
www.pbs.org/wgbh/pages/frontline/enemywithin/

——. *The Insurgency*. PBS, February 21, 2006.
www.pbs.org/wgbh/pages/frontline/insurgency/

——. *Missile Wars*. PBS, October 10, 2002.
www.pbs.org/wgbh/pages/frontline/shows/missile/

——. *News War*. PBS, February 13, 2007,
www.pbs.org/wgbh/pages/frontline/newswar.

——. *Private Warriors*. PBS, June 21, 2005.
www.pbs.org/wgbh/pages/frontline/shows/warriors/

——. *Rumsfeld's War*. PBS, October 26, 2004.
www.pbs.org/wgbh/pages/frontline/shows/pentagon./

——. *The Torture Question*. PBS, October 18, 2005.
www.pbs.org/wgbh/pages/frontline/torture/

——. *Truth, War, and Consequences*. PBS, October 9, 2003.
www.pbs.org/wgbh/pages/frontline/shows/truth/

——. *The War Behind Closed Doors*. PBS, February 20, 2003.
www.pbs.org/wgbh/pages/frontline/shows/iraq/

An Inconvenient Truth. DVD. Directed by Davis Guggenheim. 2006; Culver City, CA: Paramount Home Video, 2006.

Iraq For Sale: The War Profiteers. DVD. Directed by Robert Greenwald. 2006; Culver City, CA: BraveNew Films, 2006.

Loose Change. DVD. Directed by Dylan Avery. 2005; Oneonta, NY: Louder Than Words, Inc., 2006.

Outfoxed: Rupert Murdoch's War on Journalism. DVD. Directed by Robert Greenwald. 2004; Culver City, CA: BraveNew Films, 2004.

Una Causa Noble. Directed by Miles Merritt. Aura Studios, 2006.

Index

ORDERING INFORMATION:

SPEAKERSLIVE BOOKS

CALL: 800–736–8986

FAX: 505–986–0055

WRITE: 41 Vista Calabasas
Santa Fe, New Mexico 87506

EMAIL: info@speakerslive.com

WEBSITE: www.americasconscience.com